I0804696

THE RUSSIAN MILITARY INTERVENTION IN SYRIA

The Russian Military Intervention in Syria

OHANNES GEUKJIAN

McGill-Queen's University Press
Montreal & Kingston • London • Chicago

ISBN 978-0-2280-0829-3 (cloth)
ISBN 978-0-2280-0830-9 (paper)
ISBN 978-0-2280-0945-0 (ePDF)
ISBN 978-0-2280-0946-7 (ePUB)

Legal deposit first quarter 2022
Bibliothèque nationale du Québec

Printed in Canada on acid-free paper that is 100% ancient forest free (100% post-consumer recycled), processed chlorine free.

Library and Archives Canada Cataloguing in Publication

Title: The Russian military intervention in Syria / Ohannes Geukjian.
Names: Geukjian, Ohannes, author.
Description: Includes bibliographical references and index.
Identifiers: Canadiana (print) 20210312386 | Canadiana (ebook) 20210312408 | ISBN 9780228008309 (paper) | ISBN 9780228008293 (cloth) | ISBN 9780228009450 (ePDF) | ISBN 9780228009467 (ePUB)
Subjects: LCSH: Syria—History—Civil War, 2011– | LCSH: Russia (Federation)—Foreign relations—Middle East. | LCSH: Middle East—Foreign relations—Russia (Federation) | LCSH: Russia (Federation)—Foreign relations. | LCSH: Russia (Federation)—Military policy.
Classification: LCC DS98.6 .G48 2022 | DDC 956.9104/23347—dc23

This book was typeset by True to Type in 10.5/13 Sabon

Contents

THE RUSSIAN MILITARY INTERVENTION IN SYRIA

INTRODUCTION

Theoretical Framework, Methodology, and Structure

This book has its earliest origins in two research papers I presented at the Association for the Study of Nationalities World Convention in New York in 2017 and 2018. The papers are entitled "The Objectives of Russia's Military Intervention in Syria" and "Russia's Mediation in the Syrian Conflict: Using Leverage to Make Peace." The panels covered topics about Russia and Russian foreign policy behaviour after the collapse of the Soviet Union in 1991. The dramatic political and military events that had occurred from 1994 to 2015 were causing security threats to Moscow and threatening the national interests of Russia in the former Soviet republics (FSR), Europe and the Middle East (ME); as a result, the panels attracted a number of colleagues. What prompted me to write this book is that the Russian annexation of the Crimea in 2014 shocked many observers in the West, even scholars of the region who should have predicted Russia's behaviour. Russia's military intervention in both Ukraine and, subsequently, Syria in 2015 were a response to Russia's growing frustration with American and Western policy. This book will analyze the history of that growing frustration and provide a framework for understanding it. A number of books that have been written have attempted to explain Russia's actions in Ukraine and Syria; what makes this book different is that it provides a detailed analysis of the causes and objectives of Russia's actions in the FSR and the ME. This book highlights the relationship between status inconsistency and conflict. It demonstrates Russia's search for higher status and the conflict this quest generated with major power actors; Russia's use of military power in its foreign policy as a means to enhance status seemed highly counterproductive. This book also provides ample evidence of Russia's status dilemma dynamics and how Russia sought to restore its great power status after the end of the Cold War. This book is also different in that it examines how Russia signalled its status claims through diplomatic initiatives in Syria and the ME by using its United Nations Security Council (UNSC) seat and pursued leadership in international negotiations. Russia used power politics and tried to act as the sole power broker in the ME by mediating regional conflicts and highlighting its role in global politics, while suffering from a persistently weak economy that rendered a military intervention in Syria and its immediate neighbourhood quite costly. This book aims to present to all scholars, journalists, policy makers, and educated readers what is happening in the ME and Eastern Europe.

This book is not written for international relations (IR) specialists. The aim is not to describe the state of Russian IR theory but to give an idea of what Russia is doing in the ME. The aim is also to analyze and explain the causes of Russian behaviour and action in Syria. Interested readers, who are not IR specialists, are invited to extrapolate from their intuition. The average reader has to understand what Russia is doing in Syria and why. Equally important, this book aims to capture an audience that is interested in geopolitics, international conflict management, and conflict resolution.

In the early 1990s, Russia sought a partnership with the West in order to promote democratic values and to integrate itself in Western political and economic structures. However, in the second half of the 1990s, when Russia's interests were ignored by the West, Russian foreign policy became assertive. Russia sought to restore its lost status, prestige, and influence in global politics. In the post-Cold War era, a number of events caused tension between Russia and the United States and prompted Moscow to reorient its foreign policy away from the West. For example, the North Atlantic Treaty Organization's (NATO) enlargement policy that began in 1999, the colour revolutions in Georgia in 2003, Ukraine in 2004, and Kyrgyzstan in 2005, the Arab Spring, and NATO's 2011 intervention in Libya, which led ultimately to the ousting of Libyan authoritarian ruler Muammar Gaddafi. All of these events heightened Russia's resentment. Still, Moscow perceived the colour revolutions, supported by the West, as a challenge to Russia's exclusive status in the "near abroad." In the literature on status, Thomas Volgy described Russia as a status-inconsistent-power, more precisely status-overachiever, which has more status than capabilities.[1] Status-overachievers usually avoid conflict and try to preserve the status quo, which usually provides them with more international influence and recognition from other major powers than their resources would actually warrant. Taking action to change this status quo would mean investing significant resources and potentially losing overachiever status. Status-overachievers can become quite aggressive in their immediate neighbourhood when their regional leadership is challenged. According to status-seeking theory, Russia would be unwilling to give up its leadership position in the near abroad and therefore would risk conflict to defend it. With regard to Ukraine, in line with power shift theory, it could be argued that Russian power politics were aimed at defending the country's regional leadership.

The Syrian revolution that began in 2011 alarmed Russian leaders and antagonized them. Russia saw that the US had returned to its Cold War-era policy of regime change in foreign countries. For Russia, the loss of client regimes in Libya, Ukraine, and Syria was a major blow to its status, mainly because Russia lost part of its zone of influence and geostrategic interests in Ukraine and the ME. I will examine Russian power politics in Ukraine and Syria separately within the context of Russia's status-seeking strategy.

Some scholars of IR, such as John J. Mearsheimer, have argued that Washington's propensity to treat post-Soviet Russia "as a defeated enemy" and its failure "in managing Russia's transition from an expansionist communist empire to a more traditional great power," explains why Russia sought to achieve great power status by risking military conflict.[2] Post-Soviet Russia was a status-inconsistent power that used military force in its foreign policy as a means of status enhancement. Within this context, Russia annexed the Crimea in 2014 to maintain its interests and values in Ukraine and Eurasia in general. Andrei Tsygankov argued that Russia's conflict with Ukraine became possible, even inevitable, because the West failed to recognize "Russia's values and interests in Eurasia, on the one hand, and the critically important role that Ukraine played in the Kremlin's foreign policy calculations, on the other."[3] The Syrian conflict, which began as an insurgency in March 2011, cannot be analyzed in isolation but, rather, as another component of what appeared to be a sudden and complex regional transformation. The official justification for Russia's direct military intervention in the ME was to support the Syrian regime in its fight against terrorism and prevent a regime change. Damascus had been Moscow's ally since the Cold War period. Russia's power politics in Syria apparently meant that "Russia was once again capable of deterring any other great power, defending itself if necessary and effectively projecting force along its periphery and beyond."[4] Maria Freire and Regina Heller argued that the identity vector was crucial to understanding Russia's power politics in Syria. During the Arab Spring the ME became more important to Russia because it was a battlefield over two key issues: "setting the guiding principles of global order and preserving Russia's centrality in international conflict management as an embodiment of its international status."[5] Both issues played a key role in Russia's positioning on Syria. Moscow's decision was a key foreign policy objective, which was to prevent Syria's partition and maintain the Russian foothold in the ME. Jonathan Renshon noted that risking conflict demonstrated a number of attributes, "both material (technological prowess, fighting ability, and military and industrial capability) and psychological (toughness, resolve, and honor) that were perceived valuable" by states seeking to influence the status beliefs of others in a status hierarchy. Also, Renshon argued that "states experiencing status deficits risk conflict at a greater rate than satisfied states."[6] Thus, the militarized conflicts in Ukraine and Syria, which were public, dramatic, and salient, were a chance for the international community to calibrate its judgments on how much international standing Russia should possess. Certainly, there are other attributes that underlie status in international politics, and these are hard to measure. For example, economic weight, coercive capabilities, culture, demographic position, sociopolitical organizations, and diplomatic clout are valued attributes that signify status.[7] After the dissolution of the Soviet Union, Russia lost critical capabilities, like economic weight and demographic position, but was determined to play a role on the global stage as a major power, since it is a nuclear state that has veto power at the United Nations Security Council. While Russia's "military and economic capabilities flirted with minimal thresholds, its community-based status attribution did not diminish."[8] Other members of the major power club continued to recognize it as an equal, even giving its membership into the Group of 8 (G8) in 1998, and did not contest its permanent seat in the UN Security Council. Meanwhile, Russia increased its military capabilities and commitment in its engagement in global affairs and sought recognition of its self-defined identity as a major power. In 2008, Russia invaded Georgia and in 2014 it intervened in Ukraine by annexing the Crimea to prevent both countries from joining NATO and to stop the European Union (EU) from creating a zone of influence near Russia's borders.

Russia's annexation of the Crimea was a revisionist move, not typical of status-inconsistent powers.

This book explores a number of themes. First, Russia's preoccupation with status, a foreign policy objective, which became more visible after Vladimir Putin succeeded Boris Yeltsin in 2000. Russia's loss of its superpower status and humiliation, though it was not defeated in war, is a persistent theme in this book. In 2005, Putin declared that the collapse of the Soviet Union was "the greatest geopolitical disaster of the 20th century," and revealed his aim to restore Russia's status as a global power.[9] Thus, it is reasonable to argue that post-Soviet Russia faced a status dilemma. The Kremlin decided to seek great power status recognition by identifying new areas where Russia could assume a prominent role in global politics. No wonder Putin became more assertive and aggressive after mid-2000, although Russia continued to seek partnership with the West. Russia's partnership with Western nations was maintained as long as its fundamental values and interests were not challenged. When they were challenged, as Tsygankov wrote, "Russia tended to turn to nationalist and assertive foreign policy, especially if it possessed sufficient power capabilities."[10] Status aspirations remained a key driver of Russia's foreign policy toward the US and other Western powers.

Second, Russia's military intervention in Syria in September 2015 came at a juncture when its domestic and international circumstances weighed against such a move. By late summer 2015, the US and the EU had imposed economic sanctions on Russia in response to its annexation of Crimea; Russia had been expelled from the G8 and security cooperation within the NATO-Russia Council had been suspended. Russia's prestige as an "indispensable partner" and "reliable actor" in international politics had been severely damaged.[11] At the domestic level, a drop in oil prices in combination with the negative effects of the Western sanctions increased Russia's economic crisis, which accelerated into serious recession. Russian leaders felt threatened by the colour revolutions in former Soviet space (FSS) and the Arab world, mainly because they perceived these revolutions as sponsored by the West to bring about regime change. Changing the regimes of friendly and allied states (Libya and Syria) could threaten the unity of the Russian Federation. Russia, under Putin, is often compared with the Soviet Union in the sense that Russia is seen to have the need to maintain territorial, political, and economic control in the near abroad to safeguard its interests and values and maintain its zone of influence.[12] Thus, Russia prioritized its sovereignty and its self-defined great power status, neither expected to be recognized by the US and the EU. The eastward expansion of the EU represented a challenge to Russia, as Moscow needed to protect its values against Western values it regarded as subversive. The Russian system of values has been established as culturally distinct. Tsygankov noted that Russian values "included an authentic concept of spiritual freedom inspired by Eastern Christianity and the idea of a strong, socially protective state capable of defending its own subjects from abuses at home and threats from abroad."[13] Similarly, NATO's eastward movement that began in the mid-1990s antagonized Russia because it posed a perceived security threat to the country and endangered Russia's historical and cultural ties with its neighbours. In response, Moscow declared that there were "red lines that the Kremlin would not allow the West to cross in its attempts to incorporate Russia's neighbors."[14] From Russia's perspective, the EU Eastern Partnership program (EaP) that was about promoting democracy in Ukraine and Georgia became a source of major tension between Russia and the EU because the EU tried to undermine Moscow's sphere of influence in Eastern Europe and present itself as a civilizational choice for FSS.

Third, due to the expansion of NATO in the mid-2000s and the increasingly hawkish attitude of the Duma (parliament) and the Russian army in the second and third terms of Putin's presidency, Moscow's foreign policy became significantly more assertive in its defense of its national interests, trying to reposition Russia as a great power. Deborah Larson, Thomas Volgy Paul, and William Wohlforth noted that "a great power is considered to have a *droit de regard* in neighboring areas so that others would acknowledge, respect and defer to its special interests."[15] Russia aimed to achieve social recognition as an equal participant in various economic, political, and security projects and to address global problems with the West. Being accepted in the role of a great power implied expectations of higher task performance concerning international conflict management. Russia's intervention in Ukraine in 2014 and Syria in 2015 highlighted the importance of understanding the role of perceptions and emotions related to status in international relations. Post-Soviet Russian foreign policy behaviour was a rather natural reaction to Russia's frustration with the West and Western disregard of its national interests, values, and perceived security concerns.[16]

Fourth, in addition to its military reach, Russia was willing to assume responsibilities associated with its conflict management role in the ME by undertaking diplomatic initiatives. Russia's willingness and motivation to intervene in Syria were connected to its capabilities in both managing the conflict and setting the guiding principles of global order. Both capabilities had status implications. Yet, Russia needed to pursue cooperative conflict resolution with the US in the ME and elsewhere and not threaten the international order. Russia used a mix of military and nonmilitary instruments and leverage to achieve a particular outcome that would satisfy its economic and geostrategic interests in the ME and the interests of the regional powers of Turkey and Iran. What was new and crucial in Russia's recent military and diplomatic history was its capabilities in coalition building and coalition management in the preservation of global influence. Russia's regional diplomacy demonstrated Moscow's role in negotiating regional divides and forming alliances in fighting international terrorism that posed a common danger to the US, Russia, Turkey, Iran, Lebanon, and Jordan. Russia also established relations with rival powers in the ME, like Saudi Arabia and Iran, and concurrently maintained good relations with Israel. Russia proved that it was the major powerbroker in Syria because it was able to use leverage with Turkey, Iran, and the Syrian regime to push both the Geneva and Astana peace processes forward to end the conflict. Yet, Freire and Heller rightly argued "while Russia's policy of opposing Western actions over Syria was successful in terms of maintaining Moscow's centrality in international conflict management efforts, it did not contribute to stopping the violence on the ground."[17] While Russia sought to explain how destroying the regime in Syria would lead to chaos and instability, similar to what happened in Iraq and Libya, the US, France, Britain, Saudi Arabia, Qatar, and Turkey, as well as a wide range of Syrian opposition groups, sought al-Assad's transition from power.

The main objectives of this book are the following: First, Moscow's immediate military objective was to support the Syrian regime in its fight against terrorism and prevent the collapse of the Syrian state and the consequent takeover of Damascus, Syria's capital, by the Islamic State in Iraq and Syria (ISIS). By shoring up its ally, Bashar al-Assad, Moscow would protect its interests in the ME, which are now widely confined to Syria. Putin sought to achieve this goal through the empowerment of the Syrian army and the Lebanese Hizbullah (a Shiite group) and Iranian allies. According to the military doctrine of the Russian Federation of 2014, "Russia had the legitimate right to employ the Armed Forces, other troops and bodies to repel aggression against itself and/or its allies … in accordance with generally recognized principles and norms of international law and international treaties of the Russian Federation."[18] I argue that post-Soviet Russia was a status-inconsistent power and used power politics to enhance its status. Russia used status-seeking strategy in Ukraine and Syria "to recover recognition of its status as a global superpower and to restore, as much as possible, the influence, if not the territory, lost when the Soviet Union fell."[19] Syria's civil war and Washington's reluctance to engage more actively in Syria militarily and the perceived relative weakness on the part of the West offered the ideal context for Moscow to promote itself as an indispensable partner in fighting ISIS and managing the conflict in Syria. In addition, Russia wanted to put pressure on the West by taking the lead as the major power broker to any resolution of the Syrian conflict.

Second, fighting international terrorism at home and abroad was another objective for Russia to achieve honour and prestige. The Foreign Policy Concept of the Russian Federation that was adopted by Boris Yeltsin in April 1993 highlighted the threat of terrorism, particularly the form linked with Islamic fanaticism. In 2000, Putin promoted himself as an uncompromising leader in the fight against the Islamic terrorism that had rooted itself in the Northern Caucasus. His first term was dominated by the need to cooperate with the West especially in the context of the War on Terror to promote Russia's norms and values in the international arena. The 11 September 2001 terrorist attacks on the World Trade Center in New York created convergence of objectives between Russia and the US, and Putin was keen to link America's battle against terrorism with Moscow's campaign against rebels in Chechnya. Yet, Tsygankov argued that Russia's support for the War on Terror after 11 September had less to do with honour and was partly motivated by Putin's need to reaffirm and safeguard Russia's territorial integrity in some of its predominantly Muslim areas.[20] In 2015, Putin demonstrated willingness to fight international terrorism and asked the West to join Moscow in an unequivocal battle against terrorism and conduct antiterrorist operations anywhere in the world. However, for President Barack Obama, the dilemma remained how to rally an international coalition against ISIS without drawing the US deeper into Syria's civil war. As the Obama administration dismissed the policy of interventionism in the ME, Russia used the window of opportunity to achieve prestige. Although identity illuminates the broader picture of Russian normative positions on international order and security, it cannot fully explain why Russia was willing to use its military as a foreign policy instrument in Syria. Opportunity complements the picture here. Freire and Heller contended that the window of opportunity "consisted of a perceived relative weakness on the part of the West and offered an ideal context for Moscow to either promote itself as an indispensible partner in fighting ISIS and managing the conflict in Syria, or to put pressure on the West by taking the lead and enforce concessions and compromise."[21] Russia launched its military campaign in Syria to show that it was capable and willing to play a role not only in fighting the enemy abroad but also in navigating the Syrian civil war and building state capacity. While bolstering the endangered al-Assad regime, Putin simultaneously cultivated his image domestically as a strong leader who was able to protect the Russian people from thousands of Russian and Central Asian jihadists fighting for ISIS in Syria and Iraq.

Third, the strategic objective of the Russian intervention in Syria was "to revive the bipolar format of American–Russian cooperation and rivalry for influence in the ME and the world. It was obvious that the Kremlin would like to make Syria a template not only for bilateral relations with the U.S., but also to develop new rules of the game in a broader sense, and in other regions, like Ukraine."[22] Since the mid-2000s, Moscow's dissatisfaction had grown with the West's reluctance to respect Russia's global and regional interests and treat it as an equal partner. I argue that Russia was not only dissatisfied by its status but was also challenged and forced to respond to the EU's expansion eastward and NATO's enlargement. In June 2006, Russia considered that Ukraine's or Georgia's membership in NATO could lead to a big shift in global geopolitics. The West, by embarking on several waves of NATO enlargement, ignored Moscow's increasingly vocal demands to recognize its security interests. According to Alexander Sergunin, although Russia was "unsatisfied with the West's geopolitical and geoeconomic dominance in the world," Moscow did not want to completely destroy the existing "rules of the game," which were based on the UN's legal institutional systems.[23] The peaceful coexistence concept that was deeply rooted in Russian foreign policy thinking can be explained as the right of states to have different sociopolitical systems, as well as diverging views on international problems. I argue that Putin sought to leverage his military success in Syria and Russia's significant influence on the international conflict management in Syria via its UNSC seat into global moral clout, which the Soviet Union had once enjoyed. For example, Moscow sought to lift the Western sanctions imposed on it by the EU and the US as a consequence of Russia's annexation of the Crimea and its support of the Donbas rebels, a free hand in the FSS, and a new revision of the post-Cold War international order. For Putin, Russia's role could be leveraged to facilitate a major comeback on the global stage as a main interlocutor to the US.

Fourth, another Russian policy objective was to balance US influence and pursue multipolarity. Since the mid-1990s, Moscow's political elite adamantly opposed NATO enlargement and viewed the ME as an area of opportunity to regain a stronger standing in the world, due to the deep resentment of US policies in the region, particularly in Iraq. In January 1996, the appointment of Yevgeny Primakov as foreign minister and his promotion to prime minister in 1998 was a turning point in Russian foreign policy, mainly because it marked the systematic implementation of realism into Russian foreign policy thinking. Primakov, who was a pragmatist and centrist, did not accept US unilateralism in the world system. Jeffrey Mankoff noted that "in constructivist terms" the transition from Andrei Kozyrev (who was a Westernist) to Primakov "reflected the emergence of a new consensus about Russia's identity as a state and its role in the global system. This identity is characterized by statism (or *gosudarstvennost*) namely the idea that the state should play a leading role in the economic and political life of the country." The centrists "have a more traditional conception of Russia's national interests, rejected confrontation with the West for its own sake" and suggested that "Russia pursue a balanced foreign policy that paid much attention to its interests and obligations in the East as it did to those in the West."[24] Relations with the ME and Asia in general were crucial for Russia's immediate security concerns. The main foreign policy change was the process of rapprochement between Russia and the Arab world, India and Iran. In the second half of the 1990s, the challenge for Primakov and the Yeltsin leadership "was to balance between stifling the rise of political Islam on Russia's doorstep while promoting friendly relations with major Islamic states in the ME such as Iran and Saudi Arabia."[25] Russia began developing multi-track and multidirectional relations on the international level, which aimed to build alliances with Asian powers, such as India and China, while simultaneously preserving friendly relations with the US and Europe. I elaborate further on Russian foreign policy in the 1990s within the context of schools of thought in chapters 1 and 2.

Moscow favoured a multipolar world model where Russia could find its legitimate and rightful place. This model of the "manageable anarchy" would lead to a "concert of powers" international security system where Russia could play a significant role.[26] Sergei Karaganov noted "the unipolar world order, that was far from perfect, with the U.S. as hegemon, was withering away." Further, the unipolar order "was a source of large scale disorder not least through American support of regime change in countries near and far."[27] In February 2007, Putin's speech at the Munich conference on international security marked the moment when the Kremlin started to redesign its foreign policy in a more assertive way to meet Russia's security challenges and protect its national interests in the near abroad, East Europe, the ME, the Far East, and elsewhere. Yet, Russian foreign policy had already begun to harden in Boris Yeltsin's time when the Russian leader, in 1994, criticized the US bombing of Iraq.

THEORETICAL FRAMEWORK

The quest for status has always been viewed as an integral part of a state's behaviour in world politics. For classical realists, questions about the status of states are important issues in international politics. Yet, they have not developed a theory of prestige or status perhaps because status is perceptual in the sense that it is based on beliefs and beliefs about valued attributes have changed in different regions of the world. In this sense, prestige is located at a certain level of beliefs.[28] Renshon argued that, "Prestige was important even within a strategic approach to international relations since states might use it to judge quality or they might bandwagon, choosing who to support depending on what they expected others to do."[29] Despite highlighting the significance of prestige, the classical realists' explanation about the crucial role of prestige was unclear and sometimes contradictory. For example, Hans Morgenthau, a classical realist, thought that prestige seldom was and should not be a prime foreign policy goal.[30] This book argues strongly that prestige, self-esteem, and status were key drivers of Russian foreign policy. Certainly, status concerns create many dilemmas to which there may be no clear answer. Also, this book argues that status is a valuable resource and that Russia risked conflict in Ukraine and Syria to enhance its status. For a better understanding of Russia's intervention in Syria from a status-seeking point of view and to find out what determined Russia's foreign policy options, this book tries to give more empirical substance to the measures of attribution, willingness, and capability. With regard to attribution, I will examine the factor of identity. With regard to willingness, I will discuss the factor of opportunity. Finally, with regard to capabilities, I will examine the factor of cost.

Although claims about status and honour and their role in foreign policy have been made by researchers, politicians and diplomats, such claims lack any closer theoretical and/or empirical justification. A body of scholarly literature that explored the role of status in world politics from different IR paradigms emerged in the 2000s. Evidently, in dealing with status related issues, traditional IR paradigms, such as neorealism and neoliberalism saw status primarily as a function of states' military and economic capabilities. Also, traditional IR literature had addressed the concern states had with physical security and power maximization in shaping their international behaviour. Still, constructivism, which emphasized identities and norms, contributed to theoretical approaches that focused on psychological aspects in international relations and foreign policy making and behaviour of states.[31] The focus on psychology in constructivist research was particularly apt for capturing status.

This book is different because it uses status theories that were borrowed by IR from social psychology and social anthropology to explain and analyze Russia's seemingly irrational and unpredictable behaviour. Status theories, that best frame our analysis, focus on "drivers such as self-esteem, reputation, resentment, honor, glory and other emotional and psychological categories, which often confront each other and make a country's international course chaotic and unpredictable."[32] Within this context, I utilize Andrei Tsygankov's book on honour in international relations to pinpoint different Russian patterns of honourable behaviour in Moscow's relations with the West.[33] This book explains and analyzes Russia's power politics in both the Crimea in 2014 and in Syria in 2015 within the context of status-seeking strategy to enhance its status. In accordance with status-seeking theory Russia was unwilling to give up its leadership position in the near abroad and its increasing influence in Syria and, therefore, risked conflict to defend it. Yet, Russia's willingness to use military power in its foreign policy to enhance its status caused problems to its status-seeking strategy. Russia, deprived of its Cold War-era superpower status, believed itself to deserve great power status and risked conflict (among other strategies) to attain its goal.

In the theoretical literature on the role of status and power shift, major powers are characterized by and measured against specific attributes: strong material capabilities, including military and economic resources; activity, including the willingness to act and implement foreign policy goals regionally and globally as well as relative independence from other powers to do so; and recognition of major power status by other states.[34] According to this literature major powers' projection of power is "highly dependent on the level of prestige" and recognition as a major power by other states.[35] Power shift theory refers to major powers as "status-consistent," which means they are legitimately recognized as both having the capabilities and the willingness to become independently involved in international politics and are expected to do so. On the contrary, Vesna Danilovic and Joe Clare contended that "status-inconsistent" powers face "a gap" between capabilities, willingness, and independence on the one hand and community-based status attribution on the other.[36] Such powers may be accorded little prestige by the international community. Under such conditions, according to Thomas Volgy and Stacey Mayhall, "it is plausible that a nation's decision makers would evidence a strong desire to change the *status quo*, and failing to do so, to engage in conflict and violence."[37] Status-inconsistent powers are subdivided into "overachievers" and "underachievers." Status-overachievers do receive status power recognition but do not have the attributes to act as such. Underachievers have the power and are willing to act as major powers but do not receive recognition as such from other states.[38]

Status-inconsistency motivates states to adopt specific strategies to achieve status-consistency. Status-overachievers are usually confident with their community-based status attribution and are therefore mainly interested in staying as they are in order not to expose their power weakness. Still, they try to avoid any external activity that might change the given circumstances. However, William Wohlforth argued, in their immediate neighbourhood they can become quite aggressive, leading to conflictive behaviour, especially when their regional leadership is challenged.[39] Underachievers see their status to be generally under challenge and seek to enhance it to a level considered to be appropriate to their own role definition. Therefore, underachievers are more dangerous as they are willing to "resolve uncertainty around their status by competing more aggressively than overachievers to create larger roles for themselves in international affairs."[40]

Power transition theory (PTT) classified states into two categories, either status quo or revisionist. It was developed for the Cold War hierarchical bipolar system and when the two status quo superpowers (the Soviet Union and the US) were determined to maintain a power balance in the world. PTT argued that when a dissatisfied state rises in power and reaches a point where it is capable of challenging the dominant power for leadership and control of the international system, war becomes likely.[41] PTT suggested that status-inconsistent powers are "more willing to pay greater costs to achieve status-consistency," and they "are likely to operate in the domain of losses."[42] However, this strategy runs the risk that the costs can no longer be accommodated, particularly if the state has limited material capabilities. Thus, such a strategy is doomed to fail. If a status-seeking strategy is to be successful where there is a gap between status attribution and capability portfolio, "the increased costs of status production have to be minimized or at least mediated."[43]

It seemed power politics played a much greater role in Russia's status-seeking strategy than material capabilities of the country warranted, particularly when assessed against the backdrop of Russia's increasing economic problems. The theoretical literature on status suggests that countries with limited material capabilities primarily make efforts to strengthen their structural capability portfolio. As a matter of fact, one of the general principles of the foreign policy concept of the Russian Federation in the 2000s was to develop Russia's economic capabilities and potential, thereby acknowledging the close relationship between economic strength and international status.[44]

Russia and the West differed in their perceptions about what factors or actions would contribute to Russia's higher status. For both, Russia and the West, traditional elements of power in IR were Russia's growing GNP and its energy resources and military build up. Particularly for the West, economic development was central to the development of international influence. In addition, possessing "certain special rights and duties, namely the right to play a part in determining issues that affected the peace and security of the international system as a whole and the responsibility of modifying their policies in the light of the managerial responsibilities they bore" contribute to recognition as great power.[45] As mentioned above, Russia's power politics played a much greater role in Russia's status-seeking strategy that the material capabilities of the country warranted. To understand Russia's behaviour in its immediate neighbourhood and globally, I turn to Social Identity Theory (SIT).

SIT, a new school of thought, emphasizes the importance of status as a socio-psychological goal in itself for states with a potential for engendering conflict. This theory suggests that higher status seeking powers might emulate or compete with more advanced states or highlight their distinctive characteristics and strengths.[46] The willingness of advanced states (like the US) to accept the higher status seeking power (like Russia) depends on the legitimacy and security of their own status positions. So far, the US, the dominant power in the current international order, does not seem to accept a decline in its position and is therefore not willing to accord Russia a great power status due to its revisionist move in Ukraine that placed Russia as a status-underachiever. Concerning the ME, Moscow's power politics in Syria highlighted how its status-seeking strategy had not reversed its inconsistent power status. SIT explains the roles that perception of self play in defining status, as well as in determining behaviour towards others. These issues will be discussed in the subsequent chapters of this book.

One advantage of SIT over normative theory is that it makes more precise predictions about the conditions under which states seek to improve their status as well as the form that status-seeking strategy takes. Applying SIT to international relations, Larson and Shevchenko claimed that states could choose between strategies of social mobility, social competition, and social creativity when seeking positive self-esteem.[47] I use the strategies of social mobility, social competition, and social creativity as theoretical constructs to explain Russia's responses to identity threats. Sometimes states combine elements of the three different strategies in their foreign policy. Nevertheless, Larson and Shevchenko contended that "each strategy is driven by a different set of causal dynamics, and an aspiring state's overall foreign policy can be classified as a particular type."[48] Social mobility requires emulating the values and behaviour of member states of an elite group to be admitted to the club, such as the Group of Seven (G7). For this strategy to be workable, elite group boundaries must be open to new members.[49] For large states, such as Russia, a social mobility strategy in the second half of the 1990s became less appealing because it implied subordination and a humiliating relationship of tutelage.[50] When the opportunity for social mobility is lacking, the lower-status state may turn to the strategy of social competition with the leading or dominant state, if it regards the existing status hierarchy as illegitimate and unstable.[51] Applied to international relations, social competition aims at overtaking and surpassing the dominant state in the area of superiority, usually geopolitical power. For example, in the early 1990s, Yeltsin and Russian liberals, like Andrie Kozyrev, Anatoly Chubais, and Yegor Gaidar pursued the strategy of social mobility by trying to emulate the values of behaviour of major powers to be admitted to higher status Western clubs, such as the General Agreement on Tariffs and Trade and the International Monetary Fund (IMF). Russian leaders achieved accession to the Council of Europe in 1996, the G7 in 1997, and the World Trade Organization (WTO) in 2012. Still, the "Founding Act on Mutual Relations, Cooperation and Security between Russia and NATO" signed by the two sides in May 1997, which Russia saw a quasi-institutionalization of its relationships with the alliance.[52] Andrei Tsygangov wrote that Russia received an opportunity to join NATO and "now it had a mechanism of permanent consultations with the Alliance and the question of" NATO's "expansion was largely defused in the domestic politics."[53] Such recognition let Russia achieve prestige in a different area than geopolitical might. Russia rejected a subordinate role to the US in the mid-1990s when the Clinton administration began advocating NATO expansion.[54] Russia was disappointed and used multipolar diplomacy to restore its status by forming diplomatic partnerships to check the US, a strategy of social competition because Moscow regarded the existing status hierarchy in the world as illegitimate and unstable. Russia tried to outdo the US in its area of superiority, usually geopolitical power. Geopolitical competition could be futile as US military and technological superiority was overwhelming. Social competition could be demonstrated by rivalry and obstruction to show that the state matters.

The strategy of social creativity aimed at achieving prestige in a different domain from the dominant power. The term social creativity is borrowed from Betlina Westle, who defined it as an activity aiming at changing the rules of the game: the dimension of comparison, the evaluation of compared attributes, and others.[55] For further illustration, when Primakov became foreign minister in 1996 and then prime minister in 1998, he epitomized great power aspiration with his definition of Russia as global great power in a multipolar world. Primakov's diplomatic balancing and partnership with major powers would be based on equality, a goal that was constantly frustrated. Primakov's strategy of a multipolar world became the cornerstone of Russia's foreign policy. In addition, he made Russia's dominance in the former Soviet republics (FSRs) a key priority of foreign policy. Russia also opposed NATO expansion and continued to pursue a privileged relationship with the organization. Russia refused to be recognized as a regional power because it possessed the requisite capability and potential of a great power. Yet, to revive its global influence, Russia had to develop the non-military economic, demographic, institutional, and cultural attributes of its great power status. Freire and Heller argued that Russia "is usually depicted as a status-inconsistent power, more precisely a status overachiever, which has more status than capabilities."[56] Status-inconsistency motivated Russia to pursue strategies in order to achieve great power status. Freire and Heller contended that "status-overachievers are usually confident with the overall level of community based status attribution and are therefore mainly interested in keeping things as they are in order not to expose their own power weakness."[57] However, William Wohlforth argued that in their immediate neighbourhood "they can become quite aggressive and tend to apply more competitive strategies leading to conflictive behavior, especially when their regional leadership is challenged."[58] The Russian elite believed that Moscow should have a greater say in the management of global affairs. Tsygankov noted that in 1999–2000 Russia's political class had already arrived at a consensus regarding Russia's "grand strategy" that was viewed as a long-term plan to match military and economic capabilities. The consensus included "two central definitions of Russia's international objectives – global influence as an independent power and dominance in the former Soviet region."[59] In the early 2000s, Putin modified Primakov's social creativity strategy of a multipolar world to pinpoint Russia's traditional role as a joint stabilizer of the international system that from Russia's perspective had placed Russia on an equal status with the US during the Cold War era. In 2013, when Obama failed to engage in punitive military strikes against Syria, Putin seized the opportunity by promoting a plan to place Syria's chemical weapons under international control, thus helping the US save face by embracing a diplomatic solution to the crisis and concurrently enhancing Russia's prestige as a global power broker. This success of Russian diplomacy was an episode of social creativity. These strategies will be discussed in detail in subsequent chapters of this book.

The proper examination of status would help us understand present day international politics and its transformation. In a broader context, this book will highlight that status was a concern for all states and actors in one way or another. Since status had material and psychological implications, I use status-seeking theory and SIT to provide empirical evidence on how the dominant power (the US) and higher status seeking power (Russia) interacted with each other. The subsequent chapters of this book try to give more empirical substance to the measures of attribution, willingness, and capability. With regard to attribution, I examine the factor of identity and how ideational concerns determined Russia's status-seeking thinking. With regard to willingness, I discuss the factor of opportunity and how it influenced Russia's power politics. Finally, with regard to capabilities, I discuss the factor of cost. Russia is a useful case for considering theories about the link between status and risking conflict. I provide that status deficits significantly predict militarized conflict and war. Russia is a good case for considering status theories and assumptions about the role of status, although stronger generalizations would require comparative research.

In accordance with the theoretical framework, I advance two hypotheses. Following that, in applying the hypotheses to the case of Russia, I argue that the present major power system dominated by the US is likely to be less conflicting if the status demands of Russia are accommodated and, thereby, accord Russia a greater role in the international system.

> Hypothesis 1 (H1): The accordance of a higher status to a regional power by a dominant power is more likely when both the higher status seeking power and the dominant power do not consider each other or do not anticipate each other to emerge as primary threats.

> Hypothesis 2 (H2): The accordance of higher status to a regional power by a dominant power is more likely when both the higher status seeking power and the dominant power have a common primary threat to balance, both in security and status terms.

Accommodation is more likely if the dominant state (the US) perceives that Russia's demand for higher status is meaningful in the current international system and that Russia would not become a threat in terms of both security and status as a socio-psychological goal, especially if Russia's status goals are accommodated. The assumption is that "states are able to identify which other states are likely to be more threatening" in the near future and are willing "to rank them in terms of the potential severity of threat."[60] According to Paul and Shankar, "this assessment could be based on purely strategic and military disagreements the states might be engaged in, but might also involve more ideational sources that shape perceptions about the consequences of the ascension of the other to a role of greater influence in the international system."[61]

Given the fact that states were also concerned about status as a potentially zero-sum outcome in itself for socio-psychological reasons, it is apparent that dominant states would be much less likely to engage in status accommodation of new claimants as such an act would ensure another state's equality in status "or the likelihood of being surpassed." States were more likely to accommodate new claimants "that they expect would accept their relative dominance in the international system, rather than ones that were expected to plan to usurp the dominant state's role/status, with all the socio-psychological and material costs that might entail."[62]

While H1 ensures the permissive conditions for the dominant power to accommodate the higher status seeking power, H2 underlines conditions that require an active policy adopted by the dominant power to satisfy the aspirations of the higher status seeking power. The balancing logic means that the dominant power would rather integrate the higher status seeking power into its orbit as much as possible before dissatisfaction reaches a point where the higher status seeking power refrains from cooperation with regard to the primary threat. It is important to note that the higher status seeking power is motivated to integrate itself on reasonable terms within the current international system. This might seem workable if, psychologically, the higher status seeking power is not treated as a subordinate in a system dominated by a state that is its primary competitor. I further test H1 and H2 and elaborate on Russia's dissatisfaction of its post-Soviet status and the attempts by the US to accommodate Russia in the Western dominated international system in the subsequent chapters of this book.

METHODOLOGY

This research used a qualitative methodology because it may be impossible to measure status strategies exclusively on the basis of quantifiable criteria. It is difficult to measure prestige, honour, reputation, and self-esteem by using quantitative methods. A quantitative assessment of Russia as a status-overachiever does not tell us enough about Russia's power politics in Syria. In social science, unstructured interviews depart from surveys in terms of its concern for the perspective of those being interviewed. I used open-ended interviews with the Russian and Iranian ambassadors to Lebanon to discover the official position of the Russian and Iranian governments with regard to the Syrian conflict. Qualitative research enables us to see through the eyes of the interviewees or to take the subject's perspective.[63] This method enables the researcher to explore and clarify the topic under discussion and to expand understanding.

The qualitative method is appropriate to the nature of the study conducted for this book and the purpose and expectations of the inquiry. The aim is to gather an authentic understanding of the political experiences of the interviewees, and open-ended questions are the most effective route towards that end. The choice of the method is consistent with status theories used in this book to generate unique and testable hypotheses that help to explain patterns of conflict. I also use secondary sources like books, scholarly articles, research reports, and Russian documents to support our arguments about Russia's status-seeking strategy. As a matter of fact, the examination of Russian official documents, like the National Security Strategy of 2015, conveys the idea that Russia was unhappy with its international status, especially with regard to the insufficient recognition of its role in global politics and the lack of respect for its security interests by the United States and the West. Similarly, Russian Foreign Policy Concepts, National Security Strategies, Military Doctrines, and policy statements demonstrate a clear foreign policy priority for regional issues and threats (including terrorism and extremism) to the Russian Federation with particular reference to post-Soviet space. In addition to the interviews, I used these secondary sources to support the book's main aim of examining and analyzing the reasons for Russia's intervention in Syria and argue that Russia used a status-seeking strategy to be recognized as a great power.

STRUCTURE

This book consists of an introduction, five chapters, and a conclusion. Chapter 1, "Post-Soviet Foreign Policy, 1991–2000," aims to examine how and why, initially, Russia's Western orientation in the early 1990s caused frustration, which resulted from widespread dissatisfaction with Andrei Kozyrev's concessions to the West and the West's refusal to recognize Russia's great power identity. Chapter 1 tackles Russian foreign policy during Boris Yeltsin's presidency (1991–2000), within the context of Russian foreign policy schools. The Kremlin was determined to build a partnership with the West and join Western economic and political institutions. Yet, for Russia, partnership with the West did not mean subordination and marginalization. I argue that in the second half of the 1990s, Russian foreign policy became assertive so as to defend its core values and interests. I argue that the US and the West ignored Russia's views and concerns about the disputes, mainly NATO enlargement and international sanctions against Iraq and Libya. Russia's foreign policy towards the ME changed and Moscow tried to play an active role in the Arab-Israeli peace process to demonstrate its willingness to preserve Russia's centrality in international conflict regulation. However, it was unable to overcome US dominance in the region. This chapter will also test H1 and H2, which are about accordance of higher status, as they apply to Russia.

Chapter 2, "Russian Foreign Policy, 2001–11," examines and analyzes how Vladimir Putin dominated Russian foreign policy making and determined Moscow's role in the world and where its national priorities should lie. In its fight against international terrorism, Russia demonstrated to the US its geopolitical responsibility. However, Washington lacked an active policy to engage Moscow and satisfy Russia's higher status aspirations. I argue that US-Russian relations waxed and waned in light of arms control and the colour revolutions in Georgia, Ukraine, and Kyrgyzstan. Russia was concerned about a hidden agenda of external regime change pursued by the West. Thus, in 2008, to protect its regional or special status Russia risked international conflict by invading Georgia. In accordance with status-seeking theory, Russia would be unwilling to give up its leadership position and would therefore risk conflict to defend it. Russia's revisionist stance reflected Moscow's willingness to maintain the status quo in the post-Soviet space, implying at the same time a strategy of maintaining leverage over Georgia's politics. Chapter 2 also examines President Barak Obama's 2009 reset policy that presented the Kremlin a new opportunity to address its security perception and to clarify the motives of the Kremlin's international behaviour. I also argue that Russia demonstrated its willingness and ability to play a major role in the ME and elsewhere and to cooperate with the US to serve shared American and Russian interests. However, the US was not interested in establishing a strategic partnership with Russia.

Chapter 3, "Prelude to Military Intervention, 2011–14," explores and analyzes the Syrian insurgency that resulted in civil war and the role of external players and international attempts to stop the violence and initiate peace. I argue that Putin took advantage of America's lack of clear policy in the ME to enable Russia to "gain a non-American door to the region and to international recognition as a player on the global theater."[64] Moscow's policy in its immediate neighbourhood became more assertive, even aggressive, when its leadership was challenged. As Russian values and interests were disregarded in Ukraine, Moscow embarked on a confrontational course with the US. In 2012, as Syria became strategically important, Moscow's support of the Syrian regime complicated Russia's relations with regional players, including Turkey and Saudi Arabia, which supported the Syrian opposition by sending arms and money. In 2014, ambitious Russia applied power politics in Ukraine to prompt the West to recognize the status, interests, and values to which it aspired. In accordance with status-seeking theory, Russia would be unwilling to give up its leadership position in its immediate neighbourhood and risked conflict to defend it. Yet, Moscow's willingness to use military power in its foreign policy as a means to enhance its status seemed counterintuitive. Russia's opportunity/cost calculations were proved wrong. Russia did not achieve the expected status enhancement. Instead, Russia's action brought upon it Western sanctions that isolated Russia further. I also argue that the Kremlin sought to preserve its influence in international politics to play a significant role in conflict management in Ukraine and Syria. H1 and H2 are also tested in this chapter in regards to the likelihood of according higher status to Russia.

Chapter 4, "The Objectives of Russia's Military Intervention, 2015–17," explores and examines Russia's motives for intervening in Syria in September 2015. I argue that Russia used a mix of military and non-military instruments to achieve a particular outcome that would satisfy its economic and geostrategic interests in the ME and the interests of the regional powers of Turkey and Iran. The Syrian civil war represented an opportunity for Russia to exercise power politics and seek status enhancement. Compliant with the status-seeking strategy, Russia applied force to make other major powers recognize its self-defined great identity. I stress that the identity vector was crucial to understanding Russia's power politics in Syria. Russia's intervention had its disadvantages for Moscow, mainly because it created geopolitical conflict with Turkey and financial burdens for the struggling Russian economy. I argue that Russia's direct military intervention in Syria had a foreign policy objective of shoring up al-Assad and to assist that regime in its fight against terrorism. Also, I argue that Russia's aim was to change the political outcome in the region, which had been out of Moscow's sphere of influence for decades. For a better understanding of Russia's power politics from a status-seeking point of view and to find out what determined Russia's foreign policy options, I provide empirical substance to the measures of capability (cost consideration), status attribution (factor of identity), and willingness (factor of opportunity).

Russia wanted to assume responsibilities associated with its significant influence on the international conflict management in Syria and in the broader ME by undertaking diplomatic initiatives. Within this context, chapter 4 also highlights the Vienna process, which took place in November 2015, and the Geneva and Astana peace processes. Still, this chapter examines Russia's relations with rival powers in the ME, like Saudi Arabia and Iran, and its policy to maintain good relations with Israel. As such, Russia proved that it was the major power broker in Syria.

Chapter 5, "Russian Diplomacy, War, and Peace Making, 2017–19," examines and analyzes how the geopolitical objectives of the regional players hampered Russian peace-making efforts. Although Russian diplomacy succeeded in negotiating regional divides between Iran and Israel and between Turkey and Syria, American-Russian relations did not improve due to the international disagreement between Russia and the West over the handling of the conflict in Ukraine and Syria. I argue that issues of global security, armaments, and the US withdrawal from the Iranian nuclear deal had additional negative implications for American-Russian relations and the peaceful settlement of the Syrian conflict. Still, American-Turkish tensions over the US-backed Syrian democratic forces (SDF), Turkish incursions in Syria to blunt Kurdish expansionism, and Israeli attacks on Iranian and Syrian targets in Syria created further obstacles to Russia's willingness to negotiate a mutually acceptable agreement in Syria. In this chapter too, Russia's power politics in Syria will be analyzed vis-à-vis the three key factors of identity, opportunity, and cost. Although Russia was recognized as an indispensible geopolitical actor in the region, its status-seeking strategy did not reverse its inconsistent power status. H1 is also tested in this chapter.

The conclusion summarizes the key arguments and themes of the book and brings to the reader's attention recent (2019) political and military developments in Syria. Focusing on Russia's perceived humiliation and status dissatisfaction in the post-Cold War period gives a better account for Russia's foreign policy behaviour towards the West. Since 2011, Russia has been assertive and anti-Western despite of the imposition of Western sanctions, lower energy prices, and a reduction of European dependence on Russian gas. Power politics played a much greater role in Russia's status-seeking strategy than the material capabilities of the country warranted. Russian annexation of the Crimea in 2014 and intervention in Syria in 2015 illustrated the continued Russian bitterness in its loss of great power status. Still, Russia expected that the use of force in Ukraine and Syria would contribute to recognition of its great power status. Yet, there seems to be a gap on how Russia and the West perceived Russia's status and in particular Western policies in honouring or ignoring it.

I

Post-Soviet Foreign Policy, 1991–2000

Chapter 1 examines how and why Russia's initial Western orientation in the early 1990s caused frustration resulting from widespread dissatisfaction with Andrie Kozyrev's concessions to the West and the West's refusal to accept Russia's great power status. Russian liberals, who were labelled Atlanticists, saw Russia's fate tied to the West. A group of Russian intellectuals and politicians building on Nikolai Danilevski and Konstantin Leontyev's idea of Russia as a "special cultural-historical type" developed the notion of Russia as a principally non-European "Eurasian" civilization.[1] The Eurasianists, argued that Moscow should focus on geostrategic factors by prioritizing regions that directly bordered the Russian Federation. Another school of foreign policy thinking in Russia called Statist "equates successful foreign policy with that of strong independent state and emphasized the state's ability to respond to external threats to Russia's security."[2] This chapter tackles Russian foreign policy making during Boris Yeltsin's presidency (1991–2000), when the Kremlin was determined to build a partnership with the West and join Western economic, political, and military institutions. Yet, partnership with the West did not mean subordination and marginalization. Until 1996, the Russian leadership pursued a strategy of social mobility.

I argue that with the appointment of a statist, Yevgeny Primakov, as foreign minister in 1996 and as prime minister in 1998, Russian diplomacy became assertive. Yet, as Tsygankov rightly noted, "assertive in defending its core interests and values, Russia must also become an advocate of multilateral arrangements toward achieving international peace and security."[3] Recent experience showed that the US and the West did not take into account the views and concerns of post-Soviet Russia about the disputes, mainly Bosnia, NATO's enlargement, potentially hostile Islamic States, and international sanctions against Iraq, Serbia, Cuba, and Libya. Primakov did not accept US dominance in the world system and adopted multipolar diplomacy to balance the West. I stress that Russia's demands for social recognition as an existing great power fell under the strategy of social competition, and reinstating Russia's status in the world fell under the strategy of social creativity.

I also argue that Primakov's centrist, pragmatic, and realist approach set the stage for a new type of foreign policy that was passed on to Yeltsin's successor, Vladimir Putin. On becoming prime minister in 1999 and then president in 2000, Putin portrayed an image of decisiveness, reacting without compromise to the Chechen insurgents, often linked with international terrorism. Putin followed Primakov's policies but modified his social creativity strategy of a multipolar world to stress Russia's traditional role with the US as stabilizer of the international system. I begin chapter 1 by referring to Mikhail Gorbachev's policy in the second half of the 1980s.

The Mikhail Gorbachev era, which lasted from 1985 to 1991, brought about radical new changes in the Soviet approach to international relations. These changes were dubbed the New Political Thinking, the key principles of which included the end of the ideological confrontation between the US and the Soviet Union; fostering international efforts to solve global problems and establish collaborative projects; establishing worldwide mechanisms of interdependency that could prevent potential conflict; encouraging a multidimensional understanding of international security that included political, military, economic, societal, environmental, and cultural dimensions; overcoming political divisions and promoting the concept of "common house Europe"; and, finally, reinforcing arms control and disarmament.[4] Foreign policy under Gorbachev was "that of an empire in decline" and "his goal was to extract the highest possible price from the Americans for ending the Cold War and the arms race."[5] Internally, Gorbachev faced opposition from conservative Politburo members who rejected real change. In 1987, Yeltsin, the first secretary of the Moscow City Committee of the Communist Party of the Soviet Union broke with Gorbachev because the *Perestroika* (economic restructuring) "was only just moving from words to deed and that there were storms ahead."[6] Externally, although the US expressed empathy toward Gorbachev, Washington was unwilling to make "substantive concessions at the expense of U.S. interests, mainly rejecting Gorbachev's increasingly desperate requests for massive economic assistance."[7] After the failed reactionary coup attempt in August 1991, whose leaders wanted to prevent the dissolution of the Soviet Union, Gorbachev, the last Soviet leader, could not stop Yeltsin and the leaders of Belarus and Ukraine from dismantling the Soviet empire.[8] The collapse of the Soviet Union, in December 1991, changed the structure of the international system from a bipolar, dominated by two great powers, to a unipolar system dominated by the US. Yeltsin, Russia's first democratically elected president, was compelled to make a foreign policy with a new security and geostrategic outlook that was necessary for a country that welcomed democratic principles and wanted to be an integral part of the liberal market economy. In August 1991, the triumphant "democratic" forces stressed that in order to join the "club of developed democratic countries Russia needed to make a choice about its collective identity vis-à-vis the West and the East."[9]

Yeltsin, whose presidency lasted from 1991 to 2000, sought to build strong relations with the US for two main reasons. First, to consolidate his political position, the fragility of which became evident during the failed coup of August 1991. Second, to help the Russian economy that was already in crisis when the Soviet Union broke.[10] For Moscow, in the early 1990s, joining the Western community of nations and implementing domestic reforms was a primary foreign policy objective. Yeltsin's and Andrei Kozyrev's, the new leaders, vision of integration and strategic partnership with the West assumed that Russia would develop liberal democratic institutions and build a market economy. The West was perceived as the only viable and progressive civilization. The "main threats to Russia were to come from its economic backwardness and its association with non-democratic countries, especially with some of the former Soviet allies."[11] The new reformers or Westernizers, such as Gennadi Burbulis, Yegor Gaidar, and Andrei Kozyrev, advocated radical policies that would bring Russia in line with the political and economic standards of Western countries within a short period of time.[12] A major motivation for Russia was to integrate itself on reasonable terms within the current international system. The Westernizers were opposed by "neo-Eurasianists," the group that traced its roots to Danilevski and classical Eurasianist movement. "Neo-Eurasianism viewed Russia as a land-based civilization with strong ties in the former Soviet region, Asia, and the Muslim world, and emphasized relative cultural and geopolitical independence, or self-standing."[13]

Foreign Minister Kozyrev and other Russian liberals adopted a strategy of social mobility, aspiring to be admitted to higher-status Western clubs, such as the IMF, the G7, and even NATO. This strategy aimed to imitate the higher status group. In Kozyrev's words, Russia's "system of values was to be changed," in that "Russia was to accept the priority of the individual and the free market over society and state."[14] Clearly, the new reformers or Westernizers sought a new rank or standing for Russia within the status community of Western states that Russia perceived itself in competition with.

Within this context, three key components of Russia's asserted vision of national interest are worthy of emphasis: implementing radical economic reform, seeking membership in Western international institutions, and distancing Russia from the FSRs. Firstly, Yeltsin and Kozyrev advocated a strategy of radical economic reform, "the so-called shock therapy," so that Russia's transition to the Western-style system was quick and irreversible.[15] It was argued that in the post-Cold War period, Russia should invest its resources in the creation of a market economy and a democratic political system rather than worry about its military power and geopolitics. The Yeltsin leadership maintained a pro-Western orientation and linked the idea of radical reform to that of strategic partnership with the West. At the Washington summit in June 1992, Yeltsin and George W. Bush signed the Charter of Russian-American Partnership and Friendship affirming "the indivisibility of the security of North America and Europe" and a common commitment to "democracy, the supremacy of law and support for human rights."[16] Still, in addressing a joint session of the US Congress in June 1992, Yeltsin, reminiscent of Gorbachev's request, asked for massive external assistance to reform Russia's economy and went further in linking the success of Russia's reform to the US aid.

In Vancouver, Canada, Yeltsin and President Bill Clinton agreed to create the Russian-American Commission on Questions of Technology, and Yeltsin received the pledge of an immediate aid package of $1.6 billion, and the Paris Club granted Russia a ten-year deferral of its debt obligations due in 1993.[17] Dimitri Simes noted that "Yeltsin's radical reformers often welcomed IMF and U.S. pressure as justification for the harsh and hugely unpopular monetary policies they had advocated on their own." Also, Simes argued that the Clinton administration's "greatest failure was its decision to take advantage of Russia's weakness. The Administration tried to get as much as possible for the U.S. politically, economically, and in terms of security in Europe and the former Soviet Union before Russia recovered from the tumultuous transition."[18] Yeltsin's longest-serving prime minister Victor Chernomyrdin, who held that office from December 1992 to March 1998, a pragmatic politician with links to the country's energy sector, followed the policy of reforms that aimed toward a free market economy. The reforms sought to diversify and deepen Russia's relations with "challenger" states like China, Iran, and Iraq to bring hard currency to the Russian economy.[19] Although Chernomyrdin supported a peaceful solution to the Iraqi conflict throughout his tenure, his "approach to the ME was more complicated because of American objections" to Russia's involvement in ME conflicts.[20] But, as Tsygankov noted, in the 1990s and early 2000s, "due to domestic disorder and poverty, Russia lacked confidence and could not engage in assertive actions."[21] Moscow's alignment policies constituted a defining feature of Russian foreign policy shifts from 1992 to 2019.

Russia's second asserted vision of national interest was to join international organizations and clubs, such as the EU, IMF, and the G7, since the US and other Western nations were now "natural allies." One of Russia's most urgent priorities was to integrate into the global economy. In a world of economic interdependence and Western liberal institutional predominance, Russia would no longer need to pursue its "greatness" and "should instead prepare for a relative decrease of status" in the post-Cold War era devoid of ideological confrontation and "try to solve its problems by way of joining the Western community of civilized nations."[22] This concept of national interest would be revised in the late 1990s and 2000s.

Russia's third asserted vision of national interest assumed that Russia's integration with the West was a priority over Moscow's relationships with the FSR because the Russian Federation viewed the FSR as a heavy Soviet imperial burden. The solution came in 1991, when Russia eventually separated from the Union politically, culturally, and economically. While pursuing partnership with the West, Moscow "made no effort to negotiate for the protection of its economic and security interests in Eastern Europe or the FSR on its way out."[23]

However, this Russian isolationist policy would change in the late 1990s and 2000s. Politically, in August 1991, the leaders of Russia, Ukraine, and Belarus met at Minsk, the capital of Belarus, and created the Commonwealth of Independent States (CIS). In December, the CIS expanded to include the five republics of Central Asia, Armenia, and Azerbaijan. Georgia did not join until 1993. The organization was viewed as a mechanism for completing the republic's separation from Russia and not for supporting CIS integration. The three Westernist components of national interest shaped the new foreign policy concept of Russia that was signed into law in April 1993.

In 1993, for the first time, post-Soviet Russia adopted a comprehensive foreign policy doctrine that clearly described Russian national interests and foreign policy priorities. The document stressed the need to preserve the sovereignty, independence, and territorial integrity of Russia and to strengthen its security in every respect, to revive Russia as a democratic country, to provide favourable conditions for the formation of an efficient market economy, and to maintain the status of Russia as great power. The document suggested integrating the country's economy into the global economy in competitive forms and easing the burden of military spending.

According to its foreign policy concept, Russia was to exercise its responsibility as a great power by maintaining regional and global stability, contributing to conflict prevention, and promoting democratic principles such as the rule of law and minority rights protection. Still, the document emphasized Russia's commitment to solve conflicts by diplomatic means and negotiation rather than the use of military force. Although the Third World was viewed as the main source of threats to regional and global security, developing countries were depicted as important resources for Russia's successful global strategy. In general, the document can be characterized as liberal and pro-Western in spirit because it was prepared by the Atlanticists (Westerners) who saw Russia's fate as being tied to the West.

With regard to Russia's 1993 Military Doctrine, the document did not identify the US and NATO as primary sources of military threat. Rather, Russia called on the US and NATO not to provoke new confrontation by violating the strategic balance, military build-up and deployment in the regions bordering Russia, and NATO's eastward expansion. By implication Russia would refrain from any destabilizing behaviour. Further, the proliferation of weapons of mass destruction and international terrorism were considered part of Russian strategic priorities.[24] The 1993 Military Doctrine revealed Russia's great power aspirations as demonstrated by the powerful defense lobby. I turn now to examine Russia's policy towards the ME.

RUSSIA AND THE MIDDLE EAST

In the early 1990s, the Kremlin's policies towards the ME were broadly influenced by Russia's view of itself. Russia adopted a non-intervention policy in ME conflicts and played a minor role in the ME peace process. Indeed, in 1992, Kozyrev's non-intervention policy was most evident in the Palestinian-Israeli conflict despite Russia's official role of cosponsor of the ME peace process in the Cold War era. Following the ceremonial opening of the Madrid peace conference in the last months of the Soviet era in 1991, serious negotiations involving the Syrian, Jordanian, Israeli, Lebanese, and Palestinian delegations took place in Washington, DC. Kozyrev, who was a vocal advocate for Russia to join Western nations and build good relations with the US, conveyed to the Arab delegations that they could not take for granted Moscow's support as they had in Soviet times.[25]

The most dramatic reversal of foreign policy behaviour occurred in 1990, during the Gulf War when Moscow refrained from intervening on the side of its client state, Iraq, as it had done in the 1967 and 1973 ME crises.[26] However, in both parliament and nongovernmental circles, the Yeltsin leadership was attacked by nationalists for not preventing US airstrikes against Iraq and for Moscow's support of US policy toward the former Yugoslavia. Although Russia was a member of the Contact Group on the former Yugoslavia, in August 1995 NATO carried out sustained bombing of Serbian positions in Bosnia over Russia's staunch opposition, triggering heated rhetoric from Yeltsin about igniting war in Europe.[27] As a result of NATO's continued expansion and use of force against Serbia, historically and culturally close to Russia, the Kremlin's perception grew more militarized.

In the 1990s, Syria's relations with Russia were far from harmonious. In 1992, Kozyrev asked Syria to take an active role in the peace process that had commenced in Madrid in 1991. Syrian Foreign Minister Faruq al-Sharaa, who was then visiting Moscow, expressed his desire that the "Russian side would play a more effective role in efforts to achieve peace."[28] Russia's internal divisions and domestic struggles in the fall of 1993, between Yeltsin and his rival, Vice President Alexander Rutskoi, and parliamentary opposition, prompted Syria not to take Russian claims on the Arab-Israeli peace process seriously. Another rival of Yeltsin was Ruslan Khasbulatov, the speaker of the Supreme Soviet, who criticized Yeltsin's so-called shock therapy to establish a market economy. On 3 October 1993, Rutskoi and Khasbulatov called on protesters in Moscow to storm the Ostankino TV station and the mayor's office.[29]

While Yeltsin's supporters recommended submitting to American wishes, Rotskoi asked the Syrians to "stand up to imperialist aggression" and promised that Russia would help them.[30] The mounting standoff between rebel lawmakers, who barricaded themselves in parliament and voted to impeach the president, ended on 4 October 1993 when Yeltsin ordered the army to shell the country's legislature.[31] In December 1993, Yeltsin's victory over Rotskoi and Khasbulatov paved the way for the adoption of a new federal constitution, which remains to this day, replacing the outdated 1978 Soviet Constitution and substantially strengthening presidential powers.[32] The creation of a multiparty parliamentary system and the strengthening of presidential powers would have considerable impact on Russian foreign policy making thereafter. Yeltsin's victory marked the end of a period when Syria had been able to use Moscow to counterbalance American and Israeli powers in the region. Even earlier, in 1987, Gorbachev broke with Syria as part of his general moderation of the USSR's foreign policy line.

It is important to note that four factors determined Syrian-Russian relations. The first, and perhaps the most important factor, was that the Syrian army, largely equipped with Russian weapons, needed a continuous supply of spare parts and assistance from Russian experts. The second factor was the issue of the huge Syrian debt estimated at $7–11 billion. The third factor was Russia's desire to play "a more meaningful role" in the Arab-Israeli peace process, and, aware that the Palestinian-Israeli track was outside its power and influence, Moscow "wanted affirmation at the less politically sensitive" Syrian-Israeli track of the peace process. From a Russian perspective, Moscow's success in making peace between Syria and Israel would give "Russia's prestige a boost."[33] Russia saw that its status was connected to the resolution of conflicts and to the provision of order. The fourth factor was the deep-rooted Syrian-Russian friendship that in the Soviet era had facilitated the continuity of mutual relations despite ideological and geopolitical changes.[34]

In November 1994, Kozyrev met then Syrian president Hafez al-Assad in Damascus and stated that Russia's presence in the ME provided a "balance and a counterweight" to the US hegemony in the region.[35] The renewed links with Syria gave Moscow hope to re-enter the ME diplomatically and politically and to play a genuine role in the

Arab-Israeli peace process. Kozyrev's new policy toward Syria and the ME coincided with and stemmed from his frustration with the Clinton administration's diplomatic behaviour, which disallowed Russia from becoming a strategic partner. Still, the Clinton administration held off admitting Russia into Western clubs until it became a stable and developed capitalist democracy.[36] Alexander Motyl noted that the failure of Western efforts to help liberalize Russia in the 1990s was to recognize the distinction between a mature liberal democracy and a fledgling democratizing country.[37] Kozyrev told Strobe Talbott, who served as ambassador-at-large to the newly independent states from 1993 to 1994, "it was bad enough having you people tell us what you were going to do whether we like it or not. Do not add insult to injury by also telling us that it was our interest to obey your orders."[38] Apparently, the Clinton administration generated much resentment because it did not respect Russia and failed to treat it as an equal despite Russia's attempts to integrate with the West. Hence, Russia's status dissatisfaction, as well as emotions accompanying failure to win respect, helped to explain the shifts in Russian foreign policy beginning with the abandonment of Russia's initial post-Cold War policy of accommodating the West.[39] The failure of the US to manage the status aspirations of Russia supports H1. Accepting Russia in Western clubs would have been a gesture toward Russia's aspiring status. However, Clinton refused to accommodate Russia because the US perceived Russia could "become a threat in terms of both security and status as a socio-psychological goal."[40] Also, H2 is tested here in that the Clinton administration did not create an active policy to satisfy Russia's higher status aspirations despite Russia's attempts to integrate with the West and build a market economy.

Concerning Russia's behaviour vis-à-vis Iran, Yeltsin did not capitulate to US pressure to cease Russia's involvement in the Iranian nuclear program, especially in the construction of a nuclear reactor at Bushehr.[41] Russia had its own reasons for seeking good relations with Iran. Moscow and Tehran argued that the nuclear program was purely for civilian purposes and met Iran's obligations under the Non Proliferation Treaty of 1968. It is important to note that the Bushehr facility, which was a point of contention between Russia and the US, was estimated to bring to Russia (mainly the state owned firm Atomstroieksport) $1 billion.[42] Russia's relationship with Iran was at the centre of the talks in Moscow between US Vice President Al Gore and Russian Prime Minister Victor Chernomyrdin in July 1995. The Al

Gore-Chernomyrdin agreement ended Russian arms sales to Iran. The US succeeded in convincing Moscow that "some of its arms exports would contribute to unchecked proliferation and would threaten American long-term security interests."[43]

Russia viewed Iran as a friendly and neighbouring state. Iran not only remained one of Russia's major customers for industrial goods and conventional weaponry but also Iranian and Russian diplomacy largely coincided in the region. Iran seemed concerned that conflicts within the FSS might spill over into its territory; it thus worked with Russia to end the civil war in Tajikistan in the 1990s. The civil war in Tajikistan threatened the infiltration of extremist Islam into Central Asia. In 1993, during Kozyrev's March trip to Tehran, both Iran and Russia expressed willingness to maintain their "strategic partnership" to ensure stability in the Caucasus and Central Asia. Within this context, "as long as Iran behaved responsibly in Russia's backyard, Moscow saw no reason to accede to U.S. pressure to cut off arms sales."[44] Also, tense relations with Ukraine, Georgia, and the Baltic States increased Russia's insecurities.

The most dangerous security threat came from the Chechen republic that declared itself independent in 1991. Secessionist Chechnya (1994–96) not only threatened the unity of the Russian Federation and Moscow's authority but also "opened up the Caucasus to infiltration and domination by traditional rivals including Turkey as well as NATO and the U.S."[45] Iran took a pragmatic posture on the issue of Chechnya. Rather than supporting the separatists and sympathizing with them, Tehran saw the conflict in a geopolitical context, "fearing even more instability in the Caucasus."[46] For its part, Russia did not share the Western view of classifying Iran as a state sponsoring international terrorism. Within this context, "Moscow saw Iran as a major regional power in a different setting, seeking ways to bolster its position *vis-a-vis* its Arab and Turkish neighbors, while in a long-term confrontation with the U.S. and Israel."[47]

In 1994, Yeltsin, "in his bid for support of the army elite," ordered a full military operation to crush the Chechen rebellion.[48] Hanna Smith reiterated that, in international diplomatic terms, the use of force in Chechnya was "very peculiar" because, at that time, Russia "was building bridges, especially towards Europe, through international institutions, and the war risked to jeopardize the progress already made."[49] The year 1994 brought to Russia foreign policy achievements. Russia became a member of NATO's Partnership for

Peace Program, and in March the IMF approved a loan worth $1.5 billion to Russia – an indication of the West's keen interest in trying to keep Russia on a track toward a market economy. In July of the same year, Kozyrev attended the G7 meeting in Naples and there were hopes among the Westernizers that the G7 would become G8.[50] Although the outcome of the first Chechen war was disappointing, the war was seen as an attempt by Russia to achieve status consistency mainly because the demise of the Soviet Union resulted in loss of great power status from the point of view of the West.

The Russian application to join the Council of Europe was held up for a second time because of the Chechen war. The first application was held up in October 1993, when Yeltsin ordered the military to storm the Russian parliament. For Moscow, crushing the Chechen rebels was important to protect its sovereignty and gain international prestige. In addition, the retention of control of the pipelines transporting Caspian Sea oil to the world market was a vital Russian foreign policy objective. Chechnya had been an important link in the flow of oil from Azerbaijan's capital, Baku, to the Russian Black Sea port of Novorossiysk. Regional security was imperative because "instability in Chechnya stimulated among oil producers the prospect of building alternative pipeline routes through Georgia, Turkey and even Iran."[51]

The Russian forces were totally ineffective in winning the war. Pavel Baev rightly noted that "the near-catastrophic defeat revealed the depth of deterioration of the military structures caused by the redeployments, reductions, and under-financing, and the depth of incompetence of the High Command."[52] As a result, the prestige of the Russian military declined. Yeltsin and Kozyrev found themselves in a very difficult position and their Western policies were under attack from both the left and the right. The December 1995 parliamentary elections turned into a political defeat for Yeltsin. Yeltsin ended up with a Duma (parliament) that was not sympathetic to him. Clearly, the Westernist foreign policy orientation lost its domestic appeal and had to be modified. Shortly, significant concessions to the Statist opposition had to be made.

In conclusion, the Atlanticists believed that the West should be the main orientation of Russian diplomacy and that Russia should build a partnership with the West by joining Western economic and political institutions. The Atlanticists stressed that Russia aimed to join the club of recognized democratic states with market economies on the basis of equality. They viewed NATO as "the starting point for the formation of a new type of Euro-Atlantic Community, one which could guarantee international stability from Vancouver to Vladivostok."[53] The Atlanticists justified their isolationist policy toward the FSR on economic, political, and cultural grounds and favoured a European orientation.

REASSESSMENT OF RUSSIAN INTERESTS

As argued above, the Yeltsin-Kozyrev pro-Western policy evoked strong reactions from many Russian politicians who were disappointed by both the West's reluctance to admit Russia to its institutions and the insufficient assistance to Russia. They tried to develop alternative concepts of foreign policy that reflected the geopolitical position of Russia.

In the 1990s, the Eurasianist (*Evraziistvo*) concept became popular among Russian thinkers. Westernizers and Eurasianists represented polar opposites of Russia's civilizational identity. Eurasianist thinkers employed the language of traditional geopolitics by referring to the Eurasian continent, "the control of which would give a country the resources and transportation routes to exercise global dominance."[54] One of the most prominent advocates of the idea of a Russian Eurasian civilization was Alaxandr Dugin. His work, *Foundations of Geopolitics* (*Osnovy Geopolitiki*), was a widely read theoretical work on strategy and foreign policy in post-Soviet Russia.[55] Like Dugin, Igor Nikolaevich Panarin's ideas were ideologically informed by his opposition to the West. In his view, "geopolitics had been dominated for several centuries by the struggle between two main civilizations – the sea oriented (the British Empire and the United States) – and the continent oriented (Eurasia, Germany and Russia)."[56] Tsygankov wrote that while Westernizers had a tendency to be nihilistic about the national history, Eurasianists were prone to an exaggerated sense of pride, even glorification of Russia's past."[57]

The Eurasianists associated Russia's security concept with the notion of national interests. Thus, Russia's national interests were determined by its geography, history, culture, ethnic composition, and political tradition. The hardline nationalists, like Aleksandr Prokhanov and Alexander Dugin who were members of the radical nationalist think tank called Izborsk Club, emphasized that Russia was at the centre of a distinct Eurasian culture and advocated the development of Eurasian integration. Sergei Stankevich identified Russian national security interests with self-preservation, the prevention of further collapse, the creation of a system of democracy, and federalism that checks both imperial dictatorship and separatist tendencies, efficient guarantees for ethnic Russians who lived in the "near abroad" and the evolution of a strong and efficient state with a stable foreign policy.[58] The Eurasianists were critical of Yeltsin's government and its attention to the Western direction of foreign policy because Russia's compelling needs were in the South and East. The Eurasianists argued that Russian diplomacy should meet the challenges posed by Turkey, Saudi Arabia, and other Islamic countries. Coping with these threats and challenges was more important than engaging with the West on European and trans-Atlantic issues.[59]

Between Eurasia and the West the centrists emphasized Russia's role in FSS and advocated the consolidation of economic, political, and security ties with the FSR within the context of the CIS with a desire for productive and non-confrontational relations with the West.[60] The centrists "rejected some of the mistier notions of Russia's special identity and civilization affinities with the people of Eurasia" and suggested that Russia should "pursue a balanced foreign policy that pays as much attention to its interests and obligations in the East as it does to those in the West."[61] Such an approach to foreign policy was the foundation for the centrist tendency in Russian geopolitical thought and practice. Russia's interests consisted of improving relations with the EU and gradual integration into the European economic and political system. Still, they stressed that NATO's role and function should be reconsidered.[62] The main point of the dispute between the Atlanticists and Eurasianists was over the need to create a balance between the Western and Eastern directions of foreign policy. To illustrate, "partnership with the West would undoubtedly strengthen Russia in its relations with the East, and the South, while partnership with the East and the South would give Russia independence in its contacts with the West."[63] Russia's 1993 foreign policy doctrine was affected by their ideas, especially in shaping Russia's regional priorities.

In 1994, the Westernizer national self-image of Russia had been discredited for ignoring Russia's greatness and undermining the power and prestige of the Russian state. To appease the opposition to Yeltsin, many Westernizers had been removed from office and replaced by statists. The centre (i.e., Moscow) became dominated by the "centrists and statists" who aspired to make Russia great again. As a result, "Russian foreign and domestic policy shifted toward positions more in line with statist and national-restorationist self-image."[64] Further, the Yeltsin leadership "allowed some of the former economic and Party *nomenklatura* to privatize the lucrative energy industry, thereby turning them into the wealthiest businessmen with Western trading preferences."[65] Yeltsin also rewarded the media for helping him get re-elected in 1996 and because it was "a serious standard-setter of democratic change."[66]

Concerning the ME, in 1994, Yeltsin changed his approach to Syria as part of his effort toward an assertive foreign policy vis-à-vis the West and the ME. Contrary to his previous positions, "Kozyrev admitted that the ME was closer to Moscow than the Russian Far East."[67] Syria, Egypt, and Iraq were aware of Russia's internal problems and its weak position in global politics but, having no other choice at their disposal, tried to use Moscow as a counterbalance against the West and as a source of assistance. Kozyrev also acknowledged the importance of preserving economic and cultural ties with the FSR.

In early 1994, writing in the *New York Times*, Kozyrev clearly expressed Russia's dissatisfaction of its status. In 1995, Yeltsin distanced himself further from proponents of liberal free-market principles but kept Kozyrev in his post to avoid sending the wrong signal to the West and as an assurance that he had not succumbed to the statist, nationalist, and leftist elements in Russian politics. From 1991 to 1995, Russia's strategy of social mobility to maximize Russian interests by trying to join the Western world needed revision. The anti-Americanism fuelled by the Yeltsin government in the late 1990s stemmed from NATO's wars against Russia's client Serbia in Croatia and Bosnia in 1995, as well as Kosovo in 1999. For example, during NATO's 1995 bombing against the Bosnian Serbs, Yeltsin said, "This was the first sign of what could happen when NATO would come right up to the Russian Federation's borders … The flames of war could burst out across the whole of Europe."[68] Russia's emotional fear was on display about NATO's expansion in spite of NATO's assurances that the US-led military alliance would not take offensive action in the absence of a direct threat to any NATO member state. However, NATO's bombing was in defiance of Russia's security interests and lay outside the approval of the UN Security Council where Russia had veto power.

In spite of the war in Chechnya and a decline in his popularity, in the July 1996 presidential election Yeltsin won in the second round of voting when he obtained 54 per cent of the vote.[69] Just after the presidential election and Vladimir Putin's arrival in Moscow, the Russian military "collapsed as an effective fighting force."[70] On 23 November 1997, Chernomyrdin and Aslan Mashkhadov, Chechnya's president signed an interim agreement on the final steps to bring about peace between Chechnya and Russia, but both sides stood firm on their previous positions until the start of the second Chechen war in August 1999.[71]

TOWARD AN ASSERTIVE FOREIGN POLICY

As the Westernizer's foreign policy approach became unpopular and the statists' influence became too strong for Yeltsin to resist, on 9 January 1996 Yeltsin sacked Kozyrev and replaced him with a statist and Arabist, Yevgeny Primakov. Primakov's appointment accompanied the prevailing sentiment that foreign policy had to be more assertive because the West did not take into account Russian views and concerns about the disputes, mainly on Bosnia, NATO's enlargement, and especially the international sanctions against Iraq, Cuba, Serbia, and Libya. Contrary to Moscow's support for American strikes on Baghdad in June 1993, Russia, in October 1994, resisted the US to resume military operations against Iraq. Russian resistance was manifested both in rhetoric and practice by preventing the UN Security Council to include in its Resolution 949 the commencement of military operations against Iraq.[72] Contrary to the US, Russia advocated a peaceful resolution to the Iraqi conflict. The US's abortive attempt to revive the anti-Iraq coalition was viewed by Russia as a diplomatic success in light of its own continued status as a world great power.

In his first appearance before the State Duma's International Affairs Committee, Primakov declared that the Russian foreign policy orientation was to be based on "equality" not on "partnership where one leads and the other is led."[73] Pragmatism and Russia's international position became characteristics of Russian foreign policy. Russia's status should be reinstated and recognized by great powers. As the Western option of the liberal approach failed and NATO began its surge toward Russia's borderlands, Russia's foreign policy, from 1996 to 1999, took a confrontational tone. Externally, Russia's demand for social recognition as an existing great power fell under the strategy of social competition. In addition, reinstating Russia's status in the world fell under the strategy of social creativity. Primakov adopted both strategies because the Yeltsin-Kozyrev strategy of social mobility had failed because Western high-status clubs remained closed to Russia despite Moscow's attempts to integrate with the West.

Primakov's foreign policy course was consensual domestically and confrontational internationally mainly because he viewed the existing status hierarchy to be unstable. His policy sought to establish Russia as a great power in the international system, commensurate with its position as a permanent member in the UN Security Council with a veto power and to limit the influence of the US in FSS. He was against unipolarity and the hegemonic power of the US. Primakov advocated a multipolar approach to nurture strategic alliances with other poles of regional powers, which were "hostile to the U.S. to build a counter hegemonic bloc, such as China, India, Iran, Libya, North Korea and Cuba, albeit without result."[74] Yet, such a potential balancing coalition led by Russia was an additional reason for the US not to accord Russia higher status because Russia could be a current or future threat to the US "purely in material and security terms and/or a threat in terms of Russia's status claims, with the socio-psychological and material consequences attendant."[75] This explanation supports H1, inasmuch as Russia and the US would consider each other primary threats. Russia's national interest was defined as maintaining its global status by pointing out Russia's Eurasian geography and power and its historical role in both Europe and Asia.

In relation to Iran, Primakov continued to strengthen relations with Tehran. During his visit to Tehran in December 1996, he declared that relations between the two states were "developing along an ascending curve," in part because of Iran's role in arranging a cease-fire in Tajikistan. In 1997, Russia and Iran brokered a peace plan that ended the five-year civil war in Tajikistan, the only Farsi-speaking FSR. For its part, Tehran was also satisfied with Russia's policy toward Iran that was different from "the ultimatum-based methods of the Americans."[76] Also, in 1996, after the victory of the Taliban in Afghanistan, Russia and Iran took a posture against the extremist rulers of the country. Iran became the means of responding to Russia's perceived lack of respect in its relations with the US.

Cooperation between the two countries on regional conflicts continued into 1997, as Russia sought Iran's assistance in pressuring Turkmenistan and Azerbaijan to cooperate with Moscow in the exploitation of the hydrocarbon reserves in the Caspian Sea and in demarcating the bottom of the Caspian Sea between the five littoral states.[77] Transneft, the Russian oil transporting joint-stock company, insisted that the pipelines crossing into Russian territory should be discharging at the Russian port of Novorossiysk near Grozny. However, US policy makers only accepted the transmission of Azerbaijani oil through the Northern Route Export Pipeline to Novorossiysk, which was completed using segments of the former Soviet pipeline network.[78]

In March 1997, during a visit to Moscow, Netanyahu declared that Israel now considered Russia a "friendly state" and announced a $50 million loan for Russia's agricultural sector. Yet, there were serious disagreements between Israel and Russia, especially about Moscow's arms sales to Syria and Iran. Primakov assured Netanyahu that Russia was not supplying missiles and missile technology to Iran, and Yeltsin promised him that Moscow would not sell state-of-the-art weapons to Syria.[79] Russia wanted to be accepted as a responsible partner by all sides in the Arab-Israeli conflict. In September 1997, the US expressed concern that arm shipments to Iran would upset the regional balance in the Persian Gulf and "greatly alarm the U.S." In 1998 as the US government continued to raise the issue of arms sales to Iran, Primakov "acknowledged that some brain drain had occurred, but that it was simply not in Russia's interests to assist its neighbor in acquiring long-range missiles."[80]

After the fall of the Chernomyrdin government in March 1998, Primakov was promoted to prime minister. In the aftermath of the financial collapse in August, which left Russia impoverished and unstable, the US began to adopt a forceful policy toward Serbia, a country considered by many in Moscow and Belgrade as a Russian client. For the first time after the Cold War, the prospect of a US and Russian confrontation seemed possible when, "without authorization from NATO, a detachment of Russian soldiers seized and held the Pristina airport."[81] The Russian security establishment saw that the US would not hesitate to act outside the framework of international law and the UN if doing so was necessary to protect the national interests of the US. Jeffrey Mankoff rightly noted that as Russia "aspired to play a global role analogous to the U.S., Russia had little choice, its security establishment believed, but to equip itself to survive in an anarchic world order and be ready to respond forcefully when challenged."[82] A status conflict emerged when Russia perceived that it deserved great power status recognition, which the West failed to acknowledge. Tuomas Forsberg noted that "Russia and the West did not share the same view as to how much status Russia deserved but even more importantly, they did not perceive their mutual actions in the similar way."[83] The West treated post-Soviet Russia like a "defeated adversary" and behaved as if the West had won the Cold War.[84]

Primakov adopted a strategy of social creativity to find a "new value dimension" to gain domestic and international recognition of Russia's status.[85] Primakov criticized US unilateralism and signed declarations with China highlighting their commitment to a multipolar world while concurrently pursuing Russia's "special relationship" with NATO and equal status in other Western institutions.[86] Such a relationship was in line with Russia's National Security Blueprint of 1997 that stressed Russia's interest "in fully equal participation in world, European, and Asian economic and political structures to ensure an opportunity for Russia's full-scale inclusion in all organizations and institutions for collective management of global political processes."[87]

The rationale behind a multipolar world order to "counterbalance" the dominance of the US multipolarity "was a geopolitically motivated construct, centered in the principle of the balance of power."[88] Primakov's efforts and strategic partnership with China aimed to counteract perceived US efforts to undermine Russia's status. China continuously described Russia as an equal partner and an international great power. For its part, "Russia did not preclude cooperation with the U.S., the main thread running through it was one of soft containment through a consensus of the rest – that was, the other poles in the international system."[89] To gain recognition of Russia's role in the world, Primakov rejected the Cold War-era ideological and material conflicts and favoured competition rather than social mobility, a strategy that Yeltsin adopted in the early 1990s. As such, his "main foreign policy disposition toward the West was a reflexive one of status competition, but within a framework of cooperation with the West."[90]

Primakov's social creativity strategy of a multipolar world became the cornerstone of Russia's foreign policy. Russia would play a strategic role in stabilizing the international system and maintaining international law. In 1999, Russia's role in maintaining global stability was undermined when NATO intervened in Serbia against Kosovo, despite strong Russian objections and without approval from the UN Security Council. The Kosovo case showed that Russia could not stop the US in international matters. That said, the Kosovo case was a strong blow to Russian national self-esteem. Russia was willing to assume the responsibilities associated with great powers in global politics. Primakov described NATO's military action, under the pretext of humanitarian intervention, democracy promotion, and the use of force as a breach to international peace and order and the "rules of a great power concert system."[91] The Russian elite and the Russian people in general "came to the conclusion that they had been profoundly misled and that NATO remained directed against them."[92] Another key priority of Russia's foreign policy was Moscow's dominance in the FSR. In more than one place, Russia's National Security Blueprint of 1997 mentioned increased cooperation and integration within the CIS framework.[93]

Primakov's pragmatism, which Kozyrev lacked, was perceived by Russian elites as able to restore Russia's lost dignity on the international stage. His policy of status-driven national self-image converged with the elite aspirations regarding international status. For the conservatives, he represented the man who could bring to Russia the past Soviet reputation, power, position, and prestige. Yet, it should be stressed that status cannot be attained unilaterally; it should be recognized by higher status actors.

For Primakov, Russia could not ignore its geostrategic interests. The Kremlin became convinced that the retreat from various strategic regions, notably the ME, was interpreted by the West as a sign of weakness rather than a real attempt by Moscow to restructure international relations and integrate into Western political and economic institutions. Primakov's understanding of the ME allowed Russia to promote itself as a natural alternative to US policies in the region by being sympathetic to Arab demands.

In early 1996, Primakov's efforts focused on bringing Moscow's diplomacy back to the forefront of the Arab-Israeli conflict. Primakov visited Lebanon, Syria, and Israel in April 1996, when Israel launched Operation Grapes of Wrath against Lebanon in response to the shelling of northern Israeli settlements by Hizbullah fighters in Southern Lebanon. Contrary to Kozyrev, who had given far more attention to Israel than to its Arab neighbours, Primakov offered himself as a mediator who could exert pressure on Syria and Lebanon to de-escalate and normalize the situation. After meeting President Hafez al-Assad in Damascus in April 1996, Primakov, on 31 October 1996, met Israeli Prime Minister Benjamin Netanyahu in Tel Aviv who said that "he was keen to see Russia play an active role alongside the U.S. in the peace process," pointing out that Russia, alongside the US, had co-chaired the 1991 Madrid peace conference that adopted the formula of land in exchange for peace. Primakov made it clear that Moscow would not sell state-of-the-art weapons to Syria, but "Russia would not budge, under any circumstances, from its insistence that there had to be a Palestinian state." However, "Netanyahu was in fact abandoning all the agreements that the Palestinians had reached" with former Israeli prime ministers.[94]

In 1997, when Primakov hosted Netanyahu in Moscow he told him "bluntly that Damascus would not agree to surrender its sovereignty over the Golan Heights and that it had Russia's backing on that issue."[95] Further, Primakov stressed that the security of Israel depended on peace with Syria and the withdrawal of Israeli troops from the occupied Golan Heights. Russia's diplomatic initiatives in the ME, visible in its mediation of regional conflicts, highlighted its aspirations for great power status because status is connected to the ability to resolve conflicts and provide order, irrespective of the kinds of capabilities at its disposal.

On 12 May 1999 Primakov ceased to be prime minister. On 17 May Ehud Barak replaced Netanyahu after snap parliamentary election in Israel and the Arab-Israeli negotiations resumed without achieving a breakthrough.[96] On 5 July 1999 Hafez al-Assad visited Moscow to ask for Russian support in future negotiations and to secure a Russian agreement on a new arms deal. Syria wanted to modernize its army with Russia's help "at an expected cost of $2 billion over a five-year period," but Syria's expectations were not realized because of Israeli protests and US regional hegemony.[97] In a communiqué issued in Moscow on 7 July, Yeltsin and al-Assad "affirmed Moscow's role as a cosponsor of the ME peace process and the unity of the Syrian and Lebanese positions, thereby recognizing the special role of Syria in Lebanon."[98] The Kremlin appreciated the long-standing friendship between the two countries and Syria's role in the ME as a committed partner. However, Russia did not want to endanger its relationship with the US and Israel.

When, in August 1999, Barak visited Moscow, Russian officials pressured him to mediate between Syria and Israel, but Barak was reluctant to accept Moscow's offer. According to Israeli sources, Barak "rebuffed the offer."[99] From Barak's view "Assad wanted everything, but would not do what was necessary to change everything."[100] Once again the US dominated the Arab-Israeli peace process and Russia was left out of the Syrian-Lebanese track. Borrowing from William I. Zartman, the conflict was not ripe for resolution.[101]

In the late 1990s, Russia tried to protect its standing internationally and protect its national interests in the face of perceived Western encroachment and a growing Islamic threat from its south. In May 1999, after firing Primakov, Yeltsin appointed Sergei Stepashin as prime minister; Stepashin served for a short period. In August, Yeltsin appointed Putin as prime minister and in December of the same year as acting president. The second Chechen war was under way in early 1999 when Stepashin called for a new mission in Chechnya. According to Renshon, "for an event was capable of changing a state's place in a status hierarchy was the initiation of a military conflict that demonstrated a bundle of attributes both material and psychological."[102] Putin made a major overture to the US just after ordering troops into Chechnya. During his first meeting with Clinton in the summer of 1999, Putin claimed that al-Qaeda militants and Chechen rebels were planning terrorist operations against Russia.[103] Putin suggested that Moscow and Washington should cooperate against al-Qaeda and the Taliban mainly because the 1998 bombing of US embassies in Kenya and Tanzania caused a mortal danger of Islamic fundamentalism to the US. Putin was troubled by Chechen connections with al-Qaeda. The Taliban-ruled Afghanistan was the only country that had established diplomatic relations with Chechnya.

Chechen guerrillas, led by Shamil Basaev, were influenced by the Taliban and the Wahhabi sect in Saudi Arabia, who represented a violent Takfiri ideology and intolerant form of Islam. In the late 1990s, the Wahhabis in Russia were responsible for a series of terrorist bombings, kidnapping, and hostage takings.[104] The fight against terrorism was raised in the CIS summit in Minsk in June 1999. By linking domestic terrorism to international terrorism, Russia made the international community aware that it was impossible to fight the two separately. For Putin, "hope served as the emotional basis for engaging the West in fighting terrorism and preserving global stability. He believed that Russia and the U.S. bear a special responsibility."[105] Notwithstanding the danger of international terrorism, the Clinton administration did not collaborate with Moscow because it was "frustrated with Russian defiance in the Balkans and the removal of reformers from key posts in Moscow ignored Putin's overtures." The Clinton administration, "increasingly saw Russia not as a potential partner but a nostalgic, dysfunctional, financially weak power at whose expense the U.S. should make whatever gains it could."[106] Clinton's approach was in line with H2 because the US and Russia did not share the threat of international terrorism. Within this context, the US, the dominant power, was "expected to be motivated by the fact that on the one hand balancing the threat was likely to be easier" with the cooperation of Russia, which was seeking higher status recognition, and on the other that "the costs of not accommodating Russia might potentially include the latter adding to systematic challenges owing to its increasingly dissatisfied nature."[107] Only after the 11 September 2001 terrorist attacks on the US did cooperation between Moscow and Washington finally begin. The Clinton administration also encouraged Georgia to seek NATO membership and participate in building the Baku-Tbilisi-Ceyhan oil pipeline, running from the Caspian Sea to Turkey and bypassing Russia. It also "urged U.S embassies in Central Asia to work against Russian influence in the region."[108]

Russia's national pride was wounded and its national self-esteem was harmed because of Serbia's defeat and Washington's 1999 NATO enlargement policy that brought in the Czech Republic, Hungary, and Poland. In December 1999, Putin utilized the media to focus on his visit to Chechnya to boost the Russian army's morale. Although the EU "condemned all acts of terrorism," it accused the Russian army of committing excessive force at a time when a political solution could have been possible to end the conflict.[109] EU officials cautioned Russia by stressing that the violation of human rights in Chechnya was an obstacle to improving Russia-EU relations and that Russia's behaviour would have an impact on the acceptance of Russia by the international community as a political and economic partner. Despite European accusations and anti-Muslim fervour, Russian public opinion and the political establishment, as well as the economic elite, supported the military because a strong military was a symbol of greatness.

Given the divisions between the political groups during Yeltsin's era, Putin tried to consolidate his position and clearly state Russia's role in the world and where Russia's national priorities should lie. Jeffrey Mankoff wrote that Putin was favoured by the West because he was "a sober and responsible leader who could be expected to conduct foreign policy on the basis of Russian national interests rather than the extremes of emotion that had characterized Yeltsin's diplomacy."[110] Yet, Andrei Tsygankov noted that "emotions should be read in the context of international competition for power, status, and prestige." We should then expect that "emotions of hope would be sustained as long as Russia improved its political standing, and that emotions of frustration and fear would surface each time when Russia's political standing failed to improve."[111]

In March 2000, Putin was elected president with 54 per cent of the votes. Putin, who appealed to both liberal and moderate Westernizers, was determined to strengthen the state by encouraging state-led economic development in collaboration with business and by liberalizing government regulation. According to Putin, the purpose of modernization was to make Russia great. His vision of Russia earned him the support of statists and national restorationists.[112] Putin was well connected with the security elite of the state and enjoyed the confidence of the business elite, which enabled him to co-opt many of the components of power in Russia. In addition, "the political cohesiveness of the Putin era was to a large extent a combination of the centrist nationalist pragmatism that evolved in the late Yeltsin era and growing intolerance of diversity and variety in thinking and policy."[113] Putin followed Primakov's policies but modified his social creativity strategy of a multipolar world to stress Russia's traditional role with the US as stabilizer of the international system. In 2000, under Putin, a new national security concept and military doctrine were adopted that illustrated Russia's foreign policy behaviour. The next chapter examines and explores the foreign policy behaviour of Russia from 2001 to 2011.

Chapter 1 examined and analyzed Russia's foreign policy behaviour from Yeltsin to Putin. I argued that in post-Soviet Russia, Yeltsin initially adopted a policy of social mobility to build a strong relationship with the West to integrate Russia into liberal-Western economic, military, and political institutions. Russian liberals saw Moscow's global strategy as one of building a partnership with the West. Yet, partnership did not mean subordination and marginalization. The Kremlin's policies towards the ME were broadly influenced by Russia's view of itself in the early 1990s. The Yeltsin-Kozyrev pro-Western line faced opposition from Russian intellectuals and politicians who accused the liberals of betraying Russia's national interests in pursuing policies unbecoming to Russia's historical status and self-esteem. The statists and national restorationists rejected assimilation into the West and demanded a more global and differentiated role and status. Thus, it is reasonable to assume that Russia was dissatisfied with its status.

I also argued that Russian foreign policy behaviour changed with the appointment of Primakov as foreign minister in 1996 and then as prime minister in 1998. Primakov adopted a different identity management strategy, that of social creativity, to demonstrate Russia's assertiveness. In 1998, Russian diplomacy became assertive because the foreign policy behaviour of the US and the West did not take into account Russia's concerns about the disputes, mainly in Bosnia, NATO's enlargement, Iraq, Serbia, and Libya. Primakov, who was a statist and pragmatic politician, did not accept US domination in the world system and adopted multipolar diplomacy to balance the West. In the second half of the 1990s, Russia's policy towards the ME changed and Moscow tried to play an active role in the Arab-Israeli peace process but was unable to overcome US dominance in the region.

Perceived Western encroachments, Islamic terrorism, and the rebellion in Chechnya threatened Russia's national interests and endangered the unity of the Russian Federation. With regard to Russia's status aspirations, I provided evidence to support H1 and H2. Concerning H1, the West failed to provide the permissive conditions to accommodate Russia's status claims. As a matter of fact, the Clinton administration did not see Russia as a potential partner. Concerning H2, the US did not pursue an active policy to satisfy Russia's great power aspirations because Russia failed to develop liberal democratic institutions and build a market economy. The US did not share with Russia the belief that the Taliban and al-Qaeda were common threats to both countries, keeping in mind the material and socio-psychological consequences of Russia's status recognition. The meteoric rise of Putin, first as prime minister in August 1999 and within a few months as acting president in December 1999 portrayed decisiveness in Russia's behaviour. In the foreign policy domain, after being elected president in March 2000, Putin would emphasize a pragmatism that necessitated constructive relations with the West but would stress the need for Russia to assert itself and pursue its interests more forcefully in an unstable international system.

2

Russian Foreign Policy, 2001–11

Chapter 2 examines and analyzes how Vladimir Putin dominated Russian foreign policy development and determined Moscow's role in the world and where its national priorities should lie. This chapter explores the evolution of Russian-Western relations in light of the 2001 terrorist attacks against the US, the colour revolutions in the FSS that began in 2003, and NATO's enlargement policy. To enhance Russia's inconsistent status, Putin adopted the strategies of social creativity and social competition. Between the years 2001 and 2002, Putin attempted to enhance Moscow's bargaining power and reduce the tension with Washington by ratifying the Strategic Arms Reduction Treaty (START II) and by signing the Strategic Offensive Reductions Treaty (SORT). I argue that the American invasion of Iraq in 2003 and the Bush administration's support of the colour revolutions in Georgia, Ukraine, and Kyrgyzstan led to the deterioration of US-Russian relations. The West ideationally supported the colour revolutions as expressions of a democratization process that came from below. Yet, Russia was concerned about a hidden agenda of external regime change pursued by the West. Thus, in 2008, to protect its regional or special status Russia risked international conflict by invading Georgia. In accordance with status-seeking theory, Russia would be unwilling to give up its leadership position in its immediate neighbourhood and would therefore risk conflict to defend it. However, Moscow would face a number of negative consequences from its aggressive policy.

Chapter 2 also examines Barak Obama's 2009 reset policy with Russia and its inability to foster a strategic partnership with Moscow. Obama's attempt to reset ties with Moscow offered the Kremlin a new opportunity to address its security perception and to clarify the motives behind the Kremlin's international behaviour. I stress that status conflicts also occurred with both Presidents George W. Bush and Barak Obama when Russia was not respected and when it perceived that its international status did not correspond to the status level it thought it deserved. I argue that in 2001–02, Russia demonstrated its willingness and ability to play a major role in the ME and elsewhere and to cooperate with the US to serve American and Russian shared interests. Russia wanted to return to the ME as an active player to balance US dominance in the region and to elevate Russia's status. Russia wanted a partnership with the US but not a partnership at any price. However, the US was not interested in establishing a strategic partnership with Russia.

In March 2000, upon his election as president, Putin immediately stressed that central to his agenda were the values of *derzhavnost* (great power status) and *derzhavniki* or the *gosudarstvennichestvo* (proponents of state power). James Sherr argued that Putin sought to introduce changes in Russia's foreign policy establishment in order to restore the country's former status of great power. Under Putin the state became more centralized, securing a key role in foreign policy to the president.[1] Christian Nitoiu noted that Putin was confronted with Yeltsin's legacy "of a fragmented foreign policy, characterized by a dysfunctional clash of interests between a series of diverging schools of thought" that included the liberals, pragmatists or moderate nationalists and hardline nationalists."[2] Like Putin, his supporters, such as former exponents of economic liberalization Anatoly Chubais and Prime Minister Mikhail Kasyanov, who later became a sharp critic of the regime, sought to consolidate the state's power and to introduce economic reforms so that the state would serve as a guarantee against anarchy and instability – the traditional Russian view of the state's role. Putin advanced a vision of Russia that combined such features as "strong" and "modern," "dynamic" and "prosperous."[3]

Notwithstanding Putin's tough statements on foreign policy, his supporters argued that "his real goal was to deepen Russia's interdependence with Western economies and attain a greater level of cooperation with the West" in order to strengthen Russia internationally.[4] The Putin-led political clique, which included the financial elites who often faced competition for influence from the *siloviki* (the oligarchs whose power derived from the state security apparatus), and the military-industrial complex (VPK in the Russian abbreviation) had an important bearing on Russian foreign policy.[5] The powerful oil and gas sector lobby also played a role in foreign policy making because the oil sector "accounted for more than three-fourths of Russia's annual budget revenue."[6] Putin's success rested mainly on two factors: above all, the rising price of oil and gas and the unsuccessful transition from communism to a political system based on a market economy. Walter Laqueur noted that "from 2001 to 2007, the economy grew an average 7 percent a year."[7] Both, the financial and gas lobbies preferred a more Western-friendly foreign policy because the unfortunate Russian isolationist policy of the early 1990s undermined their business opportunities.

According to Alexander Vladislavlev and Sergey Karaganov, "the best way to define Russia's identity was to become Russian and to respect the nation's own history and values."[8] Identity definition of actors, particularly the state, is fundamental to the process of foreign policy construction. Andrei Tsygankov, whose research drew on constructivism, focused on the role of identities in Russian foreign policy. He reiterated that employing the schools of thought approach "revealed Russia's competing identities that constantly evolve, but also reproduce themselves across time and space."[9] Still, Tsygankov looked at Russian foreign policy through the lens of honour, which he defined as "what is 'good' and 'virtuous' course of action in the international society *vis-à-vis* the relevant other."[10] Like the Eurasionists, *derzhavniki* viewed the CIS and the near abroad as a top priority for Russia's security and regional policy. Thus, "a decisive component of Russia's new mission in the world was to insure, with help from the world community, that the ex-Soviet area did not become a geostrategic hole radiating instability and war and ultimately endangering the very existence of humanity."[11]

In the 1990s, the *derzhavniki* argued against an excessive reliance on Western economic aid and advocated a wide arms export policy regardless of Western opposition. The *derzhavniki* were also among the strong critics of Western policies concerning NATO's expansion. Putin never romanticized the West. For him, "the West was not an ideal; it was a vehicle for Russia's development."[12] Marcel de Hass argued that in Putin's first term, Russia's relations with the West were characterized by a sort of reluctant openness towards cooperation because his reluctance stemmed from the traditional Russian fear of the other.[13] From his political experience in the late 1990s, Putin viewed economic weakness as a handicap for national security and development, which could only be remedied with Western cooperation within the framework of Russia's modernization. Despite Putin's emphasis on economic development, there was little diversification in the country's industry that could lead to new job creation and wealth generation.

Russia's foreign policy approach has evolved since 1991 and can be traced by analyzing statements made by foreign ministers and presidents, as well as by reading key official documents. The National Security Concept of 2000 is the most significant document to aid in understanding Russia's approaches to its security policies. Despite the complicated international situation and domestic difficulties, Russia continued to objectively play an important role in global processes by virtue of its great economic, technological, and military potential and its unique strategic location on the Eurasian continent. In the international sphere, Russia's national interests lay in upholding and strengthening the country's position as a great power and as one of the influential centres of the multipolar world. In addition, Russia's interests lay in the development of equal and mutually advantageous relations with all the countries, primarily the CIS and Russia's traditional partners.[14]

The Foreign Policy Concept of the Russian Federation of 2000 aimed to achieve the following objectives: to preserve and strengthen Russia's sovereignty and territorial integrity in order to achieve Russia's firm and prestigious position in the world, consistent with the interests of the Russian Federation as a great power so as to influence general world processes with the aim of forming a just and democratic world order built on generally recognized norms of international law; to improve Russia's economy; and to prevent the emergence of potential tensions and conflicts in regions adjacent to the Russian Federation.[15]Attempts to use force under the pretext of "humanitarian intervention" and "limited sovereignty" to justify unilateral power bypassing the UN Security Council were not acceptable. Another important foreign policy task was to combat international terrorism.[16]

With regard to regional priorities, integration within the CIS framework was viewed by the Kremlin mainly in soft power terms. Relations with the EU should be determined by the framework of the 24 June 1994 Agreement on Partnership and Cooperation. Still, the problem of adequate respect for the interests of the Russian side in the process of EU expansion and reform would be dealt with on the basis of the Strategy for the Development of Relations between the

Russian Federation and the EU that was approved in 1999. Russia was open to constructive interaction with NATO on the basis of the NATO-Russia Founding Act (NRFA) on Mutual Relations, Cooperation and Security between Russia and NATO that was approved on 27 May 1997. Certainly, NATO's policies affected Russia's attitude and foreign policy. In December 1997, in his speech to the State Duma, Primakov referred to the Founding Act as a major accomplishment evidencing Russia's diplomacy in attaining its main objectives. As noted by Tsygankov, "Russia now had a mechanism of permanent consultations with the Alliance and the question of its expansion was largely defused in the domestic politics."[17]

Although Russia was unhappy about NATO's enlargement, it was prepared to overcome difficulties in its relations with the US concerning disarmament and arms control, and to preserve the infrastructure of American-Russian cooperation to achieve global influence and strategic security. Also, Russia intended to strengthen its traditional relations with India and Iran, and to stabilize the situation in the ME based on its status as cosponsor of the peace process. Indeed, Russia intended to turn the regions of the ME, the Black Sea region, Caucasus, and the Caspian Sea into a zone of peace and stability that would help advance Russia's economic interests.[18]

PUTIN'S STRATEGY TO MAKE RUSSIA GREAT

Putin followed Primakov's policy of neither rejecting the West nor denying the importance of Russia's historic greatness. In her constructivist analysis Magda Leichtova argued that Russia under Putin sent mixed messages to the West; on the one hand, showing willingness to collaborate, while, on the other, showing rather "unscrupulous pragmatism in the pursuit of national interest."[19] Despite the pragmatism of Putin's foreign policy, it remained largely a reactive one, based on recognition of Russia's proper place in the world and acknowledgement of Russia's voice in decision making.[20] By doing so, Putin was filling the psychological need to assert Russia's distinctiveness from other, lesser, European powers. Putin modified Primakov's social creativity strategy of a multipolar world to pinpoint Russia's traditional role as a joint stabilizer, with the US, of the international system. By distancing himself from Primakov's multipolarity as a substitute for US dominance, which required the cooperation and harmonization of many poles, including Europe, China, and India, Putin sought to use Russia's energy and diplomatic resources to diversify and strengthen Russia's economy and global political influence. Energy was a tool for both modernization and international influence. As Tsygankov argued, Russia had the capacity "as a global intermediary by coordinating its production with other important energy producers and offering its expertise to build energy infrastructure across the world."[21] This capacity would enable Russia to have potential influence in Asia, the Muslim world, and the FSS. Concerning diplomatic resources, Russia had already used those effectively in resolving violent conflicts in Tajikistan and Moldova in the 1990s. Globally, Russia sought "to position itself as a maker of new rules, articulating its concerns through its membership in international organizations and working to develop flexible coalitions."[22] For example, based on its involvement with the Collective Security Organization (CSO) that was established in 1992, Russia was likely to develop soft alliances with selected European powers, such as France and Germany, as well as China and Iran to promote Russia's global interests. During his first term, which lasted from 2000 to 2004, Putin's policy revealed a combination of Atlanticist and Eurasianist perspectives.

For Russian leaders, it was "multipolarity that fostered the development of democratic institutions in the international arena."[23] In place of NATO, Russia's preferred model relied on the Organization for Security and Co-Operation in Europe (OSCE) as the determiner of continental security and on the UN for global influence and security. As for Europe, Russia continued to refer to the strategic partnership with the EU, begun by Yeltsin, as a priority for Russia's integration and modernization. Thus, Putin's policies were neither purely pro-West nor purely anti-West.

Russia's arms control policy in 2001–02 was typical of Putin's strategy to enhance Moscow's bargaining power and lower tensions with the US. In his attempts at rapprochement with the US, Putin persuaded the Duma to conditionally ratify the START II, which had been under discussion since its signing in 1997.[24] In its ratification, a condition specified that the Anti-ballistic Missile (ABM) Treaty of 1972 was to be kept intact. This meant that Washington could have either START II or missile defense, but not both. Putin engaged in a "diplomatic offensive to impress on Washington both that a missile defense shield was unnecessary and that building one would be counterproductive."[25] The ratification of START II gave Moscow a card to use should Washington become determined about building an ABM system. Thereafter, and once again over the military's objections, in May 2002, Moscow signed the SORT, which also bound both sides to the establishment of a "new strategic relationship."[26] In effect, SORT ensured the maintenance of strategic parity by limiting the ability of the US to build new offensive weapons.

After his election in January 2001, President George W. Bush demonstrated a commitment to move forward with missile defense that was put on hold by the Clinton administration. The rationale behind the decision was to protect the US from possible future missile attacks by "rogue" states such as Iran, Iraq, and North Korea.[27] Russian general staff argued that a US defense against missiles would neutralize Russia's capability to retaliate against a nuclear attack. Putin's arms control policy in 2001–02 aimed to put pressure on the US and, if successful, would have helped Russia cut spending on its nuclear weapons in order to focus on modernizing its conventional weapons and deal with domestic security threats, mainly Chechnya.

Arms control was only part of Putin's strategy to counter US global domination. Another strategy was to build a "political coalition to act in concert as strategic partners."[28] In 2000, Putin visited North Korea, India, Cuba, and China in an effort to establish a multipolar world to maintain a global balance of power and to promote Russia's global interests. The Kremlin was not satisfied with the way the unipolar structure of the international system diminished Russia's global influence. In March 2000, not only did Putin sign a joint declaration with Chinese president Jiang Zemin that expressed concern over US plans to build a missile defense system but he also offered China joint development of some oil deposits in Russia as part of the Russian-Chinese subcommittee on the energy industry.[29] In March 2001, Putin met Iranian president Mohammad Khatami in Moscow to discuss ways to prevent the proliferation of ballistic missile technology. As well, Putin agreed to resume the sale of conventional weapons to Iran after an interruption of more than five years. Putin's meeting with Khatami was not overlooked by the Bush administration. Indeed, Bush extended the law imposing sanctions against Iran, banning US investment in the Iranian economy.[30] In addition to the sale of weapons to Iran, Russia signed contracts for the sale of ammunition to Libya and for the repair of armoured vehicles and air defense systems. Concerning Iraq, Russia defied US wishes to settle the Iraq issue militarily. In July 2000, to the dismay of Washington, Russia disregarded UN sanctions and invited Tariq Aziz, the Iraqi foreign minister, to Moscow in order to promote a political resolution of the Iraq conflict. Although Aziz's visit to Moscow caused a decline in American-Russian relations, Russia wanted to assume its responsibilities associated with the role of a major power status.

Moscow was eager to take diplomatic initiatives in the ME and play a role in mediating regional conflicts. In January 2000, Russia officially endorsed the US-sponsored Israeli-Syrian negotiations in Washington, DC and Shepherdstown, West Virginia, and joined Washington in pressuring Damascus to participate in the multilateral ME talks to be held in Moscow on 1 February 2000.[31] In March 2000, Russia hailed the proposed US-Syrian summit as a positive step in establishing a breakthrough in the ME peace process. However, on 26 March 2000, the Geneva meeting between President Bill Clinton and President Hafez al-Assad of Syria did not yield expected results.[32] Thereafter, on 10 June 2000, Hafez al-Assad died and his son Bashar al-Assad became president. On 18 September 2000, Putin assured the new Syrian leader that Moscow and Damascus had "mutual political will, a legal basis and a material foundation" with which they would develop their relations.[33] From Putin's statement, it is reasonable to argue that he wanted to preserve and, if possible, foster Russian-Syrian relations to demonstrate Moscow's willingness to engage in Middle Eastern affairs and to promote Russia's image as a country that is friendly toward Islamic nations.

Concerning US-Russian relations, in June 2001, Bush and Putin met in an ancient castle near the Slovenian capital Ljubljana. The meeting created an opening for Putin to highlight Russia's position and authority when Bush famously remarked that when he had "looked [Putin] in the eye … I got a sense of the soul."[34] During the meeting both leaders displayed considerable rapport but none of their differences, particularly the issue of missile defense, were resolved. Given the legacy of the financial collapse in the late 1990s and Russia's international weakness, Bush's realism made him turn to a policy of neglect. For the Bush administration, Russia was not a priority because it was viewed as "corrupt, undemocratic and weak." Simes noted that "although this assessment was accurate, the Bush Administration lacked the strategic foresight to reach out to Moscow."[35]

The 11 September 2001 attacks on the US by Islamic terrorists dramatically changed the pattern of bilateral relations between the US and Russia. Russia's "diplomatic behaviors and attitudes and its decisions, commitments, and actions" to jointly fight terrorism were associated with honour and the status of a great power.[36] Yet, Tsygankov noted that Russia's support for the war on terror after 11 September had less to do with honour and partly stemmed from Putin's need to reaffirm and safeguard Russia's territorial integrity in the context of dissent in some of its predominantly Muslim regions.[37] It seemed that "the U.S.–Russian relations took a decisive turn for the better again as optimism emerged that Russia had decided that it truly belonged to the West."[38] However, in his State of the Union speech on 29 January 2002, Bush revealed much wider US ambitions and marked the initiation of a new assertive foreign policy, described as the Bush Doctrine, which labelled Iran, Iraq, and North Korea as part of an "axis of evil."[39] The Bush Doctrine implied that the US could launch pre-emptive attacks on sovereign states if deemed necessary to protect US national security and international order.

The rapprochement between Moscow and Washington that followed the 11 September events stemmed from the convergence of interests between the two countries, both of which had suffered from Islamic terrorism and wanted to rid themselves of the Taliban regime in Afghanistan, along with its al-Qaeda affiliates. Al-Qaeda was playing an increasingly significant role in training and supporting Chechen rebels and spreading Islamic radicalism in Central Asia. To jointly fight terrorism, Putin granted the US over-flight rights across Russian territory, endorsed the establishment of US bases in Central Asia, and facilitated access to a Russian-armed and Russian-trained military force in Afghanistan. Yet, Moscow clashed with Washington over the duration of the US presence on CIS territory as part of the war on terror. The tension over the status of US troops in Central Asia and Russia's participation in the war on terrorism "were symptomatic of how the U.S.–Russian relationship continued in important ways to be driven by the traditional language of geopolitics." Certainly, after the events of 11 September, the US was "more willing than in the previous decade to actively engage in balance of power politics," especially in Central Asia, a region that was very critical to the war on terrorism.[40] However, Russia continued to view FSS as its own exclusive sphere of influence.

Hence, Moscow reinvigorated CSO, also known as the Tashkent Treaty, which had been established in May 1992. The quasi-alliance between Armenia, Kazakhstan, Kyrgyzstan, Russia, Tajikistan, and Uzbekistan was upgraded to the Collective Security Treaty Organization (CSTO) in May 2002.[41] Russia's aim was to reassert its overall control over the area's "friendly" airspace and to counterbalance US encroachments. Moscow's action to reinvigorate the CSO was an example of latent conflict of interests between the West and Russia over the status of the post-Soviet independent states.

By the mid-2000s, Russia had begun making progress toward establishing a coherent foreign policy. In addition to cooperation between Russia and the US in Afghanistan, Moscow was supportive of US initiatives against the Iranian and North Korean nuclear programs and "agreed to launch a strategic energy dialogue with the U.S. and the EU in June 2002."[42] As mentioned above, energy was a tool for both domestic modernization and international influence. Russia's agreement on a strategic energy dialogue stemmed from Russia's economic recovery led by the oil and gas sector, where large-scale export-oriented projects, including the Baltic pipeline system, the Blue Stream, and the Tengis-Novorossiisk pipelines were implemented. Still, in 2004, Russia signed onto the US-planned Proliferation Security Initiative to prevent the spread of fissile material. Both developments contributed to and raised the expectations of further cooperation between Russia and the US.

Russia's support for the US after 11 September was rewarded by full membership in the G8 and the upgrading of the NATO-Russia Council in 2002.[43] The invitation to join the G7 was issued formally in 1997 within the context of the decision about NATO's first Cold War enlargement.[44] During Yeltsin's term the format G7+1 was unsatisfactory for Russia and had led to status conflict. The NATO-Russia Founding Act and full membership in the G8 were gestures toward Russia's status. Meanwhile, Russia increased its military capabilities and demonstrated its willingness to play global roles.

For Putin's strategy of social creativity to be successful, the dominant power, the US, would have to be willing to accord higher status to the aspiring state (i.e. Russia). Despite the newfound cooperation between Russia and the US, relations remained strained because the Bush administration did not regard Russia as an equal partner. According to H2 the accordance of higher status to Russia was more likely when both the US and Russia shared the same primary threat of terrorism. The dominant power (the US) was expected to be motivated by the fact that balancing the threat was likely to be easier with the cooperation of Russia. A significant drawback of not according higher status to Russia was the resulting increase in its dissatisfaction. Although Russia demonstrated to the US its responsibility in ridding the world of terrorism, Washington lacked an active policy to engage Moscow and satisfy Russia's higher status aspirations. For its part, Russia continued to clash with Washington over the duration of US military presence in Central Asia. Russia should have realized that the common threat could not be balanced without the help of the US "and that joining hands would bring security and status." Although terrorism was a common primary threat to balance in terms of security and status, both the US and Russia failed to do so. The balancing logic meant that the dominant power (the US) did not acknowledge the enhanced responsibilities and privileges of Russia "before dissatisfaction reached a point" where Russia "might choose to assist the primary threat in its potentially revisionist goals."[45]

A number of factors contributed to the deterioration of Russia's relations with the West. First, in June 2002, the Bush administration withdrew from the ABM treaty and envisaged plans to deploy a missile defense system in Poland and the Czech Republic, which had joined NATO in 1999. The 1972 ABM treaty was the core of Cold War arms control. For Russia, the US had violated the 1997 NRFA and its commitment not to deploy significant military forces on the territories of states that recently joined NATO. The choice of the Czech Republic and Poland as the site of the initial deployment heightened Russia's anger over NATO's enlargement.[46] In addition to the military threat, "the fear was that Russia would be cut out of crucial security decisions and be isolated from the West, and that this would aid the rise of extreme nationalists inside Russia" as Kimberly Marten noted.[47] Bush's decision caused growing concern in the Kremlin, which "felt inadequately rewarded" for its support of the US after 11 September, with Washington being "reluctant to engage in bilateral negotiations on strategic stability."[48]

Second, Russia's view of the world and Russian interests and values clashed with Washington's efforts, between 2002 and 2006, to spread democracy in Iraq, Lebanon, and Syria. Moscow refused American "tendencies to override the sanctity of national sovereignty and to internationalize domestic human rights or democratic violations."[49] From 2001, the US pressured the Syrian and Iranian regimes to conform to international norms by means of UN resolutions. Apparently, the Iranian regime was providing material and financial support to the radical Iraqi Shiite cleric Muqtada al-Sadr and his followers "in a bid to tie down the U.S.-led coalition forces in Baghdad."[50] Moreover, even before the American invasion of Iraq in 2003, the Syrian regime aided the passage of Sunni Arab and Muslim volunteers from Syria to Iraq, to fight against American troops. Both, Washington and the Iraqi authorities, accused Syria and Iran of facilitating the flow of foreign fighters into Iraq. For its part, in 2003, the Bush administration imposed economic sanctions on Syria, and in 2004, the UN Security Council adopted Resolution 1559, which called for "all remaining foreign forces to withdraw from Lebanon" (a clear reference to Syria).[51] Concurrently, in a bid to isolate Iran internationally, Washington pushed the issue of Iran's nuclear activities centre stage, most notably at the International Atomic Energy Agency. Under Putin, Moscow's refusal to spread democracy in the ME and elsewhere, "strengthened authoritarian regimes by showing that rapid democratization could lead to chaos if it directly challenged the existing status quo in seeking more freedom."[52]

Third, despite Russia's continued efforts to demonstrate its great power status by finding a diplomatic resolution to the Iraq conflict, the Bush administration's decision in March 2003 to invade Iraq, a former Soviet client, without consultation with Putin was viewed by Moscow as a lack of respect. Russia, Iran, and Syria agreed that the US occupation of Iraq was a direct threat to their national interests, and they opposed it strongly. In the 1990s, Syria had already established stronger relations with Iran. Syria eased the passage of Iranian arms through its territory to the Lebanese Hizbullah, which further enhanced its military capabilities. Also, with Iranian help, Syria exerted greater influence on radical Palestinian organizations including Hamas. In a trilateral meeting in Paris on 10 February 2003 Russia, France, and Germany issued a statement saying that they would try to prevent the adoption of a UN resolution authorizing the use of force against Iraq.[53] Pavel Baev noted that "instead of consolidating Russia's profile as a *bona fide* great power, this choice set in motion Russia's estrangement and alienation from the West that culminated in the quite unsuccessful G8 chairmanship in 2006."[54] Putin described the American invasion of Iraq as a "big political mistake," but hesitated to take an entirely anti-American stance.[55]

On 18 March, Britain, Spain, and the US withdrew the draft resolution seeking UN Security Council authorization for military action to disarm Iraq.[56] Two days later, the US invaded Iraq with the "coalition of the willing." The war began without the legitimization of the UN and all that was left for Russia to do was to condemn the aggression. Washington's readiness to use force and act unilaterally without seeking agreement among its allies renewed the criticisms emanating from Russia during the Kosovo war in 1999.

Fourth, instead of showing respect for Russia's status as a regional power, with a *droit de regard* in the post-Soviet space, the Bush administration supported the colour revolutions in Georgia in 2003, Ukraine in 2004, and Kyrgyzstan in 2005.[57] For Russia, these revolutions were attempts for regime change pursued by the West and were perceived as a humiliating interference in Russia's backyard. Thus, these colour revolutions had "a malign geopolitical purpose."[58] In 2003, Georgia became a battleground. Russia was unable to prevent Western-backed Mikhail Saakashvilli from supplanting the pro-Russian Eduard Shevardnadze in the Rose Revolution. Saakashvilli, whose plan was to establish Georgian sovereignty over the breakaway regions of Abkhazia and South Ossetia, where Russian-backed separatists had declared independence in the early 1990s, alarmed the Kremlin. Encouraged by the admission of the Baltic States (Estonia, Latvia, and Lithuania) into NATO in 2003, Saakashvilli also tried to bring Georgia into the organization. In an open challenge to Moscow's leadership in the region, Saakashvilli positioned himself "as the leading regional advocate of color revolutions and the overthrow of leaders sympathetic to Moscow."[59] According to the theoretical literature on status, in their immediate neighbourhood, status-inconsistent powers "can become quite aggressive and tend to apply more competitive strategies leading to conflictive behavior."[60] To the dismay of Russia, in February 2006, Bush declared Georgia a "beacon of liberty."[61]

The Ukrainian Orange Revolution, in particular, became a source of major tension. From Russia's perspective, Western support for Viktor Yushchenko's Orange Revolution was not just about promoting democracy; it was also "an existential threat to Putin's Administration."[62] Tsygankov noted that the defeat of Moscow's favoured candidate, Victor Yanukovich, meant that Putin "lost his sought-after political influence, but found a way to remain engaged with the Ukrainian leadership and the West." However, over time, two types of conflict developed in Moscow's relations with Kiev. The first "concerned the Ukrainian aspiration to gain membership in NATO" and the second "involved issues of energy trade."[63] Still, what made Russia's conflict with Ukraine inevitable was the West's lack of recognition for Russia's values and interests in Eurasia and "the critically important role that Ukraine played in the Kremlin's foreign policy calculations."[64]

In accordance with status-seeking theory, Russia would be unwilling to give up its position in Eurasia and would therefore risk conflict to defend it. Yet, as Freire and Heller argued, it was exactly Russia's claim of exclusive leadership in the region that caused problems to the Russian status-seeking strategy in Ukraine. The more "regional states questioned Russia's primacy, the more they challenged Russia's major power identity, eventually accelerating status conflicts with the West."[65] Putin vowed to continue protecting Russian interests in Ukraine "by exerting great power influence in that country."[66] The presence of the Russian fleet in the Crimea, the rights of ethnic Russians and Russian business, and Ukraine's foreign policy orientation would continue to be of great concern to Russia. Evidently, Moscow viewed Ukraine's contemporary border, drawn in the Soviet period, as an administrative frontier that incorporated millions of Russians. The Bush administration's approach to Ukraine, namely its pressure on the Ukrainian government to request NATO membership and "financial support for non-governmental organizations (NGO) actively assisting pro-Yushchenko political parties, fueled Moscow's concern that the U.S. was pursuing a neo-containment policy."[67] Certainly, Putin felt that he had been betrayed by the US and other Western states with which he had cultivated friendships and had tried to establish partnerships. Although in the early 2000s, Putin chose not to overplay his opposition to NATO expansion and sought to organize security relations with Western countries on the common goal of fighting against terrorism, Russia's relations with the West began to shift away after Putin's re-election as president in March 2004.

Notwithstanding the above four factors that contributed to the deterioration of relations between Russia and the West, Putin engaged in a balance of power politics. Putin was able to balance the US and Europe against each other. He also balanced China against the US. In the aftermath of the American invasion of Iraq in May 2003, Putin invited the Chinese president Hu Jintao to Moscow to a summit meeting. Both leaders not only shared a similar geopolitical view of global politics, i.e., a preference for a multipolar world, but also found a common cause with the US in opposing Islamic extremism. Still, both leaders affirmed friendly relations between their countries and their joint commitment to fighting terrorism. A significant achievement of the summit was the creation of a new structure for the Shanghai Cooperation Organization (SCO), whose membership included Russia, Kyrgyzstan, Kazakhstan, Tajikistan, and Uzbekistan. This new structure would serve Russia's interests in three important ways: first, it would "counterbalance the U.S. influence in Central Asia"; second, it would "combine the weight of Russia and China in the global balance of power"; and third, it would "provide a vehicle for cooperation with those nations fighting terrorism."[68]

Concurrently, in May 2003, as a further earnest to its commitment to the strategic partnership with the US, the Russian Duma ratified SORT. Russia also supported the UN Security Council Resolution 1483 that lifted the sanctions imposed by the UN on Iraq (excluding an arms embargo) and terminated the oil-for-food program.[69] Yet, in 2004, dissatisfied Russia would adopt a confrontational posture with the West to fulfill its status aspirations.

FROM CONVERGENCE TO CONFRONTATION

Given the abortive outcome of the strategy of social creativity, Putin, after being re-elected in March 2004, adopted a strategy of social competition with the West so that Russia would be recognized as modern and great. From 2004, the policy of reducing the state's role in society was reversed. Instead, the economic sector came under the control of large organizations with many of them owned wholly or substantially by the state. The strategic energy dialogue with the US foundered when the Kremlin moved to consolidate its hold on the energy sector and use its control of energy to underpin Russia's assertive foreign policy. Indeed, in October 2003 the arrest of Mikhail Khodorovsky, a man with political ambitions, and the subsequent transfer of the assets of Yukos, a giant oil company, to the state-owned Rosneft chaired by Igor Sechin in 2004 was an indication that tensions between reform and state power were being resolved in favour of the state.[70] Putin was fulfilling the aim of *derzhavniki*, which advocated a strong and powerful state "which can maintain order and serve as a guarantee against anarchy and instability, a relatively traditional Russian view of the state's role."[71] As such, Russia's initial economic policy of diversification became rhetoric, "while the administration relied ever more heavily on resource nationalism."[72]

In his second term, from 2004 to 2008, Putin revised Russia's foreign policy with regard to the ME as well. Russia's strategy required courting Iran and the Palestinian Hamas without undermining the advantages of promoting trade with oil-rich Arab states, such as Saudi Arabia. It is noteworthy to state that the annual volume of Russian-

Saudi trade increased from $88.5 million in 1999 to $400 million, although still modest, by the end of 2005.[73] Russia also tried to improve its relations with Israel and build relations with other ME states with moderate regional policies. The positive outcome of this new strategy occurred in 2007 when Russia was granted, with Saudi backing, observer status at the Organization of the Islamic Conference (OIC). Cooperation with Muslim countries was necessary to restore international prestige and influence. The ME provided an excellent opportunity to challenge the US in addressing the complex disputes there, which offered opportunities to reenter the global stage with greater impact. America's behaviour in the region, especially in Iraq, and its failure in resolving the Palestinian-Israeli conflict, allowed Russia to exploit the developments in its favour and construct a policy that would enable Moscow to play a significant role in the ME.

Moscow's declining control in FSS continued to be troubling for the Kremlin. The second round of NATO enlargement that occurred in 2004 included Bulgaria, Estonia, Latvia, Lithuania, Romania, Slovakia, and Slovenia was not acceptable for Russia. The public, too, reacted overwhelmingly to the alliance's expansion. The Baltic states were now part of the West. Still, Moldova defied Moscow, with EU encouragement; American military advisors were positioned in Georgia; Azerbaijan and Ukraine sent troops to Iraq; the US had military bases in Central Asia; Russia lost influence in Ukraine as a result of the loss of Moscow's candidate, Victor Yanukovych, in the presidential election. Taken together, these developments constituted a significant geopolitical decline for Russia and threatened Russia's sphere of strategic interests. Putin abandoned the policy of partnership with the US and NATO. Furthermore, Putin "built up the perception that they were encroaching on or seeking to encircle Russia, and in response, announced a program of rearmament."[74] Obviously, Russia reverted from the strategy of social creativity to the strategy of social competition and became an opponent to the West. Thus, "acting on the perception of encirclement by the Western civilization Russia sought to defend itself not just on military and diplomatic grounds, but also in the area of regime consolidation."[75] For example, the "Kremlin began to position Russia as a power with its own special characteristics since the mid-2000 introducing restrictions against Western NGOs, political organizations and state-critical media."[76]

The theoretical literature on status suggested that countries with limited capabilities make efforts to strengthen their structural capability portfolio. The Kremlin, throughout the first decade of the 2000s, sought to develop Russia's economic capabilities and potential, thereby acknowledging the close relationship between economic strength and international status. Tsygankov rightly noted that "without its energy capabilities and its readiness to defend its core interests in Eurasia, Russia would not have been taken seriously by Western and non-Western powers."[77] On 27 May 2004, Putin addressed the Federal Assembly, declaring, "for the first time in a long time, Russia has become a politically and economically stable country ... Our goals are absolutely clear. They include a strengthening of Russia's position in the world."[78] The application of an assertive foreign policy to confront the US under Putin became possible through the emerging influence of Russia in the global energy sector. Oil and gas became important economic weapons used by the Kremlin to project and exert domestic and international political power and influence. The oil and gas sector required the securing of land routes for pipelines and seaports for shipping, something that further helped explain Russia's behaviour and its geostrategic view of the world. By contrast, the US was losing prestige because of its failure in Iraq. However, the US was not a weak power, and Russia was not as strong as Putin depicted. The excessive interdependence between power and energy had its drawbacks. According to Alexei Arbatov, the main problem with Putin's "managed democracy" and "executive vertical" was that "the country's present economic wellbeing and political stability rested on a very fragile and short lived foundations, because it was based on unprecedented global energy prices."[79]

Domestically, the most serious challenge to Russia's power came in May 2004 when Ahmad Kadyrov, the pro-Russian Chechen president, was assassinated and when in September 2004 Chechen terrorists took more than a thousand people hostage in a school in Beslan, North Ossetia. Shamil Basaev, a Chechen commander, took responsibility for the act, demanding the withdrawal of Russian troops from Chechnya. In the process of releasing the hostages, 330 women and children died.[80] Russia installed Ramzan Kadyrov as the new leader in Chechnya. This terrorist incident happened when the Kremlin was stabilizing the situation in Chechnya to pinpoint Russia's progress in fighting terrorism. Moscow's reaction to the Beslan incident was hardly in line with the pragmatic Westernist course.

The West criticized Moscow's use of excessive force to liberate the hostages. Yet, "governments could not fight terrorism effectively unless they sacrifice some of their democratic substance."[81] Moscow was angered "when 115 American and European foreign policy specialists and politicians published a stinging criticism of Putin's authoritarian regime and foreign policy aggression." Furthermore, the debate about human rights standards in the Parliamentary Assembly of the Council of Europe was viewed by many Russians "as an institutional setting for systematic attacks on Russia."[82] Yet, Russian identity was constructed through communication with and reference to Europe. Not only was the EU capable of exerting influence upon Russia, as it did in the 1990s, but Russia might also have some impact on Europe too.

The destruction of the secular regime in Iraq in 2003 and the termination of Saddam Hussein's dictatorship "let loose sectarianism, radicalism, and terrorism, which mutated to the new form of an Islamic state in Syria and Iraq (ISIS)."[83] The US-led invasion of Iraq in 2003 without the UN Security Council approval magnified Russia's sense of irrelevance and frustration. The divergence of interests between the US and Russia about NATO expansion coincided with an intensifying regional struggle in the ME, as Iran and Syria made a bid for regional supremacy. Moscow signalled that it was willing to return to the ME as an active player to balance US dominance in the region and engage in international diplomacy as a means to preserve its influence in international politics. In October 1994 Kozyrev had reached an agreement with Damascus on a repayment schedule of Syria's debt stretching to 2015. This agreement cleared the way for better relations between Syria and Russia, which still had a presence at a Mediterranean naval base at Tartus near the Latakia province of Syria as well as hundreds of military and civilian specialists working in the country. Putin's ability to reach a settlement with Syria set a pattern that would be replicated with Libya and Algeria, two former Soviet client states.

In January 2005, Bashar al-Assad's visit to Moscow culminated in an agreement that would reduce the Syrian debt to Russia from $13.4 billion to $3.6 billion.[84] This agreement would pave the way for Syria to purchase Russian weaponry, including advanced fighter jets and surface-to-air missile systems. What was more important, Syria allowed Russia to refurbish its naval facility in Tartus, used by the Soviet Mediterranean fleet to refuel. In the Cold War era, spreading influence in the ME was important for the Soviet posture in the region. Thus, in 2005, the resumption of the military relationship between Damascus and Moscow became crucial in rebuilding Russia's position of influence in the region.

As for Iran, Russia shared with the West a commitment of nonproliferation of nuclear weapons and tried to prevent Tehran from acquiring nuclear weapons. Concurrently, it had strong economic ties to Iran and was reluctant to impose the rigorous sanctions against Iran that the US had demanded. As noted in chapter 1, Russia had constructed a nuclear plant at Bushehr, and it would have liked to obtain new contracts for additional plants Tehran planned to build. The contentious issue between Iran and the West was Iran's program of uranium enrichment. In June 2005, Iran's newly elected nationalist president Mahmoud Ahmadinejad vowed to go ahead with uranium enrichment. This was the most damaging aspect of Ahmadinejad's foreign policy.

In fact, the nuclear issue in Iranian-Western relations became an urgent problem in the summer of 2002 when an Iranian dissident group, the Mujahedin Khalg, declared that Iran was building a nuclear enrichment facility in Natanz and a heavy water reactor plant in Arak.[85] In late 2005, a compromise was reached between Presidents Bush and Putin to permit Iran to enrich uranium in Russia under Russian supervision. Iran kept the idea as an option for further discussion. Russia, which was hoping to shield Iran from UN sanctions, was disappointed. It is out of the scope of this chapter to examine in detail the negotiations between Iran and the West on the nuclear program, yet it is noteworthy to stress that in 2006 Russia accepted the inevitability of sanctions against Iran. However, Moscow still wanted sanctions to exclude the Russian-built nuclear plant at Bushehr and its delivery of the fuel necessary for its operation to maintain dialogue with Iran. The UN Security Council Resolution 1737 had teeth. Iran was required to suspend all uranium enrichment, including research. All UN member states were "advised" to take necessary measures to prevent Iran from acquiring materials, equipment, or technology that would facilitate enrichment, reprocessing, or the development of nuclear-weapons delivery systems.[86]

In 2007, the second UN Security Council Resolution 1747 imposing additional sanctions intended to stop nuclear proliferation did not resolve the fundamental problems between Iran and the West.[87] As a result, "Putin was compelled to resume his delicate balancing act, as he sought to maintain credibility with both his Western and Eastern partners."[88] To prevent additional sanctions, Putin took the initiative to hold a meeting with Ahmadinejad. The meeting was held in Tehran and involved the five littoral states of the Caspian Sea. The participants discussed the legal status of the Caspian Sea, especially to determine each state's zone of national jurisdiction. The commitment to nuclear nonproliferation, the non-use of force among the five littoral states, and opposition to terrorism were also discussed. Although no decisions were made at the summit, Russia succeeded in enhancing its influence with both Iran and the US. It was in Moscow's interest to prevent Iran from uranium enrichment and to dissuade the US from considering the use of force against Iran. As a matter of fact, "With the U.S. Putin was a partner in keeping Iran nuclear free; with Iran he was a partner in diminishing U.S. influence in the region."[89]

In his address to the Russian Federal Assembly in 2005, Putin, without much elaboration, declared that the collapse of the Soviet Union was "the greatest geopolitical disaster of the twentieth century."[90] That said, Putin revealed his aim to restore Russia's status as a global power. In 2007, Putin's speech at the 43rd Munich Conference on Security Policy "seemed to be Russia's sole post-Soviet ideological document and key to understanding how the relationship between Russia and the U.S. reached today's nadir."[91] At the core of Putin's frustration and anger was his view of the US dangerously intervening into the affairs of sovereign states. Putin said:

> Independent legal norms are, as a matter of fact, coming increasingly closer to one state's legal system. One state and, of course, first and foremost the United States, has overstepped its national borders in every way. This is visible in the economic, political, cultural and educational policies it imposes on other nations. Who is happy about this?[92]

Putin's emotional speech at Munich should be read within the context of international competition for power, status, and prestige. Before 2005, Putin sought to avoid challenging the US and its dominance in the world because he remained hopeful of improving ties with the US even after Washington unilaterally withdrew from the ABM treaty. However, when Russia did not receive due recognition from the US Putin demonstrated an aggressive rhetorical style in relations with the US in an interview with *Kommersant*. Putin emphasized that the basis of his scepticism included the continuous military support of Georgia by the US and its unchanged intension to deploy elements of a missile defense system in Europe.[93] Putin's reactions were amplified by perceptions of the increased strength of Russia, which sought higher status.

Putin appealed to Russia's European partners "to the effect that Russia should play an increasingly active role in world affairs." With regard to the unipolar world order dominated by the US, he told the participants at Munich that "the world has changed." Hence, states "would like to interact with responsible and independent partners with whom they could work together in reconstructing a fair and democratic world order that would ensure security and prosperity for all." Putin considered the "unipolar model not only unacceptable but also impossible in today's world" because "the model itself is flawed and at its basis there is and can be no moral foundation for modern civilization."[94] Putin asserted that NATO's expansion did not relate to modernization of the alliance or ensuring security in Europe but represented "a serious provocation that reduces the level of mutual trust … against whom is this expansion intended? And what happened to the assurances our Western partners made after the dissolution of the Warsaw Pact? … Now they are trying to impose new dividing lines and walls on us."[95] In 2007, Russia reacted strongly to US plans to deploy a missile shield in Eastern Europe, ostensibly directed at Iran, in Poland and the Czech Republic. Russia felt that the US had violated its commitment not to deploy significant conventional military forces on territories of states that recently joined NATO, which was part of the 1997 Russia-NATO Founding Act. Moscow reacted by suspending Russian cooperation with the Conventional Forces in Europe Treaty, a key Cold War-era arms limitation agreement.[96] Still, in August 2007, Russia resumed regular strategic bomber patrols over the Atlantic and Pacific Oceans.[97]

US Defense Secretary Robert Gates addressed the same conference. He responded to Putin saying that the US and Russia were partners in several undertakings. However, Moscow's policies "seem to work against international stability," especially arms sales to Iran and its use of energy for "political coercion."[98] Yet, critics of the United States' handling of relations with Russia warned the Bush administration. Indeed, Ted Galen Carpenter, vice president for defense and foreign policy studies at the Cato Institute, reiterated that the US government should begin treating Russia with more respect and caution than it had in the previous years.[99]

Russia's assertive foreign policy toward the West would continue during Dmitri Medvedev's rule, elected president in March 2008. In the next section, I examine how Russia continued to struggle against the West and the EU to protect its national interests and play a role on the global stage as a major power.

RUSSIAN FOREIGN POLICY DURING MEDVEDEV'S PRESIDENCY

On 3 March 2008, Dmitri Medvedev was elected president of the Russian Federation. By no means would Medvedev's election put an end to Putin's era. On 7 May, Medvedev chose Putin as prime minister. Putin vowed that Medvedev's foreign policy would not be less assertive and less nationalist in its orientation in pursuing Russia's national interests. There should be no expectations of significant changes in Russia's threat perceptions and security policies. In 2008, the clash of interests between Russia and the West in the post-Soviet space turned into conflict.

First, in February 2008 the West recognized Kosovo's unilateral declaration of independence without UN approval. Putin had strongly opposed Kosovo's independence. Russia was still resentful of NATO's humanitarian military operation over Kosovo in 1999 and its intervention against Serbia. Russian diplomats drew parallels between Kosovo and the two Georgian breakaway regions of Abkhazia and South Ossetia. If Kosovo was allowed to be independent, why would the two breakaway regions of Georgia not be independent as well?[100] To provide empirical substance, Medvedev's pan-European diplomacy may be understood in terms of initial steps to establish a foreign policy. Medvedev, speaking in Berlin in June 2008, articulated a broad perspective on Europe "from Vancouver to Vladivostok" and proposed a new European treaty to establish a new security architecture moving beyond NATO expansion and the conflict in Kosovo. Medvedev reiterated the need to strengthen international law and "urged to move beyond Atlanticism by developing an equal partnership between the EU, the U.S. and Russia."[101] Medvedev's security initiative found strong support among Westernizers and statists. Despite sufficient backing at home, Medvedev's vision did not receive support at the international level. Some European nations, like Germany and

France remained wary of Medvedev's initiative because they found it dissatisfactory. The US also dismissed it. US Secretary of State Hilary Clinton found that a new European treaty was unnecessary. Clinton described Medvedev's initiative as reflecting "a certain envy" among "our partners."[102]

Second, in April 2008 the NATO summit in Bucharest invited Georgia and Ukraine to join the Membership Action Plan (MAP) of NATO and welcomed their aspirations for membership. The outcome of the Bucharest summit angered the Russians without satisfying the Georgians and Ukrainians.[103] Putin, who met NATO leaders at Bucharest, stated Moscow's opposition to Georgian and Ukrainian membership, to plans for missile shield in Poland and the Czech Republic, and to recognition of Kosovo. Georgian membership in NATO would put the US in the South Caucasus with direct access to the oil and pipelines of the Caspian Sea. Ukrainian membership would have been dangerous for Russia because of the historical ties between the two Slavic nations, the Russian population in Eastern Ukraine, and the location of Russia's Black Sea fleet in Sevastopol in the Crimea. Tsygankov rightly noted that "the West's geopolitical advances into what Russia has traditionally viewed its sphere of interests and the desire expressed by post-revolutionary Georgia and Ukraine to join the Western alliance exacerbated Russia's sense of vulnerability and isolation with respect to the West."[104] In his last of the twenty-eight meetings with Bush, Putin continued to argue, in vain, for a joint missile defense program in place of the US plan in Eastern Europe. Putin continued to act as a power broker and mediator between competing groups within the Kremlin. Putin was critical of the liberal school and sympathetic to the group, supported by Deputy Prime Minister Igor Sechin, which prioritized the military sector and excessively centralized energy-oriented model of development.

The EU too had been expanding eastward. In May 2008, the EU unveiled its Eastern Partnership (EaP) initiative, a program to foster economic prosperity in the FSR, such as Ukraine, and integrate them into the EU economy. Evidently, Russia viewed the plan as hostile to its interests and values in the near abroad. The European Neighbourhood Policy in general and the EaP in particular revealed a gap in perception between Russia and the EU. Andrey Makarychev noted that the EU and Russia interacted with each other in a contested area dubbed "near abroad" by Russia and, alternatively, "common neighbourhood" by the EU.[105] Within this context, James Nixey noted that the drawback in the EU's policy was that regional issues, such as "frozen conflicts," were not at the top of its agenda. Another mistake was that the EU "put a lot of effort into building bridges, the existence of which Putin denied." Nixey added that "evidence of misdemeanor was continually ignored because it did not fit the narrative of a developing partnership."[106]

In spite of the conflicts over the EaP, Moscow continued to refer to strategic partnership with the EU as a priority for Russia's modernization. It is important to match Medvedev's vision of Russia's relations with the EU with those of existing schools of foreign policy thinking in Russia. The liberal school, with close ties to Medvedev and presidential adviser Arkadi Dvorkovich, supported Medvedev's initiative of integrating Russia with European institutions, which many of them viewed as indispensable for Russia's economic development. For example, a report issued by a liberal think tank headed by Igor Yurgents presented the country as bound to the EU "by a legal treaty on strategic partnership in military, energy, political, and cultural areas." The report described the EU and Russia "as two entities with shared values, security interests, and visions of world order."[107] Russia must be "pragmatic" in devoting the country's scarce resources to the objectives of achieving global influence as an independent power as well as regional dominance "mainly in soft-power terms, rather than as imperial control over CIS states."[108] Russia was economically and culturally bound to Europe. Indeed, "Europe was the destination for 48 per cent of Russia's trade, 78 per cent of its tourists, and 80 per cent" of its energy transportation routes.[109] Those favouring the statist line of foreign policy thinking, like Fyodor Lukyanov and Aleksandr Khramchikhin, also supported Medvedev. They viewed the lack of strategic ties with the West as a tough predicament for Russia because of the nation's weakness and the rising power of China.[110] Although statists valued stronger ties with the EU or the US, such ties should not be at the expense of Russia's ability to act independently and develop relationships with non-Western countries. From a geopolitical approach, the neighbours were viewed as transit countries that constitute a "buffer zone" against the unfriendly "big other."[111] As for Russia, the EU was trying to create a "sphere of influence" in Eastern Europe. Still, "in the eyes of Russian leaders, EU expansion was a stalking horse for NATO expansion."[112]

To counter the EU's EaP initiative, on 29 May 2014 the presidents of Belarus, Kazakhstan, and Russia signed the treaty on the Eurasian Economic Union (EAEU), which came into effect on 1 January 2015. Russia's path to great power status continued to rely on distinctive elements, consistent more with a social creativity strategy than social mobility. It is noteworthy that the EAEU was created by Russian initiative to maintain Russia's influence in the former Soviet region and solve regional problems that could serve the country well. Armenia and Kyrgyzstan joined the EAEU respectively in October 2014 and in August 2015. The economic preliminary steps aimed to establish a full political Eurasian Union that "intended to provide Russia with the instruments for control in creating an alternative pole to the EU-centric order."[113] Putin stated, "today we have created a powerful, attractive center of economic development, a big regional market that unites more than 170 million people."[114] Russia's economic initiative in Eurasia would improve its regional standing. Indeed, "by engaging in architectures of cooperation, such as creating, sustaining, and participating in networks of intergovernmental organizations is consistent with a social creativity strategy of status enhancement."[115]

Russia's geopolitical idea was to restore Russia's economic and political influence on the post-Soviet space to stand up to all competitors on the world stage. By establishing the EAEU, Moscow's aim was to fulfill its ambitious goal of building a more unified version of Eurasia. As such, "Eurasianism provided the ideological glue and Russia, of course, was the self-appointed head of the Eurasian civilization."[116] If the EAEU were to succeed in its economic and political goals, "it would represent the EU's geopolitical contemporary in the East, attracting those European countries with non-Western historical and cultural roots seeking an alternative to the EU in order to support development, independence and political economy."[117]

The foreign policy concept the Russian Federation adopted on 12 January 2008 stated Russia's global priorities. First, the new world order should be based on the principles of equality, mutual respect, and mutually beneficial cooperation, as well as the norms of international law and the provisions of the UN charter. A system of bilateral and multilateral partnerships should be established to ensure the stability of Russia's international position in the face of international foreign policy volatility. Russia's "balanced and multi-vector" foreign policy stemmed from its geopolitical position as the largest Euro Asian power and the West's gradual departure from the world's economic centre. Russia would fully engage in structures, such as the G8, the Troika (Russia, India, and China), and the BRIC (Brazil, Russia,

India, China).[118] On 24 December 2010, South Africa was added to the BRIC grouping of states so that it became BRICS. Institutional integration at the regional level was also important for Russia to enhance its status.

Second, to strengthen international security, Russia reaffirmed its policy of developing multilateral foundations of nonproliferation of nuclear weapons and other weapons of mass destruction. Russia would also meet the threats of international terrorism, organized crime, the spread of weapons of mass destruction, and regional conflicts.[119] Russia possessed real capacity to play a well-deserved role globally.

Third, the document identified regional priorities that included the following: the CIS as a regional organization for multilateral political dialogue and economic development, the CSTO, and the strengthening of the Shanghai Cooperation Organization (SCO). By playing an important role in establishing international coalitions, such as the SCO, Russia's standing in the non-Western world had improved. Russia also intended to further develop its relations with Turkey, Egypt, Algeria, Iran, Saudi Arabia, Syria, Libya, Pakistan, and other leading regional states in bilateral and multilateral formats.[120]

On 7 August 2008 Georgia attacked Tskhinvali, South Ossetia's capital, to restore its sovereignty on the breakaway region. South Ossetia separated from Georgia in the 1990s and had established its own government, staffed by large numbers of Russian employees. This Georgian act provoked Russia. On 8 August Russia invaded Georgia to protect its sphere of influence among the member states of the CIS or, as Medvedev said, "Russia's zone of privileged interests."[121] In accordance with the theoretical literature on status-inconsistent powers, Russia acted aggressively in its immediate neighbourhood when its regional status was challenged. Furthermore, in accordance with status-seeking theory, Russia was unwilling to give up its position in FSS and therefore risked conflict to defend it. The 2008 Russian-Georgian war seriously undermined Tbilisi's hopes of accession to the EU or NATO. With Georgia becoming a NATO member, the strategic interests of Russia would be challenged, thus provoking Russia to defend them aggressively. Russia's power politics "was a demonstration that Russia had recovered its status as a great power and was demanding recognition as such."[122] Yet, Freire and Heller argued that Russia would face "a number of negative consequences from its aggressive policy, including Ukraine's further alienation from Russia or the increase of Moscow's partial international isolation in the form of Western sanctions." These empirical observations weaken the theoretical argument that status-overachievers "can successfully pursue aggressive policies of status enhancement in their region, thereby keeping the costs of such aggression low."[123]

The August 2008 war in the South Caucasus heralded a new stage in Russian-Western relations. Russia would no longer tolerate further expansion of NATO or expansion of US influence in FSS. The Russian posture was clearly stated by Russia's foreign minister Sergie Lavrov who said, "it is up to the American side to decide whether it wants a relationship with Russia that our two peoples deserve. The geopolitical reality we will have to deal with at the end of the day will inevitably force us to cooperate."[124]

In January 2009, Barack Obama was elected president. Obama's foreign policy toward Russia would differ from his predecessor, mainly because during his campaign he promised the American people "to make adjustments in ways that would not be so disruptive that they created uncertainty or unforeseen problems."[125] He delivered on his promise of withdrawing US troops from Iraq in December 2011. The Obama administration's policy to "reset" relations with Russia was announced by Vice President Joe Biden during his Munich speech in February 2009. The Obama administration believed that a more positive relationship with Russia would be in the interest of the US. Obama, was an internationalist and "not limited by isolationism and exceptionalism," and "his commitment to diplomatic negotiations suggested that he shared Lavrov's belief that shared interests in the face of geopolitical realities would underscore the necessity of U.S.–Russian cooperation."[126] Obama's attempt to "reset" ties with Russia presented the Kremlin with a new opportunity to address its security perception.

The US had to move on some issues of interest to Russia. Indeed, at the Moscow summit held from 6 to 8 July 2009 Medvedev and Obama signed a deal on parameters for negotiations to replace the START agreement, which would expire in December 2009, with the goal of reducing nuclear weapons, a major shift from the Bush administration's approach.[127] The American missile defense system would be reconfigured so that the US would think about intercepting short-range and medium-range missiles, rather than long-range missiles. As for Russia, it would not go ahead with plans to deploy medium-range missiles in Kaliningrad, a Russian enclave that borders NATO members Poland and Lithuania. After complex negotiations, both sides reached a compromise that allowed Moscow to withdraw from the treaty if it considered itself threatened by US missile defenses.[128]

More broadly, the Obama administration embraced a multilateral approach to tackle key transnational threats, such as terrorism. In his commencement speech in Moscow on 7 July, Obama said, "America wants a strong, peaceful and prosperous Russia. This belief is rooted in our respect for the Russian people, and a shared history between our nations that goes beyond competition."[129] Obama's foreign policy sought to address Russia's dissatisfaction with its status and reduce conflict with other European powers. Obama's reset also sought to accommodate Russia by recognizing its potential as a significant player in international affairs. In addition to the status accommodation aspects of the reset, Moscow's cooperation was motivated by recognition of the dangers of dependence on natural resource exports and the need to diversify. Moscow realized that the 2008–09 financial crisis required cooperation with the West if it were to obtain foreign investment and technology.

Obama called for a reset to refocus a relationship that "had suffered from a sense of drift" in recent years. According to Obama, the reset "must be more than a fresh start between the Kremlin and the White House, though this is important. It must be a sustained effort among the American and Russian people to identify mutual interests and to expand dialogue and cooperation that can pave the way to progress."[130]

The American gain from the July 2009 Moscow summit was a Russian agreement to allow NATO ground and air transit through its territory for troops and supplies for Afghanistan. Russian participation in the Northern Distribution Network (NDN) allowed the US to expand more efficient and direct routes that offered a strategic and vital alternative to the Pakistan routes.[131]

Another American gain was Russia's agreement on UN Security Council Resolution 1929, the most comprehensive set of sanctions against Iran to date that included tougher financial controls and an expanded arms embargo. US-Russian partnership in drafting this resolution was critical to its successful adoption.[132] Among other measures, Resolution 1929 called on Iran "not to undertake any activity related to ballistic missiles capable of delivering nuclear weapons, including launches using ballistic missile technology."[133] Equally important for Washington and Moscow was that Russia postponed its $800 million contract to sell S-300 air defense systems to Tehran.

These defense systems were a major concern to both the US and Israel. Iran accused Russia of capitulating to US and Israeli pressure. Apparently, Russia's agreement stemmed from its own growing suspicion of Iran's nuclear program and its confidence that Obama was more committed to the avoidance of military force than had been his predecessor Bush. However, Russia did not stop fuelling the nuclear reactor it built for Iran at Bushehr.[134] Both, the Bush and Obama administrations, found out "that there were limits to how far Russia would distance itself from one of its few remaining partners in the Middle East."[135]

After agreeing to replace the START agreement of 1991, Presidents Obama and Medvedev signed the new START treaty in Prague on 8 April 2010. The new treaty limited each side to 1,550 deployed strategic warheads, 700 deployed strategic delivery vehicles, and 800 deployed and non-deployed ICBM launchers, including heavy bombers equipped with nuclear armaments.[136] In their joint statement, both presidents acknowledged their commitment to continuing the development of a new strategic relationship based on mutual trust, openness, predictability and cooperation by following up on the new START treaty.

In Central Asia, the violent overthrow of Kyrgyzstan's President Bakiev in February 2010 came after he reneged on the issue of closing the American air base at Manas that was a transit centre for the NATO operations in Afghanistan. Bakiev's decision angered the Russians, and there was speculation that the Russians had a hand in his ousting. For Moscow, the outbreak of violence in the cities of Osh and Jalabad in June 2010 was viewed as an attempt by the West to provoke another colour revolution. Bakiev, who had established himself as a corrupt autocrat, tried to play Moscow and Washington against each other as rival bidders for influence. In the spirit of reset, Presidents Obama and Medvedev, on 24 June, issued a joint statement affirming their "common interest in supporting the people of Kyrgyzstan in their efforts to prevent further violence, address the current humanitarian crisis, and restore stability and democracy."[137] In October 2011 the new President of Kyrgyzstan, Alzambeck Atambaev, announced his intention to close the US transit facility when its lease expired in July 2014. In September 2012, Putin signed an agreement that extended the lease on Russia's military base at Kant. Concurrently, Atambaev planned to establish an additional base under the auspices of the CSTO in the city of Osh.[138]

If the events in Kyrgyzstan provided an unanticipated venue for US-Russian cooperation, Ukraine receded as a contentious US-Russia issue. In the presidential election of February 2010, Victor Yanukovych, who was rejected by the Ukrainians during the Orange Revolution in November 2004, defeated former Prime Minister Yulia Tymoshenko. For twenty years, "the country was irresponsibly governed, and it was far from certain that EU and IMF mandated reform would extirpate the instincts of a bloated and avaricious state."[139] After his election, Yanukovych renewed the Russian lease on the Black Sea fleet, allowing the Russian navy to remain in the Crimea until 2042. He also declared that Ukraine was not interested in NATO membership and indicated a willingness to accommodate Russia in strengthening its presence in the Ukrainian economy. Although Yanukovych argued in favour of the Deep and Comprehensive Free Trade Agreement between Ukraine and the EU that first began in 1999, the jailing of Tymoshenko created a major obstacle to looser relations with Brussels. With the NATO membership issue off the table, US policy toward Ukraine no longer aroused Russia's anger. Yet, despite the improvement of relations under Yanukovych, partnership between Russia and Ukraine remained limited because Yanukovych did not sell controlling shares of Ukrainian Naftogas to Gazprom and later on declined the customs union offer, which required agreement on common external tariffs.

The reset did little to solve the Georgian conflict that continued to remain a contentious issue between Russia and the US. The Kremlin criticized the Obama administration for its support of Georgia. Moreover, Russia and Georgia accused each other of supporting separatist groups in each other's country. The Obama administration urged restraint on both sides and refused to recognize Abkhazia and South Ossetia as independent entities. In the October 2012 parliamentary elections, Saakashvili's party was defeated. The opposition leader Bidzina Ivanishvili, who was close to Moscow, became prime minister. The US reached out to Ivanishvili in an attempt to mend Georgian-Russian relations and "moved to de-legitimize Saakashvili and the Rose Revolution." Angela Stent rightly noted that the Georgian situation "symbolized the larger issue of how to reconcile Russian and U.S. interests in the post-Soviet space, part of the broader question of how to improve Euro-Atlantic security architecture two decades after the Cold War."[140]

After the forming of the Eurasian Customs Union of Belarus, Kazakhstan, and Russia on 1 January 2010, the US and Russia intensified their discussion regarding Russia's WTO accession. The US pledged to provide additional technical assistance to help speed the process of revising Russia's WTO Working Party Report taking into account the Eurasian Customs Union. In 2012, Russia was admitted to the WTO after two decades of negotiations. Russia's entry into the WTO was a major status achievement and recognition by the international community of its importance in the world.

Despite these promising beginnings, the reset in 2011–12 appeared to be falling because it had no "contingency plan."[141] The reset was focused on obtaining agreements on particular issues, without connection to a broader vision for American-Russian relations. As observed by Thomas Graham, a former senior director for Russia in the Bush administration, the problem with the reset was that it never had a coherent answer for "what the two countries should aspire to now so as to foreclose a return to dangerous geopolitical rivalry and hold open the promise of mutually advantageous strategic partnership."[142] NATO and Russia cooperated on practical issues such as antipiracy, counterterrorist exercises, and counter narcotics in Afghanistan. However, the differences between their views remained a fundamental obstacle to cooperation. From Washington's point of view, the only way to overcome Moscow's antipathy toward NATO was to continue to engage Russia in the NATO-Russia Council, created in 2002, for joint projects and cooperation.

In June 2011, the NATO-Russia Council rejected Moscow's idea of a joint antimissile system in favour of two separate systems linked by information exchange. Russia wanted an integrated ballistic missile defense system with overlapping Russian and NATO components and shared control over missile launch detection, threat assessment, and choice of response. However, Russia's concept of shared operations and control over European missile defense differs markedly from the NATO version. On the 23rd of November 2011, Medvedev accused the US and NATO of undermining Russia's security. Russia felt humiliated when Washington refused to provide legally binding guarantees that the Obama administration's European Phased Adaptive Approach to European missile defense would not be directed against Russia.[143] Medvedev also warned "there might be grounds for our country to withdraw from the new START."[144] Russia consequently felt disrespected as an equal power and saw its legitimate security interests ignored. Although Medvedev's rhetoric was intended for domestic politics, it would be wrong to infer that his tough line was entirely campaign fodder. Russia had national security needs and concerns that were evoked by the US and NATO missile defense plans.[145]

Both Washington's refusal to provide guarantees that the European missile defense would not be directed against Russia and Medvedev's accusation that the US and NATO were undermining Russia's security provided strong evidence to support H1. Although Obama tried to address Russia's perceptions of insecurity, the US did not recognize Russia's major power identity because both the US and Russia anticipated the other would emerge as a primary threat. Russia still perceived itself as a member of the elite club of powerful states not obligated to defer to the US, however both the US and NATO did not accord higher status to Russia because they perceived Russia to be a threat "in terms of both security and status as a socio-psychological goal, especially if its status goals were accommodated."[146]

In November 2011, the Obama administration announced that the US would cease honouring its obligations under the Treaty of Conventional Forces in Europe (CFE) with regard to Russia. After three years of patiently trying to get Russia to recommit to the CFE, the US realized that Putin's decision in 2007 not to participate in the CFE treaty was final. In December 2011 the US ambassador to NATO, Ivo Daadler, stated that US and NATO plans for European missile defenses would continue with or without Russia. According to Daadler Russia's security concerns were not as important as the accelerating Iranian missile threat.[147]

Although the US and Russia were able to agree on a number of key issues, disagreements on other issues, such as missile defense, remained. The reset had limits. By the time presidential election politics began to heat up in the US and Russia in 2011, Medvedev, on 24 September, announced at the congress of the United Russia Party that the party congress would support the candidacy of Putin. In the US, the Republican Party's victory in the midterm 2010 elections and the decline in Obama's popularity raised the prospect that Obama's reelection would not be easily achieved. Meanwhile, the revolutions that began in the Arab world in December 2010 in Tunisia and extended in 2011 to Egypt, Libya, and Syria spread anarchy and uncertainty in the ME and North Africa. The protest movements in early 2011 called for democracy and freedom and advocated regime change. Chapter 3 will address the Arab Spring, the insurgency in Syria in detail, the role of regional actors, and its impact on the ME and US-Russian relations. Chapter 3 also will emphasize that as a status-inconsistent power Russia adopted a diplomatic posture in the early years of the Syrian war and tried to avoid direct military intervention that would require more substantial engagement.

It is important to note that the spread of the revolts in the Arab world coincided with the Russian State Duma elections held on 4 December 2011. The United Russia Party won a majority. The day after the elections, thousands of protesters rallied in central Moscow against what they viewed as a flawed election. The Kremlin responded by mobilizing pro-government Nashi and Young Guard youth groups to hold large demonstrations termed "clean victory" to demonstrate that minority groups would not be permitted to impose their will on the "majority" of voters. On 5 December Secretary of State Hilary Clinton stated that the US had "serious concern about the conduct of the elections," as detailed in the OSCE preliminary report and the reports of the Golos, private Russian election observers. However, Prime Minister Putin considered Clinton's comments a "signal" to the Russian opposition to "begin active work," with State Department help, to foment unrest.[148] The Kremlin was unsympathetic to Western criticism and civil society activism and felt that the escalation of the protests could destabilize society. Although the Obama administration was critical of the apparently flawed Duma elections, it called for continued engagement with Russia on issues of mutual strategic concern.

Chapter 2 examined Russia's foreign policy and the evolution of Russian-Western relations from 2001 to 2011. Putin used the strategies of social creativity and social competition to enhance Moscow's bargaining power and to reduce political tension with the US. I argued that Russia sought an arms control policy to counter US global hegemony. Putin's first term was dominated by the need to cooperate with the West especially in the context of the war on terror as a means of achieving honour and prestige. The rapprochement between Moscow and Washington that followed the 11 September events stemmed from the convergence of interests to fight international terrorism. However, in Tsygankov's view Moscow's support for the war on terror after 11 September had less to do with honour and was partly motivated by Putin's need to reaffirm and safeguard Russia's territorial integrity in the context of dissent in some of Russia's predominantly Muslim areas. Russia also tried to build a political coalition with North Korea, China, and Cuba to establish a multipolar world and maintain a global balance of power. Russia's attempts to establish a strategic partnership with NATO were unsuccessful because NATO's enlargement policy in 2004 disregarded Russia's leadership and interests in FSS. Russia continued to view FSS as its exclusive zone of influence to preserve and promote its values and interests. The findings in the first part of this chapter supported H2. Although Russia demonstrated responsibility with the US in fighting against international terrorism, Washington lacked an active policy to engage Moscow and satisfy Russia's higher status aspirations.

The American invasion of Iraq in 2003, without UN Security Council approval, and the Bush administration's support of the colour revolutions in Georgia, Ukraine, and Kyrgyzstan led to a deterioration of US-Russian relations. I argued that Moscow's loss of influence in Georgia and Ukraine constituted a geopolitical decline for Russia in Eurasia. Consequently, Putin adopted a strategy of social competition with the West so that Russia would be recognized as modern and great. In 2005, the resumption of the military relationship between Damascus and Moscow became crucial to rebuilding Russia's position in the ME.

Chapter 2 also examined Russia's strong reaction to US plans to deploy a missile shield in Eastern Europe, ostensibly directed at Iran, in Poland and the Czech Republic. Furthermore, Russia viewed the EU's EaP initiative as hostile. In 2008, the clash of interests between Russia and the West in post-Soviet space turned into conflict. Russia invaded Georgia to enhance its status and maintain its values and influence in the South Caucasus. In 2009, Obama's reset policy with Russia failed to reconcile American and Russian interests in post-Soviet space and Russian and NATO views on missile defense. Russia lost an opportunity to address its security perception. The findings in the second part of the chapter support H1. Although Obama tried to accommodate Russia's security fears, the US did not accord higher status to Russia because both powers anticipated each other could emerge as threats. In 2008, Medvedev's proposal of a new all-European treaty to establish a new security architecture by moving beyond NATO expansion did not appeal to US and European leaders. By 2011, the reset largely exhausted its agenda. The West could only engage Russia as an equal contributor to shaping the global system if Moscow did not harbour revisionist plans that might represent a threat to Western interests.

3

Prelude to Military Intervention, 2011–14

Chapter 3 examines the Syrian insurgency that transformed into civil war, the external players in the conflict, and international attempts to stop the violence and to initiate peace (the Geneva Communiqué or Geneva I in 2012 and Geneva II in 2014). Chapter 3 also examines the lack of US policy in the ME and Russia's power-based foreign policy to fill the vacuum in light of American diplomatic retreat. The US, along with Saudi Arabia, Qatar, and Turkey supported the insurgents battling al-Assad whose external military backing had so far come from Russia, Iran, and its Lebanese proxy Hizbullah. Since late 2011, Russia had been assertive and anti-Western despite lower energy prices and reduced European dependence on Russian gas. In 2014, ambitious Russia applied the strategy of using force in Ukraine to prompt the West to accept its aspired status gain – a strategy of social competition. While suffering from a persistently weak economy that rendered military intervention quite costly, Moscow's willingness to use military force in its foreign policy as a means to enhance its status seemed highly counterproductive. In this chapter and within this context, H1 and H2 are tested. From Moscow's perspective, regime changes in the FSR and ME would pose a direct threat to the Russian regime. In 2012, Moscow's diplomatic and military support of the Syrian regime complicated Russia's relations with international and regional players, including Turkey and Saudi Arabia, which supported the Syrian opposition by sending arms and money.

In 2014, Putin expressed willingness to join the Western-led coalition to fight against Daesh or ISIS as such a coalition would allow al-Assad's regime to survive, break Moscow's isolation by lifting the Western sanctions that were imposed on it after it annexed the

Crimea in March 2014, and allow Moscow to maintain its political presence in the ME. From Moscow's perspective, the removal of al-Assad by the externally backed and financed opposition could not be a prerequisite for any deal to end the civil war. The Kremlin believed that it possessed the right and duty to play a role in determining the potential outcome of the Ukrainian and Syrian conflicts that would affect the peace and security of the international system as a whole. From the Kremlin's perspective, Moscow's significant influence on the international conflict management in Syria via its UNSC seat would preserve its influence in international politics.

I argue that Putin took advantage of America's lack of clear policy in the ME to allow Russia to "gain a non-American door to the region, and to international recognition as a player on the global theater."[1] After NATO's military intervention in Libya in 2011 and the fall of the Muammar Gaddafi's authoritarian regime, another regime change in the ME could lead to a catastrophe in the region. Moscow's permissive posture concerning Western intervention in Libya "provoked a much more anti-Western position, taken by the Russian diplomacy in blocking outside humanitarian intervention in Syria."[2]

RUSSIAN, AMERICAN, AND ARAB DIPLOMACY IN 2011–12

In the early spring and summer of 2011 tens of thousands of peaceful demonstrators in the southern town of Deraa and elsewhere, initially called for democracy and reform rather than regime change.[3] The Deraa protests began in between crucial episodes of the Arab Spring: the crackdown on the Shiite opposition in Bahrain and the UN Security Council (SC) Resolution 1973 on 17 March 2011, which paved the way for the US and NATO intervention in the Libyan conflict. There was a dispute between Putin and Medvedev over the non-veto of the resolution in order to bargain preferences in Russia's relations with the West. In 2011, Moscow still hoped to improve its relationship with Washington and keep its military contracts with France.[4] However, President Putin believed that Moscow was betrayed in 2011 when NATO interpreted Resolution 1973 as a mandate to pursue regime change in Libya. Putin would not allow the "Libyan scenario to be reproduced in Syria."[5] The Western-led Libya intervention that led to the fall of Gaddafi not only cost Russia billions of dollars in arms sales and jeopardized oil and infrastructure deals but also reactivated Russian concerns over a hidden agenda of regime change pursued by the West. According to Maria Zakharova, Russia's foreign ministry spokesperson, another regime change in the ME could be a catastrophe that "could simply turn the whole region into a black hole."[6] Freire and Heller argued that "the identity vector" is important in understanding Russian power politics in Syria. During the Arab Spring the ME became more crucial for Russia as it came to be interpreted as a battlefield over two key issues: "setting the guiding principles of global order and preserving Russia's centrality in international conflict regulation as an embodiment of its international status."[7] The events in Syria could not be dealt with in isolation but rather as another trend of what appeared to be a sudden and complex regional transformation.

Until March 2011 the Syrian government had relied on its anti-Israeli and anti-Western rhetoric to protect itself. Slogans about the Israeli-Palestinian conflict were rarely heard in Tunisia and Egypt. Tunisian president Zein al-Abideen bin Ali left the country and in Egypt the pro-American President Hosni Mubarak was ousted by a popular revolt. In Syria, the angry anti-al-Assad demonstrators initially had no predilection for violence. They wanted reform, democracy, and freedom. In his speech in the Syrian parliament on 30 March 2011 al-Assad failed to unveil specific reforms that the international community had urged him to take and left the country in a state of uncertainty. Instead, al-Assad said that Syria was "being subjected to a big conspiracy, whose threads extended from countries near and far."[8] His speech lacked substance. The opposition demanded radical change in the way al-Assad ran the country. The protestors wanted the release of thousands of political prisoners, the right to free speech, and a multiparty system to replace the Baath Party, which had ruled since 1963.

This chapter does not focus on the internal dynamics of the conflict, the brutality of the regime, or the power struggle between the various factions of the Syrian opposition. Rather, it focuses on the role of regional and international actors in fuelling the conflict and on Russian diplomacy via its UNSC seat intended to prevent Western intervention in Syria. Certainly, the Syrian conflict is complex and multidimensional, and there is an evident interaction between internal and external actors. I offer a different interpretation and analysis of the conflict by giving the international and regional factors a more central role in the failure of Russian and American attempts to resolve the conflict. The US supported the protestors' democratic aspirations ideationally, but Washington's reluctance to get involved militarily stemmed from winding down the war in Iraq and fighting the Taliban in Afghanistan.

When the regime's internal security force responded to the peaceful demonstrators in Deraa with its usual brutality, the protests snowballed and spilled over to other cities and were met similarly by regime violence. In March to April 2011, the government organized pro-regime counter demonstrations in Aleppo, Homs, Hama, and Hasakah to illustrate its legitimacy. When the regime's security forces, military, Mukhabarat, and Shabiha(loyal militias) were given free rein to attack the rebels, the massacres began. Consequently, the peaceful insurgency took on a sectarian nature between the Alawites and the Sunni Muslims.[9] The US and the West along with Saudi Arabia, Qatar, and Turkey supported insurgents battling to topple al-Assad, whose external diplomatic, military, and financial backing had so far come from Russia and Iran and its Lebanese ally Hizbullah (Party of God). In an interview with the author, Walid Jumblatt the leader of the Progressive Socialist Party in Lebanon said, "Hizbullah is an extension of Shiite Iran in Lebanon and it enjoys a special standing in Iran."[10]

Turkish Prime Minister Recep Tayyep Erdogan's foreign policy over the previous decade had been to eliminate Turkey's problems with neighbouring states, increase trade with those states, and establish itself as a regional power. Accordingly, Erdogan urged al-Assad to choose reform over repression and the killing of unarmed civilian protestors after the regime used tanks to crush the rebellion. Initially, Erdogan's reluctance to take sides stemmed from Turkey's sizable business interest in Libya and Syria. The revolt in Syria posed the biggest test for Turkey as it competed with Iran for influence in Syria.

The conflict between opposition groups and the brutal regime that escalated destructively made a peaceful resolution highly improbable. Turkey and Iran supported their proxies in Syria in order to gain more territory and power. Turkey's continuous military support of the opposition served several purposes, most notably Ankara's policy to prevent the Syrian Kurds from gaining territory and establishing an autonomous Kurdish region in Syria, as that could embolden Kurdish militants of the Kurdistan Workers Party (PKK), which has been fighting for autonomy in Turkey. Turkey also would not close its borders to Syrian refugees and urged the Syrian government to be more tolerant towards the protestors and refugees. Iran, on the other hand, deployed its elite military force, the Islamic Revolutionary Guard Corps (IRGS), and Shiite militias from Iraq into Syria. It also provided equipment and technical support to help the al-Assad regime suppress the rebellion. Iran's long-term plan was to create a land corridor extending from Tehran all the way through Iraq to Syria and Lebanon in order to use its leverage in the Israeli-Palestinian conflict. Therefore, the expansion of the Iranian and Turkish zones of influence significantly shifted power balances in the ME, hindering Russia's peacemaking efforts.

On 19 May 2011, in his Arab Spring speech, Obama stated that al-Assad was "isolating himself from the international community due to his egregious actions. It was up to al-Assad to lead the political transition or to leave."[11] Obama's blueprint of what al-Assad should do in order to survive included "stop shooting at the demonstrators, release political prisoners, allow human rights monitors to have access" to Deraa and other besieged cities, and open "serious dialogue" with the opposition about a democratic transition. Obama's speech was his first major attempt to place the antigovernment protests that swept the ME in the context of US national interests. In relation to the Israeli-Palestinian conflict, Obama said that any agreement creating a Palestinian state must be based on borders that existed before Israel captured the West Bank in 1967 Arab-Israeli war but "with mutually agreed swaps" of land.[12]

Notwithstanding the international pressure on Syria, Syrian Foreign Minister Walid al-Moallem ruled out foreign military intervention and a no-fly zone of the kind NATO had imposed over Libya. Moallem reiterated Syria would not accept demands from "outside Syria" and blamed European and American sanctions for delaying reforms in the country.[13] Moallem's statement stemmed from the geopolitical position of Syria and the sanctions against Syria that would harm the region. He also urged Turkey, a vocal critic of al-Assad, to reconsider its stance.

By June 2011 violence and counterviolence escalated to such an extent that the chance of peaceful discussions and dialogue between the regime and the opposition became extremely unlikely. Concurrently, the regime opted for a so-called "security solution" to the conflict.[14] In July 2011, the formation of the Free Syrian Army (FSA) was officially announced. It became the opposition's largest military organization but was not powerful enough to bring other military factions under its command in order to coordinate their actions. Western countries recognized the FSA as a moderate and secular organization with which they were willing to cooperate against the regime. The FSA headquarters was in southern Turkey, not inside Syria proper, which turned out to be a weakness in terms of both efficiency and legitimacy. The FSA depended, to a great extent, on the military assistance of various supporting countries that the FSA did not coordinate and which did not provide the FSA with the weapons necessary for them to defend themselves, let alone defeat the regime.

After Obama's speech in May, the new US policy was articulated in Secretary of State Hilary Clinton's blunt statement on 11 July that al-Assad had "lost legitimacy" and that "our goal is … a democratic transition."[15] The Obama administration wanted to encourage the Syrian opposition inside the country to unite, develop a clear political agenda, and build an inclusive leadership. Freire and Heller rightly noted that "while the West saw a chance of democratization, Russia and China feared longer-term chaos and instability through political turnover."[16] Internally, the violent crackdown by the regime compelled the protestors to shift their demands from political change to the outright downfall of the regime. Al-Assad made a series of overtures to ease the growing outrage. In addition to lifting the old emergency law and granting nationality to thousands of Kurds, on 25 July 2011 the government endorsed a draft law that would allow the formation of political parties. However, these concessions failed to stop the momentum of the rebellion, which dismissed them as either symbolic or far too late. As the regime weakened, al-Assad allied himself ever more with the stridently anti-Western regime in Iran. Jumblatt reiterated that "although the Persians did not like the Arabs, without Iran's military intervention the regime would have collapsed."[17]

After weeks of talks, on 3 August the UNSC adopted a nonbinding presidential statement that "condemns the widespread violations of human rights and the use of force against civilians by the Syrian authorities."[18] Since March, China and Russia had threatened to veto any formal resolution. Like any major power, Russia had interests. Moscow was concerned about the spread of the democratic movements to its near abroad and even to Russia itself. Russia had had political, economic, cultural, and educational ties with Syria for decades and would not allow the West to do in Syria what it had in Libya. President Medvedev urged al-Assad to find a compromise with the opposition, "urgently conduct reforms and restore civil peace."[19] Yet, Moscow warned the West against interfering with Syrian affairs and objected to a UN binding resolution. The Russian ambassador to Lebanon, Alexander Zasypkin, disclosed to the author that "from the beginning of the protest movement, Russia supported reforms."[20]

Syria faced near complete diplomatic isolation when in August Saudi Arabia, Kuwait, and Bahrain recalled their ambassadors from Damascus. The Arab League's secretary general, Nabil al-Arabi, urged Syria to launch a "serious dialogue" with the opposition that so far remained divided and without clear leadership or an agenda beyond toppling al-Assad.[21] For its part, Iran vowed to help Syria and stop the US from interfering in regional affairs and "accused Washington of trying to destabilize the Iranian ally."[22] Egypt and Turkey also became increasingly critical of Syria over the bloodshed and urged al-Assad to implement reforms. Damascus appeared suspicious of Turkey's intentions and ruled out Ankara's meddling in Syria's internal affairs. Syrian authorities continued to ignore the calls to reform and blamed the unrest on extremists and terrorist groups who sought to destabilize the country.[23]

The beginning of the civil war in late 2011 coincided with the internationalization of the Syrian crisis. In August, Obama took a harder stance and, without the intent to enforce it, called for al-Assad to step down. In addition to the EU as a collective body, Britain, France, Canada, and Germany also demanded that al-Assad go. The US decision reflected the conclusion that al-Assad was incapable of reform because reform would signify a gradual collapse and result in the end of al-Assad rule. Jumblatt rightly noted that the "Alawite regime cannot sustain without al-Assad family."[24]

Joost Hiltermann convincingly argued that "at the core of the Syrian war, inexorably internationalization stands the fundamental disagreement between the U.S. and Russia over the fate of the regime."[25] Although Obama had little intention of following up with military action, Russia and Iran saw the US weighing in against their ally and added their determination to support the regime. Qatar, Saudi Arabia, and Turkey, who were hostile to the regime, would proceed to take action in Syria on the assumption that the US would eventually intervene and force a regime change. This positioning of the external actors not only reflected the regional dimension of the war but also served to escalate the sectarian divisions within Syria.

The Syrian war was devolving into a regional proxy war. Syria was a key pillar of Iran's regional policy and a key land bridge through which Iran provided money and weapons to Hizbullah to resist Israel.

From Iran's perspective, the "resistance axis" of Iran-Syria-Hizbullah against Israel had given the Syrian regime domestic and regional legitimacy.[26] To counter Iranian influence, Saudi Arabia pumped money to Sunni fighters in Syria. David Ignatius described Syria "as the fault line for Sunni-Shiite tensions, and for the confrontation between Iran and the U.S. and Israel."[27]

After six months, on 18 September 2011 opposition figures met in Istanbul and formed the Syrian National Council (SNC); in November 2012, the SNC became the Syrian National Coalition, to steer a transition in case al-Assad was toppled and to establish ties with Western powers that had condemned the crackdown.[28] The main aim of the SNC was to topple al-Assad. The opposition consisted of a variety of groups with often conflicting ideologies, including Islamists, secularists, and dissidents from the regime.

Meanwhile, a Russian parliamentary delegation headed by the deputy chair of the Russian Federation Council, Ilyas Rogachyov, arrived in Damascus to conduct talks with political, social, and religious figures and to convince the regime to implement the series of reforms that al-Assad had promised, including constitutional changes, a new electoral law, and the annulment of the state emergency law. The Kremlin believed that "if the Syrian government was unable to hold on to power, there was a high probability that radicals and representatives of terrorist organizations would become entrenched."[29] The theoretical literature on status policies suggest that in 2011 Russia as a status-overachiever adopted a strategy or preserving influence in Syria through diplomacy instead of undertaking a risky military intervention. At this phase of the conflict in Syria, Russia was interested in maintaining international relations as they were, as it benefited status-wise from them without investing too many resources. It was reported that Russian investments in Syria in 2009 were valued at $19.4 billion, mainly in arms deals, a friendly government, infrastructure, commercial opportunities, energy, and tourism.[30] In addition, since the Soviet era, Russia has been operating a naval and maintenance base in the Syrian coastal city of Tartus. The port at Tartus has strategic and geopolitical interest and could prove valuable if conflict with Ukraine or Turkey obstructed the operations of the Russian Black Sea fleet. The Soviet navy began using the port at Tartus for submarines and surface vessels under its 1971 agreement with Damascus.[31] The Russian naval facility at Tartus was the only base outside the territory of the former Soviet Union. The port was undergoing a major refurbishment, which after 2012 would grant Russian vessels a permanent base in the Mediterranean warm waters.

On 4 October 2011, Russia and China vetoed a Security Council draft resolution condemning Syria's crackdown on protestors because it did not emphasize "the non-acceptability of military intervention, and that the collapse of Assad's government could destabilize the entire region."[32] In line with the theoretical argument of status-inconsistent or status-overachiever powers, Russia engaged in international diplomacy as a means to preserve its influence in international politics and as a counterweight to Western, in particular US, dominance in the UNSC. The Russian ambassador to the UN Vitaly Churkin said, "we are not advocates of the Assad regime." He added that violence was unacceptable, but "part of the Syrian opposition had not hidden its extremist bent." The Russian Federation would continue to work with "patriotic" opposition groups who opposed foreign interference, which could include NATO.[33] In an interview with the author, Zasypkin said:

> In addition to the ruling Baath Party there were other political parties, which had secular and national orientation. There was also the Muslim Brotherhood and many opposition factions, including the al-Qaeda terrorist organization. The international community misunderstood our position at the UN due to false reports. We supported the national opposition, international legitimacy, and opposed foreign intervention. Those who encouraged armed opposition were responsible for the continuance of violence.[34]

The prospects of dialogue seemed dim when in October 2011 an Arab League delegation headed by Qatari Prime Minister Sheikh Hamad al-Thani visited Damascus and failed to convince al-Assad to hold talks with the opposition at the League's headquarters in Cairo.[35] The Arab League peace plan called on al-Assad to release all prisoners held since February, withdraw security forces from the streets, permit deployment of Arab League monitors, and start dialogue with the opposition groups under the auspices of the League. The plan was "backed by neither meaningful incentives nor credible threats in case the regime reneged on its commitments or played for time."[36] The League meeting in Morocco on 12 November suspended Syria's membership after al-Assad failed to honour the terms of the peace plan and imposed sanctions on Damascus. Sheikh al-Thani warned that the League "was coming near the end of Arab diplomacy for Syria." Washington's welcoming the suspension and Moscow's calling it "incorrect" reflected US-Russian disagreement on the prospects of ending Syria's war.[37] The US also accused Russia of blocking UN action and condemned the crackdown by Syrian authorities.

Syria's conflict had a regional dimension as well. Al-Assad's commitment to dialogue was unlikely without ensuring the interests of his key allies, Iran and Hizbullah, who became intimately intertwined with his own fate. The Tehran-Damascus-Hizbullah defensive alliance was threatened by the Israeli-American regional hegemony. Thus, the fall of al-Assad could lead to a regime change in Iran. Israel was attempting to push the US into war against Iran to halt its nuclear program. Turkey's foreign policy endorsed the SNC and dissident army factions, and Turkey's support of the FSA engaged Ankara in a proxy war with Damascus. Syria's reactivation of ties with Kurdish insurgents battling Turkey further polarized relations between Ankara and Damascus. Thus, Turkey's attempts to mediate the Syrian conflict were doomed. Turkey's cooperation with Iran in 2010 as Tehran sought a diplomatic solution to its nuclear power program turned to rivalry. Both, Turkey and Iran, "who spar over the future of the Syrian regime, took opposite sides on NATO's anti-missile defense shield, and competed for influence in the Arab world."[38] From an Iranian perspective, Turkey's decision to install NATO's antimissile early warning facility in the Turkish city of Malatya aimed to neutralize Iran's deterrent capacity vis-à-vis Israel, thereby threatening the likelihood of an Israeli or US strike against Iran's nuclear facilities.

To avoid Western criticism, on 15 December 2011 Moscow presented a draft UNSC Resolution, which strongly condemned the violence by "all parties, including disproportionate use of force by Syrian authorities, and the illegal supply of weapons to the armed groups in Syria."[39] Concurrently, on 19 December, Syria was prompted, on the advice of Russia, to sign a protocol with the Arab League to deploy Arab monitors to inspect areas gripped by violence and present a report about the mission's progress.[40] On 22 December, the first monitors arrived in Damascus, followed few days later by the mission's head, Sudanese General Mohammed Ahmad al-Dabi. Although the al-Assad regime made some concessions to the observers, including the release of nearly 800 prisoners, the delivery of humanitarian aid to embattled regions, and temporary withdrawal of tanks from hotspot areas, like Homs, the army continued its violent campaign to squash peaceful protests, particularly in Homs. Shortly, the first round of the League's handling of the Syrian crisis proved disappointing. The observers were ineffectual in ending the suffering of civilians because they had no power and were not protected by the authorities. Al-Assad emphasized that "crackdown on terrorists who were collaborating with foreigners would continue unabated." He also reiterated "the West was not interested in reforms. It wanted to change Syria's behavior."[41] In a rare public appearance on 11 January 2012 al-Assad vowed to crush the "foreign conspirators, and win without any doubt."[42] Despite Western criticism, a large Russian naval flotilla led by an aircraft carrier docked in the port of Tartus to support its beleaguered ally in the ME.

The disappointed SNC gave up on the Arab League's efforts to stop the violence and appealed to the UN to handle the crisis. However, on 22 January the League foreign ministers, who met in Cairo, voted to extend the controversial observer's mission for another month.[43] In their second round of diplomacy, the foreign ministers also agreed on a new political roadmap that called al-Assad to delegate power to his Sunni first deputy Faruq al-Sharaa in order to establish a unity government as a prelude to early parliamentary and presidential elections to be held within three months. The unity government would establish a constituent body to draft a new constitution that would be put to a referendum.[44] The plan that aimed at a negotiated solution was reminiscent of an agreement for transfer of power in Yemen. While the UNSC was split on how to address the crisis, with Western powers demanding tougher sanctions and an embargo on weapons, Russia preferred to leave the Arab League to negotiate a peaceful outcome.

The new Arab peace plan would extract no concessions from al-Assad as Russia wielded a veto power on the Security Council, and continued to hold close ties with Damascus and sign a new arms deal. Indeed, the Syrian government rejected the decisions of the League and considered them "a violation of its national sovereignty and a flagrant interference in its internal affairs."[45] By the end of January, as fighting appeared to move closer to Damascus (in the Ghouta area), the Russian foreign ministry took the initiative to hold informal talks in Moscow between the opposition and the Syrian government.[46]

THE ROAD TO AN INTERNATIONAL PEACE PLAN

On 4 February 2012, Russia and China vetoed a second UN draft SC resolution that backed the Arab peace plan and called on al-Assad to step down. Churkin explained Moscow's stance by saying the draft resolution "sent an unbalanced signal to the Syrian parties."[47] Al-Assad was bolstered by the Russian and Chinese vetoes. Russia undertook its position at the UN to reinforce its views on the Syrian conflict and its position in the contemporary international system.

Recalling the colour revolutions in FSS, the Kremlin considered protests and calls for regime changes destabilizing. As the Russian presidential election was scheduled on 4 March 2012, Putin, in a front-page article in the daily *Kommersant*, wrote "we need to renew the mechanisms of our democracy. But, real democracy is not created in an instant and cannot be copied from an external model."[48] Putin, who regarded Syria as a domestic issue too, did not mention the protest movement that erupted in December 2011 when tens of thousands of people marched in central Moscow behind the banner "Russia without Putin."[49] Following Putin's return to the presidency in March 2012 and particularly following the Euromaidan revolution in Ukraine, Putin consolidated restrictions against Western NGOs, political organizations, and media that were critical of the state that had been introduced in mid-2000. The Kremlin now presented Russia as a special civilization, committed to defending its values, interests, and principles relative to those of the West. On 12 December, in his address to the Federal Assembly, Putin stated "in the 21st century amid a new balance of economic, civilizational and military forces Russia should preserve its national and spiritual identity, its sense of national unity. It is essential to give every support to the institutions that have enshrined our traditional values," especially family and schools."[50]

As noted above, Russia wanted to advance its national interests and assert its authority at the global level. Authority mattered for Russia because Moscow advocated multilateralism and rejected the past world domination of the US. Russia also wanted to wield authority over states and regions within its respective sphere of influence. The crisis in Syria and the failure of Western attempts to punish the al-Assad regime was an excuse and opportunity for Moscow to display its displeasure with US and NATO policies in Libya and Iraq. With regard to Egypt, Russia tried to establish relations with the popularly elected leader of the Muslim Brotherhood, Mohammed Morsi. By blocking UN resolutions, Russia was flexing its muscles to reassert its global influence while ignoring human rights violations in Syria.

Its failure to stop the violence prompted the Arab League to formally end its observation mission to Syria on 12 February. At that point, most Arab countries encouraged the Syrian opposition factions to unite before they would formally recognize the SNC as the representative of the Syrian revolution. Meanwhile, on 26 February the Syrian regime held a referendum on a new constitution, which would lead to a multiparty election in three months.[51] However, al-Assad had lost credibility and was delegitimized by the West and the opposition.

After the failure of the Arab League peace plan and the deadlock over UN efforts to stop the bloodshed, the UNSC endorsed former UN Secretary General Kofi Annan's plan (Annan had been appointed joint UN–Arab League envoy to Syria in February 2012). Annan's six-point plan, unanimously adopted as a UN presidential statement on 21 March and backed by both Russia and China, pressured the al-Assad regime to commit by 25 March.[52] The plan called for a sustained cessation of armed violence in all its forms by all parties with an effective UN supervision mechanism including provision of humanitarian assistance to all areas, freedom of movement for journalists, the right to demonstrate peacefully, the accelerated release of prisoners, and a commitment to an inclusive Syrian-led political process to address the legitimate aspirations and concerns of the Syrian people.[53] Most importantly, it steered well away from Russian and Chinese vetoes by including no condemnation of Syria, no specific timetable for a political transition, and no threat of intervention if Syria failed to comply with the Annan plan. The presidential statement represented a considerable blow to al-Assad, who had counted on the Security Council's divisions in rebuffing previous resolutions.

In light of renewed international dynamics, Turkey hosted a "Friends of Syria" meeting of mostly Western and Arab foreign ministers on 1 April. Representatives from around eighty-three countries tried to envisage a new way to make Damascus halt its repression of dissent. The statement that emerged from the meeting backed Annan's plan but lacked enthusiasm for arming the opposition despite strong demands from the SNC.[54] The Europeans did not have the means to get involved in a new conflict after what happened in Libya, and some Arab countries were part of the cold war between Iran and the alliance between Saudi Arabia and Qatar who wanted to prevail in the region.

A UN-backed ceasefire between the regime and the opposition on 12 April paved the way to the successful deployment of an advanced team of a UN Supervision Mission in Syria (UNSMIS). Three hundred monitors were dispatched on 21 April.[55] The unarmed monitors who belonged to neutral countries, were stationed in Aleppo, Damascus, Deir al-Zour, Hama, Homs, Idlib, Deraa, and Tartus to monitor and report on the implementation of Annan's plan. The US and European countries then announced new sanctions against Damascus because the Syrian government was not complying with the six-point peace plan. After two weeks, the fragile ceasefire began to break down. The international community was horrified by reports of a massacre that was committed by pro-regime Shabiha in the village of Houla near Homs on 25 May. The FSA commander, Riad al-Asaad, asked the protestors not to cooperate with the monitors mainly because it was "no longer possible to abide by the peace plan brokered by Kofi Annan."[56] Turkey, Qatar, and Saudi Arabia, who were lending support to the armed opposition, had been critical of Annan from the beginning for not including in his plan a mechanism to oust al-Assad. Russia was unwilling to accept a transition that excluded al-Assad.

Lavrov called for a thorough investigation but acknowledged that "both sides participated in the killing of civilians." Annan, in his turn, called on the al-Assad regime to take "bold steps" in an effort to salvage his faltering plan.[57] Putin, who took over the presidency from Medvedev on 7 May 2012, would take a harder line, projecting distrust and disdain, and publicly blaming Washington for inciting protests against him in Moscow. Russia was not respected when Obama pointedly withheld a customary congratulating phone call to Putin until days after his election. Putin responded by skipping the G8 meeting that Obama hosted later that month at Camp David. Gideon Rachman rightly noted that Putin, who was "hypersensitive about any reminder of Russia's declining global reach, was also clearly determined to preserve his country's strategic relationship with Syria."[58]

As his plan appeared to hit a dead end, Annan wanted to revive it by creating a "contact group" of world and regional powers to try to break the deadlock and draft a transition plan. Annan's initiative threw a gauntlet down to the opponents of al-Assad, including Western nations, the Gulf States, and Turkey, and the supporters of the regime, including Russia, China, and Iran. Syria was in a civil war. Meanwhile, the UN team decided to suspend its eight-week-old mission, citing concerns about the security of its monitors. Herve Ladsous, the UN's under-secretary for peacekeeping operations, described the situation on the ground when he said, "keeping a peacekeeping force when there is no peace to observe – that summarizes the situation."[59]

On 18 June 2012, Obama and Putin met on the sidelines of the G20 summit in Mexico to try to resolve their differences over the solution to the Syrian conflict. The joint statement issued by the two leaders was notable for the fact that it did not call "for an immediate cessation of all violence," and expressed "full support for the efforts of Annan, including moving forward on political transition to a democratic, pluralistic political system."[60] For Russia, the Syrian regime was engaged in a war with Islamist radicals like its own against the Chechens. For the US, Russian help had been indispensible in getting military supplies into Afghanistan, especially after Pakistan closed the route through its territory in November 2011. In the longer term, Obama wanted Russia's cooperation in nuclear disarmament and non-proliferation. However, any Russian help in resolving the Syrian conflict and the Iranian nuclear power program would come at a cost. Due to its active diplomacy, Russia succeeded in not marginalizing itself from global politics. Tsygankov contended that "all significant powers needed Russian cooperation – the West for Afghanistan and Iran, China for energy and stability in Central Asia, and Turkey for economic and political security in the Caucasus."[61]

The Syrian situation was a Russian foreign policy priority. According to the Moscow-based military think tank CAST, the Russian backing of al-Assad appeared to be more emotional than rational. CAST characterized the Kremlin's Syria policy as a consensus of elites who "had rallied around the demand not to allow loss of Syria," which would cause "the final disappearance of the last ghostly traces of Soviet might" in the ME.[62]

On 30 June 2012, Annan's "Action Group for Syria" meeting was endorsed at the Geneva conference (also known as Geneva I) composed of the secretaries general of the Arab League and the UN, the EU's high representative for foreign and security policy, and the foreign ministers of the US, UK, France, China, Russia, Turkey, Iraq, and Qatar. Neither Saudi Arabia nor Iran nor any Syrians were invited.[63] All participants signed a communiqué (known as the Geneva Communiqué) that reiterated support for the six-point plan and agreed on a set of principles and guidelines for a Syrian-led transition. Crucially, it called for the

> Establishment of a transitional governing body that can establish a neutral environment in which the transition can take place, with the transitional governing body exercising full executive powers. It could include members of the present Government and the opposition and other groups and shall be formed on the basis of mutual consent.[64]

Zasypkin disclosed to the author that, "In Geneva, Russia supported national dialogue to establish national unity in Syria. Initially, Russia counted on possible U.S. cooperation, but Washington hindered agreements. Syria was strategically important for the region. Therefore, we took a firm and strong position to prevent regional chaos. This was Russia's strategy in Syria."[65]

For the regime, "establishing a transitional governing body with full executive powers" became the main point of dispute. For the US, al-Assad could not take part in such a transitional body, whereas Russia said no transition plan could presuppose that al-Assad would step down. The Syrian opposition strongly rejected any role for al-Assad in the transitional period. International pressure on al-Assad escalated, when the regime sought to assert its authority in the face of rebel offensives. In July 2012, for the first time the regime appeared seriously shaken when the rebels launched their first major assaults on Damascus and Aleppo. On 18 July a bomb exploded in the national security headquarters in Damascus killing four top officials, including al-Assad's brother-in-law Assef Shawkat.[66] An Islamist rebel group, Liwa al-Islam, claimed responsibility for the attack.

On 19 July 2012, Russia and China, for the third time, vetoed a draft UNSC resolution that sought to threaten sanctions under chapter 7 of the UN charter unless al-Assad implemented the peace plan.[67] Russia had put forward its own resolution, extending the UN monitor's mandate set to expire on 20 July, without any threat of punishment for the regime, but it was not put up for vote. Russia and China argued that imposing sanctions could lead to a regime change. Russia also rejected external military intervention without a UNSC mandate. Freire and Heller contended that, "while Russia's policy of opposing Western actions over Syria was successful in terms of maintaining Moscow's centrality in international conflict management efforts, it did not contribute to stopping the violence on the ground."[68] Preserving Russia's centrality in international conflict management and

Moscow's role in setting the guiding principles of global order played a key role in Russia's positioning on Syria. Russia had been an advocate of multipolarity and a supporter of multilateral action through the UN.

A frustrated Kofi Annan resigned on 2 August. In an article that summarized the difficulties in Syria, he wrote, "only a united international community could compel both sides to engage in a peaceful political transition." He added, "a political process was difficult, if not impossible, while all sides, within and without Syria, got an opportunity to advance their narrow agendas by military means."[69] In further signs of failed diplomacy, during a landmark visit to London to watch the Olympic judo competition, Putin and the British Prime Minister David Cameron did not hide their differences over Syria. The level of US assistance to the rebel supreme military council (SMC) remained modest, with "about $25 million for non-lethal equipment and humanitarian aid."[70] The US and its regional allies Saudi Arabia, Jordan, and Israel feared the rise of extremist groups on their borders. With more Arab fighters joining the armed struggle against the regime, the FSA had become an umbrella of "increasingly religious and radicalized groups."[71] Andrew J. Tabler rightly noted that non-lethal assistance would "neither force the downfall of the regime nor earn Washington the loyalty of the opposition."[72]

REGIONAL AND INTERNATIONAL DYNAMICS AFTER GENEVA I

At the regional level, Tehran vowed to fight terrorism and not allow the resistance axis (Syria-Iran-Hizbullah) against Israel to break. If al-Assad fell, Iran would lose the balance of power in the ME. According to the Iranian Ambassador to Beirut Mohammad Jalal Firouznia,

> The Iranian–Syrian alliance aimed to fight against terrorism and the extremist and Takfiri groups, like al-Qaeda, to prevent the collapse of the Syrian state. Some nations thought that Syria would be partitioned. Iran supported al-Assad because it was against partitioning Syria. This was Iran's position in Iraq too. Iran was against changing the borders of Iraq and successfully prevented the creation of a Kurdish state. The Takfiri groups were a threat to all the states in the region.[73]

The Iranian posture with regard to Syria was analogous with the Russian posture. Zasypkin reiterated, "there was a Western plan to partition Syria. Russia believed that there was a conspiracy to partition all the states in the region."[74]

Tehran's policy was predicated on keeping al-Assad in power. Iran also viewed the conflict in Syria as the extension of a sectarian power struggle with its regional rival Saudi Arabia, as well as the US-led campaign to halt its nuclear ambitions by imposing sanctions. After Annan's failure, Iran sought a diplomatic role and offered to host talks between the Syrian government and the opposition. However, the US ruled out Iranian mediation because Iran was part of the problem in Syria and the broader ME. Although Washington viewed Turkey as the key player in supporting the opposition, like Ankara, it was worried about the PKK and al-Qaeda terrorism. It is worth nothing that in July 2012, the Kurdish Democratic Union Party (PYD) seized control of major Syrian Kurdish towns and key strategic resources, when the Syrian military and security forces withdrew from most Kurdish areas.

The UN withdrew UNSMIS on 17 August because the conditions required continue the mission were not fulfilled and announced that Lakhdar Brahimi, a former Algerian foreign minister and a veteran UN diplomat, would serve as UN–Arab League peace envoy. On the humanitarian front, the UN faced the problem of 221,000 Syrian refugees registered in camps in Turkey, Jordan, and Lebanon.[75] On 1 September 2012 the UNSC did not endorse a Turkish proposal to create a foreign-protected "safe zone" or "liberated zone" to cope with the growing exodus of Syrians into its territory because it was difficult to provide credible protection for "liberated" areas that would require no-fly zones patrolled by foreign aircraft.[76] In addition, China and Russia would have opposed such a plan.

Brahimi, who took over as envoy from Annan on 1 September, reported to the UNSC that the situation in Syria was worsening. He said that al-Assad acknowledged, "something must change." However, al-Assad wanted only to return to "the old Syria," which he and his father had ruled for more than forty years.[77] On the 25th of that month, in his speech to the UN General Assembly (UNGA) Obama said that the US could not solve all the world's problems nor "dictate the outcome of democratic transitions abroad."[78]

Obama's realist foreign policy avoided adventurism, such as the 2003 invasion of Iraq. The president was not a liberal interventionist. The interventionists made geopolitical arguments. For example, the fall of the regime would be a blow to Iran. Obama told the UNGA that the US wanted to resolve the Iranian nuclear issue "through diplomacy." On the Israeli-Palestinian conflict, Obama said, "the road was hard, but the destination was clear: A Jewish state of Israel and an independent, prosperous Palestine." The US "would walk alongside all who were prepared to make the journey."[79] Obviously, the US had no will for military intervention in Syria and Iran just as Washington had wound down the US war in Iraq and was largely pulling out of Afghanistan by 2014. Obama's calculus was right because, like Iraq and Libya, a Western air campaign would not end the fighting in Syria.

Obama warned al-Assad not to cross the red line and unleash chemical weapons against the rebels. Turkey in its turn, asked NATO to deploy Patriot missiles and troops along Syria's border with Turkey to protect against potential attacks. In northern Syria, the radical Islamist group, Jabhat al-Nusra, or the Nusra Front, linked to al-Qaeda in Iraq, assisted other rebel groups in seizing swathes of territory and regime command centres in Aleppo and elsewhere.

As part of its efforts to achieve great power status, Russia used the strategy of social competition to demonstrate its military and economic potential in the region. Indeed, Russia unveiled $4.2 billion in arms deals with Iraq during Iraqi Prime Minister Nuri al-Maliki's first visit to Moscow on 9 October 2012. Iraq also approved new investments from Russia's energy giants Rosneft and Gazprom, as well as Lukoil to explore oil deposits near Basra.[80] Arms and energy exports would bring revenue to the Russian weak economy. Still, by offering its expertise in the energy field Russia would gain potential influence in the region. The powerful Shiite Maliki enjoyed Iran's support. Russia sought to rekindle its ties with Iraq and win regional backing for its position on Syria.

Various opposition figures, who were meeting in Doha, endorsed the formation of a Syrian National Coalition and elected the Islamist progressive Ahmad Moaz Khatib to head the new group on 11 November.[81] Khatib was backed by Qatar and Turkey. Restructuring the Syrian opposition was a US and Gulf States initiative to enable it to win international recognition and support. Also, the Syrian National Council, which feared marginalization, elected the veteran Christian dissident George Sabra as its leader. However, the SNC was absorbed into the Syrian National Coalition (thereafter SNC) in which the Muslim Brotherhood was dominant. The US, the EU, and the Friends of Syria group, during their meeting in Morocco on 12

December, recognized the SNC as the legitimate representative of the Syrian people. Yet, Washington's designation of the Nusra Front as a terrorist organization remained a matter of dispute between the SNC and the US.

After Obama's re-election in November 2012, US-Russian tensions over Syria, as well as the issue of the Magnitsky Act, increased. In December 2012, Russian political circles were enraged when Obama signed into law the Sergei Magnitsky Rule of Law Accountability Act, which denied visas to Russian officials implicated in "gross human rights violations" and froze their US assets.[82] Moscow considered the Magnitsky Act an intolerable interference in Russia's internal affairs. The Russian ambassador to the US wrote that the Magnitsky Act was an "unwillingness to show respect."[83] It should be noted that Western and US criticisms of Russia grew in response to the Kremlin's handling of protesters, such as Pussy Riot, and the case of the Russian lawyer Sergei Magnitsky who exposed corruption among state officials, was arrested, and died while in detention. Washington sought to increase the pressure on Moscow to not support the regime, although both the US and Russia had shared interests in Syria, mainly in order to avoid extremism and a sectarian war that could spill over throughout the ME and Central Asia. However, both great powers were still far apart on their positions about what the transition in Syria should look like.

On the sidelines of an international security conference in Dublin on 6 December 2012, Brahimi blamed internal divisions in the UNSC for the lack of progress in ending the violence in Syria. He also stressed that a peace process must be based on the Geneva Communiqué because it was the only recognized diplomatic negotiating track. Syria "urgently needed a cease-fire and a large peacekeeping force," he said. Russia suggested that al-Assad could go but "we need really to find responsible people on both sides … to swallow their pride."[84] Apparently, Russia was trying to distance itself from al-Assad for being incapable of finding a compromise with the opposition and, in turn, was losing control in the country. Yet, Russia wanted assurances that it would not lose its geopolitical and strategic interests from al-Assad's exit.

Backing down could mean that Russia had given in to the West and the US in particular. This was not the image that "Putin wanted to convey either to Russians or to his country's allies."[85] Protecting the principle of national sovereignty was a Russian foreign policy priority. As argued in chapters 1 and 2, post-Soviet Russia's objective had been to become an independent centre of power and influence by creating flexible international coalitions. Russia would work hard to preserve its significant influence on the management of international conflict in Syria via its UNSC seat.

RUSSIAN, AMERICAN, AND REGIONAL INTERESTS IN SYRIA, 2013–14

In early January 2013, Brahimi's patience with al-Assad seemed to be wearing thin. On 10 January he announced that "instead of taking the lead in responding to the aspirations of his people," al-Assad seemed "uncompromising."[86] So far, Brahimi had failed to bring both key players, the US and Russia, to an agreement on the transition plan. Ahead of Brahimi's remarks, on 6 January, al-Assad, in a public speech and in a defiant tone, branded the opposition as terrorists and Western puppets who would Balkanize the country.[87] The SNC and the tolerated internal opposition, the National Coordination Body for Democratic Change, rejected al-Assad's remarks and ruled out dialogue with the regime.

On 20 January Russia unleashed its largest naval exercises in the Mediterranean and the Black Sea since the collapse of the Soviet Union in 1991.[88] Moscow flexed its military muscles so as to remind the West of its interest in Syria, where it had repeatedly argued against outside intervention. The drills also coincided with Russia's aim to increase its naval presence and the inauguration of a new class of submarine it would rely upon as a bulwark of its strategic nuclear force. Putin vowed to build Russia's sea power to demonstrate that Russia was great. It is worth noting that in 2011, Moscow had announced "a ten year modernization program that included $360 billion in new military procurement."[89]

Fulfilling Ankara's request, NATO deployed six Patriot missile batteries, provided by the US, Germany, and Netherlands, to help bolster security along Turkey's 850-kilometre border with Syria.[90] The deployment sent two signals to Turkey. First, it reassured a NATO member about its security and protection. Second, given that Turkish public discourse had become increasingly aggressive, the deployment of the Patriot missiles indicated a NATO attempt to prevent any unilateral military action by Turkey.

The UNSC was likely to remain paralyzed by the reticence of China and Russia. However, the Western countries also were at a complete loss as to what actions to take in order to unseat al-Assad. A solution to the stalemate would not be achieved without serious consideration being given to the regional power dynamics. A solution to the Syrian conflict could not be achieved without taking Iran's policy perceptions and sensitivities seriously, including its strategic alliance with al-Assad and Hizbullah and its nuclear power program.

Washington's overly cautious approach, to not arm the rebels, left the field open for extremist groups to lead the rebellion. This explanation might be right. However, US Defense Secretary Chuck Hagel, during a congressional hearing on 19 April, expressed reservations about arming the rebels by saying "once you are into it, there is not any backing out, whether it is a no-fly zone, safe zone … whatever it is."[91] Meanwhile, Hagel revealed that "some 150 US military specialists had been deployed in Jordan since 2012" and that he had ordered the US army headquarters team to bolster the mission, bringing the total American presence to more than 200.[92] With the US out of Iraq, American influence in the ME appeared to be diminishing. Yet, the US preferred to build its global strength through domestic economic and social reforms, concentrating on what Obama called "nation-building at home."[93]

On 6 March 2013, the communiqué issued by the Arab League's ministerial meeting in Cairo "stressed the right of each state according to its wishes to offer all types of self-defense, including military to support the resistance of the Syrian people and the FSA."[94] The decision of arming the opposition was a major shift in the League's policy. Lebanon, Iraq, and Algeria refused to endorse the League's statement. At the Doha summit on 26 March, al-Araby invited the SNC, headed by Khatib, to occupy Syria's seat at the League that was held by Damascus until its suspension from the organization in November 2011. Consequently, the SNC opened its first embassy, raising its green, white, and black rebel flag, in Doha. Brahimi became increasingly frustrated with the League's moves because by recognizing the SNC the League undermined his role as a neutral mediator. While al-Assad appealed to the BRICS countries for help to resolve the conflict, the Russian Foreign Ministry expressed "bewilderment" and considered the League's decision contradictory to international law.[95]

In March 2013, the Nusra Front in alliance with the radical Islamist Ahrar al-Sham captured the eastern city of Raqqa. Chechens from the North Caucasus region, who participated in Chechnya's war in the mid-1990s, alongside with fighters from Libya, Tajikistan, Turkey, Jordan, and Saudi Arabia, were fighting on the side of the opposition.[96] Moscow was likely to ensure that Chechen fighters in Syria be prevented from returning to Russia because they could threaten the Winter Olympics scheduled for Sochi in February 2014. Russian deep involvement in Syria aimed to balance the destabilization of the political situation in the ME and, more globally, in Eurasia to defend its interests and be taken seriously by Western and non-Western powers.[97] For Putin, Russian national interests would be protected by supporting Damascus, establishing close relations with Tehran, and rapprochement with Egypt. The Kremlin thus sought to demonstrate to the US and the EU that Moscow's mediation in the conflicts in the ME would play a crucial role in the settlement of existing international issues.

The Chinese President Xi Jinping's visit to Moscow on 22 April highlighted the strategic partnership between Russia and China through the signing of energy, trade, and political deals. After two months, Russia, which wanted to diversify its energy customers away from Europe, signed a $60 billion contract with China on oil supplies on 20 June.[98] Both countries had vetoed three Western-backed UNSC resolutions that pressured al-Assad to end violence. As a result of US ambivalence, Putin sought to "blunt" US influence in the ME while China was grappling with the expanded military and economic interest that Obama had displayed in Asia since 2011 in an effort to rebuild America's global strength. Obama's "Pivot to Asia" strategy was redirecting the focus of American foreign policy to build power in China's immediate sphere of influence. In an increasingly multipolar world, both China and Russia would "decisively defend the principles of the UN Charter and the commonly accepted norms of international relations, to protect justice and equality in the world."[99] Putin needed oil revenues to cement Russia's economy and its global standing on the basis of superior economic performance.

At the domestic level, chemical weapons were deployed in Khan al-Assal, near Aleppo, on 19 March 2013. The issue moved forward on 20 March, when UN General Secretary Ban Ki-moon established a UN independent mission to investigate the chemical attack. Separately, in July a Russian inquiry indicated that the opposition and not the regime had used sarin gas in Khan al-Assal.[100] However, action by the US was pending the submission of a report by the UN mission. Meanwhile, Iran continued to supply the regime with military assistance and financing estimated $500 million a month.[101]

Iran's regional rival, Turkey, became more concerned, when in July 2013 the PYD captured the Syrian town of Ras al-Ain on the border with Turkey. Ankara feared that the emergence of an autonomous region in Syria could embolden homegrown militants of the PKK, which was then fighting for autonomy in Turkey. Indeed, in November 2013 the PYD, many of whom were PKK fighters, unilaterally announced the formation of a transitional administration in the territories it possessed as the autonomous region of Rojava (western Kurdistan) in northern Syria.[102] The Kurdish National Council, which included a broad spectrum of parties, considered the act an obstacle to the Syrian opposition.

Diplomacy got another chance after lengthy talks in Moscow between Lavrov and US Secretary of State John Kerry, to resolve the deadlock, on 9 May 2013. Lavrov and Kerry agreed to call for a second international conference dubbed Geneva II. For two years, Washington's demand that al-Assad step down had not been helpful. Indeed, Washington's demand "had marginalized the U.S. more than it had Al-Assad," as Christopher Hill noted.[103] Thus, the US should work with Russia to narrow their differences so that a peace conference could be held.

During an icy encounter at a G8 summit in Northern Ireland on 17 June, Obama and Putin disagreed over how to end the Syrian conflict. There were already growing disputes over other international issues including the ME, Russia's efforts to strengthen its influence in Eurasia, and nuclear arms control. New politically explosive issues caused further tension in US-Russian relations, most notably over Moscow's granting a temporary asylum to former US intelligence contractor Edward Snowden. Both leaders shared an interest in reducing violence, ensuring that chemical weapons were not used, and working on Geneva II. A US-Russia dialogue on Syria and other global issues, such as missile defense in Europe, disarmament, Iranian and North Korean nuclear programs, and emerging cyber security threats, was urgent. Until then, Washington had approached negotiations with Moscow by pushing Russia to abandon its support of al-Assad, while Moscow expressed a justified concern that the US had no alternative strategy. Russian foreign policy identity aimed to support state survival from extremist and Islamist groups because Russia's domestic stability required strong leaders, who could keep extremists and terrorists in check. Hence, Putin's ME policy rested on close relations with the al-Assad regime, Iran, and Israel. Moreover, the Kremlin supported

Egypt's strong man Defense Minister Abdel Fattah al-Sisi who had ousted the democratically elected Morsi through a military coup in July 2013. In addition, Russia was dissatisfied with its status and was afraid of being marginalized in the international environment. Apparently, Obama was cautious "against squandering more political capital to salvage a reset the Russian side never fully embraced."[104]

On 18 August 2013, the UN independent mission arrived to investigate alleged chemical attacks by rebels on regime positions in Khan al-Assal. Three days later, on 21 August, 1,429 civilians were killed in a chemical attack in the rebel-held Ghouta area of Damascus.[105] A year before, Obama had declared that the use of chemical weapons by the regime would constitute a red line for the US, evoking a military response. After Kerry presented an unclassified US intelligence report about the regime's guilt in the gruesome attack, Obama declared that the US was in the process of planning for a "limited narrow" military response that would not involve "boots on the ground" in order to punish al-Assad and deter future use of chemical weapons.[106] Rallying for international support at the G20 meeting in early September in St Petersburg, Obama appeared weak when Putin argued that responsibility for the attack was not clear and insisted that only the UNSC could legitimately authorize the use of force. Putin's posture was endorsed at the meeting of the SCO, in Bishkek on 13 September.

The Gulf States and the Syrian opposition were surprised, when on 12 September Kerry and Lavrov met in Geneva to discuss dismantling Syria's chemical weapons. As the US Congress debated military strikes as a response to the chemical attack, Lavrov proposed that Syria put its chemical weapons under international control. The survival of the regime was a red line for Russia. In addition, keeping US military power at bay was crucial for Putin's effort to reassert Russian influence, particularly in the ME. Kerry, who still kept the military option on the table, reiterated that the US was ready to consider the Russian proposal provided that surrendering the chemical weapons must be "real, comprehensive and verifiable."[107] Concurrently, the UN received Syria's application to join the Chemical Weapons Convention established in 1997. The regime had spent decades building a chemical arsenal to deter Israel. Seizing the opportunity to promote Russia's position in front of a worldwide audience, Putin took the unusual step of publishing an op-ed in *The New York Times* on 11 September. He warned that a strike "would increase violence and unleash a new wave of terrorism. It could undermine multilateral efforts to resolve the Iranian nuclear problem, and the Israeli-Palestinian conflict and further destabilize the Middle East and North Africa." He added, "we are not protecting the Syrian government, but international law."[108]

Obama declined to intervene and strike Syrian regime targets, in favour of avoiding involvement in the Syrian civil war. In the autumn of 2013, the US and Russia agreed on a plan, and Putin convinced al-Assad to surrender his chemical weapons to the Organization for the Proliferation of Chemical Weapons based on UNSC Resolution 2118.[109] Resolution 2118 demanded the destruction of Syria's chemical stockpile, thereby "rescuing Obama from his dilemma while rescuing al-Assad from the consequences of American force."[110] Given the situation of conflict escalation and Russia's obstruction of any move against al-Assad, the US agreed to Russia's proposal to cooperate on the destruction of Syria's chemical weapons. The opposition and Turkey felt betrayed by Obama. Putin had another self-serving objective. If al-Assad's chemical weapons were not in safe hands, Russia could not be confident that some would not fall into the hands of rebel groups and Chechen fighters, who could threaten the Winter Olympics scheduled for Sochi in February 2014.[111] Putin not only protected the Syrian regime but also gained honour, a main component of status, and international prestige for his adroit diplomacy. He also highlighted Russia's great power status and ability to continue to play a major role in the ME and cooperate with the US to serve American and Russian shared interests.

Russia's soft power in preventing the US from striking Syria could be considered an attribute of status. Similarly, Russia's entry into the WHO and the G8 were gestures toward Russia's status. Yet, in accordance with H1, the US did not accord Russia higher status in the current international system because Russia could become a threat in the medium or long term in terms of both security and status as a socio-psychological goal. Revisionist Russia was viewed by the US as a primary threat. The American assessment was based purely on strategic and military disagreements between the US and Russia since the late 1990s. Russia's heavy-handed approach to political disputes in Eurasia is a case in point. Still, Medvedev's perspective on Europe "from Vancouver to Vladivosdok" and his proposal of a new all-European treaty to establish a new security architecture by moving beyond NATO expansion was dismissed by the EU and the US because Washington expressed full confidence in the NATO-centred security system in Europe. Another case is that Russia did not exploit an opportunity when Obama attempted to "reset" relations with Moscow to address its security perception.

In November 2013, the new Islamic Front, composed of thirteen groups, was announced with Saudi Arabia's approval.[112] The FSA had been losing ground as it battled al-Assad's forces and groups linked with al-Qaeda. The Obama administration had rightfully been careful to supply only nonlethal arms to moderate rebel groups. In 2013, the CIA trained only about 1,000 moderate rebel fighters.[113] The rise of the Islamist radicals at the expense of the mainstream opposition, SNC, whose leader became the Saudi-backed Ahmad al-Jabra, bolstered al-Assad's argument that the alternative to his rule was a Syria ruled by al-Qaeda.

The continuing bloodshed and the West's disastrous foreign policy toward Syria were starting to threaten the political stability of Iraq, Lebanon, and Turkey. Still, the more than 40,000 foreign jihadists and terrorists fighting in Syria on the side of ISIS posed a potential threat to the national security of the US and Europe. ISIS did not become a major issue in Syria until 2014. The US and the UK shifted their focus from Syria to Iraq by arming the "fervently pro-Iranian and pro-al-Assad regime" of Iraqi Shiite Prime Minister Nouri al-Maliki as his government struggled to fight the Sunni al-Qaeda-linked militias. The US had withdrawn from Afghanistan and Iraq, but the military gains so painfully won were being reversed. Al-Qaeda was back and was fighting for its own proto state in western Iraq and eastern Syria. The previous Western hostility to the Syrian regime, at least for the time being, lessened in the face of what was perceived as a worse threat. The main concern now seemed to be defeating al-Qaeda rather than al-Assad. That said, former US ambassador to Iraq and Syria Ryan Crocker wrote, "the West should engage al-Assad on counterterrorism."[114] Moscow and Washington, which emerged as the leading pro- and anti-al-Assad powers, urged both sides to initiate confidence building measures, including local ceasefires, access for aid, and prisoner exchanges before Geneva II.

On the Iranian front, international diplomacy achieved a breakthrough when, in Geneva in November 2013, Iran struck a historic agreement with the P5+1, accepting strict constraints on its nuclear program for the first time in a decade in exchange for partial relief from Western-imposed sanctions.[115] For Iran, the interim deal reduced the threat of war, eased punishing sanctions, and bolstered its role in the ME. For the US, the deal gave a boost to Obama's noninterventionist policy that stated global security threats could be addressed by diplomacy.

The tension between Russia and the West increased when Ukrainian President Victor Yanukovych, under pressure from Moscow, refused the association agreement with the EU at the Vilnius summit in Lithuania on 28–29 November 2013. The Kremlin saw the Eastern partnership program as a geopolitical competitor to the Eurasian Union. Tsygankov argued that the more the EU presented Ukrainian membership in the organization as a "'civilizational' choice, the more Putin and his associates viewed the Eurasian Union as a values-based community."[116] This was followed by political turmoil in Ukraine, where protesters tried, and once again failed, to topple Russian-backed Yanukovych. The mass protests in late 2013 became the "Euromaidan revolution."[117] Yanukovych's last minute U-turn was attributed to a deal with Putin on a $15 billion bailout and a big cut in the cost of Russian gas supplies to Kiev. The EU had signalled that Ukraine stood to receive between 600 million and 19 billion Euros over seven years. Yet, Brussels made Yanukovych's choice harder by insisting that he free former prime minister Yulia Tymoshenko, his political rival.[118] Evidently, Moscow had the upper hand in a region that was still considered its own backyard. Russia refused to be isolated in FSS. Still, FSRs, "which traditionally found themselves in Russia's sphere of influence might sign on initial agreements deepening their cooperation with the EU was seen by Moscow as a threat to both its symbolic status and to its real geopolitical position in the region."[119] During the meeting of the Valdai Club Putin further "defended independence and sovereignty in spiritual, ideological and foreign policy spheres as an integral part of our national character."[120]

In addition to achieving its policy goal in Ukraine, the Russian policy of keeping al-Assad in power did not change. Since 2011, Moscow's ME diplomacy was based on standing up for the principles of international law and upholding the role of the UN. In 2014, as Western support for the FSA was growing increasingly wary because of the role played by foreign militants, Russia continued to raise its diplomatic and economic influence in the ME as a major provider of conventional weapons to Syria to keep al-Assad's army fighting apace. On the ground, the regime launched vicious barrel-bomb attacks on Aleppo and other cities. Dozens of Russian Antonov 124s transport planes had been bringing in armoured vehicles, surveillance equipment, radars, electronic warfare systems, spare parts for helicopters, and guided bombs for aircraft. In December 2013, the Russian oil and gas company Soyuzneftegas signed a $90 million deal with Syria's oil ministry for oil exploration and production in a 2,190-kilometre area of Mediterranean waters off the Syrian coast between Tartus and Banias.[121]

With the spread of radical Islamist ideology in the region and worldwide, Syria became a problem for global security. A year and a half after Geneva I was held in June 2012, the second international conference (Geneva II) opened in Switzerland on 22 January 2014. Syria's government and opposition delegates met at the UN peace talks along with foreign ministers from some forty countries. Iran, which was a key foreign player, was not invited because it did not accept the June 2012 Geneva Communiqué as a basis for a negotiated solution. Kerry, in his opening remarks, emphasized, "al-Assad would not be part of the transition government." Lavrov, expected that "all external players would be encouraging the Syrians to reach agreement, would refrain from attempts to prejudge the final agreements. The threat of turning Syria into a hotbed for international terrorism had become the most serious problem." Ahmad Jabra, the president of the SNC considered the Geneva talks "a prelude to the removal of al-Assad."[122] He called on the Syrian government to immediately transfer power to a transitional governing body with full executive powers. However, for Russia the transitional government did not mean categorically that al-Assad must give up power immediately. Russia had repeatedly said that only the people of Syria could decide al-Assad's fate. The key issue of a transitional government blocked any progress.

Moallem tried to steer the focus away from a transitional governing body to a discussion of countering terrorism. He stressed that "fighting terrorism would pave the way for the start of the political process and an internal Syrian dialogue without any foreign intervention."[123] Envoy Brahimi, who acted as communicator, met separately with the government and opposition delegations to keep the process moving. The first round of talks failed to narrow the gap between the government and opposition delegates. The Friends of Syria, an alliance of mainly Western and Arab Gulf countries, met in Geneva shortly after the first round of talks ended and urged the regime not to obstruct the second round of talks.

At the 50th Munich Security Conference that took place from 31 January to 2 February 2014, the matter of Syria was that of helplessness. Brahimi reported that there was no progress. Ukraine had been in turmoil since November 2013 when Yanukovych turned down a EU accord in favour of a Russian bailout and announced his decision to postpone an association agreement with the EU. In response, mass demonstrations took place in Kiev protesting Yanukovych's decision. Jude Dempsey wrote that, "the EU's soft power tools of civilian assistance, diplomacy, and sanctions had so far been no match for the kind of Russian hard power that was now engulfing parts of eastern Ukraine." She added, "that mismatch highlighted the West's general lack of strategic direction, which has huge implications for global security."[124]

By ignoring Russia's interests and values in FSS, European Council President Herman Van Rompuy said, "the future of Ukraine belongs with the EU," while Kerry reiterated that the US backed Ukraine's "fight for democracy." In an apparent swipe at Moscow, Kerry added that the future of the majority of Ukrainians "did not have to lie with one country alone, and certainly not coerced." Presumably Lavrov did not expect such a statement from Kerry. Hence, Lavrov asked, "What does incitement of violent street protests have to do with the promotion of democracy? Why do we not hear condemnation of those who seize government buildings and attack police and use racist, anti-Semitic and Nazi slogans?"[125] Similar to the NATO enlargement and EU expansion since the beginning of the 2000s, the Western policy of democracy promotion in FSS was perceived by Russia as a threat to its values and interests. Russia cooperated with Western nations when its fundamental values and interests were not challenged.

In Ukraine, on 21 February 2014, the government and the opposition struck a deal that allowed Yanukovych to stay in power until new elections were held. However, the deal quickly fell apart, and Yanukovych fled to Russia the next day. The Kremlin blamed Western governments for the collapse of the deal and refused to recognize the new government because it was "pro-Western and anti-Russian to the core, and it contained four high-ranking members who could legitimately be labeled neofascists."[126] Washington's involvement in the coup came to light. Assistant Secretary of State for European and Eurasian Affairs Victoria Nuland and Republican Senator John McCain participated in antigovernment demonstrations, and US Ambassador to Ukraine Geoffrey Pyatt proclaimed that Yanukovyche's toppling was "a day for the history books." Still, as a leaked telephone recording revealed, "Nuland had advocated regime change" in Ukraine.[127] Rather than accommodating Russia's great power aspirations and acknowledging its international conflict management role in the ME, the EU and Washington not only dishonoured Moscow but also provoked Putin to use power politics to protect Russia's borders and national interests.

For Putin, it was time to confront the West and achieve Russian foreign policy ambitions. Putin used the strategy of social competition to attain regional hegemony in Eurasia and to re-establish Russia's lost great power status. Russia's foreign policy behaviour was in line with the theoretical concept of status-overachievers who become quite aggressive and tend to apply more competitive strategies in their immediate neighbourhood. Shortly after 22 February Putin ordered Russian forces to take the Crimea from Ukraine, and soon after that he annexed it to Russia. He also supported the insurgency in the Donbas region in eastern Ukraine from March 2014 by sending thousands of Russian troops to the Ukrainian border.[128] Russia's annexation of Crimea was framed in terms of consolidating Russia's centuries old "civilizational and sacred significance."[129] Tsygankov noted that Putin made his decision to intervene in Crimea in close consultation with the nationalist coalition that had a tough stance toward the new government in Kiev. The nationalist coalition "included security hawks like Nikolay Patrushev and Sergey Ivanon, who were known for their close ties with Putin and tough opposition to NATO expansion."[130] The crisis in Ukraine brought relations between Russia and the West to their lowest point since the Cold War. The US and the EU imposed several rounds of crippling sanctions against Moscow to push Russia into isolation. In terms of costs, Russia faced a number of negative consequences from its aggressive policy in Ukraine. Freire and Heller contended that the Kremlin did not follow "a clear strategy on cost-calculation regarding status-seeking."[131] The economic costs associated with Western sanctions from 2014 to 2018 amounted to about US$40 billion, the Russian ruble devalued, oil prices remained low, and millions in economic assets left the country."[132] In political terms, Russia's relations with Western nations sunk to an unprecedentedly low level. Unlike Russia, the US and the EU leaders endorsed the new government of Ukraine, promising political and economic support and demanding that Russia withdraw its troops and cease assistance for protestors inside Ukraine. Still, Mark Urnov argued that Russia's use of power politics to regain great power status recognition had not changed its inconsistent status and was "unlikely to have any lasting effect."[133]

Russia was sensitive to potential threats near its borders. Putin was also fixated on the notion that the US wanted to overthrow his regime. However, Obama's foreign policy relied on diplomacy over military intervention to resolve global conflicts like Ukraine and Iran and pledged to boost support for Syria's opposition.

Due to the expansion of NATO in the mid-2000s and the increasingly hawkish attitude of the Duma and the Russian army, it was no coincidence that in his second term Putin adopted an assertive foreign policy. Putin was condemned by the US and NATO for annexing Crimea and violating international law. Yet, back in 1999, when faced with a Russian veto of a potential UNSC resolution in the case of Kosovo, NATO used force and justified its action, legality aside, on moral grounds. In addition, there was the US invasion of Iraq in 2003, which was a clear example of the violation of international law. Putin rejected Western criticisms and argued that Russia's "primary concern was humanitarian to prevent what he claimed would be further cases of violence by Ukrainian extremists against Russian-speaking Ukrainians."[134] The Kremlin demanded that Kiev initiate institutional changes and guarantee the protection of Russian speakers. Putin also insisted that the interests and position of Russia and other nations should be taken into account to stabilize the global situation. According to the independent polling group Levada Center, Putin's domestic approval rating surged to 80 per cent after incorporating the Crimea.

Al-Assad and China supported Russia's actions in Crimea. During a April 2014 meeting in Damascus with the Imperial Orthodox Palestine Society, headed by former prime minister Sergei Stepashin, al-Assad praised "the important role that Russia was playing on the international scene and its contribution toward drawing up a new map for a multipolar world."[135] Al-Assad told Stepashin, "this year, the active phase of military action in Syria will be ended. After that we will have to shift to what we have been doing all the time – fighting terrorism."[136] He also asked Stepashin to "tell Putin that I am no Yanukovych and that I will not go. The project of political Islam has failed, and there should be no mixing between political and religious work" in Syria.[137] Since 1963, secularism has been a characteristic of the authoritarian Syrian regime.

Few would dispute that the US experienced a relative decline. Its status-seeking strategy in Ukraine and Syria demonstrated that Russia was ascending militarily and politically. Putin was defying the US in

Syria. As argued in chapter 2, Putin was willing to create a new world order where Russia would have an equal say on common global issues. The US could not be complacent. As diplomat and historian Charles Hill observed, "no international order had proved immortal."[138]

Back in Syria, the delay in removing a large shipment of chemical weapons that was due in February prompted Western criticism that Damascus was seeking to gain leverage during the peace talks. The director of US national intelligence, James Clapper, noted that al-Assad was in a "strengthened position by virtue of the agreement to remove the chemical weapons."[139] Yet, Russian Deputy Foreign Minister Gennady Gatilov rejected such concerns. Clapper's admission that al-Assad was getting stronger was an implicit confirmation that Obama's claim that the chemical agreement represented a diplomatic breakthrough was wrong. With Russian acquiescence, al-Assad needed to buy time. For the first time in the three-year old conflict, Russia hosted Jabra to hold discussions about Geneva II, but Moscow did not yield to Jabra's demand of removing al-Assad.

The second round of talks resumed in Geneva on 10 February but the only tangible result was the agreement on evacuating civilians from Homs. While the regime had no incentive to discuss transitional government, Russia accused the sponsors of the rebels of pushing for regime change. Still, the majority of the rebel groups had little interest in a political solution. In a move that would further discourage the opposition to talk to the government delegation, Syria's parliament unanimously approved a new election law on 13 March, allowing multiple candidates to run for president.

The war in Ukraine and the rise of ISIS exposed the weaknesses of the West. Brahimi appealed to the US and Russia for help. Yet, reluctant Western leaders could not provide security in conflict zones. For Russia and the regime, terrorism was no less threatening than the humanitarian crisis in Syria. Syria became a magnet for jihadists and Islamic radicals. The crisis in Syria would not stop without bridging the Sunni-Shiite schism that required a regional security agreement that reconciled the national interests of Saudi Arabia and Iran. This regional balance, in turn, required new security architecture between the US and Russia. The Saudi and Israeli governments urged the West to halt the Iranian nuclear threat to the region. In Vienna on 20 February the deal that was reached between the P5+1 and Iran on the framework for comprehensive negotiations over Tehran's nuclear program presumably could ease the Iranian-Saudi tension in the region.

Although the Western powers insisted that "any final agreement would be contingent on Iran taking concrete verifiable steps that prevent it from ever obtaining a nuclear weapon," Riyadh's perception of a pivotal threat was not matched in Washington.[140]

Amid regional rivalry and no clear US policy on Syria, violence was likely to continue. However, on the humanitarian front on 22 February the UNSC unanimously adopted Resolution 2139, which called "on all parties, in particular the Syrian authorities, to promptly allow humanitarian access for the UN agencies and its partners, including cross conflict lines, and to ensure that aid reached people."[141] Damascus welcomed the resolution that condemned terror attacks by all al-Qaeda-linked terrorist organizations. There was an agreement between the US and Russia that the jihadists were a common foe. Within this context, Russia warned Saudi Arabia not to plead for greater US engagement in Syria by supplying the Syrian rebels with shoulder-launched surface to air missiles and antitank systems.[142]

Russia's strategy of diplomatic and military support to the regime did not change. For the first time in February 2014 the Syrian army started to use longer-range Russian Smerch and Uragan rockets. Syria also intensified the use of MiG-29 fighter jets with ground attack capabilities to win the war. Another significant development in the conflict was the use of US-made BGM-71 TOW antitank rockets by Harakat Hazm, the Syrian Rebel Front and the Martyr Ahmad Abdo Battalions and Brigades, which were secular insurgent factions.[143] Apparently, the TOW rockets were provided to the rebels by Saudi Arabia with American consent.

Al-Assad's defiance of opposition demands to step down and pave the way for a peaceful political transition, reflected his growing confidence that he had turned the tide of the war, which had killed 150,000 people and displaced nine million from their homes. The opposition remained fragmented and not ready to govern, even if al-Assad fell. The opposition's military wing lacked a unified command-and-control structure, and the Muslim extremists were gaining a foothold in the south, just as they had in 2012 in northern Syria.

On 8 May, the Syrian army took full control of the Old City of Homs after a deal between the government and the rebels to evacuate about 2,250 fighters and civilians in return for freeing seventy Lebanese and Iranian prisoners that were being held by the Islamic Front in the province of Aleppo.[144] However, in a diplomatic blow to Russia and al-Assad's legitimacy, the US State Department upgraded the SNC's informal liaison office in Washington and increased non-lethal assistance to the opposition's SMC by $27 million. Overall US support amounted to $287 million.[145] The Syrian opposition would open a formal diplomatic mission in Washington under US law, but the office would not be an embassy. Kerry also met Jabra in a public show of support but did not provide details on weapons. As noted above, the CIA reportedly participated in a secret program to train moderate rebels in Jordan.

On 28 May Obama delivered a key foreign policy address at the US Military Academy in West Point. He laid out his approach to foreign affairs for the rest of his presidency built on a commitment to act in concert with other nations and shifted the fight against terrorism from Afghanistan to more "decentralized al-Qaeda affiliates and extremists" around the world. Obama announced a $5 billion proposal to serve as a "partnership fund," which would allow the US "to train, build capacity and facilitate partners on the front lines" in Syria, Yemen, and Libya. About Syria, he reiterated that the US should help the Syrian people and "stand up against a dictator who bombs and starves his people." Obama pledged to work "with Congress to ramp up support for those in the Syrian opposition who offer the best alternative to terrorists and a brutal dictator."[146] Conspicuously absent in Obama's remark was any direct mention of al-Assad, for whose resignation he had previously called.

Washington was struggling to formulate an approach based on fighting terrorism as diplomatic options stalled. According to Joshua Landis, Obama's overarching goal in the ME was counterterrorism to fight the jihadists, an argument used to back Egyptian President Abdel Fattah al-Sisi who was elected in May 2014.[147] Yet, Daniel Byman noted, "by fixating on counterterrorism, the U.S. overlooked opportunities to prevent or mitigate civil wars and regional conflicts."[148] Supporting al-Assad aside, Russia was trying to mitigate the conflict in Syria to demonstrate its significant influence on international conflict management. Geneva was not on the table, and Brahimi resigned on 31 May. A Swedish Italian diplomat, Steffan de Mistura was appointed in July 2014 to mediate the conflict. From Brahimi's perspective, neither Russia nor the US convinced their allies to participate in the negotiations with serious intent. The failure of Geneva II meant that UNSC Resolution 2139 to ensure humanitarian aid access represented "the ceiling of diplomacy" for the time being.[149]

Obama's speech coincided with the dubious re-election of al-Assad, in the middle of a war, in June 2014. Voting did not take place in opposition held areas, effectively excluding millions of people. Al-Assad's Syrian and foreign opponents dismissed the election as a sham. The US and its allies insisted that al-Assad had lost legitimacy and could not be part of any future Syrian government. Russia, which had been at odds with the West over al-Assad's future, said that only the Syrian people should decide if he stepped down. The West should drop its demand about the political exit of al-Assad if it wanted a genuinely international coalition against ISIS. In that month, the offensive spearheaded by ISIS, including Sunni tribes and ex-Baath party elements, which took swaths of northern and western Iraq and the major city of Mosul on 10 June, prompted Obama to send up to three hundred US military advisers to help the country's beleaguered army. After overrunning Mosul and Tikrit, ISIS advanced toward Baghdad and the Kurdish areas that produced 10 per cent of Iraqi oil and were home to a CIA base. The American-trained Iraqi troops melted away when confronted by militants. Concurrently, Washington asked al-Maliki to form an inclusive government to bridge sectarian splits between the Sunni and Shiite population and to tackle Islamist militant forces threatening the unity of Iraq. The Obama administration found itself in a foreign policy dilemma with the apparent entry of Syria into the Iraqi conflict, and active Iranian military support for al-Maliki. The Syrian air force targeted ISIS on the Syrian side of the border, across from the Iraqi town of al-Qaim. Iraq's other neighbours, Jordan, Kuwait, Saudi Arabia, and Turkey, bolstered their defenses.

On 26 June, Kerry met with the foreign ministers of Saudi Arabia, the United Arab Emirates (UAE), Jordan, and Israel to ease their fears about the potential convergence of US, Iranian, and Syrian policies to defeat ISIS. Obama's request to Congress to provide $500 million in equipment and training to "appropriately vetted" moderate Syrian opposition forces was the most significant US move so far to support those fighting against al-Assad.[150] Yet, the question was how Washington was going to vet the dispersed opposition of 1,500 separate insurgent groups in Syria? There were liberal and democratic people in the opposition. Unfortunately such moderates barely had contact with, let alone influence over, the groups fighting on the ground. Thus, creating a moderate opposition could be too late to influence events in Syria. In his meeting with the Saudi King, Abdullah, and Jabra, in Jeddah on 27 June, Kerry said, "the moderate opposition in Syria had the ability to be a very important player in pushing back ISIS's presence not just in Syria but also in Iraq."[151] Certainly, Russia did not share Kerry's view. Through Syria, Russia was interested in sharing global power with the US and defending its international presence.

On 28 June, ISIS, which carved out large chunk of territory that effectively erased the borders between Iraq and Syria, declared itself an Islamic caliphate and laid the foundations of its proto state. ISIS would govern by Sharia law. The terrorist group renamed itself the Islamic State (hereafter IS) and proclaimed its leader Adu Bakr al-Baghdadi as caliph.[152] The proclamation was a bold move claiming legitimacy as a successor to the first Islamic rule created by the Prophet Mohammad in the Arabian Peninsula fourteen centuries ago. (The caliphate had been abolished by the Turkish ruler Mustafa Kemal Ataturk in 1924.) Following the group's announcement, IS militants paraded with their black flag in their stronghold of Raqqa and along the banks of the Euphrates River from which they expelled the rebel groups in the spring of 2014. Yet, the announcement of IS was condemned elsewhere in Syria by rival Islamist groups, who had been fighting the terrorist group since January 2014 across northern and eastern Syria. IS was greeted with disdain by many Iraqis too. According to the Iraqi government "the world now bears a big and ethical responsibility to fight those terrorists, who made Iraq and Syria their battlefield. We are fighting them not for the sake of Iraq only, but for the sake of the whole world."[153]

The IS threat prompted Russia and Iran to step in to bolster the Iraqi government. Iran deployed hundreds of troops from its IRGC under the command of Iran's feared Quds (Jerusalem) Force, Qassem Suleimani, to reenforce the al-Maliki government. In late 2014, "Iran had spent more than $1billion in military aid to Iraq in the approximately six months after the June IS Offensive." In its turn, Russia delivered the first Sukhoi fighter jet to the government vowing that it would prevent Iraq's collapse.[154] Both, Iran and Russia wanted to confirm their regional reach. According to Ambassador Firouznia,

> We [Iranians] and the Russians were concerned about the developments in the ME, especially after the appearance of the takfiri and extremist organizations, like ISIS. The Russians sought to play a bigger role in the ME. Iran cooperated with Russia in Iraq and Syria to defeat the terrorist groups.[155]

In early July 2014 IS seized the Al-Omar oil field in the oil rich Syrian province of Deir al-Zour. With its agricultural land and crude petroleum, Deir al-Zour provided IS "with critical resources to finance its war and governance, and buy the loyalty of hard-pressed tribes and local communities."[156] Controlling most of the oil and gas fields in Syria allowed IS to recruit more local and foreign fighters and control the areas it conquered.

In early August the US embarked on a long-term mission to defeat IS in Iraq. The new Iraqi prime minister-designate Haidar al-Abadi, who was trying to form a power-sharing government, advocated effective partnership and a counterterrorism strategy with the US and its allies. While al-Abadi was trying to form an inclusive government, US airstrikes enabled the joint Iraqi and Kurdish forces, which were battling IS, to liberate a large part of the Mosul Dam, which had great strategic value as it supplied electricity and water to a large part of the country.[157] On 15 August the UNSC voted unanimously on a resolution aimed at weakening extremist groups in Iraq and Syria. Although Syria's ambassador to the UN Bashar Jaafari insisted that the government "had been fighting terrorists for the past three years, Jordan's representative, Ambassador Mahmoud Hmoud, maintained that, "terrorism in Syria had been exacerbated by Syria's marginalization of moderate opposition groups."[158] In addition, the West had held al-Assad, in large part, the cause of terrorism in Syria and certainly he could not, therefore, be the solution to it. Although Syria and the US found themselves on the same side of the battle against IS, a common enemy was unlikely to mean collaboration.

Obama urged countries in the ME to join Washington to "extract the cancer" of the IS jihadist ideology. Moallem welcomed Obama's call to fight terrorism provided that military and security collaboration with the US could not take place without a political deal with Damascus.[159] Russia, in its turn, urged Western and Arab nations to overcome their distaste for the Syrian government and engage with it to fight the jihadists. Lavrov noted that the West would "have to choose what is more important: to change the regime and satisfy personal antipathies with the risk that the situation will crumble, or find pragmatic ways to join efforts against the common threat, which is the same for all of us: terrorism."[160] British Prime Minister David Cameron agreed to "step up Britain's involvement in the fight against the IS by sending military trainers to Baghdad to help the Iraqi security forces."[161] The irony was that in August 2013, in the wake of a chemical attack on the Ghouta suburb of Damascus, the US did not call for a similar global response against heinous crimes and massive violations of human rights.

Obama's foreign policy was thrown into disarray because Washington was to deal with an incredibly dangerous situation in Iraq, Syria, and Libya. There was a terrorist proto state in the ME posing a direct threat to the West. The clashes in the ME were asymmetric conflicts for which the West was not equipped. Obama was thinking about a new strategy to defeat IS but the US had no clear Syria plan. As noted above, the US was not willing to be the world's policeman. There was also Russia's meddling in Ukraine, where, in May 2014 newly elected pro-Western President Petro Poroshenko's government was fighting to put down pro-Moscow separatists in the east and south of the country.[162] Inspired by the Russian annexation of Crimea, the separatists took control of government buildings and refused to cooperate with the government in Kiev by appointing their own governors in the regions of Donestsk, Lugansk, and others. In terms of costs, the Western sanctions imposed by the US and the EU on Moscow had damaged the Russian economy that had already been battered by declining commodity prices. Yet, Moscow deployed to eastern Ukraine more soldiers and new heavy armour to maintain influence. The Kremlin managed to strengthen public support for its policy by appealing to Russian nationalists and evoking the narrative of an independent and strong Russia that sought to defend its values and interests in Ukraine.[163] From Moscow's perspective, Ukraine's allegiance was important to Putin's effort to establish his Russian-led Eurasian Union as an alternative to the EU. But the Eurasian Union's main downside was that it entailed creating new barriers with the outside world. Moreover, the Kremlin had always viewed Ukraine as an important security buffer. Ukraine was also a transit route for the energy exports on which Russia's economy depended. In revisionist Russia's view, in an emerging new world order Moscow should have a strong say in the ME and maintain its leadership when it is challenged in FSS.

The situation in Iraq, the role and mission of NATO, the crisis in Ukraine, and the relationship with Russia were priorities during the discussions of the NATO summit that took place in Wales on 4–5 September 2014. NATO's General Secretary Anders Fogh Rasmussen noted that "our peace and security are once again being tested, now by Russia's aggression against Ukraine … and the criminal downing of the Malaysian MH-17" in eastern Ukraine "has made clear that a conflict in one part of Europe can have tragic consequences around the world." In his turn, Obama declared that several NATO states were forming a "new coalition of the willing" to combat IS in Iraq.[164] To avoid further tension with Russia, Ukraine was not admitted into NATO as a member. Yet, NATO members approved of an action plan to form a "very high readiness force," which would be deployed in the Baltic countries with permanent detachments of three hundred to six hundred soldiers.[165] This was a breach of the Founding Act on Cooperation and Security, which NATO and Russia signed in 1997.

After Obama met ministers from ten European nations on the sidelines of the NATO summit, Hagel unveiled what he called the "core coalition" to fight IS militants.[166] Obama was also weighing airstrikes in Syria. On 7 September, Arab foreign ministers, who met in Cairo, "agreed to take the necessary measures to confront terrorist groups including" IS.[167] In a change of position, the final statement called the Syrian opposition groups to hold talks with the regime to create a reconciliation government. After one day of Obama's decision to strike both sides of the Syrian Iraqi border, Kerry, who met Saudi King Abdullah in Jeddah on 11 September, won the backing of the Arab countries – Egypt, Iraq, Jordan, Lebanon, and six Gulf States – for a coordinated military campaign against IS.[168] Obama's decision to confront IS militarily in both Syria and Iraq marked a "major victory" for Saudi diplomacy. The Saudi's agreed to allow the US training of five thousand Syrian rebels inside the kingdom and participated in the US-led airstrikes against IS targets inside Syria. However, both sides still risked a falling out over their respective goals. For the Saudis, the overriding goal remained the removal of al-Assad, while Obama's goal was to "degrade and destroy" IS in Iraq and Syria.[169] For the US, a lasting solution to Syria's civil war would be an inclusive political transition.

Iran, Russia, and Syria criticized the international coalition for excluding them. Iran continued its efforts to back al-Assad and strengthen its clout with Iraq's government. It is worth noting that when Washington sought to remove al-Maliki from power, it was Iran that made it happen. Further, in Afghanistan in late 2001, Iran's cooperation with the US was important in routing the Taliban and installing the new Afghan government of Hamid Karzai. Notwithstanding setbacks suffered by the Russian-backed Syrian army, it remained the strongest player in the war. Meanwhile, al-Assad, who met the UN envoy de Mistura in Damascus, stressed that the success of the diplomat's mission depended on ending terror.

The US's emerging strategies were to work through partners and allies and have them do the fighting on the ground. Meanwhile, the US had opened a back channel to Iran to de-escalate potential clashes as both countries used air power to attack IS targets. It was impossible to bypass Iran in the search for defeating IS. Russia should have been engaged too because the West and Russia did not want a sanctuary for Islamist fanatics in the heart of the ME. Joseph Nye rightly argued while the West must resist Putin's challenge to the liberal order and "the norm of not claiming territory by force, it must not completely isolate Russia, a country with which the West has overlapping interests concerning nuclear security, non-proliferation, anti-terrorism, the Arctic region, and regional issues such as Iran and Afghanistan."[170] Defeating IS was a bigger challenge than al-Qaeda because the caliphate had set for itself a quasi state and had ample financing, sophisticated weapons, and a highly competent military command.

Extending on H1, the dominant power, which was the US, was to accede to Russia's status demands, especially when Russia sought participation in a balancing coalition against the actual common primary threat that was IS. However, Russia was excluded from the coalition of the willing. IS was a threat to both the US and Russia in purely national security and stability terms. In short, the US and Russia shared the same primary threat of terrorism according to H2. Within this context, on the one hand, the US was expected to be motivated by the fact that balancing the threat was likely to be easier with the cooperation of Russia, which was seeking higher status recognition. On the other hand, the costs of not accommodating Russia potentially included "the latter adding to systemic challenges owing to its increasingly dissatisfied nature."[171]

On 28 September, Lavrov said, as the truce in Ukraine was holding and "as talks between Russia, the EU, and Ukraine started, including gas talks," it was time for a "reset 2.0" with Washington. He criticized NATO's "Cold War mentality" and explained that "Moscow needed to modernize its conventional and nuclear arms" without causing "a new arms race." Rejecting American domination, Lavrov reiterated that Washington "could no longer act as the prosecutor, the judge and the executioner in every part of the world." Lavrov added, despite Western sanctions, Russia did not feel isolated. But, "having said that, I want to emphasize that we do not want to go to extremes and abandon the

European and American directions in our foreign economic cooperation." On the US-led air campaign in Syria against IS, he accused Washington of a "double standard for refusing to cooperate with the regime."[172] It is probable that Lavrov signalled that Russia wanted a gradual resumption of dialogue with the US. Yet, his remarks showed that the era of American pre-eminence had ended, ushering in a multipolar international system that could be tense and less orderly. What was also becoming apparent was the collapse of the region's old order too, which had existed unchanged since the end of World War I.

The US had gone into battle in Iraq and Syria. However, this time military action against Muslim targets was joined by a coalition of Arab states: Saudi Arabia, the UAE, Jordan, Bahrain, and Qatar. Although Obama insisted that there would not be American combat "boots on the ground," about 1,600 US troops had been deployed to Iraq to train local security forces and help safeguard US personnel.[173] On 24 September 2014 the UNSC unanimously adopted Resolution 2178 on stemming the flow of foreign jihadists to Iraq and Syria.[174] After talks between Kerry and Lavrov on 26 September, US-led coalition that included Belgium, Denmark, and Britain, hit IS's infrastructure in Syria. Russia could gain from the US-led airstrikes against IS, which had been joined by Chechen fighters from the north Caucasus. Washington's strategy was incoherent. When it sought to destroy IS, the Nusra Front, and the Khorasan Group, it would indirectly strengthen their rival, al-Assad. As the terrorists lost ground, the Russian-backed Syrian army was able to take the advantage more easily than were the disorganized moderate rebels. Al-Assad voiced his support for any international antiterrorism effort. Rebel groups expressed their anger with the US strategy of targeting jihadist groups while leaving the regime forces untouched.

Turkey, a NATO ally, belatedly agreed to join the international coalition but continued to argue that creating a safe zone was vital to accommodate the Syrian refugees, ensure security, and train moderate Syrian rebels to topple al-Assad. Ankara manipulated the ongoing battle in the strategic border town of Ain al-Arab (Kobani) as part of a geopolitical struggle. Turkey's real fight was for the removal of al-Assad and the weakening of the PYD, which was defending Ain al-Arab. Mona Alami disclosed that when al-Assad did not fall, "Ankara provided free passage to jihadists to cross to Syria."[175] Alami's evidence illustrated the murky relationship between Turkey and IS. Contrary to Turkey, the US engaged with the Kurdish fighters because it did not consider the PYD a terrorist organization. The Kurdish fighters were the only forces on the ground standing between IS and Ain al-Arab. On 20 October, in a significant shift, Turkey's Foreign Minister Mavlut Cavusoglu announced that Turkey was helping Iraqi Kurdish Peshmarga fighters cross into Syria to support the PYD. Cavusoglu's announcement came after US military C-130 cargo planes made multiple drops of arms and supplies provided by Iraqi Kurdish authorities to the PYD forces in Ain al-Arab.[176] FSA fighters arrived, too, to combine forces with the Peshmarga.

It is plausible to argue that Washington was moving closer to Russia's position on the Syrian conflict. *Rossiiskayagazeta* wrote that "Russia and the U.S. agreed to exchange intelligence on the actions of extremists in the Islamic State group." After a three-hour meeting in Paris on 14 October between Kerry and Lavrov, it became clear that Russia was helping the Iraqi forces "by providing arms and training."[177] Cooperation between Moscow and Washington was important to address global security issues, including terrorism. Their agreement in 2013 to remove Syria's stockpile of chemical weapons was an example. Both Russian news agencies, *RIA Novosti* and *Tass* quoted Medvedev as saying that Washington was "already not insisting" that al-Assad stepped down. In addition to intelligence sharing, the US blacklisted three entities in Syria that could pose a security threat to Russia. The first was the IS military emir Umar Shishani. The other two were Chechen-led factions, Jaish Al-Muhajireenwal-Ansar and Murad Margoshvili (Muslim Abu Walid Shishani).[178] Both factions were wanted in Russia.

Concerning peace-building attempts, on 10 November UN envoy de Mistura proposed local truces to improve aid access and alleviate the sufferings of the Syrian people in local areas, starting in the Waer neighbourhood of Aleppo. He stressed that the "freeze" proposal was an action plan, not a peace plan.[179] The action plan was to stop fighting and de-escalate violence. Within this context, while meeting Khatib, who was still an influential opposition figure, in Moscow on 7 November, Russia repeated the need for intra-Syrian dialogue that could be held in Moscow, without Western participation, to end the war. Russia floated the idea that al-Assad could stay in power for two years with a provisional government before presidential elections in which he could stand again along with other candidates. However, Khatib could not make a decision without the consent of the different groups affiliated with the external and internal oppositions. The

EU, Russia, Iran, and Syria supported de Mistura's effort to freeze the fighting in Aleppo, while the armed opposition voiced scepticism because the proposed truce would play into the hands of al-Assad. Aleppo could face the same fate as the City of Homs, where regime forces had largely regained control.

Meanwhile, the US doubled the number of American ground forces in Iraq. Obama's new authorization allowed for the deployment up to 3,100 troops to train and assist Iraqi forces as they pressed ahead with gains on the ground. The government of Iraq asked for more airstrikes and weaponry. IS was on the defensive but still able to launch limited attacks. US Vice President Joe Biden's visit to Ankara on 24 November to overcome differences in the fight against IS achieved little in the way of deeper military cooperation. For Washington, fighting IS was a priority. Its reluctance to confront al-Assad, who was backed by Iran and Russia, was compounded by the fear of failing negotiations over Tehran's alleged nuclear program. There were also differences over the objective of the trained rebels. Moreover, there was no guarantee that Turkey's Incirlik air base could be used for coalition airstrikes. Yet, Turkey facilitated the travel of FSA and other moderate rebels (called Mujahedeen Army) to Qatar where they were trained at Al-Udeid, the largest US air base in the ME. The Mujahedeen was one of the biggest mainstream groups left in northern Syria. Training in Qatar was part of an ostensibly covert CIA program to offer military support to vetted factions in the opposition.[180]

After months of discussions on the need for a unified military body to counter the fragmentation in rebel ranks, the Revolutionary Command Council (RCC) was created on 30 November in Gaziantep, Turkey. The RCC was a merger of militias fighting under the banner of the FSA and the Islamic Front. The formation of the RCC was a clear sign of rising Islamist influence in opposition-controlled northern Syria particularly, the Salafist group, Ahrar al-Sham. Charles Lister noted that the RCC was a "complex organism" headed by Qais al-Sheikh, a judge from Deir al-Zour, who expressed displeasure with the performance of the SNC.[181] Clearly, the RCC would remain hampered by its ties to Turkey and the Islamist Ahrar al-Sham.

Knowing well the ME's "treacherous divides," Russia "transformed itself into a paragon of pragmatism."[182] Despite acknowledging their differences over the Syrian conflict, Putin and Erdogan agreed in their meeting in Ankara on 1 December to fight IS. Both leaders "managed to compartmentalize their relations."[183] That was down to realpolitik.

The issue of energy was on top of their agenda. Turkey was Russia's second largest European importer of natural gas after Germany, and its importance as a customer increased given the political tensions with the EU and the US over Russia's intervention in Ukraine. Putin and Erdogan signed a protocol on energy cooperation and hoped that both countries could "reach $100 billion in annual bilateral trade by 2020."[184] Traditionally, Russia kept its economic, political, and military relations in the region. Russia's foreign policy aimed to meet with all sides to assert Moscow's position in the ME.

Chapter 3 examined and analyzed the regional and international dimensions of the Syrian conflict and the postures of the external actors who took sides with the regime and the opposition. The war in Syria became a proxy war between the supporters of the opposition and the Syrian regime backed by Russia and Iran. Two international conferences (Geneva I and Geneva II) did not achieve a breakthrough because the fate of al-Assad remained a matter of dispute between the internal and external actors. The key issue of transitional government blocked any progress. I argued that the fractured opposition, which served Turkish, Saudi, and Western agendas, was not an alternative to al-Assad's rule. While the US lacked a clear Syria policy, Russia's strategy of preserving influence in Syria and the boarder ME through diplomacy had remained unchanged since 2011. Russia's diplomatic and military support to the regime was associated with Moscow's strategic vision in the ME. Through Syria, Russia would reassert its role and position in the ME and protect its strategic interests.

Although fighting terrorism and preventing foreign fighters who joined IS to return to their home countries was a common policy goal between Russia and the US, both powers disagreed over the solution in Syria. Russian foreign policy was against regime change by force and military intervention outside the UNSC authorization. I emphasized that Russia had significant influence on the international conflict management in Syria via its UNSC seat. In Syria, Russia was "engaged in international diplomacy as a means to preserve its influence in international politics and as a counterweight to Western, in particular U.S., dominance in the UNSC."[185] Fighting terrorism and safeguarding the principle of national sovereignty remained constants in Russian foreign policy.

I also argued that the crisis in Syria could not stop without bridging the Sunni-Shiite schism, which would require a regional security agreement that reconciled the national interests of Saudi Arabia and

Iran. This regional balance, in turn, required new global security architecture between the US and Russia. In light of the deteriorated relationship between Russia and the US, owing to disagreements over arms control, missile defense, and human rights, instability in the ME would persist. In addition, in a changing world order, the Kremlin believed that it possessed the right and duty to play a role in determining the outcome of the Ukrainian and Syrian conflicts that affected the peace and security of the international system as a whole. I provided an empirically grounded interpretation of Russia's policy by considering its values and interests, which guided Russia's actions toward Ukraine. The Kremlin's assertive foreign policy, whereby Russia adopted a unilateral approach in order to promote its norms and values in the international arena, was a pattern of honourable behaviour. Russia's annexation of Crimea was a revisionist move not typical for status-inconsistent powers or status-overachievers. In terms of costs, Russia was subject to Western economic sanctions. Russia's use of military power in its foreign policy to enhance its status seemed highly counterintuitive. With a greater say on global security issues, including NATO and arms control, Russia would be able to protect its strategic interests and satisfy its status aspirations provided that the West would accommodate Russia's fears. Revisionist Russia could not step backward from its posture in Syria. The next chapter will address the objectives of Russia's military intervention in Syria from a status-seeking point of view to find out what determined Russian policy options.

4

The Objectives of Russia's Military Intervention, 2015–17

Chapter 4 explores and examines Russia's motives for intervening in Syria in September 2015. Russia used a mix of military and non-military instruments (i.e. leverage) to achieve a particular outcome that would satisfy its economic and geostrategic interests in the ME and the interests of the regional powers of Turkey and Iran. Certainly, Russia's direct military intervention in the Syrian civil war was a foreign policy objective to shore up al-Assad and the Syrian regime in its fight against terrorism. Also, the aim was to keep Syria unified as a state and to maintain the Russian foothold in the ME. I argue that Russia's intervention in Syria aimed not only to strengthen al-Assad's position but also to change the political outcome in the region that had been out of Moscow's sphere of influence for decades. From Moscow's perspective, the exercise of power politics in Syria would enhance Russia's place in a status hierarchy. Compliant with the status-seeking strategy, Russia applied force to make other major powers recognize its self-defined great power identity. Yet, Russia's intervention had its disadvantages for Moscow, mainly because it created geopolitical conflict with Turkey and financial burdens for the struggling Russian economy.

I also argue that Russia projected force beyond its periphery to confirm Russia's great power identity and to return to its rightful place among the world powers. As Freire and Heller noted, the "identity vector" was crucial to understanding Russia's power politics in Syria.[1] In addition to Moscow's willingness to use military power in its foreign policy, chapter 4 also analyzes how Russia's regional diplomacy demonstrated Moscow's role in negotiating regional divides and forming alliances to fight international terrorism, a common threat to the US, Russia, Turkey, Iran, Lebanon, and Jordan. Still, Russia sought to demonstrate its centrality in international conflict management as an embodiment to its international status. However, satisfying Russia's status aspirations depended on US policies. In this chapter, I provide evidence to support H1 and H2. What was new and crucial in Russia's recent military and diplomatic history was its capability in coalition building and coalition management. Both capabilities had status implications. Russia wanted to assume responsibilities associated with its significant influence on the international conflict management in Syria and in the broader ME by undertaking diplomatic initiatives. Yet, Russia needed to pursue cooperative conflict management with the US in the ME and elsewhere to demonstrate that Russian hard power status-seeking strategy did not threaten the international order.

I will discuss the nature and scale of the Russian intervention in Syria, the Vienna process that took place in November 2015, Russia's relations with rival powers in the ME like Saudi Arabia and Iran, and its policy to maintain good relations with Israel, which was targeting pro-regime Iranian facilities in Syria. As such, Russia tried to prove that it was the major power broker in Syria. Moscow used leverage with Turkey, Iran, and the Syrian regime to push the Geneva and Astana peace processes forward in order to end the conflict. For a better understanding of Russia's power politics from a status-seeking point of view and to find out what determined Russia's foreign policy options, the following sections try to give more empirical substance to the measures of capability (cost considerations), status attribution (factor of identity), and willingness (factor of opportunity).

RUSSIAN MEDIATION AND REGIONAL DYNAMICS

As discussed in chapter 3, Russia watched the US policy on Syria and gauged the depth of the global rivalry over Syria, not least the clashing agendas of Saudi Arabia, Qatar, and Turkey. Russia realized the political and military fatigue in the ME and internationally with the seemingly intractable Syrian conflict. The regime had created an enormous humanitarian problem that its regional rivals, and the US no longer insisted on al-Assad's exit. According to the UN, the number of Syrian refugees had grown by 704,000 in the first six months of 2014.[2] For Russia, the more pertinent matter was how long the regime could last.

In light of deafening diplomatic silence from the Obama administration, from 26 to 29 January and from 6 to 9 April 2015, Russia used its leverage and hosted two meetings in Moscow (the so-called Moscow 1 and Moscow 2 meetings) between Syrian opposition members and representatives from the Syrian regime.[3] The regional priority for the US was to conclude a deal with Iran over its alleged nuclear program and defeat IS by helping the Iraqi army and by training the moderate Syrian rebels. That said, beyond just fighting IS, the US had no commitment to resolve the Syrian conflict. Turkey, which signed an agreement with the US to train Syrian rebels fighting IS, expected that the trained rebels would also fight the Syrian regime.[4] Although Damascus and Tehran officially welcomed both Moscow meetings, they remained suspicious that Russia might come to terms with the Syrian opposition and its foreign supporters. Iranian President Hassan Rouhani, in his televised speech marking the anniversary of the 1979 Islamic Revolution, linked the ongoing nuclear talks to resolving the bloody conflicts in Iraq and Syria. He emphasized Iran's influence and regional role by saying "you have seen in Iraq, Syria, Lebanon and Yemen that the power that could help those nations against terrorist groups was the Islamic Republic of Iran."[5]

During the Syria talks in Moscow, Russia, which wanted to boost its standing as a mediator and honest broker for peace, tried to promote the idea that a settlement could be achieved through intra-Syrian dialogue between the non-radical groups and the regime to achieve consensus. The moderator of the Moscow meetings, Vitaly Naumkin, considered them an important achievement. Apart from acknowledging Syria's sovereignty, unity, and territorial integrity, the rejection of foreign interference, the struggle against terrorist groups, and settling the conflict by peaceful means, the Moscow meetings did not offer a practical and workable roadmap to settle the Syrian conflict (see appendix A). Apparently, Moscow tried to reinforce the idea that the regime should be part of the solution. Moscow also tried to demonstrate to both the US and the EU the importance of Russia's role in international conflict management and its values in the settlement of current international problems.

A number of constraints hindered Russia's mediation. First, Russia's leverage in influencing Damascus was limited because al-Assad demonstrated a lack of flexibility in the search for a compromise through cooperative means. Second, the Turkey-based SNC boycotted the talks. Internally, the Building the Syrian State Party, the so-called domestically tolerated opposition that was headed by Louay Hussein, announced that "the regime no longer had the capacity for reconciliation or negotiating a serious solution."[6] Third, representatives of the regime and the opposition who participated in the talks failed to work out confidence-building measures (CBMs) that would allow them to implement the terms of the agreement. Fourth, both the regime and the opposition still believed that a military solution in Syria was the only solution. Fifth, Russia was unable to launch a national dialogue on its own but could be an effective player in an international team of players, including the US, to solve the conflict.

On 15 January 2015, in Geneva, UN envoy de Mistura urged the international community to ensure that the Syrian conflict did not get placed on the "back burner" and the UN to respond to the humanitarian situation in the war-ravaged country. He added that a truce in Aleppo should be reached and "movement toward some kind of political solution should take place."[7] Since October 2014, de Mistura worked on a plan to broker local freezes starting from Aleppo. Yet, the regime had no reason to agree to a freeze in Aleppo as its aim was to force the rebels to surrender. The rebel forces in Aleppo rejected de Mistura's plan for a freeze, too, because it did not bring a comprehensive solution to the conflict.

The US and European governments, which closed their embassies in Damascus in early 2012, did not show any signs that they were ready to resume diplomatic relations with al-Assad. For the first time, the UN envoy acknowledged that al-Assad should be part of the solution. Al-Assad became increasingly reliant on Iran and Hizbullah to supply him with fighters and on Russia to protect him from international pressure at the UN. Already Russia had been engaged in international diplomacy as a means to preserve its influence in international politics and as a counterweight to US dominance in the UNSC. Russia's and Iran's common opposition toward US foreign policy and their joint support for the Syrian regime provided the basis for cooperation between the two countries. In January 2015, Russian Defense Minister Sergey Shoigu visited Tehran and signed a military cooperation agreement with Iran that pertained mainly to military personnel training exchanges, counterterrorism cooperation, and naval visits.[8] Russia agreed to sell Iran the S-300 air defense missile system. In April, Turkish President Erdogan visited Iran too. Officials from both countries signed new agreements for commercial, economic, and industrial cooperation. Both regional powers,

Turkey and Iran, agreed that regional cooperation was needed to stop the bloodshed, despite their deep differences over the conflicts in Yemen and Syria.

In March 2015, John Kerry, in a stunning reversal of policy, said that Washington would have to negotiate with al-Assad for a political transition in Syria. Kerry's comments during an interview with CBS News in Egypt did not repeat the standard US line that al-Assad had "lost all legitimacy" over the four-year civil war and had to go. Al-Assad dismissed Kerry's comments and accused the US of undermining peace efforts. He also reiterated that foreign countries should stop supporting "terrorist groups." Kerry's remarks were quickly qualified by State Department spokeswoman Marie Harf who insisted that Washington's policy had not changed and the format of the peace talks remained in adherence with the 2012 Geneva Conference, whose last session ended without results. That said, the US continued to face a serious problem with its Syria policy. According to the director of the CIA, John Brennan, Washington had reason to worry about who might replace al-Assad if he fell, given the rise of IS and other jihadist groups in Syria. Brennan said of those groups, "the last thing we want to do is allow them to march into Damascus."[9]

On 20 January 2015, Obama, in his 2015 State of the Union speech, praised the "American leadership, including the military power," for stopping the advance of IS, and called on Congress to authorize the use of force against IS.[10] The US National Security Strategy of 2015 made it clear that the US "mobilized and was leading global efforts to impose costs to counter Russian aggression in Ukraine, to degrade and ultimately defeat ISIS, to squelch the Ebola virus at its source, to stop the spread of nuclear weapons material, and to turn the corner on global carbon emissions."[11] For his part, Lavrov described the fight against IS as a primary task because it "posed the main threat to the ME and North Africa." Beyond the ME, IS was a principal foe to Russia too because "hundreds of Russian nationals were fighting alongside the militant group in Syria and Iraq."[12] On 21 January, in his annual press conference, Lavrov advocated Moscow's position stating that dealing with the rise of Islamic extremism in Syria should take priority over calls for regime change.[13] Moscow had used the narrative of war against terror to advocate not only collaborative action to be taken against IS in agreement with Damascus but also to reiterate that the peace talks should not address al-Assad's departure but should rather focus on combating IS and terrorism.

After four months of fierce battles, on 26 January the YPG, with the help of US-led air raids and a group of fighters from Iraq's Kurdish Peshmarga forces, drove IS from the Syrian town of Ain al-Arab on the frontier with Turkey. Meanwhile, across the border with Iraq the Iraqi army liberated the Diyala province from IS.[14] After an Israeli attack near Qunaitra, in southern Syria, pro-regime forces spearheaded by Hizbullah and IRCG launched an offensive in Deraa, which was largely under the control of rebels and Nusra Front. The dual aim was to secure southern Syria, which was essential for the control of Qunaitra, and to extend the Iranian battleground against Israel from Lebanon to Syria. By positioning Iranian forces in closer proximity to the Israeli-occupied Golan Heights, Tehran hoped to retain leverage in the Arab-Israeli conflict. So far, the Syrian army was unable to crush the rebels on important front lines such as Aleppo. What mattered to al-Assad was useful Syria, the corridor stretching north from Damascus through Homs and Hama and then west to the coast with the cities of Latakia and Tartus, the strongholds of the Alawite regime. However, the regime's broader military situation deteriorated and its army withered away through combat and attrition.

As there was no discernible end in sight for the conflict and as the provincial capital of Iblib fell to an alliance of rebel forces and jihadist militias called the Army of Conquest in March 2015, al-Assad welcomed an increased Russian military presence at Syria's seaports, including Tartus. Al-Assad appeared to be exhausted after four years of fighting and was no longer able to hold some contested areas. The regime also lost the northwestern strategic town of Jisr al-Shughur and one of its few remaining footholds in Deraa and Swaida provinces in the south. Russia had supplied the regime with arms since the conflict began in 2011and persisted with its strategy of preserving influence in the region through diplomacy. From 18 to 20 June 2015, at the St Petersburg International Economic Forum, Putin said that Russia had made the right decision in supporting al-Assad and that it "would be difficult to expect us to take any other line" to prevent the disintegration of the state. Zasypkin disclosed to the author, "Russia's primary goals were to protect the Syrian state and defeat terrorism."[15] Concurrently, Russia was "ready to engage in dialogue with President Assad about carrying out political reforms together with the healthy opposition forces."[16] On 30 June, during his meeting in Moscow with Walid al-Moallem, Putin stressed that Russia would continue to help Syria politically, economically, and militarily. Putin also urged other Middle

Eastern countries to help Syria fight IS. In the same month, close Russian ally, Iran, sent 15,000 fighters made up of Iranians, Iraqis, and Afghanis to reverse the regime's recent battlefield setbacks.[17] Firouznia disclosed to the author that "Iran intervened militarily first to prevent the disintegration of the Syrian state. Russia joined the axis of resistance in a later stage. Iran was convinced that the Russian intervention would complement the axis of resistance."[18]

In May 2015, US trainers were in Turkey on a training and equipping program aimed at adding fighters to counter IS and bolster moderate rebel forces in Syria. Ignoring the US concerns about aiding extremist groups, Turkey and Saudi Arabia set aside their differences and agreed on a new strategy to bring down al-Assad. The agreement led to a new joint command centre in Idlib province, where a number of rebel groups, including the Nusra Front and Islamist brigades such as Ahrar al-Sham, which Washington viewed as extremist, depleted the regime forces.[19] David Ignatius wrote, "Jordan and Israel had developed secret contacts with members of the Nusra Front along the borders."[20] In addition to the city of Ramadi in western Iraq, on 21 May, IS militants once again took control of the Syrian central city of Palmyra, which had been recaptured by the regime in 2013, and seized the Al-Tanf border crossing with Iraq, southeast of Palmyra.[21] Thus, IS was potentially poised for advances toward the capitals of Syria and Iraq. Yet, in June 2015, the Kurdish-led YPG militia dealt IS its worst defeat by seizing the town of Tal Abyad on the Turkish border, cutting a supply route to the jihadists' capital of Raqqa. The YPG was the only significant partner for the US-led alliance in Syria.[22] Cooperation between the US and the YPG had deepened since 2014 when they joined forces to repel an IS attack on Ain al-Arab. Alarmed by the Kurds' advances against the IS militants, Erdogan once again raised the prospect of a Turkish military intervention in Syria to create a buffer zone in Syria's Jarablus region in order to prevent the formation of a Kurdish state. Above all, Ankara wanted Washington to rein in Kurdish aspirations of statehood and increase the pressure on al-Assad. However, the US did not want rebel groups, including the Nusra Front, to topple al-Assad because such an alliance could put a more dangerous radical Islamist regime in al-Assad's place. Against this turbulent and fast-changing regional environment, and in light of the nuclear deal between Iran and the West on 14 July 2015, Obama held talks with Gulf leaders in the White House and at Camp David to stress that there was no broader détente with Iran's destabilizing support for proxy groups in Iraq, Syria, Lebanon, and Yemen. Concerning the negotiations with Tehran, Obama highlighted that a nuclear deal with Iran would be in the security interests of the Gulf and "would help remove a primary source of tension and might foster greater cohesion in dealing with sources of conflict and instability in the ME."[23] Meanwhile, in July Turkey made a dramatic turnaround by granting the US-led alliance to use its air bases and bomb targets in Syria. The Turkish decision stemmed from a US-Turkish plan to create an "Islamic State free zone" in northern Syria, using warplanes flown from Turkish air bases to take the area with a ground force of Syrian rebels, presumably including trainees of the Pentagon's program.[24] Despite Turkish misgivings, the US would continue to provide air support when needed for YPG fighters.

Although the prospects for a political solution were slim, in May 2015 de Mistura launched wide-ranging consultations in Geneva with regional and domestic players, including Iran, to revive the stalled peace talks. As labelled by de Mistura, the "low key, low profile" talks aimed to take stock of the various sides' positions "to assess progress and decide on the next step."[25] In July, de Mistura aimed to set up four thematic working groups to address safety and protection, counterterrorism, political and legal issues, and construction, a plan that was supported by a UNSC presidential statement.

In mid-July, during the BRICS-SCO summits in the Russian city of Ufa, Putin praised the efforts of member states who had been working "under the principles of mutual respect, equality and open dialogue." Putin reiterated that multilateralism was the only foundation "to seek and find solutions to acute international problems and to respond to the threats that were relevant to all of humanity such as the spread of weapons of mass destruction, terrorism, extremism and international crime."[26] The summits were an attempt by Moscow to show that it was not isolated despite its conflict with the West over Ukraine and Syria and to demonstrate Russia's standing in the non-Western world. In the first half of 2015, the Kremlin was preoccupied with the fallout of diplomatic and military operations in Ukraine. Tsygankov emphasized that since the mid-2000s Putin, "could no longer ignore those inside Russia who had long insisted on protecting the country's values and security from what they saw as dangerous encroachment by the West."[27] In addition, the threat to its ally al-Assad and the Russian base at Tartus seemed to have spurred Moscow to action.

In August, more than four years after the beginning of the Syrian civil war, Putin began preparing the ground for military intervention in Syria. On 26 August, during his meeting with Egyptian President Abdel Fattah al-Sisi in Moscow, Putin emphasized the vital importance of "creating a broad anti-terrorist coalition involving key international players, which would include Syria, to fight the Islamic militants" in the ME.[28] To expand Moscow's influence in Egypt, Putin also reiterated Russia's commitment to include Egypt in the Russian-led EAEU free trade zone. Earlier, on 9 August, after two meetings with Kerry, Lavrov addressed the US to cooperate with al-Assad to fight IS by forming an international coalition. From a Western perspective, Putin's call for a broad international coalition, including both Syria and Iran appeared "disingenuous." Moscow hoped that "it could get the U.S. and European partners to persuade Turkey and Saudi Arabia to acquiesce; but considering this would have required a shift in foundational aims of the U.S.-led coalition. It was more likely that the Kremlin understood it would be rejected."[29]

In early September, in his call to Lavrov Kerry expressed concern about enhanced Russian military build up in Syria including the transport to a Syrian airfield of prefabricated houses for hundreds of people. Moscow's diplomatic and increased military and logistical support of al-Assad prompted a reassessment in Israel about how to handle fallout from the conflict without risking a clash with Moscow. Israel had occasionally fired across the Golan Heights in response to spillover shelling and bombed advanced arms it suspected were to be delivered to al-Assad's Lebanese ally, Hizbullah.

Moscow staunchly backed al-Assad and supplied the Syrian army with military equipment and humanitarian aid. In the summer of 2015, Russia initiated a peace plan for Syria that envisioned cooperation between the governments of Syria and Iran in the anti-IS coalition. It appeared that the Kremlin was testing the water for its next move: beefing up its military presence in Syria. Still, Russia contemplated the possibility of joining the US-led anti-IS coalition to eradicate IS, which had been launched at the NATO summit in September 2014, and to achieve rapprochement with the West while hoping as well to win a few key concessions. It is important to note that the launching of the international coalition against IS in 2014 had bypassed Russia and shifted attention to the military domain. Yet, in accord with H2, the US could accede to Russia's status demands if Moscow ensured its participation in a balancing coalition against IS and was more effective in explaining its objectives to the outside world. Russia should realize that the common threat of IS could not be balanced without the help of the dominant power (i.e. the US) and that joining hands could bring security and status recognition. Such a coalition would allow al-Assad's regime to survive and enable Russia to maintain its political influence in the ME. For decades the ME has been a zone of US influence. However, the US was unlikely to pursue an active policy to satisfy Russia's higher status aspirations, because the balancing logic meant that the US would much rather subordinate Russia into its orbit while it could. Yet, Russia was unlikely to submit to a subordinate role. Alexi Malashenko, the ME expert with the Carnegie Endowment's Moscow office, rightly noted that Putin's foreign policy behaviour was "unpredictable" and driven by emotion, something that is compatible with the status-seeking strategy.[30] In accordance with status-seeking theory, Russia would be unwilling to give up its position and would therefore risk conflict to defend it.

Strategically, Moscow would like "to avoid a frontal collusion with/isolation by the West, and not go back to the old pattern of EU-Russia relations, when Brussels was a norm giver."[31] Russia wanted recognition of its values and interests in the world. However, Washington was "reluctant to accept proposals from Putin whom it wanted to contain."[32] As Joseph S. Nye argued "American policy makers would need to follow a flexible strategy of 'containment plus nudging' because the U.S. had various interests in the region, including Israel's security, nuclear non-proliferation, and human rights."[33] Evidently, Obama's foreign policy preferences for global goals over regional ones created an opening for Russia in the ME. The US hard power could do little to overcome ethnic conflicts and tribalism. Further, Washington's reluctance to cooperate with Moscow stemmed from the fear that Russia could harness coalition forces into eradicating all rivals to the al-Assad regime, which "would then become Moscow's dedicated clients in the ME."[34] Putin's plan to use Syria to improve ties with Washington and achieve status recognition was unlikely to succeed because the US wanted to impose its will unilaterally and had no incentive to accommodate Russia. When a few rounds of negotiations with the US and Saudi Arabia brought no visible results, Moscow decided to beef up its military presence in Syria in order to play an active role in world politics. It has been argued that military power was "traditionally assumed to be a prime shaper of foreign policy because it was the most immediately employable power asset for protecting populations, controlling territory, and coercing others."[35]

In mid-September, Russia was solidifying its foothold in Syria by sending ships, armoured personnel carriers, and naval infantry to support the Syrian army, whose military capacity was eroding steadily. Escalated Russian military involvement in Syria was an indication that al-Assad's regime was in dire need of help. Responding to Western criticisms that Russian involvement in the Syrian conflict would complicate its solution and attract foreign fighters, Lavrov reiterated that supplying its ally with military equipment and humanitarian aid was taking place under existing contracts. The resumption of the military relationship between the two countries was critical to the Russian posture in the ME. Building up its military in Syria would restore Russia's identity as great power and give Moscow more bargaining power in subsequent international negotiations on Syria. Yet, as Frederic Hof noted, for the time being, talk of the political process was "empty and useless as long as atrocities were ubiquitous."[36] Military supplies to al-Assad's beleaguered regime would continue because, from Russia's perspective, al-Assad's removal by the externally backed and financed opposition was not up for discussion by Moscow for domestic reasons. Also, regime change could not be a precondition for any deal to end the civil war.

In the second half of September 2015, Russian forces, after expanding the tarmac of the Humeimeem airport in Syria's coastal province of Latakia, deployed twenty-eight combat planes at the air base, battle tanks, as well as ammunition, and other military equipment in quantities for the first time since the end of the Cold War in 1991.[37] Raising the stakes in a military build up put Washington on edge and led to the first talks between US and Russian defense ministers to discuss mechanisms for de-escalation, i.e., avoid accidental military interactions between American and Russian aircraft flying in the Syrian airspace. The former Cold War enemies had a common adversary in IS, but Russia might want to target the opposition fighters too, which were supported by the US, seeing them as a threat equal to the al-Assad regime. David Ignatius wrote, "the CIA-backed fighters could not stop the dominance of Al-Qaeda's Syrian affiliate Nusra Front. Opposition groups might pretend otherwise, but they were fighting alongside Nusra, which branded itself in 2016 as Jabhat Fatah al-Sham."[38]

On 21 September, during a visit to Moscow, Israeli Prime Minister Benjamin Netanyahu agreed to coordinate military actions over Syria.

Israeli jets had occasionally bombed suspected targets in Syria to prevent Iranian and Hizbullah potential security threats to Israel. According to Putin, "without Russia's support for Syria, the situation in the country would have been worse than in Libya and the flow of refugees would have been ever bigger."[39] It is worth noting that 470,000 Syrian had been killed since the civil war began in 2011, and the war resulted in a situation where there were nine million internally displaced Syrians and five million refugees, two million of which were seeking refuge in Europe.[40] For Obama, Putin's status-seeking strategy in Syria was "doomed to fail," and "further support, military or otherwise for the al-Assad regime was destabilizing and counterproductive."[41] Yet, the US could not bring stability to Syria unilaterally. Trying to do so had arrayed other powerful countries, including China and Russia, against it. It has been argued that, like the US, Russia had a strong interest in defeating IS, but "it had no interest in allowing the U.S. to install its choice of regimes in Syria or elsewhere."[42] Putin, who was cultivating geostrategic relationships with Egypt and Israel, was not likely to yield to American political pressure and refrain from military intervention. The Russian political scientist Sergei Karaganov argued that Russia was "being pushed to the wall by more than two decades of Western expansion – be it in Europe or NATO enlargement – into a part of Europe that it considered vital to its national security."[43] By late summer 2015, Russian status came under pressure. Russia had been expelled from the G8 and security cooperation within the NATO-Russia council had been suspended. Freire and Heller reiterated that "Russia's prestige as an 'indispensible partner and reliable actor' in international politics had been severely damaged."[44] In addition, a dramatic drop in oil prices in combination with the negative implications of the Western sanctions accelerated Russia's domestic economic crisis.[45] These domestic and international circumstances weighed against a military move in Syria. Yet, Russia believed that it had the moral high ground in defending its values and national interests globally. The Kremlin came to the conclusion that Western expansionism could be reversed only with an "iron fist," as Karaganov put it in 2011.[46]

The FSA, a loose alliance of insurgent groups supported by the US, Saudi Arabia, and Jordan via the Military Operations Centre (MOC) in Jordan and by the joint Operations Centre (MOM) in Turkey, posed additional threats to the regime.[47] Clearly, the regional actors were fighting in Syria by proxy. It is worth noting that the MOC and MOM were CIA covert assistance programs established in 2013 that "pumped many hundreds of millions of dollars to many dozens of militia groups." Yet, the program was "too late, too limited and too dependent on dubious partners, such as Turkey and Saudi Arabia."[48] Putin mocked the $500 million US effort to train anti-IS fighters. On 26 September, Putin launched a new coalition composed of Russia, Iran, Syria, and Iraq to battle IS in Syria as he prepared to confront Obama at the UN. Without this coalition, as Firouznia explained to the author, "Russia's role on the ground to shore up al-Assad could have not succeeded."[49] Russia's leadership role in coalition building to fight against terrorism was a key symbolic and tangible recognition of its new status.

In his address to the UN General Assembly on 27 September 2015 Putin said, "it is hypocritical and irresponsible to make loud declarations about the threat of international terrorism while turning a blind eye to the channels of financing and supporting terrorists." It was "an enormous mistake to refuse to cooperate with the Syrian government and its armed forces, which were valiantly fighting terrorism face to face … Russia could not allow these criminals, who were fighting under the banner of the so-called ISIS, to return back home and continue their evil doings." Putin was referring to thousands of recruits from FSR who were fighting for IS. Concerning the world order, Putin said that Russia "could no longer tolerate the current state of affairs in the world" and that Russia proposed an order that should be "guided by equality, common values and common interests rather than ambitions."[50] Putin also referred to Ukraine, to NATO's policy of enlargement, mainly by absorbing countries that previously were a zone of Russian influence, and the situation in the ME and North Africa, where the power vacuum was starting to be filled with extremists and terrorists. Putin's appeal at the UNGA meeting went unheeded. The following sections explore the evolution of Russia's military campaign, Russia's objectives in Syria, regional dynamics, and Moscow's approach to a political settlement.

RUSSIAN MILITARY INTERVENTION IN 2015

Shortly after the UNGA meeting, on 30 September, Russia launched airstrikes against Syrian rebels who fought the government forces in and around the cities of Homs and Hama, well outside the territory held by IS, supposedly the target of the military intervention.

By equating terrorist and non-terrorist opposition, Moscow signalled that any sustainable settlement would require the defeat of all parts of the opposition. Not since the end of the Cold War, a quarter-century before, had Russia been so assertive and interventionist outside its borders. Washington was acquiescent. After Moscow's helpful role in the Iran nuclear talks in July, Obama and Kerry, who welcomed greater Russian diplomatic involvement in the region, did not anticipate that Russia would seek to bolster al-Assad on the battlefield. By launching its air campaign on 30 September, Russia deviated from its position, held since 2011, that the international community should abstain from any attempts to intervene in what Moscow considered an internal conflict. Russia's military intervention was an indicator that Moscow was using status-seeking strategy to enhance its status that included efforts to outdo the US in its area of strength, i.e., geopolitical power in the ME. Russia was a stats-inconsistent power that used power politics as a means of status enhancement. Yet, Russia's willingness to act militarily contradicted the status-overachiever theoretical assumption that "Russia as an overachiever was interested in maintaining international relations structures as they were, as it benefited status-wise from them without investing too many resources."[51] But according to power transition theory, status inconsistent powers are "more willing to pay greater costs to achieve status-consistency, as they are likely to operate in the domain of losses."[52] After Ukraine, Russia decided that the next place to put down the "iron fist" would be Syria.[53] The official justification for the military intervention was to support the Syrian regime in its fight against terrorism and to "stabilize the legitimate authority" al-Assad.[54] Other than the memorandum of understanding to avoid accidentally shooting each other in the skies over Syria, Moscow and Washington were otherwise not cooperating. US Secretary of Defense Ashton Carter said, "we were not able to associate ourselves more broadly with Russia's approach in Syria because it was wrongheaded and strategically short sighted. It attempted to fight extremism while not also at the same time working to promote the political transition" away from al-Assad.[55] However, Zasypkin argued that, "there were many opposition groups and the West did not know to which opposition political transition should happen."[56]

Since 2000 Putin had been the dominant politician in the making of Russian foreign policy. I argue that in light of the Arab Spring,

Syria became more important to Russia as it came to be interpreted as a battlefield over two key goals: setting the guiding principles of global order and preserving Russia's centrality in international conflict management as an embodiment of its international status. As the US stepped back in the ME, the vacuum was filled by Russia and Iran, the new masters in the region. Therefore, opportunity complements the identity vector in understanding Russian power politics in Syria. Both countries saw "the promotion of Western values as an insidious plot to bring about regime change in Moscow and Tehran."[57] The Syrian intervention aimed not only to strengthen al-Assad's position but also to change the political outcome in a region that had been out of Moscow's sphere of influence for decades. Zasypkin stressed to the author that, "Syria was important in the ME and that was why Russia was steadfast."[58] Putin was willing to take major strategic risks to demonstrate that Russia was a strong nation and could project hard power beyond its own borders. Yet, Putin would face the challenge of preventing the deterioration of the Russian economy and restoring order in a region that was long influenced by the US. Since 2014 there had been a dramatic drop in oil prices. Russia's economy had shrunk and over the previous decade state spending had risen from 35 per cent of GDP to a staggering 70 per cent.[59] Brian Michael Jenkins, a senior advisor to the president of the RAND Corporation, contended that, "economic weakness at home might accentuate Russia's aggressive behavior abroad as a distraction." However, Russia's invasion of Georgia in 2008 suggested that, "the state of its economy was not the sole determinant of Russian policy."[60]

Moscow's immediate military objective was to shore up al-Assad, prevent the defeat of the Syrian army and the consequent takeover of Damascus by IS, and protect its interests in the ME. Still, Moscow's campaign was initially designed to rout the opposition groups that had threatened al-Assad's control over key cities like Homs, Hama, and Aleppo, which was retaken by the Syrian army in December 2016. Putin sought to achieve this goal primarily through the empowerment of the Syrian army and its Lebanese Hizbullah and Iranian allies. Russia intended to bolster the regime's enclave in the western coastal area, the heartland of the Alawite sect, and fight international terrorism. Putin believed that the regime's forces, which currently controlled a quarter of Syrian territory with 60 per cent of the population, must be reinforced to ensure that Russia could exert a dominant role in negotiations on a political settlement.

The bombing campaigns against what Russia claimed were IS targets in Syria became known as Operation Vozmezdie (Retribution). Initially, Russian airplanes bombed the western-backed FSA and Sunni rebel groups with a known connection to IS under the guise of the war on terrorism. The US backed some Sunni groups in the rebel alliance, such as the FSA, Sham Legion, Jund al Aqsa, Jaish al-Sunna, and the Turkish-backed Ahrar al-Sham. Apparently, Russia adopted key aspects of al-Assad's strategy, "which was focused on crippling its non-jihadist opponents and pounding their popular base into submission, or displacement, via a combination of military defeat and collective punishment."[61] Russia's military operations that aimed solely at providing Russia with mastery over Syrian airspace and protecting its interests on the ground, bolstered efforts to defeat IS too. For Putin, fighting IS seemed to be a crucial matter, especially for a Russia with a large and growing Muslim population.[62] If Russia was the re-enforcer against IS, "this could mean a fundamental change in power relations in the ME with Russia bidding to become the protector not just of al-Assad, but of a Europe that was frightened of terrorism, refugees and energy supplies."[63] For Russia, "the connection between civil war in Syria and the European refugee crisis had the potential to put the EU under pressure and undermine the sanctions regime."[64]

On 7 October 2015 four missile ships of the Russian Navy's Caspian Flotilla fired twenty-six calibre cruise missiles at militant targets in Syria 1,500 kilometres away, and on the next day the Syrian army launched a large-scale offensive.[65] Russia's use of cruise missiles in Syria and other military displays showed that Russia was a great power and was catching up with the West in advanced weapons systems. It could be argued that although "Russia's military forces remain materially weaker than NATO armies [they] were gaining technological ground aided by Putin's aggressive command."[66] Putin reiterated that Russia's military modernization program was being successfully implemented, with defense plans churning out new jets, missiles, navy ships, and other weapons.[67] In November 2015, NATO Secretary General Jens Stoltenberg, speaking at a news conference during NATO war games in Troia, south of Lisbon, said he "believed that the buildup of Russian military might lead to Moscow's ability to limit the access of the U.S. and its allies to certain regions."[68] In May, NATO had condemned Russia's plans to deploy nuclear-capable missiles in Kaliningrad, a Russian region sandwiched between Lithuania and Poland, as well as its increased number of nuclear bomber flights. Yet, the Kremlin protested the US-led missile shield voicing concern that it could become capable of intercepting Russia's nuclear intercontinental ballistic missiles, thus weakening Russia's nuclear deterrent. It is worth nothing that Russia used the air campaign in Syria to showcase an array of new weapons, including state-of-the-art cruise missiles. Indeed, Russian Tu-160 strategic bombers flew from the base on the Kola Peninsula over the Norwegian Sea, the North Atlantic, and the Strait of Gibraltar and into the Mediterranean to launch long-range cruise missiles on targets in Syria, demonstrating the Russian military's global reach.[69]

The Kremlin could not withdraw its support for al-Assad because that would be seen by the whole world as the abandonment of a loyal ally since the Soviet period in the ME, as well as submission to Western policies. The loss of a client regime would imply a major blow to Russia's influence in the ME. In addition, Syria accounted for 7 per cent of Russia's total of $10 billion in arms deliveries abroad in 2010, according to the Russian defense think tank CAST. Further, Fyodor Lukyanov noted that giving in on Syria would deepen discontent in the arms industry and enhance the campaign rhetoric of Russia's electoral rivals, the Communists and the nationalist Vladimir Zhirinovsky's LDPR against Putin.[70]

In addition to its military and financial support for the al-Assad regime, Russian intervention in Syria stemmed from Syria's geostrategic location in the ME. Russia as a great power had the incentive to mediate the conflict and reach a settlement that would be favourable for maintaining Russian geostrategic and national interests. For Russia, status-seeking strategy was connected to the capability to regulate conflicts as an embodiment to its international status. Putin aimed to embrace a political process that would enable him to demonstrate Russia's central role in shaping the future of the ME and the global order. David Ignatius wrote that if "Primakov, in the late 1990s, dreamed about reviving Russian power in the ME and globally, Putin was now doing it."[71] However, in order to achieve successful mediation, Russia should use its leverage to balance the interests of regional actors in Syria.

International cooperation was a necessary ingredient for successful mediation and negotiation in the Syrian conflict. On 30 October world and regional powers, including Iran, met in Vienna and agreed to launch a new peace effort involving Syria's government and opposition groups. Throughout the conflict, the US disagreed with Russia on al-Assad's role in the transitional governing body with full executive powers. Russia's unilateral use of force since September to weaken the opposition and bring it to the negotiating table did not yield tangible results, mainly because the US and the regional actors continued to support the rebels. Such a unilateral action, as Stephen M. Saideman noted, increased the costs of intervention and decreased the chances of success.[72] Zasypkin disclosed that "Russia counted on the possibility of cooperation with the Americans, but the U.S. aborted all the agreements."[73] For the first time, the US deployed a small number of Special Operation Forces (SOP) on the ground. Russian military intervention in the war gave the regime a decisive edge over the opposition. Moscow claimed that Russian jets used coordinates supplied by some opposition groups and hit targets close to Palmyra, Deir al-Zour, and eastern Aleppo. The US-led anti-IS coalition and Russian intervention increased the stakes for regional actors and deepened their relationship with opposing sides in the civil war. Russia wanted the Syrian government and the opposition to agree on launching a constitutional reform process lasting up to eighteen months, followed by early presidential polls. Thus, Russia's policy was in line with Moscow's centrality in international conflict management as an embodiment of its international status. The eight-point plan drawn up by Moscow before international talks on Syria in November 2015 included a popularly elected president, agreement on a list of terrorist groups, and a future conference to be organized by the UN (see appendix B).

Given the large number of tasks associated with the peacemaking and peace-building processes, it is unreasonable to assume that Russia would perform them on its own or could shoulder the full responsibility of guaranteeing that the eight-point plan would succeed. For third parties with limited leverage, "the costs and risks of intervention would usually outweigh the foreign policy benefits to be gained by involvement. This argues for a multilateral approach to conflict resolution, whereby the costs and risks of intervention could be shared within a larger group."[74]

On 13 November the terrorist attacks in Paris marked a watershed moment in Russia's relations with the West. Putin hoped that Moscow's cooperation with France in attacking IS in Syria would end Russia's isolation over the Ukraine crisis and lift Western sanctions. The West's strategy was to engage Russia where possible yet continue to punish it over Crimea and Ukraine until it fulfilled its obligations under the Ukraine peace deal reached in February 2015.[75]

On 14 November, the International Syria Support Group (ISSG), consisting of twenty states and organizations including Iran and Saudi Arabia, met in Vienna and "expressed [a] unanimous sense of urgency to end the suffering of the Syrian people, the physical destruction of Syria, the destabilization of the region, and the resulting increase in terrorists drawn to the fighting in Syria."[76] Washington and Moscow were the key powers in the Vienna process. The ISSG acknowledged the close linkage between a ceasefire and a parallel political process pursuant to the 2012 Geneva Communiqué. Yet, the foreign players failed to reach agreement on al-Assad's departure and the transitional period sought by Western states. Nonetheless, the talks set out a blueprint to move the peace process that included a framework for a transitional government, a new constitution, and elections.

At Vienna, Russia insisted that only the Syrian people should decide whether al-Assad would step down or not. For Russia, the West should drop its demand for the political exit of al-Assad if it wanted a genuinely international coalition against IS. The participants at the Vienna talks agreed to ask the UN to broker a peace deal between the regime and the opposition, to clear the way for a new constitution and UN-supervised elections. This was endorsed by UNSC Resolution 2254 on 18 December 2015. Pursuant to the 2012 Geneva Communiqué and consistent with the 14 November 2015 ISSG statement, Resolution 2254 called for a start of negotiations between the opposition and government with a target of early January 2016. The resolution was designed to reunify the country following an eighteen-month transition period, after which democratic elections would be held under a new constitution.[77]

On 15 November 2015, at the G20 meeting in Antalya, Turkey, which came just days after the terror attacks in Paris that killed at least 129 people and after IS blew up a Russian passenger plane over Egypt on 31 October in revenge for Syria, Obama urged Putin to focus on combating the militant group. Putin seemed cooperative when he said that, "life moved forward, everything changed. New problems, threats and challenges arise which were difficult to resolve on your own whoever you were. We needed to unite."[78] Putin, who also met Saudi Arabia's King Salman, said that Russia was ready to support Syria's opposition with airstrikes in their fight against IS. Putin did not want to harm Russian relations with the Saudi-led Gulf Cooperation Council, whose financial resources were still considered by the Kremlin a potential source of investment in the Russian economy.[79]

So far, Moscow's rapprochement with the West was confined to Syria. In the wake of the attacks on Paris and after French President François Hollande called on the US and Russia to join the global coalition to destroy IS, French and Russian warplanes conducted air strikes on Raqqa, the stronghold of IS. Putin also ordered the Russian missile cruiser Moskva to start cooperating with the French military.[80] However, Hollande and Putin remained at odds over the fate of al-Assad. Western dissatisfaction with Russia's sustained political and military support for al-Assad thwarted any diplomatic progress on the conflict. The Russian strategic Tu-22 and Tu-160 bombers also struck targets in Idlib, Aleppo, and Deir al-Zour provinces. The Russian military tested new types of weapons in actual combat for the first time. Indeed, in December Kalibr cruise missiles that were launched by the Rostov-on-Don submarine in the Mediterranean Sea successfully hit the designated targets in Raqqa.[81]

Apparently the logic behind Putin's overtures was clear. Russia had achieved its objective in Ukraine: a frozen conflict that would provide Moscow with a continuous role in the country's politics. However, the Russian attempt to link Syria to Ukraine did not pay off. At the time of writing, Western sanctions remain in force and Russia's relations with the EU have not normalized. From Putin's perspective, the West should join Moscow in an unequivocal battle against terrorism and should conduct antiterrorist operations anywhere in the world that they are deemed necessary. The interventions in Ukraine and Syria demonstrated Russian foreign policy ambitions to be recognized as great power. Yet, Russia's use of the military in its foreign policy placed Moscow in direct opposition to Europe and the US. In keeping with H1, the US was unlikely to recognize Russia as a great power because Russia would become a threat in terms of security, especially if its status goals were accommodated. Obviously, the Europeans would not concede to Russia, and the EU policy of sanctions would persist unless Russia was convinced to observe the Ukraine agreement (Minsk Protocol, September 2014) and withdraw its troops from the border, and help facilitate local elections under international standards.[82] It could be argued that Russia used the Paris attacks to split European solidarity on the issue of sanctions.

However, there would be no political détente with Russia and no European nation was prepared to give Russia a free hand in FSS.

The short informal meeting between Obama and Putin did not narrow the rift on Syria and Ukraine because Russia was exposing its assertive foreign policy ambitions. The dilemma for Obama was figuring out how to rally the international coalition against IS without drawing the US deeper into Syria's civil war. According to Fen Oslen Hampson, "the prospects for conflict resolution thus depend significantly on the ability of great powers to accommodate their divergent preferences or one great power's ability to prevail over the other."[83] So far, neither Russia nor the US was able to overcome their divergent preferences over the prospects of ending the war in Syria. Obama's foreign policy had treated Syria as a trap to be avoided.

The intervention in Syria had its disadvantages for Moscow. There were a number of costs that the Kremlin apparently did not consider at the beginning of the air campaign. In November 2015, Turkey shot down a Russian Sukhoi Su-24M bomber near the Syrian-Turkish border, threatening the international escalation of Syria's civil war. While the Turkish army said that the bomber was shot down after it violated Turkish airspace ten times within a five-minute period, Putin branded the shooting down of the aircraft a "stab in the back committed by accomplices of terrorists" and warned that the tragic event would have "the gravest consequences."[84] It is worth noting that Ankara had expressed anger at the Russian operations near Turkey's border, saying that they caused the displacement of thousands of Turkmen Syrians, an ethnic minority in the Latakia province and strong ally of Turkey. Another factor that caused significant deterioration in the relationship between Ankara and Moscow was the Kremlin's decision to deploy some of Russia's sophisticated fighters and bombers to the Gyumri Russian military base in Armenia, a country in the South Caucasus with which Ankara had no diplomatic relations. Since its campaign that began on 30 September, Russia achieved one of its central goals of stabilizing the al-Assad regime with minimal casualties. Domestic fiscal woes aside, Russia covered the operation's cost, estimated at \$1–\$2 billion a year. According to a US intelligence source, the war was being funded from Russia's regular annual defense budget of about \$54 billion.[85]

Russia refrained from military retaliation, but its relations with Turkey, a major economic partner, suffered a crushing blow when

Moscow imposed restrictions on trade and curbed travel by Russian tourists to Turkish resorts. Turkey was central to Russia's energy strategy. Putin accused Ankara of being complicit in the smuggling of oil into Turkey and supplying weapons to Islamist groups. The political damage was much higher. Until the incident, Turkey had been an important regional partner. For example, Ankara had not supported Western sanctions against Russia following the annexation of Crimea. On 30 November, on the sidelines of the Paris climate summit, Obama, in a closed-door meeting with Putin, expressed regret over the death of the Russian pilot and called for a calming and de-escalation of the inflamed tensions between Russia and Turkey.[86] Both leaders also discussed efforts to bring about a ceasefire and political resolution to the Syrian conflict. Shoigu announced that the S-400 antimissile system would be deployed to the Russian air base in Latakia province to put an end to regular incursions by Turkish jets in Syrian airspace. Putin demanded a clear apology from Turkey's top leadership or an offer of compensation for the damage. Russia was the largest destination for Turkey's exports, and the two countries were bound by plans for the new Turkish Stream pipeline that would allow Russia to export gas to the EU through Turkey and reduce its reliance on transit through Ukraine. Currently, Turkey was dependent on Russia and Iran for 80 per cent of its gas. Moscow carefully calibrated its response to Turkey not to jeopardize its main objective in the region that was to rally international support for its view on how the conflict in Syria should be resolved. As Tsygankov reiterated, Turkey was important for Russia, "with the two countries converging on common perception of world order, developing ambitious energy plans, and cooperating to improve security in the black sea area."[87] During his visit to Tehran on 23 November Putin and the Iranian Supreme Leader Ayatollah Ali Khamenei jointly announced their opposition to external attempts at regime change. Moscow coordinated its air campaign with Tehran. Russian airplanes began flying over Tehran and Iraq to avoid the airspace of Turkey. Putin also relaxed an export ban on nuclear equipment and technology to Iran and ordered a start to the process of supplying Tehran with an S-300 antiaircraft system. Meanwhile, Russian troops expanded the runways of the Shayrat air base about forty kilometres southeast of the city of Homs.

From late September 2015 through mid-February 2016 Russia's high intensity air campaign succeeded in preventing the al-Assad regime's fall, which was a military and political objective, halted the opposition's momentum, and allowed the pro-Assad forces, facilitated by Iran, to take the offensive. Firouznia argued that, "the Russian air campaign was crucial but without Iranian help Russia would be unable to achieve a military and political victory."[88] The US prediction that Russia would be bogged down in a quagmire in Syria proved a "historic misjudgment."[89] With the help of Russian officers and military experts, the pro-Assad forces cut off the rebel's supply lines to the Turkish border at Bab al Salameh, in their most successful offensive of the war. They also gained rural territory in the western coastal province of Latakia and in the north and retook military bases around Aleppo and Damascus.[90] Regime troops supported by Hizbullah fighters also advanced in the eastern Qalamoun Mountains. The northern city of Aleppo fell completely under siege with tens of thousands of people fleeing toward Turkey, NATO's southern flank. Russian air support for the Syrian government offensive transformed the balance of power in the five-year-old war. With Putin associating all Sunni rebel groups with IS, the conflict in Syria took on an extra dimension as a proxy war between Russia and the US. While bolstering the endangered al-Assad regime, Putin simultaneously cultivated his image domestically as a strong leader who was able to protect the Russian people from thousands of Russian and Central Asian jihadists fighting for IS in Iraq and Syria. Putin dismissed concerns that Russia's airstrikes would prompt retaliatory terrorist acts at home. Chechen spies loyal to Moscow had infiltrated IS in Syria and gathered intelligence for Russian air force bombing strikes.

Still, Russia's air campaign made Putin a major player in the Syrian conflict, and Russia's influence over al-Assad gave it a central role in diplomatic efforts to negotiate a political solution. Hence, another political objective was to seek a resolution in Syria and restore stability in the extremely volatile ME. Therefore, Russia was to adjust its status-seeking strategy in Syria to push the conflict toward an initial settlement, especially with Moscow's decision to help implement a cessation of hostilities. Russia facilitated local ceasefires in rebel-held areas around Damascus with the aim of creating a secure buffer zone around the capital. Russian mediators who "worked in the shadows" also helped the Syrian government broker deals with rebels seeking to lay down their weapons or to relocate to insurgent strongholds in Idlib and Raqqa.[91]

The diplomatic drive that followed UNSC Resolution 2254 on 18 December, which aimed at ending the Syrian conflict, also motivated opposition groups and regional powers to distance themselves from Salafi and jihadist terrorist groups. For example, in the wake of the Vienna talks Jordan could coordinate military activities with Russia against IS. Already there was a joint Jordanian-Russian military coordination centre in Jordan that could facilitate a ceasefire in the south between the rebels and the al-Assad regime. Still, on 8 December opposition groups including Ahrar al-Sham attending the Riyadh conference in Saudi Arabia agreed to set up a thirty-four-member secretariat to supervise peace talks. The Riyadh conference's final statement called for a new "pluralistic regime that would represent all sectors" in Syria.[92] Yet, Syria's opposition wanted to see CBMs from Damascus including the release of prisoners, a halt to the bombardment of towns and cities, and the lifting of regime blockades on rebel-held areas. On 5 January 2016, after meeting Saudi Foreign Minister Adel al-Jubeir, de Mistura said that the Saudi-Iranian regional tensions would not have a negative impact on the momentum of the forthcoming talks on the continuation of the political process in Geneva. De Mistura also visited Damascus to lay the groundwork and prepare the peace negotiations between al-Assad and his opponents. The Geneva II conference in 2014 failed to bring about a settlement. The ME was in a situation in which regional and global powers alike, along with empowered opposition groups and terrorist organizations, all engaged energetically in political and military actions in different battlefields.

Notwithstanding the great powers' rivalry, the Geneva peace talks (known as Geneva III) began on 1 February 2016 but were quickly suspended due to Russian- and Iranian-backed government offensives against rebel-held territory around Aleppo chocking the supply lines from Turkey to the city. Damascus's goal was to totally liberate Aleppo and then to seal the northern border with Turkey. The offensive could not stop, as doing so would be tantamount to defeat. John Kerry urged both sides to seize the opportunity to make progress and reiterated that "while battlefield dynamics can affect negotiating leverage, in the end there is no military solution to this conflict. Without negotiations, the bloodshed will drag on until the last city is reduced to rubble."[93] Representatives of the Saudi-backed HNC headed by Riad Hijab, which included political and militant opponents of al-Assad, met de Mistura whose attempts to convene the first peace negotiations in two years were planned to begin as "proximate talks" with government and opposition delegations in separate rooms.[94] The HNC did not want the PYD to join the negotiations because it was considered an ally of the regime. In addition, the HNC insisted that the Syrian regime should first comply with UNSC Resolution 2254.[95]

The entire process of getting the talks going was entangled in regional power jockeying and geopolitics. Amid a push by the Kremlin to include the Kurds in the talks, Syrian Kurds opened an office in Moscow despite Turkey's objections. Ankara, which supported the rebels and provided assistance to the refugees, rejected the PYD's participation in the talks and criticized the US for supporting the YPG (the armed wing of the PYD) and for failing to recognize it as a terrorist organization. Turkey had taken in three million Syrian and Iraqi refugees and had spent $10 billion on Syrian refugees, while the UN had given only $455 million.[96] It is important to stress that the YPG was a key ally to the US in its fight against IS. Now the YPG was branded as the Syrian Democratic Forces, the most effective fighters in this conflict. The SDF numbered about forty thousand and included seven thousand Arabs. Although the SDF was attacking IS positions near Aleppo, the Turks were shelling YPG positions in northwest Syria. Under the circumstances and with an emerging alliance between Russia, Syria, Iran, Lebanon, and Hizbullah the so-called Shiite Crescent alliance, threatening other states in the region, Turkey and Israel vowed to cooperate to manage the threat from Iraq, Iran, and Syria as well as from IS.

The Syrian government's delegation head, Bashar al-Jaafari, said that Damascus was considering options such as ceasefires, humanitarian corridors, and prisoner releases, but that those were pending the result of the talks – not as a condition for negotiations to begin.[97] The government's delegation completely ignored the discussion of a political transition and UNSC Resolution 2254 because, from its perspective, they had little value for the intra-Syrian talks in Geneva. Apparently, Moscow and al-Assad saw no point in serious negotiations, at least as long as they advanced against the rebels on the ground. Although Kerry urged the opposition to drop their preconditions, the HNC walked away from the talks because it felt "betrayed and abandoned [by its] Western supporters."[98]

On 11 February Kerry's attempt to arrange a ceasefire with Russia and Iran and coordinate support for the ongoing talks during the 52nd Munich Security Conference was aborted because Moscow and Tehran would not compromise on their fundamental support to al-Assad. At Munich, the discussions focused on the war in Syria and the refugee flow from the war that was causing a political crisis in Europe.

As argued above, Russia's military campaign in Syria had broader objectives. Concerning the prospects for solving key international issues, Lavrov, at the security forum, criticized NATO's and the EU's approaches toward conflicts and their non-cooperative behaviour with Russia. As I emphasized, the identity vector was crucial to understanding Russia's power politics in Syria. Setting the guiding principles of global order was a key issue for Russia. Lavrov added that, "a reform of the world order should be negotiated, because such NATO-centric egotism, which reflects political nearsightedness, does much damage to seeking solutions to real, not invented, threats."[99] Moscow demonstrated that the West should recognize Russia as an indispensable global player and any effort to resolve the Syrian crisis must take Russian interests in the ME and FSS into account.

Russia saw mediation as a way of extending and enhancing its own influence by becoming indispensible to the parties in the conflict. Frederic C. Hof wrote that "the State Department spokesman insisted on the relevance of Russian commitments to ceasefires, humanitarian access, peaceful negotiations and the like, but proved unable to make a very simple and truthful statement" that "Russia imperiled diplomatic prospects as a cover for military operations and objectives; Russia was fully to blame for the suspension of the Geneva talks."[100] The Kremlin rejected claims that it had abandoned diplomacy and vowed to continue providing military aid to al-Assad.

Roughly two weeks prior to Putin's withdrawal announcement, Russia changed course and diverged from key aspects of the regime's strategy that it had been emulating. On 27 February 2016, Obama, who was reluctant to engage in military-to-military cooperation with Russia, negotiated a cessation of hostilities, however fragile, with Putin. The deal largely followed the blueprint set by Washington, Moscow, and the ISSG at the Munich Security Conference earlier in February. The truce did not cover IS and the Nusra Front and other militias designated as terrorist organizations. In early February 2016, a Russian military adviser and eight Russian army officers were killed by mortar fired from IS positions near Latakia.[101] Russia and the regime significantly reduced the scope and intensity of their attacks, but the Salafi-jihadist factions would continue fighting because the agreement did not apply to them. To explain the substance of the US-Russian brokered ceasefire, Putin embarked upon a round of telephone diplomacy, speaking to al-Assad, the Saudi king, the Iranian president and the Israeli prime minister. Direct military intervention was Russia's best strategy to achieve strategic objectives, as had been the case in Georgia and Ukraine where decisive military intervention substantially altered the situation in Moscow's favour. Obama, who met Jordanian King Abdullah II at the White House on 24 February, also discussed Syria and necessary steps to reduce tension between Israel and the Palestinians.

The deal set up a "communications hotline" and the concerned parties could report violations to the working group being cochaired by the US and Russia.[102] The agreement required Russian and US military experts to exchange information on opposition groups abiding by the ceasefire. The US-Russian brokered ceasefire allowed Putin to achieve a primary foreign policy goal by raising Russia's global profile to appear as an equal to the US in mediating the – now international – Syrian conflict. Russia was treated by US diplomats with respect. Kerry and Lavtov spoke almost daily to make a deal over Syria. As Alexander Baunov, a senior associate at the Carnegie Moscow Center, noted, Russia seemed to have "returned to the global board of directors. It returned to the table where world and regional powers decided the fate of others' conflicts and Russia was clearly not a local but a world player."[103] The agreement was a gesture to Russia's great power status as a main international player because Moscow compelled the US to talk to it while keeping the Ukraine issue, temporarily, off the agenda. Russian Prime Minister Dmitry Medvedev outlined the world order in which the world's powers could come together in "a fair and equal union" to maintain peace.[104] Apparently, Medvedev intended to initiate dialogue between the EU, Russia, and the US to enhance international strategic stability. Medvedev's stance stemmed from his proposal in June 2008 of a new all-European treaty to establish a new security architecture that would move beyond NATO expansion. However, his pan-European diplomacy did not succeed.

Obama considered the cessation of hostilities "a potential step in bringing about an end to the chaos" and facilitate humanitarian assistance.[105] For now, the US was holding its side, warning that if the Syrian opposition undermined the ceasefire it would face consequences. However, the barrier to implementation of the ceasefire stemmed from the inability of Russia and the US to put real pressure on the regional players of Turkey, Qatar, Saudi Arabia, and Iran, whose interests diverged on the fate of al-Assad.[106]

The US campaign against IS continued, but Washington had no appetite for deeper military intervention. Obama was known to be reluctant to risk a new confrontation, "limiting Washington's ability to credibly put pressure on Putin or even al-Assad."[107] The US needed more leverage to match Russia and establish a credible political and military balance to consolidate the ceasefire. Cooperation between both regional powers, Iran and Turkey, was crucial to end the civil war in Syria. Ahead of talks in Geneva, and despite their differences and backing of opposing sides in the Syrian conflict, Rouhani met Davutoglu in Tehran on 6 March 2016 and stressed that both countries should support the current ceasefire and preservation of Syria's territorial integrity. He added that the regional issues "should be settled by regional countries." For his part, Davutoglu stressed the importance of both countries in developing a "common perspective" to end the "region's fight among brothers, and stop the ethnic and sectarian conflicts."[108] According to Firouznia, "the change in Turkey's policy stemmed from the success of the Russian and Iranian strategy on the battlefield."[109] The talks between Rouhani and Davutoglu reflected a will on both sides to manage their differences, mainly to reach regional stability and to reap trade benefits from the easing of international sanctions against Iran. Turkey would also serve as a key transit for Iranian energy supplies to Europe.

Reorienting toward the political path and after having derailed the first peace attempt at the Geneva III talks, Moscow, motivated to preserve Russia's centrality in international conflict regulation, paved the way for a second attempt that began on 14 March 2016. While the US and the opposition remained sceptical of Moscow's intensions in Syria, Russia was emerging as an important diplomatic and security partner of the US in Syria. Improved ties and coordination between Moscow and Washington now included regular diplomatic, military, and intelligence contacts. Yet, it is worth nothing that in the National Security Strategy document of the Obama administration for 2015 Russian aggression, specifically in Ukraine, was singled out as a threat to America's vision of the international order. For Obama, "the willingness to work with Putin was an act of foreign policy realism or desperation. Some would argue that in Syria, the two converged."[110] In keeping with H1, the US would not accord Russia higher status because it perceived Russia as aggressor and a primary threat to Washington's vision of the international order. Russia's annexation of Crimea was a revisionist move, not typical of status-inconsistent powers.

On 14 March, Putin also ordered the Russian military to withdraw the main part of its aerospace forces from Syria. Shoigu claimed that "a significant turning point in the fight against terrorism" had been reached.[111] Yet, Russian forces would stay on at the Mediterranean naval base at Tartus and at the Humeimeem air base from where they could deploy if the Syrian regime came under dire threat. It appeared that the withdrawal was limited, with estimates ranging between 10 and 25 per cent of Russia's forces remaining in Syria. It was reported that in the two weeks after Putin's withdrawal announcement Russia shipped more equipment and supplies to Syria than it had actually withdrawn.[112] Putin was inscrutable and unpredictable, and his decision to withdraw from Syria was no exception. Notwithstanding Putin's withdrawal announcement, if Russia felt that its newfound global influence and the Syrian regime were threatened, it could use the two military bases left behind to maintain its military and strategic achievements. Putin said that the objectives of the operation had been "generally accomplished" and the main task now was "to comprehensively assist a peace settlement."[113] Putin's surprise pullout announcement was made to make clear to al-Assad that it was time to negotiate seriously and that he would not have Moscow's support for the military solution he spoke of in February 2016 when he vowed to retake all of Syria. Yet, Russia did not want to push him over the edge. The Russians would probably keep him until they could bring about a managed change that preserved their interests, while also enhancing their cooperation with the US.

With Russia's direct military objective in Syria achieved, the pullback would allow Putin to play the role of peacemaker on the ground and help ease tensions with Turkey and the Gulf monarchies, which had opposed Moscow's military action. According to the Russian Defense Ministry spokesman Igor Konashenkov more than ninety towns and villages and fifty-two rebel groups had signed local truces with government forces.[114] Yet, Russia's credibility was tied to the success of the peace process. The Syrian regime was no longer in immediate danger, creating a new situation that necessitated a reassessment by Turkey of its Syria policy.

Apparently, the regime rejected investment in a political process whose objectives Damascus rejected out of hand. The Kremlin had made it less likely that Russia would be dragged into a potential regional conflict with Turkey and Saudi Arabia. In March, Moscow calmed tensions with Turkey, preparing the ground for dialogue with

Ankara, mainly because the Syrian peace talks were underway in Geneva. Engaging with Turkey became an unavoidable necessity for Russian diplomacy since Turkey was a key player with significant capacity to influence the situation in Syria. Moscow also sent a meaningful signal to Ankara by discarding traces of any ambivalence on Syrian Kurds. Erdogan seemed ready to forge strategic ties with Moscow rooted in energy exports.

Unlike the previous round, the talks had run for a week without any hint of collapse and al-Jaafari acknowledged that he had given de Mistura a document entitled "Fundamental Principles for a Political Solution" in Syria.[115] The document listed familiar goals such as maintaining a secular state and Syria's territorial integrity and the importance of fighting terrorism. However, it included nothing about the political transition. The opposition, which was represented by the HNC, questioned the government's commitment. The regime viewed any meaningful political transition as an existential threat and would do whatever it could to prevent this from happening. Meanwhile, in western Syria on 27 March, the Russian-backed Syrian army recaptured the ancient desert city and archaeological site of Palmyra, which had been lost to IS in May 2015. This victory was used by the regime to bolster its negotiating position at the peace talks. The liberation of Palmyra was the biggest blow so far to IS militants, who had declared a caliphate in Syria and Iraq in 2014, and was a major coup both for Damascus and Moscow. For the first time since it had launched its operations in Syria in September, Moscow admitted that it had Special Forces on the ground as part of the offensive. Putin could now provide the world with proof that Russia was a partner in the war against IS and apparently trying to coordinate with the US to launch airstrikes against terrorists. Further, as Frederic Hof contended, "Russia wanted an open-ended peace talks to anaesthetize the West and to keep alive its objective of reconciling al-Assad to Washington for the sake of an anti IS united front."[116] However, the US refrained from doing so. The US-Russia brokered ceasefire, which came into effect in late February, had helped reduce violence, but it was steadily eroding. Shoigu warned that Russia reserved the right to unilaterally strike militants refusing to abide by the ceasefire, as well as weapons and militants crossing into Syria from Turkey, starting from 25 May 2016. The commander of the Russian forces in Syria, Alexander Dvornikov, said that the recapture of Palmyra would "open up the road to Raqqa and Deir al-Zour and create conditions for reaching and taking control of the border with Iraq."[117] In eastern Syria, the US-backed SDF alliance, which was dominated by the Kurdish YPG militia, was waging a campaign aimed at attacking Raqqa. Both the US and Russia were fighting IS but were in disagreement regarding the political solution in Syria. Russia was not planning to abandon al-Assad but was offering him a chance to win the civil war.

According to Vladimir Frolov, the strategic objective of the Russian intervention was "to revive the bipolar format of American-Russian cooperation and rivalry for influence in the ME and the world." Still, "it was obvious that the Kremlin would like to make Syria a template not only for bilateral relations with the U.S., but also to develop new rules of the game in a broader sense and in other regions, like Ukraine," Frolov added.[118] Yet, the activation of a ballistic missile defense shield in Romania and preparation of a new deterrent in Poland in May 2016 by the US and NATO, intended to protect Europe against Iranian ballistic missiles, increased the tension between Russia and the West.[119] Although not aimed against Russia, Moscow considered the deployment of the defense system onto its periphery a perceived threat to its nuclear arsenal. For its part, Moscow deployed nuclear-capable Iskandar missile units to Kaliningrad, a Russian enclave between Poland and Lithuania, in response to NATO's activation of a US-built missile shield in Poland. During NATO's summit in Warsaw on 8 and 9 July 2016 Moscow criticized the organization's decision to put four battalions in Poland and the Baltic States to bolster its eastern flank after Russia's annexation of the Crimea and the Ukraine conflict. The Warsaw summit communiqué signalled that dialogue with Russia should complement deterrence, not replace it. Moscow's stance was in line with Russia's updated national security strategy of 2016 that considered NATO's "military activization, its continued expansion, the approach of its military infrastructure to Russian borders, all created a threat to national security."[120] The US dismissed the Russian view of establishing a strategic balance and blamed Moscow for breaking off talks with NATO in 2013 that were aimed at explaining how the shield would operate. Putin sought to leverage his military success in Syria and Russia's indispensable role in the Syrian peace process into more global clout, of the sort the Soviet Union had enjoyed. For example, Moscow sought the lifting of Western sanctions, a free hand in the FSS, and a new revision of the post-Cold War international order.

Reasserting Russia's global status was crucial to Putin. As argued above, he sought a new multipolar world order where other powers would counterbalance US influence. More broadly, as Sergei Karaganov noted, "the unipolar world order, that was far from perfect, with the U.S. as hegemon, was withering away." He added that the unipolar order "was a source of large scale disorder, not least through American support of regime change in countries near and far."[121] Putin seized the opportunity when the ASEAN-Russia summit was held in Sochi on 19 and 20 May 2016 to show that Russia still had friends on the international stage, despite being sanctioned by Western nations over the conflict in Ukraine. Russia still had few chances to host major international gatherings that were regarded as status enhancing. The Comprehensive Plan of Action to develop further cooperation in 2016–20 signed by ASEAN and Russia stated that both parties would enhance ASEAN and Russia's role in the regional security architecture by emphasizing international norms, mutual respect for sovereignty and integrity, non-interference, non-use of force, and joint efforts to counter terrorism and international crime.[122]

In conclusion, more than nineteen months had passed since Russia's military intervention in Syria. Obviously, Russian airstrikes, Iranian ground forces, and Hizbullah fighters had immunized al-Assad from political transition. I have argued that Russia's military and strategic objectives went beyond rescuing the Syrian regime. Russia once again counted in the ME and in global politics. I have emphasized that the identity vector was crucial to understanding Russian power politics in Syria. I also stressed that the window of opportunity that opened in late September 2015 was used by Russia to enhance its status in Syria. This opportunity "consisted of a perceived relative weakness on the part of the West, and offered an ideal context for Moscow to promote itself as an 'indispensable' partner in fighting the IS and managing the conflict in Syria."[123] It is important to note that to date Washington's response to Russian bombing attacks on Syrian residential neighbourhoods and the Syrian regime's atrocities was, "no more than [to] rehearse diplomatic phrases."[124] The next section of this chapter examines the new military and diplomatic dynamics from mid-2016 to mid-2017 within the context of Russia's status-seeking strategy and the factors of identity, opportunity, and costs.

NEW MILITARY AND DIPLOMATIC DYNAMICS, MID-2016 TO MID-2017

The Obama administration grudgingly accepted that military achievements did indeed influence diplomatic outcomes. This meant that Washington no longer expected Syrian political transition to take place in the few months left before the US presidential elections, and that fact would provide Russia with more opportunities throughout 2016 to continue its military actions in Syria without major resistance from the international community. Washington hoped that a cessation of hostilities could reduce violence and spur humanitarian aid. Yet, "all cards of any value were in Russian, Iranian and al-Assad regime hands."[125] While the West insisted that no military solution existed for Syria, the al-Assad regime's effort to encircle and besiege Aleppo's rebel-held zone took effect. Concurrently, Syrian government forces advanced toward Raqqa, and the US-backed SDF major offensive on Manbij cut the road to IS-held Jarablus to the north at the Turkish border and to Raqqa to the south. There was a race by both the SDF and the Syrian government forces to reach Raqqa. In Iraq, Washington's main target was the northern city of Mosul. In his address to the newly elected parliament on 7 June 2016, defiant al-Assad vowed to liberate every inch of the country lost to rebel groups. In his speech, al-Assad hardened his position on the peace talks, stressing that Syria would be ruled by a "unity government" not a "transitional governing body" as called for by the opposition.[126]

Concerning NATO's policy towards an assertive Russia, on 8 June former NATO Supreme Allied Commander for Europe General Philip M. Breedlove said at an event on "The Future of NATO Enlargement and New Frontiers in European Security" that it was important not to close the door to Russia. He pointed out that Putin's "No 1 goal was really to crack either the EU or to crack NATO, because if he did that he would get everything else he wanted." A starting point for Putin to create cracks in the EU and NATO was to try to break Western sanctions. Breedlove also reiterated that, "we have to, in a very determined way, begin to establish quality communications with the Russians. If we waited for it to fall into our lap we were going to fail and this risked more problematic developments."[127] Within this context, after NATO's Warsaw summit on 13 July, the NATO-Russia Council (founded in 2002) met at Brussels and discussed the situation in Ukraine and

Afghanistan. The meeting's purpose was to keep dialogue with Russia open despite deterrence. A peaceful settlement of the conflict in eastern Ukraine would contribute to an overall improvement in the relations between NATO and Russia.

Apparently, keeping the door open with Russia was advice following from former US Defense Secretary Chuck Hagel, who said on 10 May 2016 that the next US president should prioritize engagement with Putin, something that the Russian president was seeking. A cooperative US-Russian relationship would provide status-elevating opportunities for Moscow. Russia would be recognized internationally as a great power and a major player along with the US in global politics. On 17 June, in his talk at the St Petersburg International Economic Forum, Putin said that the US was probably the world's sole superpower. However, "Russia wanted to and was ready to work with the U.S."[128] Yet, the US was wary of working too closely with Russia because Washington did not want to be seen as entrenching al-Assad. Putin's statement was an acknowledgement of the role the US held in international politics and a signal to Washington to accommodate Russia. Yet, the deployment of US troops into Poland in early January 2017 and Montenegro's joining NATO in June 2017 created additional tension and perceived security threats to Russia.[129] However, these material threats could be undermined if US President-elect Donald Trump (inaugurated on 20 January 2017) accommodated Russia's status aspirations and engaged Moscow on key security and economic issues.

In relation to Russia-Turkey relations, seven months after Turkey shot down a Russian Su-24 bomber over Turkey's border with Syria, on 27 June 2016, Erdogan sent a letter to Moscow expressing sorrow and regret over the loss of a Russian pilot.[130] Ankara's foreign policy move came in light of the triple suicide bombing at Istanbul's international airport in June, the increasing tense relationship with Europe over the Mediterranean migrant crisis, and the disdain for Obama's ME policy and Erdogan's conviction that the US, NATO, and the EU were not doing enough to help Turkey confront Kurdish militants and Islamist terrorism. Yet, one wonders how IS fighters, weapons, and equipment had been moving from Turkey, which was NATO territory, into Syria without being detected. After Russia ended a ban on the sale of package tours to Turkey in the first step to ending broader sanctions slapped on Ankara, on 1 July, Lavrov met his counterpart Cavusoglu on the sidelines of a regional economic cooperation conference in Sochi. Both Lavrov and Cavusoglu agreed to restart "a working group on fighting terrorism" and discuss "even the most difficult issues" including "the task of not allowing Turkish territory to support terrorist organizations in Syria."[131]

Russia and Turkey reached a common understanding in Ankara when Lavrov and Cavusoglu recognized that IS and the Nusra Front were terrorist organizations that should be fought. This understanding was in line with Russia's foreign policy concept of 2016 that called for the creation of a broad antiterror coalition amid a global threat posed by IS.[132] Both countries also agreed that opposition groups should withdraw from the territories controlled by the terrorists to escape Russian and Syrian airstrikes. According to Lavrov, "Turkey accepted the new rules of the game in Syria" which could turn the tide of the Syrian war in favour of the regime. Further, Aaron Stein noted that Turkey was looking to a "narrowing of its goals in Syria" and that "its priority would be subduing Kurdish rivals and weakening the IS, aims for which it could expect Russian support for Ankara dropping its demand for regime change in Syria."[133] Turkey was concerned with the alliance of the US and Syrian Kurds, which resulted in uncontrollable arms smuggling from northern Syria to both the pro-Turkey moderate opposition and the PKK, which Ankara considered a terrorist organization. Turkey also considered the YPG, backed by the US in its fight against IS, to be an extension of the PKK.

The coup attempt against Erdogan in July 2016 signalled a new and uneasy phase in the relationship between the US and Turkey because the Turkish government linked the coup to Fethullah Gulen, an Islamic preacher based in the US. Although Kerry categorically rejected charges in the Turkish press about US complicity in the coup attempt, Turkey halted US bombing operations against IS from Incirlik air base in southern Turkey. Unlike the EU, with whom Turkey had a deal to stem the flow of refugees, the Kremlin was quick to express solidarity with Erdogan immediately after the failed coup. Russia's stance reflected Putin's intentions to mend bilateral ties. Western leaders had criticized Turkey for the crackdown in the aftermath of the coup. Ahead of his meeting with Putin and in an interview to *Tass* on 7 August, Erdogan said, "I recalled his [Putin's] high-principled position with gratitude and I thank him on behalf of myself and the Turkish people."[134]

Obviously, Erdogan's letter to Putin was a signal that Turkey was ready to change its policy in Syria. Indeed, Ankara began to abandon its previous policy to topple al-Assad and its support to radical opposition groups. For its part, in August 2016 Russia approved Turkey's Euphrates Shield operation against IS in northern Syria and assured Ankara that Kurdish militias would not gain more territory in Syria. In February 2017, Turkish troops backed by Syrian rebel fighters entered the centre of IS's bastion of Al-Bab city.

Russia was compelled to make adjustments to its diplomacy to secure Iran's and Turkey's cooperation in and outside the ME. For example, on 7 August Putin took part in a trilateral summit with his Azerbaijani and Iranian counterparts in Baku. The three leaders discussed joint efforts to fight terrorism, settle regional conflicts, work together on Caspian related issues such as south Caucasus stability, and develop ties in the energy sector, transport corridors, and pipeline infrastructure.[135] Moscow wanted to strengthen its relations with Tehran, a key partner for Russia in Syria and the Caspian region. Russia and Iran would also begin the construction of two new nuclear reactors at Iran's Bushehr nuclear power plant. Russia had signed a cooperation contract to help in building the two new reactors in 2014. The three states could no longer ignore each other's views on a wide range of issues including Western presence in the post-Soviet Central Asian republics, the legal status of the Caspian Sea, and barriers to a trans-Caspian pipeline. It was the first time since the beginning of the Syrian conflict that these issues were being given equal political weight. It is noteworthy that the Baku summit was a reaction to a meeting held in Washington few days before between Kerry and the ministers of Foreign Affairs of the Central Asian republics. Russia wanted to demonstrate that it was eager to maintain its interests in Central Asia and that Moscow, not Washington or other states, was the key power broker in Caspian issues. In the ME, Putin also wanted to host an Israeli-Palestinian summit to revive peace talks.

On 9 August, in his first foreign trip after the failed coup, Erdogan met Putin in St Petersburg. Although the summit between the two leaders aimed to normalize relations following Ankara's apology for shooting down the Russian Su-24 fighter jet in Syria, it raised concerns about whether Turkey might be turning its back on the West. Both Russia and Turkey reinstated their annual bilateral trade target of $100 billion, which had been abandoned after Russia imposed sanctions.[136] The summit took on a broader geopolitical significance mainly because tension between Turkey and its NATO allies was beneficial to Russia. Erdogan would try to leverage his rapprochement with Putin in his relations with the West. Moscow and Ankara would move on to restore their defense cooperation because Turkey did not receive the expected support from its NATO allies following the failed coup. Both leaders also tried to find common ground on Syria and agreed to revive the Turkish Stream gas pipeline that would bolster Russia's position in the European energy market. This project, aimed at delivering Russia's natural gas to Turkey and parts of Europe by bypassing Ukraine, had been announced in late 2014.[137] Concurrently, during a meeting between the Turkish and Iranian foreign ministers in Ankara on 11 August, Cavusoglu said that Turkey and Iran agreed on maintaining Syria's territorial integrity. Ankara would also cooperate with Iran to resolve the Syrian conflict.

On the battlefield, the US-backed SDF took full control of the city of Manbij, a transit point along the IS supply route all the way from the Turkish border to Raqqa. Following the SDF victory and with the approval of Russia, on 24 August Turkish troops with Syrian rebels launched operation Euphrates Shield and achieved two interconnected goals. They seized Jarablus and drove the IS fighters and the US-backed SDF out of the border area and prevented Syrian Kurdish forces from seizing more territory that would have linked other Kurdish areas in Afrin, in Syria's northwestern corner.[138] Meanwhile, US Vice President Joe Biden, who was visiting Ankara, failed to mend fences with Erdogan in an effort to have Turkey refrain from attacking the SDF. Both Turkey and the US ordered the YPG to withdraw to the east bank of the Euphrates River to avoid further escalation. Turkey's incursion strengthened Erdogan's stance, who raised the issue of a safe zone once again with Obama and Putin at the G20 summit in Hangzhou, China on 6 September. For the first time, Russian strategic bombers used the Shahid Nojeh airbase in Hamadan in northwest Iran to strike targets in Aleppo, Deir al-Zour, and Idlib provinces in Syria. By seeking clearance to use airspace over Iran and Iraq to launch cruise missiles, "Russia was signaling to its adversaries that its power politics in Syria had legitimacy and had been approved by other countries."[139]

For its part, the US-led coalition sent aircraft into northern Syria in a "very unusual" move to protect US special operation ground forces and US-backed SDF positions from attacks by the Syrian regime jets.[140] The perception that Obama kept the US out of the Syrian war was false. The Russian, Iranian, Hizbullah, and the Syrian regime alliance would spell doom for Syria's besieged opposition. Still, Russian-

Iranian coordination suggested that Tehran was not sidelined. Russia's use of Iran's airbase, for a short time, to launch air strikes in Syria sparked cautious debates between Iranian parliamentarians on the sensitive issues of Iran's sovereignty and constitutional provisions that banned establishing a foreign military base in the country. The Russian move was a message to the West that despite having different long-term strategies in Syria and divergent regional alliances, currently there was convergence of interest with Iran over Syria. Russia's relations with Israel and Moscow's reluctance to take Iran's side in its conflicts with Saudi Arabia and Yemen made the Iranian ruling elites question Russia's commitment to the partnership with Iran.

On 14 September 2016 Kerry and Lavrov, who met in Geneva, agreed on a new ceasefire in Syria to de-escalate violence between the government forces and rebels and open humanitarian corridors in Aleppo. But airstrikes on major frontlines in Hama and Homs provinces continued. For his part, de Mistura blamed the government for not providing the proper permits for humanitarian aid convoys. The next stage of the agreement was to coordinate military strikes against Jabhat Fatah al-Sham, previously known as Nusra Front, and IS militants.[141] Sadly, airstrikes on UN convoys in Aleppo by regime forces and possibly Russia contributed to the collapse of the ceasefire. Russia and the US blamed each other for the attack. It was apparent that a path toward peace was not an option for the time being. Capturing the rebel district of Aleppo and crushing the revolt in its last major urban stronghold would be the biggest victory of the war so far for al-Assad. Echoing al-Assad, Hizbullah's leader Sayyed Hassan Nasrallah said, "there were no prospects for political solutions … the final word was for the battlefield."[142] Russia came under fire at the UN when US Ambassador to the UN Samantha Power said, "instead of peace, Russia and Assad made war. Instead of life-saving aid to Syrians, Russia and Assad were bombing hospitals and first responders. What Russia was sponsoring and doing was not counterterrorism, it was barbarism."[143] Western countries also accused Russia of war crimes. Moscow rejected these accusations and offered evidence that showed a US drone in the vicinity of the attack. Moscow's accusations echoed earlier denunciations of US airstrikes on a camp of Syrian soldiers in Deir al-Zour.

Amid the major assault on Aleppo by government forces and its allies that began in late September, Kerry threatened to withdraw the American team from Geneva, where Russia and the US had established a centre to collaborate on two separate ceasefires.[144] The Kremlin's spokesman, Dmitry Peskov, described Kerry's threat as "awkward" and said that the "war on terror" in Syria would continue.[145] The Kremlin argued that the US had failed to ensure that mainstream rebels disassociate from Jabhat Fatah al-Sham. Russia would not stop the bombing because it was targeting Jabhat Fatah al-Sham. Still, Russia sent more warplanes to ramp up its campaign of airstrikes. Russian weapons now included thermobaric bombs, incendiary munitions, cluster bombs, and bunker busters. Putin assumed that Obama, who had long refused to approve direct military intervention in Syria, was unlikely to confront Russia in his final months in office. It is plausible to argue that Russian airstrikes on IS positions and Western-backed rebels were aimed to ensure Russia's place at the international negotiation table and legitimize Moscow's external power politics. Putin's status-seeking strategy in Syria was aimed to restore Russia's great power identity. Mikhail Troitskiy rightly noted that "Russia continued to seek ways to boost its authority and a positive assessment by Western counterparts of Moscow's contribution" to setting the guiding principles of global order.[146] Yet, Russia's foreign policy since 2014 had resulted in a worsening confrontation between Russia and the West over Ukraine and Syria. Thus, it was unlikely that Russia's status-seeking strategy would reverse its inconsistent power status. With the growing tensions in US-Russian relations and the suspension of talks with Russia on trying to end the violence in Syria, Putin, on 3 October, issued an executive order to suspend Russia's participation in an agreement on the disposal of plutonium that had been concluded in 2000 as one of the framework disarmament deals.[147] The US called Russia's decision a "big mistake."[148] Putin wanted to use nuclear disarmament as a new bargaining chip with the US over Ukraine and Syria. Putin set preconditions for the nuclear accord to be resumed. These conditions included lifting the sanctions imposed on Russia, paying compensation for the damage they had caused, and reducing US military presence in NATO member states in Eastern Europe. Russia also confirmed that it had deployed an S-300 antiaircraft missile system to its Mediterranean naval base at Tartus.[149]

Putin, in his address to the State Duma on 5 October after a sweeping victory of his ruling party, United Russia, in the parliamentary elections in September and in light of Russia's suspension of its nuclear agreement with the US, vowed "to strengthen the security and defense capabilities of our country to assert its position on the international stage." In an attempt to mobilize domestic support to his foreign policy Putin also said, "we must all unite, coordinate our efforts, obligations and rights to maintain Russia's historical supreme right, to be strong."[150] Putin was less interested in resetting relations with the West through a deal to cease hostilities than he was in ensuring Russia's influence from its western borders to the ME through Ukraine and Syria. Given Putin's power politics, the EU was now less likely to ease the sanctions on Moscow over Ukraine. On 6 October 2016, Russia's parliament ratified a treaty with Damascus that allowed Russian troops to stay indefinitely in Syria. In January 2017, Moscow and Damascus also signed an agreement on modernizing and expanding Russia's naval facility at the port of Tartus. Russia also considered reopening Soviet-era bases in Vietnam and Cuba. The first Russia-Egypt antiterrorism drills that kicked off in Egypt on 15 October signalled the return of Russia as a major geopolitical player.[151]

For the fifth time in six years, on 8 October 2016 Russia vetoed a UN SCR that sought to "immediately end all aerial bombardments of and military flights over Aleppo city."[152] Russia considered the draft put forward by France unacceptable because it was "politicized and one-sided."[153] As noted above, Russia used its veto power in the UNSC to preserve its influence in international politics and as a counterweight to US dominance in the UNSC. In a second vote, the council defeated a rival resolution drafted by Russia that urged the immediate implementation of the cessation of hostilities but did not call for a halt to the bombings that Russia's military was participating in. In addition to Ukraine, the failure of the resolutions deepened divisions at the UNSC between Moscow and Western powers to levels unseen since the end of the Cold War. Both, Russia and the Syrian government endorsed a proposal by de Mistura to evacuate al-Qaeda-linked militants from east Aleppo. For its part, Turkey, which owed its gains in Syria to Russia, showed willingness to respect Russian sensitivities in Aleppo by agreeing to evacuate Jabhat Fatah al-Sham from the city. To this end, Putin offered a humanitarian pause in Aleppo, urging rebels to use it to leave the city's besieged districts. Meanwhile, US presidential candidate Donald Trump criticized Clinton for her stance on Syria and Obama's weak foreign policy and his failure to bomb Syria if al-Assad used chemical weapons. Obama would be unable to deliver on his promise to degrade and ultimately destroy IS before he left office in January 2017. Trump said that the only US interest in Syria was defeating IS. Trump also suggested that he might leave Syria's fate to Russia and Iran.[154] Meanwhile, a simultaneous attack was launched on Raqqa and Mosul by US-backed Iraqi and Kurdish Peshmarga forces. Fighters in the Iranian Popular Mobilization units were also engaged in the battle for Mosul, which was the biggest since the US-led invasion of Iraq 2003. Turkey, which was seeking warmer ties with Russia, also took part in the Mosul offensive, despite Iraqi and US warnings to stay out, and was hoping to participate in the US-led coalition's assault on Raqqa. Erdogan spoke of Aleppo and Mosul as former Ottoman regional capitals. The outcome of Turkey's policy would accord well with Russia's strategic goals in Syria.

Outside the ME, Russia also tried to spread its influence in Central and Eastern Europe by using soft power. For example, the publication of *The Kremlin Playbook: Understanding Russian Influence in Eastern and Central Europe* in October 2016 disclosed that Moscow had co-opted sympathetic politicians, strived to dominate energy markets and other economic sectors, and undermined anticorruption measures in an attempt to gain sway over governments in Bulgaria, Hungary, Latvia, Serbia, and Slovakia.[155] The authors of *The Kremlin Playbook* argued that Russia discredited the Western liberal democratic model and undermined trans-Atlantic ties. The publication coincided with an unprecedented debate in the US over whether Russia had tried to interfere in the 8 November 2016 presidential election through cyber attacks and the release of emails from the campaign of the Democratic Party candidate Hilary Clinton. Even after US intelligence agencies accused Russia of hacking US political parties to destabilize the election, Trump praised Putin for being a strong leader. Concerning his comments on al Assad, Trump said, "he was much smarter than her [Clinton]." He also added that if the Syrian opposition prevailed, "you might very well end up with worse than Assad."[156] The US had not yet taken any covert action to respond to Russian cyber attacks. As argued above, Russia tried to establish a sphere of influence in Eurasia to maintain its values and interests and to prevent NATO from steadily moving closer to Russia's borders. Richard Haass noted that although Russia's "sphere of influence was controversial to good reason, it could be and to some extent was a source of order."[157] Within this context, the leaders of the CSTO, who met in Yerevan, Armenia on 16 October, emphasized the role of the organization in maintaining security in the FSS and vowed to counter perceived security threats from Europe to Central Asia. Belarusian President Alexander Lukashenko stated the need to "force" NATO to recognize the CSTO.[158]

The US-Russia stalemate was an obstacle in the path toward Syrian peace. The map of the external players further complicated the situation. Obama had only a short time left in office and could not make a foreign policy shift. Yet, after six years of conflict in Syria, retreating from the region was not an option. Al-Assad wanted to remain in power; Russia wanted to demonstrate its identity as a great power; Iran wanted to increase its regional influence, secure access to the Mediterranean, and carry on its proxy campaign against Israel; and Turkey wanted to participate in the Raqqa offensive and bid for Al-Bab to set up a free zone inside Syria and trample Kurdish aspirations. For Ankara that would mean a long-term Turkish presence in Syria. That said, peace in Syria could not be delivered by the US and Russia on their own despite Russia's significant influence on international conflict management in Syria. From a Russian perspective, the next US administration should begin with a clear understanding of how the Kremlin looks at the world order, treat Russia as an equal, work with Moscow to satisfy its status aspirations, and solve world crises.

When on 8 November 2016 Trump was elected as America's forty-fifth president, Western leaders expressed anxiety over how he would handle problems from the ME to an assertive Russia, Europe, and Asia. His stated views during the campaign, including "America First" in foreign policy, future relations with NATO, joint military efforts with Russia and al-Assad to defeat IS, and renegotiation of the Iranian nuclear deal, represented a sharp break with US foreign policy orthodoxy. Yet, it was likely that great power relations with China and Russia and the turmoil in the ME would dominate Trump's foreign policy agenda. The incremental approach to the ME taken by Bush and Obama meant that the US had failed to keep pace with events.

It is plausible to argue that Trump's election was a symbolic victory for the Kremlin in its resistance to US pressure to establish a Western-style democracy in Ukraine and Georgia. Putin had blamed Clinton as fomenting protests in Russia in 2011–12 because Russia feared the spill over effect of democratization and its impact on the regime. As noted above, the Kremlin had presented Russia "as a special civilization, committed to defending particular values and principles relative to those of the West."[159] President-elect Trump indicated that he would align US policy on Syria more closely with Russia. Putin would be pleased if the US dropped the sanctions it had imposed on Russia for its annexation of the Crimea. In addition to a plunge in oil prices, the US sanctions had been a strong factor in Russia's economic decline. In terms of costs, the IMF country report stated that pressure on the ruble had intensified since 2014 "as geopolitical tensions rose and oil prices tanked. The ruble fell by 50 per cent between 2014 and 2015."[160] Falling under pressure to legitimize its external power politics, the Kremlin "tried to dispel domestic concerns of a too costly military intervention from the beginning by justifying it as a contribution to the fight against the IS."[161]

On 14 November 2016, Putin and Trump spoke over the phone and discussed a number of issues including combining efforts in the fight against "international terrorism and extremism and strategic economic issues." Putin, who congratulated Trump on his victory, expressed readiness to "establish a partner-like dialogue with the new administration on the basis of equality, mutual respect and non-interference in domestic relations."[162] Joseph Nye rightly noted that sanctions were necessary for deterrence but, "Trump was correct to avoid complete isolation of Russia with which the U.S. had overlapping interests when it came to nuclear security, non-proliferation, anti-terrorism, the Arctic, and regional issues like Iran and Afghanistan."[163] It was important to discuss ways to improve the current unsatisfactory relations with Russia after Trump took office on 20 January 2017. For Russia, the inauguration of Trump could start a new era of détente between Russia and the US that could change the current liberal international order. Multilateralism still mattered because the problems, challenges, and opportunities that countries faced had no regard for national borders. The prospect of a shift in US policy came at a difficult time for the Syrian rebellion. Trump signalled that he could abandon the rebels to focus on fighting IS. It was significant that just hours after Putin spoke to Trump Russian bombers launched a new offensive on Aleppo. Moscow's aircraft carrier, the *Admiral Kuznetsov*, joined land-based aircraft in bombing targets in Syria. Russia used the Syria campaign to test several new designs of cruise missiles, fighters, and bombers in combat for the first time. On 5 December Russia and China vetoed a UNSC Resolution that would have demanded a seven-day truce in Aleppo, with Russia arguing that it would allow rebels to regroup and that time was needed for talks between Washington and Moscow.

Putin, who spoke to top military generals and defense industry officials in Sochi on 18 November, vowed to oppose attempts to disrupt the strategic balance around the world, such as NATO's US-led global antiballistic missile defense system. The Kremlin would continue the military modernization drive it had pursued since 2008, after Russia's war with Georgia, because it gave Russia "a usable instrument of foreign policy which Moscow did not have for a quarter century."[164]

Putin criticized the termination of previous agreements, referring to the withdrawal from the ABM Treaty in 2002 by President Bush. He added that the strategic balance in the late 1940s and 1950s prevented a major military conflict between the opposing camps during the Cold War.[165] Putin's statements indicated Russia's dissatisfaction of the current US-dominated world order. Russia wanted to establish strategic parity with the US. Russia's foreign policy concept of 2016 indicated that Moscow was ready to discuss the stage-by-stage reduction of nuclear potentials. Talks on strategic arms reduction were possible only if all factors influencing strategic security were taken into account. According to the document, Russia was interested in mutually beneficial relations with the US as both Moscow and Washington were responsible for international security. Russia did not recognize US attempts to implement its jurisdiction beyond its borders as it contradicted international law. The new foreign policy concept also stressed the importance of defending the country's cultural distinctiveness in the context of new international challenges and attempts by the US to preserve global dominance. In addition, the document underlined that Russia would build its relations with NATO based on the alliance's readiness to hold an equal dialogue.[166] The document also said that Russia stood for the peaceful settlement of the Syrian conflict.

Putin, in his annual address to the Federal Assembly on 1 December 2016, once again expressed the hope of joining efforts with the US in the struggle against international terrorism. Putin expected to discuss a multilevel integration model, similar to the Eurasian model, and partnership with the EU countries. The bilateral EU-Russia economic relationship could be dissolved into an overarching grand Eurasian partnership. For Moscow, the EU would have to give up the current principles of its EaP and its present neighbourhood policy. That said, "The EU could agree that the normative activity must be carried out in cooperation by all countries of the region and take into account the values and interests of all parties."[167] Putin attributed "the main reason for Russia's economic slowdown to internal problems and lack of investment resources." Yet, Russia "ensured macroeconomic stability, which was very important, and had maintained financial reserves." Concerning defense, Russia "carried out far-reaching modernization at its defense industry enterprises. In 2016, Russia "expected growth in the defense industry to reach 10.1 percent, and a labor productivity increase of 9.8 percent."[168]

In terms of political costs, on 19 December 2016, the assassination of Andrei Karlov, the Russian ambassador to Turkey, by a former Turkish police officer, threatened to undermine the Russian-Turkish rapprochement that had begun in June after Erdogan expressed regrets to the Russian people. As the assassin pulled the trigger he shouted, "do not forget Aleppo! All those who participated in this tyranny will be held accountable."[169] Meanwhile, it should be noted that regime forces with its allies retook the eastern part of Aleppo in mid-December. Ankara and Moscow reached a deal to get the opposition out of Aleppo and bring it to the negotiating table in Astana, Kazakhstan, without the US and the UN. Putin, who had leveraged Russia's role in Syria, wanted to boost its diplomatic muscle as an attribute of major power. On 19 December, the UNSC approved the deployment of UN monitors to Aleppo to observe the evacuation of fighters and civilians from northern Aleppo to Idlib.

Aleppo's fall was proof that al-Assad prevailed and Iran sustained its influence. Iran secured a land corridor that connected Tehran to Beirut, allowing it to send weapons to Hizbullah in Lebanon. Yet, whether Iran could maintain such a large sphere of influence in the region (the Shiite Crescent) was uncertain because it posed a threat to Israel and a geopolitical challenge to Saudi Arabia. Complete victory in Aleppo belonged to Russia, which once again counted in the ME. Russia's brutal air campaign stirred memories of Putin's destruction of Grozny in 1999–2000. The supporters of the Syrian opposition outside and inside Turkey were outraged by the Ankara-Moscow agreement, which became an initial step toward resolving the Syrian crisis diplomatically. It is reasonable to argue that both the June terrorist attacks and Karlov's assassination were a message to Turkey to stop its advancement in Syria against Kurdish militants and to undermine its strategic cooperation with Moscow. As the regime forces and its allies focused the bulk of their firepower on fighting the rebels in western Syria, IS militants managed to retake Palmyra, once again challenging al-Assad who had vowed to re-establish control all over Syria.

The killing of the Russian diplomat did not halt Russian-Turkish cooperation. Increasingly, warm ties with Ankara would also strengthen Russia's ability to counter Western efforts to politically isolate Moscow over its actions in Ukraine. On 20 December, the foreign ministers of Russia, Iran, and Turkey met in Moscow and adopted a document they called the Moscow Declaration, which set out principles they thought any Syrian peace agreement should adhere to. They also backed a new ceasefire across Syria, the free movement of humanitarian aid, and the movement of civilians on Syrian territory.[170] Lavrov announced that a new series of peace talks were set to take place in January 2017 in Astana, capital of Kazakhstan, and that the priority in Syria was to fight terrorism and not to remove al-Assad from power – something that brought Iran into the idea of three-way peace push. Lavrov's announcement was pertinent to the Russian foreign policy concept of 2016 that "aimed at neutralizing threats that emanate from international terrorist groups" and "prompt political and diplomatic settlement of conflicts in regional states."[171] In mid-January 2017, the first joint Russian-Turkish airstrikes against IS militants in the town of Al-Bab signalled improving ties between the two countries.

On 30 December, talks between Turkish and Russian officials and rebel representatives in Ankara called for a new ceasefire across Syria. Both agreements highlighted Russia's role as the main international player in Syria. After the major victory in Aleppo, Moscow was pushing from a position of strength for the expected Astana talks.[172] Russia, Turkey, and Iran expressed their readiness to act as guarantors of a future settlement between the Syrian regime and the opposition. Russia positioned itself as a mediator between the internal actors in Syria and the external ones. Putin's desire was to consolidate his influence in the ME and set the guiding principles of the global order. For the time being, by sidelining the US and playing the lead role in trying to broker a settlement, initially, with Turkey and Iran, Putin would bolster Russia's posture as a world power and strong ME player.

Obama waited to react until the last week of December, punishing Russia for cyber attacks by directing new sanctions against Moscow and expelling thirty-five Russian diplomats under the pretext of intimidation and its hacking of the emails of institutions like the Democratic National Committee in July 2016 to influence the American presidential election. As part of the sanctions, Russia would also close two compounds in New York and Maryland that were used by Russian personnel for "intelligence related purposes." It is worth noting that in addition to Russian demands for equal partnership and recognition as a great power, cyberspace was a potential area for status satisfaction. For Obama, Russia's act was a breach of national security and an "effort to undermine established international norms of behavior."[173] Putin refrained from taking retaliatory action. He said, "further steps toward the restoration of Russian-American relations would be built on the basis of the policy which President Trump would carry out."[174] Maria Zakharova called the US administration "a group of foreign policy losers embittered and narrow minded."[175]

According to Vladimir Frolov, an international relations analyst, Putin's act was "an attempt to show that he was a figure not just of worldly scale, but of planetary," and it was suggested that, "he refrained from retaliation because he wanted Trump to have room to maneuver when he attained office."[176] Putin expressed hope that Trump would improve US-Russian cooperation.[177] Putin, made no secret of the fact that he would like to establish a multipolar world divided into great powers' spheres of influence. Apparently, Russia had the potential to be a great power and the cyber attacks underscored that a state did not need nuclear weapons to assert global influence. Putin could bring the US back into Syria and forge a new deal on fighting IS. Trump, in his presidential campaign, had already stated that he wanted to join forces with Russia in defeating the terrorist groups. Apparently, Putin looked "strong in relation to the U.S. and he had freedom to maneuver, and he could do what he wanted to demonstrate that the U.S. should recognize that Russia was not a regional power but a great power that should be taken into account."[178] For its part, Moscow should also recognize that the US was a "democracy guru and a security provider to the smaller powers."[179]

On the diplomatic front, on 23 and 24 January 2017, Russian, Turkish, and Iranian officials met in Astana to consolidate the new ceasefire that had been reached between Russia, Turkey, and rebel representatives on 30 December 2016 in Ankara. In Astana, rebel representatives and the regime delegation held indirect talks to de-escalate violence and help prepare an environment conducive to intra-Syrian political talks.[180] The trilateral initiative was sponsored by Russia, Turkey, and Iran – the states that possessed leverage on the ground. The US attended only as an observer, and there was no participation at all from Saudi Arabia, reflecting that "the talks were in Russia's geopolitical backyard, and the ball was now largely in Moscow's court."[181] The statement made by Alexander Lavrentiyev, head of the Russian delegation, that Russia "gave birth to the Astana process" demonstrated that Moscow had become the main power broker since its intervention in September 2015.[182] Yet, the question was, would Russia go further than it had done to date in pressing for a suitable ceasefire supported by Turkey, accepted by Iran, and adhered to by the regime and the non-jihadist rebels? Saudi Arabia would like to end its military intervention in Yemen, and Turkey sought an outcome to the Syrian conflict that would align with its own policy towards the Kurds. Firuznia disclosed that "the U.S. did not support the Astana process, but Astana managed military and political issues and prevented destructive escalation in the region."[183] It should be stressed that Russia, Turkey, and Iran, as Syria's conflict brokers, in their different ways, had credibility problems with the internal conflicting parties.

The final communiqué issued at the conclusion of the two-day talks stated that the three countries would jointly monitor the ceasefire and "ensure full compliance to it, prevent any provocation and determine all modalities of the cease-fire."[184] The final communiqué also mentioned reviving the political talks in Geneva under UN Resolution 2254, and the three countries agreed to continue fighting the jihadist groups and separate them from other armed opposition factions. Obviously, the Astana talks were a diplomatic victory that underlined the growing ME clout of Russia, Iran, and Turkey and Washington's diminished influence at a time when Trump was still determining his foreign policy goals. De Mistura, who attended the meeting, endorsed the ceasefire, praised Russia, Turkey, and Iran for coordinating the truce talks in Astana, and reiterated that "the UN was the main player in regards to the political process that should continue in Geneva" and that the UN "could not allow another cease-fire to be, in a way, wasted because of a lack of a political process."[185] The Astana talks on the ceasefire would reinforce Geneva and vice versa.

The Astana talks exposed the limits of what Russia, Turkey, and Iran could achieve in their efforts to resolve the conflict without the full involvement of the US and the Gulf States. While Moscow would welcome Washington joining the process, Tehran would not accept such a proposal. Thus, the third parties, as Charles King noted, "had, in many instances, been unable to translate cooperation at the strategic level into conflict resolution on the ground."[186]

In line with our argument, resolving the Syrian conflict required international cooperation. According to Bruce Jentleson, successful conflict prevention necessitated developing "a fair but firm strategy" and getting the external powers to act.[187] He argued that third-party interveners must deliver on their promises and their threats. However, as Saideman noted, the problem was that the external powers "might not want to hurt the side that they preferred but punish the side they disliked."[188] For example, all external powers advocated harsher measures against IS but disagreed with each other due to conflicting preferences. Jasmine El-Gamal, senior fellow at the Atlantic Council, stated that although Russia's and the US's interest in Syria was to defeat IS, "Russia's foremost interest was to exert strategic and tactical dominance over the U.S. in Syria."[189]

Trump, in his inaugural address, pledged to eradicate IS "from the face of the earth" and emphasized that a better relationship with Moscow would be beneficial for the West.[190] At a meeting with Russia's Federal Security Services on 16 February, Putin also said that it was "in everyone's interest to restore dialogue between the intelligence agencies of the U.S. and other members of NATO. In the area of counterterrorism all relevant governments and international groups should work together."[191] In the same vein, Lavrov, at the Munich Security Conference from 17 to 19 February 2017, reiterated that US-Russian relations should be "pragmatic" and marked by mutual respect and acknowledgement of a shared responsibility for global stability.[192] Both, Putin's and Lavrov's statements were in line with Russia's status-seeking strategy. US policy on Syria and its relations with Russia remained unclear. Nothing had changed since the Munich Security Conference in 2007 when Putin delivered an inflammatory speech detailing Russia's deep dissatisfaction with the world order. As Pavel Baev argued, Putin could not be treated as "an equal" because the West still widely recognized Russia as a deeply entrenched corrupt autocracy.[193] Upgrading Russia's bilateral relations with the US to the status of "equals" had in fact been one of Putin's goals since 2007. According to de Mistura, "at the moment there was no clear U.S. strategy on a political solution in Syria."[194] American officials ruled out cooperating with Russia militarily until the US could persuade Damascus to take a broader view on the conflict and grant concessions to the opposition. At the global level, as the new US national security adviser Herbert Raymond McMaster stated, Moscow's broader goal was to "collapse the post-Cold War security, economic and political order in Europe and replace that order with something that is more sympathetic to Russian interests."[195] More broadly, the unipolar world order, with the US as the dominant power, was withering away. There is reason to believe that a new global order might be on the horizon and that

Russia would be one key pillar in setting the guiding principles of the new order.

The second round of the Astana talks took place on 15–16 February, ahead of the Geneva IV talks, with the participants agreeing to set up a ceasefire monitoring group comprising Iran, Russia, and Turkey that would report to the UN.[196] On 23 February 2017, Syria peace talks restarted in Geneva (known as Geneva IV) after ten months of freeze, but familiar disagreements surfaced despite big changes in the military and political context that had occurred since the Geneva III talks in April 2016. The regime forces had gained key territory and Turkish troops backed by Syrian rebel fighters entered the city of Al-Bab on 12 February. Obviously, the opposition pressed for prisoner releases, the lifting of government sieges, and above all for a political transition leading to the removal of al-Assad. However, the future of al-Assad depended on the agreement between Russia, Iran, and the US. As argued above, for Russia the fight in Syria was primarily against the forces of extremism and terrorism and not a fight for representative democracy and to depose Russia's strong ally, al-Assad. In his turn, de Mistura was determined to focus on reforming the governance of Syria, introducing a new constitution, and holding elections under UN supervision. Diplomats from the ISSG, which united twenty regional and world powers and was led by the US and Russia, attended the talks. Trump signalled that he was more concerned with fighting IS than with removing al-Assad.

Still, US Secretary of State Rex Tillerson said during a visit to Ankara that the "long-term status" of al-Assad should be decided by the Syrian people. Also, US Ambassador to the UN Nikki Haley commented that "our priority was no longer to sit there and focus on getting al-Assad out."[197] Haley also reflected on Trump's concern over Crimea and Washington's sanctions on Russia. These statements revealed a change in the US stance on Syria and the ME. Trump, while hosting Netanyahu, declared that the US would no longer insist on the creation of a Palestinian state as part of a peace deal between Israel and the Palestinians. Trump's position on a two-state solution "discarded a policy that had underpinned America's role in ME peacemaking since the Clinton Administration."[198] Trump appeared to have withdrawn from the US-Russian co-leadership that drove diplomacy under Obama's administration. Putin, in his turn, the most potent international power broker in Syria's conflict, expressed hope for the success of a political settlement that would help to defeat international terrorism. Quoting from Saideman, these statements also demonstrated "the crucial role of international political dynamics in managing conflict."[199]

The Geneva IV talks that centred on UNSC Resolution 2254 did not achieve a tangible breakthrough and the parties did not meet face-to-face. Nasr al-Hariri, a senior member of the opposition delegation, singled out Iran, for its continuous violations of the ceasefire, as the biggest obstacle to settling the conflict. Yet, the question of political transition was seriously addressed for the first time and the issue of counterterrorism, which was pushed by the regime's delegation, was added to the agenda. De Mistura handed both delegations a working paper on procedural issues that could help to begin the political process. He reiterated that the issue of fighting terrorism and the ceasefire should be held in the parallel talks in Astana. However, the members of the armed opposition, who participated in the two previous rounds, refused to attend the third round of talks in Astana that took place on 13 March 2017, asking Russia to change its policy if it wanted a peaceful solution.

Meanwhile, the seizure of Al-Bab from IS by the Syrian rebel forces was accompanied by a deployment of Turkish troops, tanks, and artillery inside Syrian territory to oust the US-backed SDF from the city of Manbij. Turkey's aim was to stop the YPG from crossing the Euphrates westward and linking three mainly Kurdish cantons it held in northern Syria, preventing it from establishing a self-government analogous to Iraq's autonomous Kurdish region. It is important to note that the US had about five hundred special operations forces (SOFs) in Syria helping to organize, advise, and assist the SDF and the YPG.[200] In March 2017, the US, which had no frontline role, deployed an additional four hundred Marine and Army Ranger forces in and around the city of Manbij as part of a new role to ensure that the different parties in the area did not attack each other but instead focused on fighting IS.[201] Turkey had been pressing Washington for a role in the final assault on Raqqa. In another blow to IS, on 2 March Russian-backed Syrian government forces recaptured Palmyra.

The regional dimension of the Syrian conflict and the geostrategic interests of the external players were a key source of difficulty in reaching a political settlement. Netanyahu, during his visit to Moscow on 9 March 2017, made it clear to Putin that Israel was opposed to any agreement on Syria that would allow "Iran and its proxies [to have a] military presence in Syria."[202] On 17 March, Israeli warplanes attacked a weapons convoy destined for Hizbullah in Lebanon, but Israel did not wish "to intervene in the Syrian civil war or provoke a confrontation with the Russians."[203] Firouznia disclosed to the author that, "neither Iran nor Russia could stop Israel from bombing targets in Syria because there was a red line that the Russians could not cross. Still, Russia did not want to confront the West."[204] On 10 March, after concluding his meeting with Erdogan in Moscow, Putin hailed "efficient and close contact" between their militaries and intelligence agencies around Syria. Both leaders insisted that preserving the territorial integrity of Syria was a "necessary condition for the full-scale peace settlement in the country."[205] Russia's stance stemmed from the military doctrine of the Russian Federation that was approved in December 2014. Moscow had formed an unlikely alliance with Ankara since 2016, envisioning Turkey as part of a solution to the Syrian conflict. Erdogan's direct contact with Putin stemmed from the lack of commitment on the part of the US and NATO in helping Turkey fight terrorism to defend itself and create its own missile defense system. On 28 March, Putin also hosted Rouhani in Moscow. In addition to their cooperation on Syria, energy and defense ties had deepened between both countries in recent years. Russia would build nine of Iran's twenty proposed nuclear reactors and had emerged as a long-term arms partner, supplying Tehran with its S-300 air defense missile system.[206] The rapprochement with Iran and Turkey was the achievement of an assertive foreign policy goal for Putin, who wanted to demonstrate Russia's greatness and influence in the ME and the world. Turkey was also interested in purchasing the Russian-manufactured S-400 missile system capable of intercepting all types of modern air weaponry. Turkey's interest stemmed from enhancing its defensive strategic capabilities. Concerning geopolitics, Russian-Turkish defense cooperation faced limitations because of Moscow's relations with PYD/YPG groups in Syria, which posed a significant national security threat to Turkey because of their affiliation with the PKK terrorist organization.

Russia would not be dragged into a potential conflict with Turkey and Saudi Arabia. In October 2017, the landmark visit to Moscow by the Saudi monarch King Salman and his agreement on joint investment deals worth several billion dollars at a time when the Russian economy was battered by low oil prices and Western sanctions was an indication of rapprochement between Moscow and Riyadh.[207] Engaging with Turkey, a NATO ally, and Iran became an unavoidable necessity for Russian diplomacy since both states were key players with significant leverage in Syria. On 26 November 2017, the trilateral Putin-Erdogan-Rouhani summit in Sochi was the culmination of that effort. There seemed to be convergence between Turkey's, Russia's, and Iran's Syria policy, as Erdogan seemed ready to forge strong strategic ties with Moscow rooted in energy exports.

Notwithstanding the obstacles to making peace, on 23 March 2017 the fifth round of talks resumed in Geneva (Geneva V) amid much speculation as the regime forces launched an offensive around Hama and the Damascus neighbourhood of Jobar. SDF fighters supported by the US were also on the offensive in the IS-held town of Tabqa in the Raqqa province. De Mistura urged Russia, Turkey, and Iran to "retake the situation in hand" amid a recent escalation of fighting on the ground.[208] The regime delegation submitted a paper on basic principles to launch any dialogue about the constitutional process, but the discussions centred on ceasefire violations. Meanwhile, Turkey announced the end of the Euphrates Shield operation in northern Syria. The talks in Geneva descended into bureaucratic wrangling and de Mistura acknowledged that no peace deal was foreseeable in the near future. As noted by David Lake and Donald Rothchild, the external powers did not exert enough pressure on both sides "to moderate their demands." That was why "intervention by itself would not necessarily enhance the prospects for agreement."[209] Still, the weak commitments of the external powers produced ambiguous policies that exacerbated rather than ended the war. Ambiguity and vacillation apparently persuaded al-Assad that "the external powers did not possess sufficient stamina" and that the regime too "might improve its position by continuing to fight."[210] This ambivalent commitment was the true tragedy of the external power's policies in Syria.

On 4 April 2017 the chemical attack by the regime forces on the rebel-held town of Khan Sheikhun, in northern Idlib province, revived international outrage at a time when Trump was still formulating his policy on Syria. The regime denied carrying out the chemical attack and blamed the militants; Russia ruled out al-Assad's responsibility and rejected the UNSC draft resolution on chemical weapons in Syria, considering its "anti-Syrian nature" risked making the negotiations process impossible.[211] Notwithstanding Russia's stance, Ambassador Haley, at the UNSC meeting on the situation in Syria, said, "it was time for all civilized nations to stop the horrors that were taking place in Syria and demand a political solution."[212] The

Kremlin's spokesman, Dmitry Peskov, reiterated that Russia would continue "the consistent line of the decisive fight against terrorism, which Putin had been conducting for years. We had repeatedly said that we lack international cooperation; and that happened not due to our fault."[213]

Although Trump did not publicly draw a red line concerning the use of chemical weapons, as Obama had in 2013, he spoke out against military action against al-Assad before his presidency. The scale of the chemical attack compelled him to take strong action to prove he was tougher than Obama. Trump, on 7 April, ordered a cruise missile strike on the Shayrat airbase, southeast of Homs.[214] Trump's decision, which opened up a rift between Moscow and Washington, was his biggest foreign policy decision since taking office in January. But, what was next? Turkey welcomed the US missile strike but did not consider it sufficient. Ankara's stance set Turkey at direct odds with Russia less than four months after the two powers brokered a ceasefire in Syria and peace talks in Astana. The US used the de-escalation line to warn Moscow that the strike was coming in order to avoid a military confrontation with Russia. In the aftermath of the attack, Moscow's decision to suspend the hotline and its cooperation in the information-sharing campaign signed with the US in October 2015 signalled its readiness to raise the stakes. Putin described the attack as an "act of aggression against a sovereign state in violation of international norms and under an invented pretext," and the Kremlin considered it to be in the interests of IS and terrorist groups.[215] Notwithstanding tensions between Russia and the West, on 2 May 2017 German Chancellor Angela Merkel's visit to Putin in the Black Sea resort of Sochi indicated that Russia was not isolated. Despite their differences over Syria and Ukraine and Russian respect for civil rights, Merkel stressed that talks between Berlin and Moscow should continue. Equally important, after being elected president on 7 May, Emmanuel Macron hosted Putin at the Palace of Versailles on 29 May and told the Russian president that any use of chemical weapons in Syria was a "red line" for France and would be met by "reprisals" and "immediate riposte" from France, whose airplanes were still participating in bombing IS targets in Syria and Iraq.[216] Macron's election victory offered an opportunity for Paris to retool its foreign policy on Syria because the previous administration's policy was too intransigent and left Paris isolated. Macron's remark that there was no legitimate successor to al-Assad and that France no longer considered al-Assad's departure a precondition to resolving the conflict showed acquiescence to Russia's assertive foreign policy in Syria. Macron's positioning on Syria was an opportunity for Russia, too, to address Western sanctions and seek rapprochement with the EU. Macron appeared to fight terrorism, while seeking better ties with Russia, which he considered a long-term partner rather than a threat to Europe.

As argued above, it was a Russian foreign policy objective to protect the Syrian regime so that Syria would not suffer the same fate as Iraq and Libya. Iran's Syria policy would not be affected either. Vladimir Frolov rightly noted that "fighting ISIS was supposed to be the low-hanging fruit for both the U.S. and Russia to re-launch their relationship under Trump, a President, who even exhibited some willingness to work with Assad on fighting terrorism."[217] It is plausible to argue that after both sides made their largely symbolic moves, the moment had arrived to return to diplomacy and to de-escalate tensions. Indeed, Moscow was looking forward to reengaging with Washington in the fight against terrorism. Obviously, the US intervention intended to deter future chemical attacks and was not an expansion of the American role in the Syrian war. Removing al-Assad from power was no longer a US priority. The military action was a signal to Russia, as well as countries such as Iran, China, and North Korea, where Trump faced foreign policy tests, that he was willing to use force. Yet, without having a clear strategy, a bombing strike against al-Assad was very unlikely to change anything in Syria's messy civil war. Foreign policy required strategic thinking. Trump "showed no evidence of it; in fact, his policy impulsiveness risked digging an even deeper hole for Syria, into which the U.S., Britain and Russia would be sucked."[218] According to Frederic Hof, "frustrating and complicating Assad's strategy of terror and mass homicide must be at the heart of an American strategy aimed at marginalizing and eventually neutralizing the regime. But, this was complicated by Russia's presence." Further, Washington "must aim diplomatically for a complete Syrian political transition away from a mafia family that was destroying the Syrian state and making the country safe for other forms of violent extremism."[219]

On 12 April 2017, the tense talks that Tillerson held in Moscow did not seem to narrow the gap with Russia on Syria.[220] Tillerson tried to challenge Russia to distance itself from al-Assad and his Iranian backers, an idea that the Kremlin dismissed as absurd. Both rival powers failed to bridge the deep gap in trust. Russia could not accept al-

Assad's demise because that would deprive Moscow of its only ally in the ME and one that hosted Russian air force and naval assets. Even more crucially, abandoning al-Assad would cast Russia as a loser in the six-year-old Syrian conflict, dealing a blow to its aspirations to regain Soviet-era global clout and prestige. It is reasonable to argue that Washington should have reinvigorated its role in the UN-supervised Geneva peace talks and consulted with Russia about a political outcome in Syria that respects Russian interests in the ME and Europe.

In March 2017, the US Senate ratified Montenegro's accession to NATO. In its first expansion since Albania and Croatia joined the Western military alliance in 2009, Montenegro became the twenty-ninth member of NATO on 5 June.[221] Montenegro's accession to NATO further angered Russia and diminished Moscow's influence in southeast Europe. Another issue that angered Russia and limited Trump's flexibility regarding sanctions on Russia were the congressionally mandated trade sanctions on Russia and Ukrainian separatists on 20 June. Lavrov denounced the act and called it "Russophobe obsession."[222] If Trump had really wanted to improve relations with Russia, he should have persuaded NATO to stop its eastward expansion and urged the US congress to ease sanctions. Such an American posture would lessen the distrust and tension between Moscow and Washington and help build a sustainable peaceful global order. To enhance regional security, it is worth noting that the SCO at its meeting in Astana on 9 June accepted Pakistan and India as full members to expand the organization's security role and influence into south Asia.

In northeast Syria, meanwhile, on 24 April, the US-backed SDF entered the IS-held town of Tabqa in the Raqqa province, the militant group's de facto capital. American armoured vehicles were deployed in areas in northern Syria along the tense border with Turkey a few days after a Turkish airstrike that killed a number of SDF fighters. The US role was to establish a buffer between the SDF and the Turks. In May 2017, the Trump administration decided to arm Syria's Kurdish fighters despite intense opposition from Turkey, which saw the YPG as a terrorist organization.[223] The assault on Raqqa to liberate it from IS began in early June 2017. Turkey's Prime Minister Binali Yildirim stated that, "my country would respond if an offensive by the SDF in Raqqa posed a security threat to Turkey."[224]

On 4 May 2017, once again Russia proved that it was the major player in the ME when in Astana, Russia, Iran, and Turkey signed a memorandum on establishing four "de-escalation" or "safe zones" in rebel-held territory in the northwestern Syrian province of Idlib, in parts of Homs province, in the opposition enclave of eastern Ghouta near Damascus, and in southern Syria, particularly Deraa and Quneitra provinces, to shore up the ceasefire and set the stage for a later settlement.[225] The US sent a senior State Department official to the Astana IV talks for the first time after Trump and Putin had signalled greater cooperation to end the violence in Syria. Shoigu noted that Moscow had been discussing safe zones in Syria with several nations including the US, Israel, and Jordan.[226] Zasypkin disclosed that, "establishing de-escalation zones was a combined Russian–U.S. idea. Initially, de-escalation would facilitate a political settlement."[227] Compliant with its status-seeking strategy, Russia was moving from a military posture to that of a mediator trying to reach a solution to gain status recognition through achievements in areas other than military power.

The deal called for "rapid, safe and unhindered humanitarian access" in the four areas as well as measures to restore basic infrastructure and allow the "safe and voluntary return" of the displaced people and refugees."[228] However, Russia's peacemaking efforts would face the same obstacles as past efforts to reduce the violence in Syria because al-Assad was entrenched, Iran and its proxy Hizbullah resisted any compromise to reduce their role, and the Syrian opposition was divided and influenced by the terrorist and extremist groups which resisted any peace deal that did not include al-Assad's removal. The Syrian government's alternative to stalled negotiations had been the implementation of reconciliation agreements in many parts of the country. For example, in May 2017 Syrian rebels and their families left the city of Waer, in Homs province, under a Russian-brokered deal between the regime and rebel forces. It is important to note that in June 2017, Russian and US special envoys Alexander Lavrentiyev and Michael Ratney met a number of times in Jordan to strike a deal on the boundaries of the proposed de-escalation zone in Deraa because the US wanted no role for Iran in the area, which was of strategic interest to the US, Israel, and Jordan.[229] On 2 May, after Putin and Trump discussed working together in their first phone call since the US strikes in Syria, it appeared that the US wanted to work more closely with Russia because a plan that targeted Russia's allies was fruitless. In July 2017, Russia deployed military police and set up two checkpoints and four observation posts to monitor two safe zones in the southwest and in eastern Ghouta. Russia had informed Israel of its deployment. The nearest Russian position was thirteen kilometres from the demarcation line between Israeli and Syrian troops in the Golan Heights.[230] For the time being, it was unclear if Trump would keep some US troops inside the country to help stabilize Syria after the jihadists were defeated. Trump, like Obama, expressed scepticism about permanent US wars in the ME. However, pulling out US troops from bases east of the Euphrates could create a vacuum that might trigger a new wave of jihadist violence and regional proxy wars.

On 16 May 2017, a new round of peace talks opened in Geneva (Geneva VI). De Mistura suggested forming a team of technocrats headed by UN experts and "qualified representatives from both the Syrian government and the opposition" to lay the foundations for a new constitution.[231] However, as in previous talks, no tangible results were achieved. Clearly, regional cooperation was still lacking to negotiate an end to the Syrian civil war. For example, during Trump's two-day visit to Saudi Arabia and his meeting with more than fifty Arab and Muslim leaders on 21 May, King Salman described Iran as a source of terrorism that should be confronted by the Arab nations and the US, while Trump also urged the Arab leaders to unite to defeat militants and accused Iran of fuelling "the fires of sectarian conflict and terror."[232] The point of Trump's strategy was to isolate Iran and support Saudi Arabia in the belief that it would be able to fight terrorism and stabilize the region. Trump's visit to Saudi Arabia also served as "a reset with the region following his presidential campaign, which was frequently punctured by bouts of anti-Islamic rhetoric."[233]

On 6 June, the SDF, by US SOFs, entered the city of Raqqa supported. On 9 June, Russian-backed progovernment forces that had been advancing in the direction of Albukamal along the Syrian-Iraqi border avoided a direct confrontation with US-backed forces based at Al-Tanf. Russia criticized the US deployment of the truck-mounted high-mobility artillery rocket system (HIMARS) to defend Al-Tanf base where the US-led coalition was training Syrian rebels to fight IS.[234] For the first time since 2015, Iraqi forces, after capturing the Al-Waleed crossing point with Syria, met pro-Syrian troops. The link between the Iraqi and Syrian forces would allow pro-Iranian militias to move inside Syria and help the regime's campaign against IS. Russia's midterm plan was to improve the capabilities of the regime forces, which would allow Russian troops to relocate to Russian bases in the country. According to Putin, the experience acquired by the Russian army in Syria was "priceless."[235] What was lacking in the peace process, as Stephen John Stedman noted, was "the implementation of a successful strategy that depended on the custodian's ability to create an external coalition for peace, the resources that the coalition brought to its responsibility, and the consensus that the coalition formed about the legitimacy (or lack thereof) of spoiler demands and behavior."[236]

This chapter has examined and analyzed the immediate and strategic objectives of Russia's intervention in Syria mainly to set the guiding principles of global order and preserve Russia's centrality in international conflict management as an embodiment of its international status. Both factors played a key role in Russia's positioning on Syria. I have argued that Russia's power politics in Syria aimed to enhance its inconsistent status. For a better understanding of Russia's power politics in Syria from a status-seeking point of view I discussed the factors of identity, opportunity, and cost. Putin's assertive foreign policy demonstrated that Russia was able to protect its national interests in the ME and FSS. Russian and Iranian policy aimed to protect the Syrian state and defeat terrorism. I also argued that Putin, who cultivated geostrategic relationship with Egypt, Israel, and Saudi Arabia, was unlikely to yield to American and Western pressure. After Ukraine, Putin used Syria to achieve great power status. Yet, Russia's use of military power in its foreign policy as a means to enhance its status seemed counterintuitive. Russia's military intervention in Syria that aimed to support the al-Assad regime's fight against terrorism showcased Russian power politics in action and highlighted how Moscow's status-seeking strategy did not reverse its inconsistent power status.

Russia wanted its position to be respected and be treated as an equal to the US. However, the West was not willing to recognize Russia as a great power because it considered Russia an aggressor and a security threat. Within this context, I tested H1 and H2. By negotiating ceasefires with the US and Turkey and undertaking diplomatic initiatives in Geneva and Astana, Russia was willing to play a leading role in conflict management and peacemaking in order to acquire status symbols. To fulfill its desire for enhanced status, Russia pursued more active policies, such as organizing the Astana process in 2017 and establishing the de-escalation zones in Syria. Russia also used its leverage to balance the interests of the regional actors in Syria in an effort to resolve the conflict and establish order.

Although Russia and the US were fighting a common enemy they did not reach an agreement on Syria, Ukraine, missile defense, NATO enlargement, and the sanctions imposed on Russia. The prospects of improving American-Russian relations hinged on stopping NATO enlargement and removing the sanctions. The idea that Russia would force Iran out of Syria was unrealistic. American strategy was to reduce Iranian influence in Syria. However, Russia would not cooperate in the undermining of its influence in Syria for the sake of a partnership with the US. Russia was back as a global force after decades of humiliation, and the US, after the election of Trump, seemed divided and still had no clear strategy on Syria. Stabilizing Syria required an American-Russian agreement and cooperation between the regional actors, including Saudi Arabia, Iran, and Turkey, to end the conflicts in Yemen and Iraq. Shortly, if the US wanted stability in the ME, it should help broker a new balance of power to end the proxy wars and accommodate Russia's status aspirations. The next chapter will further examine Russia's status-seeking strategy, regional diplomacy, its key role in the Syrian peace process, and its growing clout in the ME.

5

Russian Diplomacy, War, and Peace Making, 2017–19

Chapter 5 examines and analyzes diplomatic and military developments from 2017 until 2019 within the context of Russia's status-seeking strategy. I examine how the geopolitical objectives of the regional players hampered Russia's conflict management and peacemaking efforts. The regional players tried to shape the Geneva talks in their interests. Although Russian diplomacy succeeded in negotiating regional divides between Iran and Israel and between Turkey and Syria, American-Russian relations did not improve due to the international disagreement between Russia and the West over the handling of the conflict in Ukraine and Syria. Issues of global security, armaments, and the withdrawal of the US from the Iranian nuclear deal had additional negative impacts on American-Russian relations and the peaceful settlement of the Syrian conflict. I argue that American-Turkish tensions over the US-backed SDF, Turkish incursions in Syria to blunt Kurdish expansionism, and Israeli attacks on Iranian and Syrian targets in Syria created further obstacles to Russia's willingness to negotiate a mutually accepted agreement in Syria. In this chapter too, Russia's power politics in Syria will be analyzed vis-à-vis the three key factors of identity, opportunity, and costs. I also argue that although Russia was recognized as an indispensible geopolitical actor in the region its status-seeking strategy did not reverse its inconsistent power status. Russia still believed that achieving great power status was connected to its capability and significant influence on the international conflict management in Syria. In addition to Moscow's status-seeking strategy, Russia used the strategies of social competition and social creativity to enhance its current status. Yet, acknowledging Russia's self-defined great power status entailed eliciting acts of recognition by others.

Syria's internal conflict was entirely intertwined within regional and international dimensions. It was impossible to reach a settlement without constructive dialogue among the external powers. Russia seemed to accept that there could be no military solution to the civil war and that boosting ties with the US would help bring stability to Syria and the ME. Presumably, the US would also address problems in its relationship with Russia and explore opportunities where both powers could work together in areas of common interest around the globe, like disarmament and fighting terrorism. On 7 July 2017, Trump discussed the Syrian conflict with Putin on the sidelines of the G20 summit in Hamburg, Germany and reiterated that "now it was time to move forward in working constructively with Russia."[1] Putin sat down as an equal to Trump, while attending the gathering with more than a dozen other top leaders from Europe. Russia could hardly be called isolated. The most concrete deliverable from the meeting was a ceasefire in southwestern Syria near the cities of Deraa, Qunaitra, and Swaida.

This agreement was significant mostly because the region was of interest to US allies Jordan and Israel. Both countries share a border with the southern part of Syria and had been concerned about violence from Syria's war. As such, the ceasefire was a small win for Trump. Meeting with Trump was also a win for Russian diplomacy. This opportunity allowed Putin "to showcase his own skills as a negotiator, holding firm to Russia's longstanding positions on hacking, Syria and Ukraine, but also putting the final nail in the coffin of the previous U.S. Administration's policy of isolation."[2] Moscow hoped that Trump could act to roll back the sanctions. However, amid investigations into possible collusion with Moscow by Trump's campaign, any deal with Putin would expose Trump to more criticism by Congress. For example, Trump was not sure whether the joint US-Russian cyber security group he discussed with Putin might really be created.[3] Elizabeth Rosenberg, a senior fellow at the Center for a New American Security, reiterated that, "there was a tremendous and unprecedented effort by Congress to assert its influence in Russia and foreign policy because it did not trust the President."[4]

The deal marked "a new level of involvement for the U.S." in trying to resolve the Syrian conflict.[5] Yet, it was unclear whether this separate ceasefire would be a model for wider US-Russian cooperation in Syria and commit the US to the multilateral Astana process. It could be argued that Washington was willing to cede territorial and strategic control of Syria to Russia. The most telling sign of this was that Russia, by using its leverage, had signed multiple bilateral agreements with opposition factions to de-escalate violence in the safe zones.

To break the stalemate, President Emmanuel Macron reversed France's stance by saying that there was "no legitimate successor to Assad at this time" because if al-Assad was weakened IS and Islamists would gain strength.[6] Evidently, the French position stemmed from Macron's willingness to initiate dialogue with Russia in light of the vacuum left by the US, which had no clear policy beyond defeating IS.

Given the change in the French, Russian, and US positions after six failed rounds of UN-brokered peace talks in Geneva, the seventh round (Geneva VII) began on 10 July 2017. De Mistura tried to reconcile the Saudi-backed HNC and the opposition groups, known as the Cairo and Moscow platforms, to come up with "a more inclusive and perhaps even more pragmatic approach" to negotiations.[7] The Moscow and Cairo platforms were named after the cities where they first convened with Russia's approval and support. Both platforms were less opposed to al-Assad than the HNC. The Geneva talks focused on four topics: a new constitution, governance, elections, and fighting terrorism. There was no breakthrough.

The Geneva talks coincided with talks held in Amman between Jordanian, Russian, and US experts, who agreed on a memorandum to monitor the de-escalation zone in the southwest of Syria in Deraa, Quneitra, and Souweida. These talks were the first peacemaking effort by the US government in the war. Tillerson stated that the de-escalation zones could serve as a foundation for future US-Russian cooperation toward a broader political settlement.[8] Preceding the Geneva VII talks, the regime and rebel delegates who met in Astana (Astana V) on 4–5 July 2017, failed to reach an agreement on the exact boundaries of the de-escalation zones. In Astana, Turkey and Iran reportedly wrangled to bolster their influence, the rebels refused to have Iran monitor the safe zone in Homs province and Russia hinted that there could be a need to involve the US and Jordan in southern Syria.[9] On 24 July, Russian forces succeeded in setting up checkpoints and observation posts in the southwest and in eastern Ghouta, near Damascus, that had been under opposition control for much of the six-year-old conflict.

The regional and international players in Syria continued to pursue their geopolitical agendas. On 13 July, Turkey, at odds over the US-backing of the SDF in Syria, agreed to pay $2.5 billion for Russia's

S-400 air defense system. By doing so, Turkey violated the US sanctions on Russia. Russia would transfer some of the technology to Turkey, which was one of Ankara's consistent requirements. Turkey wanted to show NATO that it had a strategic choice in its relationships.[10] Russian-Turkish military cooperation would boost Moscow's influence in the ME. In Syria, Russia and Turkey needed to cooperate with each other to achieve their security and geostrategic interests, mainly for economic and political security in the Caucasus. Turkey also leaked the locations of ten US bases in northern Syria. Still, Ankara refused to allow a German delegation to visit German troops in Turkey's important NATO base, Incirlik. The Turkish moves were an indication of the strained relations between Turkey and the West. Geopolitically, "Turkey used its relationship with Russia as leverage vis-à-vis European and NATO partners; whereas Putin saw Turkey as a wedge he could drive into NATO and transatlantic solidarity."[11]

As for the US, Washington unveiled new economic sanctions against Iran because it was concerned about Tehran's "malign activities" in the ME that undermined US interests in Iraq, Yemen, and Lebanon. The Trump administration said that although Iran was complying with the nuclear agreement of July 2015 it was in "default of the spirit of the accord and Washington would look for ways to strengthen it."[12]

As part of US efforts to improve relations with Russia and to stabilize Syria, on 20 July 2017 the Trump administration decided to halt the CIA's covert program to equip and train certain rebel groups in Syria that were fighting the al-Assad regime. David Ignatius wrote, "the CIA-backed fighters were so divided politically, and so interwoven with extremist opposition groups, that the rebels could never offer a viable political future."[13] In addition, the defection of Jordan and Turkey from the anti-Assad alliance had rendered the US-supported rebels more isolated and ineffective. It should be noted that the Russia-Ukraine conflict posed the largest impediment to restoring a more normal relationship between Russia and the US. Moscow, which understood Israel's security concerns, did not prevent Israeli aircraft from bombing Iranian targets in Syria. Netanyahu was caught on a live microphone making a rare public admission that Israel had targeted Iranian arms convoys in Syria bound for Hizbullah, Iran's proxy, "dozens and dozens of times."[14] The airstrikes came amid heightened tensions over Iran's growing reach in Syria. Firouznia, disclosed that "Iran and Russia were unable to stop Israel from intervening in Syria because there were 'red lines.' Moscow did not want a confrontation with the West."[15] Firouznia also disclosed that "Hizbullah was an extension of Iran in Syria. Hizbullah had a particular position and there are lines to provide the needs of the party."[16]

In response to a US Senate vote on 27 July to impose tougher sanctions on Russia for its meddling in the 2016 presidential election and to further punish Russia for its 2014 annexation of the Crimea, the Russian foreign ministry ordered the US to reduce its diplomatic and technical staff at its embassy in Moscow and diplomatic missions in other Russian cities to 455. The US had 1,200 employees in Russia at the time.[17] The staff cuts were actually a delayed response to Obama's decision in December 2016 to expel thirty-five Russian diplomats and seize diplomatic compounds in the US. Russia's retaliation would put Trump in a position where his administration would not be able to strike any "grand bargain" with Moscow because the US Congress "would have to sign off. That included deals like trading Russia's cooperation in Syria, Afghanistan and North Korea for acquiescing to Russian interests in Ukraine."[18] In addition, Trump's advisers clashed over the direction of US foreign policy toward Israel and Iran. Moscow was forced to retaliate against the US Congress's tough new sanctions legislation. Lavrov confirmed that Russia was still ready to normalize bilateral relations and "cooperate on the most important international issues." However, cooperation was possible "only on the basis of equality, mutual respect, and balancing of interests."[19]

Calling the proposed sanctions "extremely cynical" Putin said the demarche looked like an attempt by Washington to use its "geopolitical advantages at the expense of its allies." Putin added that "it was very sad" to sacrifice US-Russian relations at the expense of resolving internal policy issues in the US. It was "a pity" because both powers acting together "could solve jointly the most acute problems that worry the peoples of Russia and the U.S. much more efficiently."[20] On 3 August Trump signed the sanctions bill "for the sake of national unity" as he said.[21] By the end of August, the Trump administration ordered Russia to close its consulate in San Francisco and two diplomatic annexes in New York and Washington. However, "the Administration seemed eager to contain the fallout, casting the move as a straightforward return to diplomatic parity between the countries rather than the latest volley in an increasingly combative relationship."[22]

The new sanctions on Russia did jeopardize the dialogue between Putin and Trump that had begun at the G-20 summit in Germany.

Sanctions relief was important to Russia's broader objective of being recognized as great power. Russia's ambition to be on equal footing with the US had already suffered a setback in 2014 when Obama authorized sanctions against sectors of the Russian economy. Russia's overreach aimed at undermining and hollowing out the US-led international order, "with its norms of economic openness, democratic accountability and the rule of law."[23] For the Kremlin, setting the guiding principles of global order was a key foreign policy issue.

Concerning the Russian forces in Syria, Putin signed a law ratifying a deal with the Syrian government allowing Russia to keep its forces at the Humeimeem air base for forty-nine years with the option of extending the arrangement for twenty-five-year periods.[24] On the military front, IS was quickly losing territory in Syria in separate campaigns waged by the Russian-backed regime forces and the US-backed SDF, whose main enemy was Turkey. Yet, after the liberation of Raqqa, the SDF would have no choice but to abandon the city to the regime forces in exchange for informal autonomy for the Kurdish cantons because there was no guarantee that the US would stick around in Syria once IS was defeated. Zasypkin stressed to the author that, "it was in the interest of the Kurds to approach the regime to negotiate on the prospects of establishing autonomy if the issue was put on the agenda." Zasypkin disclosed that, "Russia collaborated with the Kurds and the Turks to fight terrorism. The Turks were struggling to deport the terrorists." The Russian ambassador also acknowledged that, "the external parties to the conflict had divergent interests."[25] In effect, the US was offering victory to al-Assad and his allies. The next section of this chapter examines military and diplomatic developments in 2017.

WAR AND PEACE-MAKING ATTEMPTS IN 2017

The identity vector is crucial to understanding Russia's power politics in Syria. Moscow wanted to preserve its centrality in international conflict management as the embodiment of its international status. Maximizing Russia's leverage, on 3 August 2017 Moscow reached an agreement with the moderate opposition regarding the third de-escalation zone north of the city of Homs, paving the way for the delivery of sorely needed humanitarian relief to rebel-held areas.[26] However, beyond these de-escalatory tactics and notwithstanding the al-Assad regime's military momentum, a political solution appeared distant. By taking advantage of the truce in Deraa, the Russian and

Iranian-backed regime forces marched eastward to the IS-held Deir al-Zour province bordering Iraq, whose oil resources were critical to the state. The Syrian regime and its supporters would work assiduously to prevent the US-backed SDF from reaching the al-Omar oil field. In the recent prior months, militants fleeing US-backed offensives in the Iraqi city of Mosul and Raqqa had fled to Deir al-Zour. All the while, US and Russian military officials had been communicating regularly in order to draw a line on the map separating US- and Russian-backed forces, which were waging parallel campaigns in Deir al-Zour province. The Euphrates River divided the zones of control: Russia and the regime to the south and west, and the US and SDF to the north and east. So far, negotiations had failed because, as Barbara Walter rightly argued, "the outside enforcers [in this case Russia] did not guarantee the terms and the commitments to disarm, demobilize and disengage" the adversaries' military forces and prepare for peace.[27]

The regional and Western rebel patrons recognized that al-Assad was staying. Thus, In August, at a two-day meeting in Riyadh, the Saudi-backed HNC was told to bridge differences between the opposition groups and formulate "a new vision" in light of the new political and military reality.[28] However, the HNC and the Cairo and Moscow platforms were on full display. The disagreements reflected the changing priorities of the different oppositions' main backers – the US, Europe, Turkey, Qatar, and Saudi Arabia, which were now more concerned with preserving their own narrowly conceived strategic interests than they were with toppling al-Assad. Saudi Arabia wanted to contain its regional archrival Iran as well as reduce the influence of Qatar, which was seen as a key backer to the HNC. Likewise, Turkey's top priority was to contain the US-backed Kurdish PYD in northern Syria.

No doubt, defeating IS was important for Russia and the US, but the US, according to Frederic Hof, "should focus on post-IS stabilization in the east of the country if it hoped to block widening Iranian control" and make peace.[29] In addition, the prospects for cooperation between the US and Russia hit a low level when Trump signed the new sanctions bill. However, Russian Prime Minister Dmitry Medvedev reiterated that Moscow remained "open for cooperation with the U.S. in the spheres where it saw it useful for Russia and international security, including the settlement of regional conflicts."[30]

While the regime forces and the US-backed SDF alliance advanced in separate offensives in Deir al-Zour, on 15 September 2017 Russia, Iran, and Turkey struck a deal in Astana to jointly police the fourth de-escalation zone around rebel-held Idlib province on the border with Turkey and called for the end of hostilities in mainly opposition-held areas. The Astana VI talks were also attended by representatives of the regime and opposition, the UN, and observers from the US and Jordan.[31] Russia had so far deployed military police to patrol the boundaries of three agreed zones in the south, in eastern Ghouta, and in part of central Homs province. Russia increasingly sought to depict itself as a peacemaker and humanitarian donor in the war-devastated country. Borrowing from Ronald Fisher, the question was how Russia, Turkey, and Iran would coordinate to enhance the effectiveness and efficiency of the Astana process. The hope was that they could coordinate by "information sharing, resource sharing, collaborative strategizing and collaboration through partnership" in order to contribute to the conflict resolution effort.[32] It should be stressed that the agreement on creating de-escalation zones was the result of Moscow's diplomacy and leverage to "safeguard its own interests in Syria, while giving Russia's allies and rivals the impression of also satisfying their respective agendas."[33] Evidently, the agreement on the de-escalation zones would help formerly legitimize the Russian-Iranian-Syrian strategy to surround and ultimately defeat rebels in eastern Ghouta and in northern Homs.

Since its military intervention in 2015, Russia had changed the balance of power on the ground and adopted a policy of dealing with the external and internal actors. After stabilizing the al-Assad regime, Russia's strategy foresaw that the ultimate success for a peace settlement hinged upon a stable regional environment and cooperation between neighbours who would support the peace process. Thus, Turkey's agreement to buy Russian S-400 air defense missile systems and its acknowledgment that the Astana process was achieving results, and Saudi Arabia's cooperation with Russia in coaxing the opposition to unite for peace talks had greater merit. Russia also kept open channels of communication to all sides, from Iran to Saudi Arabia and the Palestinian Hamas movement to Israel. Internally, to prevent risks that would come from spoilers and to regain its global clout, Russia negotiated intraregional divides in different parts of the ME.

Concurrently, at the global level and to back its status-seeking strategy with shows of force, Russian nuclear-capable TU-95MS strategic bombers flew a rare mission around the Korean Peninsula in August 2017 while the US and South Korea were conducting joint military exercises to the infuriation of North Korea.[34] In the meantime, North

Korea fired a midrange ballistic missile that flew over Japan and splashed into the northern Pacific Ocean. Trump warned that all options were on the table for the US to respond to North Korea's actions. For its part, North Korea, a former Soviet satellite state, vowed to never give up its nuclear program because it was necessary to counter hostility from the US and its allies. Apparently, North Korea's race to test missiles was an effort to prepare the strongest possible bargaining position before negotiations with the US. Trump's warning was hollow, as he needed both Russia's and China's help to avoid war with North Korea. China could stop the smuggling of oil to North Korea. To gain Russia's help on North Korea and Syria, Trump seemed "to give Putin a pass." During his Asia trip in mid-November 2017, in a Hanoi news conference Trump said, "people don't realize Russia has been very, very heavily sanctioned. It's now time to get back to healing a world that is shattered and broken … And I feel that having Russia in a friendly posture, as opposed to always fighting with them, is an asset to the world."[35] Russia, as a status-seeking power, would be willing to assume responsibilities associated with mediating international conflicts, such as the standoff between the US and North Korea.

On 4 September 2017, the BRICS countries, at a summit in China, denounced North Korea's nuclear test, called for tougher measures against terrorist groups, and stressed that the only lasting peace to the crisis in Syria was through an inclusive "Syrian-led, Syrian-owned" political process which safeguards the sovereignty and territorial integrity of the country. Also, the declaration issued by the BRICS leaders "strongly supported the Geneva peace talks and the Astana process."[36] Russia and China used the summit as a showcase for their growing international status and as Tsygankov noted for their "proposed solutions to issues in world politics."[37] Similarly, the BRICS countries sought to enlarge the organization's presence on the world stage and called for a "comprehensive reform" of the UN and the Security Council "with a view to making it more representative and efficient.[38]

As the world grappled with North Korea's nuclear and ballistic missile development, Trump, in his speech to the UN General Assembly on 20 September 2017, called the UN-backed Iran nuclear deal "an embarrassment" to the US. Trump also called Tehran a "corrupt dictatorship" and a "murderous regime." For his part, Rouhani declared that Iran would "respond decisively and resolutely to" the violation of the nuclear deal "by any party." He added that it would be a pity if the agreement was destroyed by "rogue newcomers to the world of politics." Responding to Netanyahu's allegation that Iran had embarked on a "campaign of conquest across the ME," Rouhani said, "While Iran had continuously rejected nuclear weapons it was reprehensible that the Zionist regime threatening the region with its nuclear arsenal had the audacity to preach to peaceful nations."[39] On 22 September, during a military parade in Tehran that commemorated the Iran-Iraq war in the 1980s, Iran's Revolutionary Guard unveiled its latest ballistic missile, which was capable of reaching much of the ME, including Israel. Addressing the parade, Rouhani vowed that Iran would not halt its missile program, which was not strictly prohibited by the nuclear deal, to boost its military capabilities. He added that Tehran would keep supporting the "oppressed peoples of Yemen, Syria and Palestine."[40]

Compliant with the strategy of social creativity, Russia moved from a military posture to that of a mediator and took new steps to establish bilateral agreements directly with armed opposition groups on the ground in the same areas where the Astana de-escalation agreements were announced. For example, Russia signed separate agreements with Jaish al-Islam and Jaish al-Tawhid. Russia's mediatory role would enable Moscow to achieve prestige. However, the de-escalation agreements that were based on Russian unilateral guarantee lacked an international guarantor for the opposition and were without international legal mechanisms such as the UNSC. Evidently, as Dmitry Trenin wrote, Moscow sought "a balance in the region that would maximize its gain without losing credibility with either party."[41]

Regional powers acquired greater potential to affect the situational dynamics of the Syrian conflict. On 5 October 2017, Putin hosted Saudi King Salman for talks at the Kremlin to cement a relationship that was crucial for stabilizing world oil prices and to decide the outcome of the conflict in Syria. King Salman, who was a US ally, tried to persuade Moscow to scale down its ties with Tehran and said that Iran "must stop meddling in the internal affairs of the countries in the region and halt its activities to destabilize" the ME.[42] Iran had spread its influence in the region, particularly in Iraq and Syria. Saudi Arabia was at war with Iranian-allied rebels in Yemen and embroiled in a diplomatic standoff with Qatar, which was supported by Tehran. Trump, in defiance of world powers and to get tough on Iran, decertified the 2015 nuclear deal despite Tehran's compliance with its terms. For Trump, Iran "was not living up to the spirit of the deal."[43] Trump's ambiguous approach toward Iran suggested that the US wanted to get a better deal. However, there was no indication that Russia would support the US position and sacrifice Iran or change its posture in Syria although arms sales to Iran suggested that Moscow had some leverage over its client.

Multiple regional interests posed an obstacle to ending the Syrian civil war. Indeed, on 13 October Turkey's military began setting up observation posts in Idlib which was largely controlled by Hay'at Tahrir al-Sham (HTS). Western powers, Iran, and Russia considered HTS a terrorist group that must be destroyed. Turkey's deployment of about thirty military vehicles into Idlib, through the Bab al-Hawa crossing, was facilitated by an understanding between Ankara and HTS to stop the YPG from linking Afrin with a larger area that it controlled in northwestern Syria.[44] The deployment allowed the Turkish military to surround the YPG-held territory from all sides, enabling Ankara to besiege the area.

Within this context, on 16 October, the US-backed SDF seized the city of Raqqa from IS. This was a major blow to the militant group, which had long used the city as the de facto capital of its self-declared caliphate. The SDF also focused their operations in rural Deir al-Zour and seized a major natural gas field. In the same month, Russian-backed Syrian troops and Iranian-backed fighters took nearly all of the provincial capital of Deir al-Zour.[45] The military moves of the regime and its allies reflected a convergence of military and political interests. The regime needed to retake Deir al-Zour and its natural resources to improve its vision for a solution in Syria. Iran also needed to take control of the area to protect its investment in the Syrian war. As for Russia, it wanted to preserve its position within the balance of power in Syria and to exploit that balance in negotiations with the US in the framework of a comprehensive peace agreement that would protect its national interests and its posture globally at a time when the US administration had no comprehensive strategy for Syria. Given the overlapping interests of the regional powers, it is reasonable to argue that the US had to lay out a broad blueprint for any future negotiations at the regional level.

From an American perspective, the ousting of IS from Raqqa was a milestone in the US fight against terrorism and a step toward a political transition and a lasting peace in Syria. It should be noted that when the Trump administration came into office it espoused the view that the departure of al-Assad was not a prerequisite before the transitional process began. At the regional level, Rouhani declared that Iran's position in the ME had never been stronger. He reiterated that, "in Iraq, Syria, Lebanon, northern Africa and the Persian Gulf region no action could be taken without Iran."[46] Firouznia, for his part, also stressed to the author "Iran's stabilizing role in Iraq and Syria and preventing the partitioning of both countries."[47] As noted by Barry Buzan, most civil wars were usually embedded in the politics of a "regional security complex" that had significant implications for both peacemaking and conflict resolution.[48] This suggests that the success of a peace settlement in Syria was inextricably tied to the interests of neighbouring regional powers and their overall commitment to the Geneva and its parallel Astana peace processes. Renato Corbetta and Molly Melin supported the notion that "conflict management efforts … required the presence of strategic interests."[49] Both authors asserted that mediators' activities were targeted towards broadening their zone of influence, resources, and power. Thus, the peace-builder had a role in influencing the disputed outcome and in reshaping the political environment according to its own benefits (i.e. its strategic interests). Therefore, Iran and Turkey could stand in the way of the Geneva peace process if they felt that their strategic interests were threatened by a settlement.

After the defeat of IS in Raqqa on 30 October 2017, a new round of talks began in Astana (Astana VII). Russia's chief negotiator, Alexander Lavrentiyev, disclosed that Russia was ready to host a Congress of National Dialogue, inviting both regime and opposition delegates to the Russian city of Sochi.[50] The congress could be considered a CBM between the warring parties. For the first time, the Kurds would be invited too in a major diplomatic push to end the war. However, objections came from Turkey, which viewed the SDF as a national security threat and from two main opposition groups, the SCN and the HNC. Both groups considered the congress an attempt to circumvent the Geneva process.

At the systemic level, good relationships between the great powers and the changing dynamics of their competition at the global level had a major impact on the possibilities of diplomacy and resolution of regional conflicts. At the subsystemic level, changes in the behaviour of both the regional actors Iran and Turkey was crucial for the success of the peace process in Syria. Putin's visit to Iran on 1 November 2017 should be analyzed within this context. Putin, who was accompanied by Azerbaijani President Ilham Aliyev, hailed cooperation with Iran on the Syrian conflict mainly because both Moscow and Tehran wanted to marginalize US hegemony in the region and establish a balance of power. Putin also vocally backed the 2015 Iran nuclear agreement and called for the improvement of transport links, trade, and energy cooperation between the three Caspian States. During the visit, Russia's state-owned Rosneft oil firm and the National Iranian Oil Company signed a roadmap deal to develop joint projects in Iran worth up to $30 billion.[51]

Russia and the US advocated the expansion of the 7 July ceasefire in the southwestern zone bordering Israel and Jordan. After they met on the sidelines of a regional summit in Vietnam on 10 November, Putin and Trump issued a presidential joint statement saying there was "no military solution" to the war in Syria.[52] Yet, Israel, which had expressed to Putin concern about Iran's presence in Syria, signalled that it would keep up military strikes across its frontier to prevent any encroachment by Iranian-allied forces, even if the US and Russia tried to consolidate the ceasefire. It is plausible to argue that the US could tell Russia to do its part to prevent the widening of regional conflict. In terms of opportunity and in exchange, "Washington could offer Russia a chance to be treated as a world power and on an equal footing with the U.S., a longtime priority for Putin."[53] Yet, Russia's violation of the 1987 INF Treaty by testing intermediate-range ground, air, and sea launched cruise missiles on 26 October 2017 confronted the US.[54] Moscow claimed that Washington had already violated the treaty in the sense that the launchers for the US SM-3 missile interceptors in Romania could hold ground-launched cruise missiles, in violation of the INF Treaty.

In light of the overlapping interests of the regional powers it remained unclear if Russia's power politics in Syria could win the peace and enhance its status. The difficulty for Moscow was to balance its military success with a political process and put an end to the war. The dilemma was that al-Assad wanted to control all of Syria, while Russia wanted a negotiated solution with the opposition. On 9 November, the Syrian army spearheaded by Hizbullah fighters captured Albukamal, IS's last stronghold on the border with Iraq, bringing the self-declared caliphate close to complete downfall. The regime did not respect de-escalation zones unless they suited its agenda. After his visit to Iran, on 14 November Putin hosted Erdogan, his Turkish counterpart, in Sochi in an effort to create conditions for dialogue that would help resolve the Syrian conflict.[55] Despite calling for al-Assad to step down, Ankara was now more compromising behind closed doors in Sochi. Firouznia attributed Turkey's "compromising position to the military and political achievements of Russia and the axis of resistance. Iran's joint work with Turkey and Russia would continue irrespective of policy differences over Syria."[56] It was more important for Turkey to keep its say in the future political negotiations. On 20 November in Sochi, Putin also hosted al-Assad ahead of a summit between Russia, Turkey, and Iran. The next day Putin called Trump and informed him that al-Assad was ready to abide by a political settlement, including constitutional reform and the holding of parliamentary and presidential elections.[57] In an apparent flurry of diplomacy on Syria, Putin also spoke with Saudi King Salman, Israeli Prime Minister Netanyahu, and Egyptian leader al-Sisi. Putin had put himself at the centre stage of talks over Syria's future. On 16 November, Russia politically protected the regime by vetoing for the tenth time a US-sponsored UNSC Resolution calling for the renewal of an international inquiry into who was to blame for chemical weapons attack in Syria.

These meetings were followed by a trilateral summit between Putin, Erdogan, and Rouhani in Sochi on 22 November 2017. Putin emphasized that the Syrian people should decide their fate and that the political process necessitated concessions from both the regime and the opposition. He also reiterated that cooperation between the three powers prevented the partitioning of Syria and the defeat of the terrorist groups.[58] There seemed to be a greater convergence between Turkey's Syria policy and Russia's and Iran's Syria policy. However, at the same time, Ankara and Washington shared an interest in countering Russia's and Iran's influence in Syria and in shaping the country's future as the UN-backed peace talks were due in Geneva. The resolution of the Syrian conflict required a combination of regional and international strategies to deal with the communal, regional, and geopolitical dimensions of the conflict. Hence, on 23 November Riyadh hosted a meeting of opposition groups backed by the Gulf countries, Russia, and Egypt in order to unify the stance of the opposition and reach common ground between the divergent views on al-Assad's role in the transitional period.[59] Al-Assad's role had always been the sticking point in previous rounds of talks. The various opposition groups chose Nasr Hariri as head of the HNC, replacing the more hardline opponent of al-Assad Riyadh Hijab to lead the opposition delegation in the coming Geneva talks. For the first time since the beginning of the conflict the opposition called on the UN to arrange direct talks with the Syrian government.

On 28 November 2017, the eighth round of the peace talks in Geneva (Geneva VIII) got underway with an expanded opposition delegation, which met de Mistura and asked him to pressure al-Assad to engage in reaching a political solution within six months. Russia, which wanted to politically seal the military advances it had achieved, conducted back-channel diplomacy with key world powers. The government delegation quit the talks and would not return unless the opposition withdrew a statement demanding that al-Assad play no role in any interim postwar government. Even if the opposition and its supporters managed to remove al-Assad, there was no guarantee of a successful outcome. One could argue that Russia had become the primary mediator, which resulted in one-sided negotiations. De Mistura, who refused preconditions, wanted an "inclusive process" and stressed that the talks would be guided by UNSC Resolution 2254, which mandated a political transition for Syria that was becoming more unrealistic. De Mistura sought the support of the five permanent members of the Security Council to achieve progress.[60] On the agenda there were four main issues: elections, governance, drafting a constitution, and fighting terrorism. De Mistura published a document suggesting twelve principles for future Syria including that the country "shall be democratic and non-sectarian" and hoped that the two sides would agree.[61]

The latest round of the Geneva VIII talks collapsed, with a deflated de Mistura admitting that "a golden opportunity" had been missed. De Mistura blamed the government delegation because it refused to discuss two potential agenda items: a constitutional process and presidential elections, insisting instead that it would only discuss terrorism. Moreover, there would be no progress in the UN-sponsored talks "if the government was not willing to meet anyone who had a different opinion."[62] With a military advantage on his side and without pressure from his Russian sponsor, comfortable al-Assad was not interested in real negotiations. Also, there was no mutually hurting stalemate (MHS) because the regime was confident of winning the war. Apparently, Russia's leverage on al-Assad was limited. The collapse of the talks meant the political initiative to negotiate a settlement now rested largely with Putin – mainly because the balance of power undeniably favoured Russia – who convened a Syrian Congress of National Dialogue (CND) in Sochi.

In a surprise visit to Syria's Humeimeem air base on 10 December 2017, Putin declared victory over IS on both banks of the Euphrates River and over the Western-backed rebels, adding that the focus would then switch to the political process. He declared that a "significant part" of the Russian force could return home. Russia's partial withdrawal of its troops was unlikely to cause much concern in Tehran. Iran would still be able to operate in Syria and reap the rewards of its intervention by planning the direction of the offensives on the ground. Evidently, "Putin was keen to leverage the heightened ME influence that Syria had given him to cast himself as a leader who could do diplomacy as well as military force."[63] A real test for Russia was how the Syrian and Iranian ambitions would play out in the de-escalation zones so that Russia could balance its desire to step back with the need to stand behind its allies. Putin, who sought to bolster his support at home by reviving Moscow's global clout, announced that he would seek re-election in March 2018.[64] Putin's visit to Syria came amidst a flurry of ME diplomacy and after Trump's decision on 6 December to recognize Jerusalem as Israel's capital. Trump's decision reversed decades of US and international policy on Jerusalem and angered US allies in the region and worldwide. Although for Israel Trump's decision was "an important step toward peace" it would aggravate conflict in the volatile ME.[65] Palestinian President Mahmoud Abbas called the US a "dishonest mediator" and said the Palestinians "would no longer accept" an American-sponsored peace process.[66] Although Israel was still Russia's friend, Moscow could do little in the Palestinian-Israeli conflict because its priority remained Syria and its posture on the world stage. After his visit to Syria, Putin flew to Egypt and Turkey to discuss the next steps of the Syrian peace process.

The release of the US National Defense Strategy (NDS) of 2018, on 18 December 2017, emphasized that, "inter-state competition, not terrorism, was now the primary concern in U.S. national security." The strategy said that China and Russia "challenge American power, influence and interests, attempting to erode American security and prosperity." The NDS classified China and Russia as "revisionist powers" that wanted to change the global status quo and "to shape a world consistent with their authoritarian model." The strategy detailed that rogue regimes such as North Korea and Iran were destabilizing regions through their pursuit of nuclear weapons or their sponsorship of terrorism. The NDS acknowledged an "increasingly complex global security environment characterized by overt challenges to the free and open international order and the re-emergence of long-term, strategic competition between nations."[67] Thus, the US should not presume that engaging with its rivals "would turn them into benign actors and trustworthy partners."[68] The way within which Russia was described in the US NDS supports H1. The US, being the dominant power, was unlikely to accommodate Russia's aspirations for higher status because Russia was seen as a revisionist power and a threat in terms of both security and status as a socio-psychological goal, especially if its status goals were accommodated. Russia's annexation of Crimea was a revisionist move, not typical of status-inconsistent powers. In Syria, Russia's use of power politics as a means to enhance its status seemed counterintuitive. Yet, it was unlikely that Russia would change its power-based foreign policy because Syria was of strategic interest to Moscow. But Russia would bear the costs of status-seeking strategy and, potentially, the risk of conflict with the US over global issues.

US National Security Advisor General H.R. McMaster recognized the US-led global order and criticized the "sphere of influence" strategy in which the US retreated and allowed Russia and China to extend their global influence. Russia used Syria to set the guiding principles of global order. From his perspective, recognition of a Russian or Chinese sphere of influence would dishonour the US.[69] Such rhetoric suggested that great power military competition would not "facilitate conflict resolution and settlement processes by bringing pressure to bear on client states and other parties to the conflict" in Syria and elsewhere.[70]

The Kremlin responded to McMaster's statements by saying that his allegations "were groundless and not backed by facts, and that Russia did not indulge in sophisticated subversion in the U.S."[71] Still, the Kremlin denounced "the imperialist" character of the document and "its refusal to renounce a unipolar world." Beijing and Moscow had been promoting a vision of a multipolar world in which countries respected each other's national interests and did not try to impose their preferred systems through military force. However, the US viewed multipolarity as an encroachment on its unique status. China too described Trump's NDS as showing a "cold war mentality with an imperialist character."[72] On 17 December, Putin called Trump and expressed gratitude for the CIA information that helped prevent a series of planned terrorist attacks in St Petersburg. Yet, Putin's spokesperson, Dmitry Peskov, denounced the NDS saying that Moscow could not accept that Russia was "treated as a threat to the security of the U.S."[73] Ironically, the NDS contrasted significantly with Trump's previous friendly face-to-face encounters with Putin. Moscow considered the document as both "confrontational" and "anti-Russian."[74] Russia also hit back at a decision by EU leaders to extend the sanctions for six months, which mainly targeted the Russian banking, defense, and energy sectors.[75] In terms of costs, the sanctions had been imposed on Russia since its annexation of the Crimea in March 2014. Fighting in Syria would continue unless the US actively participated in helping create genuine negotiations and an equitable and legitimate political settlement.

After Putin ordered a partial withdrawal of Russian forces in Syria, the eighth round of the Astana talks (Astana VIII) began on 21 December 2017. The opposition delegation, along with representatives of the regime, Russia, Turkey, and Iran, discussed the list of invitees to the CND. De Mistura emphasized that "any political initiative by international actors should be assessed by its ability to contribute to and support the mandated political process under the UN in Geneva."[76] The Russian envoy, Lavrentiyev, saw no reason for US forces to remain in Syria. After having completed a partial withdrawal, Russia would keep three battalions of military police and officers at the Russian Center for Reconciliation (RCR) in Syria, as well as its two military bases in the country. At its base, the RCR routinely held peace talks with armed factions. Russia used "capability leverage" that relied on material coercion to impose "a settlement or carrots and sticks to alter disputants' bargaining range."[77] That is why Russia did not achieve long-term success.

Based on the above, the prospect of a settlement was dim, and the Syrian conflict was likely to bleed through 2018 and beyond. I argued that the postures of the regional powers were unlikely to change mainly because of their geopolitical and geoeconomic interests. Similarly, empowered al-Assad would seek to control all of Syria rather than render concessions to the opposition. Peace making attempts in the Geneva and Astana talks failed because the regime was not interested in real negotiations, and Russia was not willing to push al-Assad to the edge. Russia remained the main peace broker in Syria and succeeded in keeping the balance of power in the region by maintaining good relations with Turkey, Iran, Israel, Egypt, and Saudi Arabia. Yet, it failed to stop the violence on the ground. Although Russian mediation was not successful, Moscow still hoped that the CND could bridge the differences between the regime and opposition. However, without US-Russian dialogue on Syria, Ukraine, and global security issues, Moscow's power politics would not enhance its status.

The next section will address military and diplomatic developments from 2018 until 2019 within the context of Russia's status-seeking strategy.

WAR AND PEACE MAKING ATTEMPTS IN 2018–19

While the US and Russia were recalibrating their relationships and interventions in the ME, Turkey, Iran, and even subnational groups like the Kurds were trying to enhance their political impact in Syria. In January 2018, Russia, Syria, and Turkey strongly criticized a US plan to create a Kurdish-led border security force of 30,000 personnel in the Afrin area to "defend and preserve" part of northern Syria that was controlled by the US-backed SDF and prevent any IS resurgence there.[78] Currently, the SDF alliance, of which the YPG was the strongest, controlled roughly 25 per cent of Syrian territory in the north and east of the country. Tillerson argued that "the U.S. should keep, train and assist forces in northeast Syria to aid stabilization there."[79] Trump maintained and implemented an Obama-era policy to arm the YPG for the assault on Raqqa. With the battle over in 2017, Trump told Erdogan that the US would stop supplying weapons to the YPG. Yet, in practice the US engagement continued, though now it was apparently aimed more at weakening al-Assad than overthrowing him. While Ankara sought to prevent the potential legitimization that a border force would bring to the YPG, Damascus considered the plan a breach of Syria's sovereignty and territorial integrity.

Although Syria opposed Turkey's intervention, on 20 January 2018 an infuriated Turkey launched Operation Olive Branch to expel the YPG from Afrin and prevent the establishment of a Kurdish autonomous enclave. The US urged Turkey, whose forces approached Afrin, to exercise restraint and insure that the offensive was "limited in scope and duration."[80] Russia, which accepted Turkey's security concerns, blamed the crisis on US unilateral action and acknowledged the role of the Kurds in the peace process. However, according to Lavrov, "that role must work on a common platform" in that "all members of the Syrian political settlement must respect the sovereignty and territorial integrity of Syria."[81] Turkey, in return for Moscow's forbearance, would turn a blind eye to Russian and Syrian attacks on the rebels in Idlib province who were nominally allied with Turkey against the regime. Despite being officially demarcated as a de-escalation zone, regime forces made significant advances in Idlib, where most of the remaining jihadists were gathered. In mid-January, the government forces recaptured the strategic Abu Dhuhur airbase that had been under HTS control since 2015 and secured the road linking Damascus with Aleppo. The discord between the US and its NATO ally Turkey would rehabilitate Russia's relationship with Turkey and extend its diplomatic influence in the region. Politically speaking, the events playing out around Afrin served Russian, Iranian, and Turkish interests and significantly boosted the Astana process.

As Turkey threatened to expand the operation eastward to Manbij, where the US had deployed troops after Kurdish forces took control of the town in 2016, Washington acknowledged the "legitimate concerns" of Turkey and discussed with Ankara the creation of a thirty-kilometre security zone to ensure Turkey's border security.[82] Manbij was a disputed territory between the US and Turkey. Washington assured Turkey that the YPG would withdraw from the city and adjacent areas west of the Euphrates River. However, the YPG retained control of the area. On 22 January, Tillerson accused Russia and the Syrian government of violating the 21 August 2013 agreement on the removal of chemical weapons from Syria, when government forces allegedly used chlorine gas against the rebel-held eastern Ghouta.

The regional and international dimensions of the conflict had been the key source of difficulty in reaching a political settlement in Syria. On 26 January, while the ninth round of peace talks were being held in Vienna, which the SNC attended, five Western and Arab states that backed the rebellion – the US, Jordan, Britain, France, and Saudi Arabia – made recommendations to de Mistura for what they called a "practical approach" that would lead to a "slow political process." The five states' proposal, while not addressing al-Assad's fate, called for changes to the UN-led talks focusing on reforming the constitution, on holding elections for Syrians inside and outside the country, and on creating a "safe and neutral environment" for the vote. Furthermore, "all external supporters of the political process, should encourage both the opposition and government delegations, engage genuinely in the talks and at least initially, set aside other issues."[83] The document also called for the departure of all foreign militias, an apparent reference to the Iran-backed Shiite groups. The Vienna talks failed because the resolution of hostilities in Syria clearly required a combination of communal and international strategies to deal with the various communal, regional, and geopolitical dimensions of the conflict.

After the Vienna talks, on 29 January, Russia hosted the Syrian CND in Sochi with the primary aim of establishing a mechanism for drafting a new constitution. Compliant with the strategy of social creativity or to find new value dimensions in which Russia would be superior to the US as the most engaged global power in international conflict management, Russia's goal was to reshape the diplomatic process to fit the military and political reality. Although it was boycotted by the SNC, 1,500 delegates and few opponents of the Syrian regime, including some Kurds on an individual basis, attended the CND. Lavrov stated that the conditions were ripe to turn "a tragic page" in Syria's history.[84] According to Richard N. Haass's definition of ripeness in terms of "the prerequisites for diplomatic progress" or "the circumstances conducive for negotiated progress," Lavrov's statement could not be right.[85] Yet, "a shared perception of the desirability of an accord" and a willingness on the part of the conflicting parties to reach a compromise was questionable.[86] Although the absence of a MHS was one possible impediment to successful talks, Russia's efforts were hampered by the US, France, and Britain, who did not attend and said that talks must fall under UN auspices in order to reach a resolution. Thus, the Sochi talks showed the limits of Russian diplomacy as a means to preserve its influence in international politics and as a counterweight to US dominance. The Sochi Congress agreed to establish a 150-member committee representing most of Syrian society to draft a new constitution for the country without specifying how it would happen. In Vladimir Frolov's view, the Sochi talks were a "success in propaganda terms for both Moscow and Damascus, who sought to legitimize a substitute for the real talks with a fake opposition that had no followers on the ground."[87]

After the battle against IS was largely finished, the external powers shifted their focus of the conflict. Their struggle for regional influence, oil, and territory intensified. In February 2018, Turkey intensified its military campaign against the Syrian Kurds in Afrin, who proved to be a more reliable proxy of the US. The YPG sought help from the Syrian government to resist the Turkish thrust. Turkey would never tolerate a Kurdish military presence on the country's southern border and threatened to expand its Operation Olive Branch to the town of Manbij, calling it a bastion of terrorists and demanding that Kurdish and US forces withdraw to the east of the Euphrates River.[88] Turkey's war on the YPG in Afrin, to reshape military alignments in northern Syria and around Manbij, highlighted the true complexity of the Syrian crisis. Turkey and the US, both members of NATO, now faced a real risk of escalation that could lead to direct confrontation between their armed forces. The dilemma for the US was to find a way to reassure Turkey without abandoning the Kurds. After all, as Christopher R. Hill noted, "Western countries would need Turkey to counterbalance Russia, whose broader strategic agenda went beyond the ME."[89]

In another development, the Russian military fired cruise missiles from ships in the Mediterranean at rebel positions near Idlib in retaliation for the downing of its fighter jet.[90] As militants rejected an evacuation deal, similar to eastern Aleppo and Homs, Russian and Syrian warplanes pounded eastern Ghouta, which had been under siege since 2013. Two rebel groups, Jaish al-Islam and Failaq al-Rahman, were fighting in Ghouta. As the conflict endured, the biggest loser, meanwhile, was the civilian population, which had been the main victim of the civil war.

Israeli airstrikes against Iranian and Syrian forces were another indication of how dangerously tensions had escalated. Russia criticized the Israeli airstrikes but did not mention an Iranian drone's incursion into Israeli airspace. On 8 February, the US-led coalition hit back hard with airstrikes from US SOFs near oilfields on the east side of the Euphrates against troops supported by the regime, striking a headquarters of SDF and their partners.[91] It was likely that the regime would attempt to capture the lucrative gas and oil fields in the SDF-controlled area. The US had roughly two thousand troops in the country. Although the US military showed its overwhelming dominance in the areas it controlled in eastern Syria, the incident "demonstrated the fragility of the U.S. role in Syria politically and diplomatically."[92] Further escalation could involve Turkey, the US, Israel, Iran, and Russia. The US pledged not to withdraw from key strongholds in northern Syria where the SDF currently maintained control, so as to have any hope of maintaining influence, checking Russia in the great power competition in the region, preventing Iranian hegemony from Iran to Lebanon, and maintaining leverage for bargaining in Geneva. In order to prevent escalation and confrontation between Israel and Iran in Syria, "in theory, it fell to Russia, which entertained good relations with all the parties, to use its channels to help establish understanding between adversaries of each other's threat perceptions and red lines."[93]

Dissatisfied with its status, once again Russia turned to the strategy of social competition with the US to surpass Washington in its area of superiority, mainly strategic missiles. On 1 March 2018, three weeks before the presidential election, Putin used his state-of-the-nation address to unveil a new arsenal of hypersonic missiles and nuclear-capable underwater drones that would be impossible to intercept. Putin said that Russia also tested a new heavy intercontinental ballistic missile, called Smart, with a range that allowed it to fly over both the North and South poles to reach any target. By issuing defiant warnings to the West, Putin said that Russia could have taken such measures in 2004, but "no one listened to us then. So listen to us now."[94] Taking a stab at the US antimissile systems like the Aegis, whose elements Washington placed in Eastern Europe, Putin said, "I want to tell all who have fueled the arms race over the last 15 years, sought to win unilateral advantages over Russia, introduced unlawful sanctions aimed to contain our country's development. You have failed to contain Russia."[95] The Trump administration vowed to expand US nuclear strength and missile defenses at a cost of hundreds of billions of dollars while criticizing Russia's build up. In November 2018, Trump threatened to pull out of the 1987 INF Treaty with Russia, citing alleged violations of the accord by Moscow.

Underscoring the tension between Russia and the US, it was unwise for Washington to suddenly cancel talks on cyber security that were planned for late February 2018. Engaging Russia and preventing an arms race were undeniably crucial for global security. The Kremlin responded by cancelling planned discussions about strategic stability. Yet, both powers continued to hold consultations on de-escalation in the contested battle space of Syria.

Notwithstanding his warning, Putin left the door open to discuss new weapons systems with the US. Russia's military reach, beyond the regional context, gave Russia an opportunity to become a major power in the highly unequal international system. As argued above, Russia was following more power-based foreign policy to enhance its status. Putin stressed that "the growing Russian military power would guarantee global peace."[96] Although he talked about domestic matters and promised to cut the poverty rate, Putin chose to cite nuclear weapons, not economic achievements, as a crucial attribute of Russia's self-defined major power identity. How to drive diversification in an economy that was still dependent on oil and gas would be a major challenge for Putin.

In Syria, the two offensives, one backed by Russia and the other led by Turkey, showed how the external powers were trying to reshape the map of control after the defeat of IS. On 16 March 2018, the conquest of eastern Ghouta with the help of Iran marked another milestone in al-Assad's effort to crush the rebellion and the terrorist threat as the war entered its eighth year. Similarly, on 19 March Erdogan announced that Turkey's Operation Olive Branch had achieved its aim in Afrin and that the allied Turkish and rebel forces could push to take over Manbij to eliminate the terrorist threat where the US and its SDF allies had a presence.[97] Yet, the US had reason to keep Manbij under its control "to check Russia in the great power competition in Syria; to prevent Iranian hegemony across the land bridge from Iran to Beirut; and to maintain leverage for the bargaining in Geneva."[98] The rebel-held northeastern province of Idlib, where Turkey had deployed observation posts to monitor the de-escalation zone, would be at the heart of the contest between Turkey and Russia. It was very likely that Idlib's fate would be determined by Russian-Turkish cooperation because if the Syrian army tried to seize the province hundreds of thousands of people would be displaced.

Putin won a fourth term as Russia's longest-serving president since Joseph Stalin in a landslide victory on 18 March, in which he claimed 76.7 per cent of the vote. The Kremlin sought to ensure a large turnout to bolster Russia's "managed democracy" and Putin's popular image as a defender of Russia against its foreign enemies.[99] Since the mid-2000s, and in light of the increasingly hawkish attitude of the Duma and the Russian army, Putin in his third term would also adopt an assertive foreign policy in trying to position Russia as a great power. The election came amid escalating tensions between Russia and the West, with accusations that Moscow was behind the 4 March nerve-agent poisoning that left both former Russian double agent Sergei Skripal and his daughter Yulia in critical condition. The United Kingdom and Russia announced tit-for-tat diplomat expulsions over the spy case. Two dozen countries, including the US and EU nations expelled more than 150 Russian diplomats in solidarity with Britain. Despite advice to the contrary from his aids, Trump called Putin to congratulate him on his re-election and suggested they have the first meeting in Washington. Trump kept the focus of the call on "shared interests" between the two countries and refrained from raising Moscow's role in the poisoning and its alleged meddling in American elections.[100] Putin's new mandate would give him little incentive to seek entente with the US, especially as Washington imposed another round of sanctions on Russian entities on 15 March and as the investigation of alleged Russian interference in the 2016 presidential election intensified.[101] Putin struck a softer tone toward the West after his election victory, saying that he had no desire for an arms race and would do everything he could to resolve differences with other countries using diplomatic and political channels. Putin was unlikely to introduce any substantive foreign policy reversals, especially after his election and after Russia's geopolitical and military victory in Syria. Russia's intervention in Syria strengthened Moscow's foothold in the ME and preserved Russia's centrality in international conflict management as an embodiment of its international status. Yet, Moscow's willingness to use military power in its foreign policy as a means to enhance its status seemed unlikely.

The conflict in Syria seemed more and more to be about the country's future as a pawn in the struggle between the regional and international actors. On 4 April 2018, the Turkish, Iranian, and Russian presidents met in Ankara for their second tripartite summit to reaffirm their commitment to Syria's territorial integrity and the continuation of the local ceasefires.[102] Despite being on different sides of the Syrian civil war, they cooperated to ensure their influence in Syria once the conflict ended. The tripartite summit was preceded by a meeting between Erdogan and Putin on 2 April. Both leaders launched the construction of Turkey's first nuclear power station in Mersin. The capture of Afrin increased Turkey's influence on the ground. However, Russia still remained important in managing the rivalries between Turkey and Iran and in pushing forward the Astana process. But so far, Russian efforts had failed to resolve the Syrian conflict. Any agreement, as Hampson noted, "should serve multiple regional and national interests, with substantial involvement of the region in the implementation processes."[103]

While Trump vowed to withdraw US troops from Syria, an alleged chemical weapons attack took place on the rebel-held town of Douma in eastern Ghouta on 7 April. What to do next in Syria was a crucial test for Trump, "who had shirked America's traditional leadership role" in the region.[104] Russia, once again, vetoed a US-drafted resolution to create a new inquiry to investigate the attack because it could be a prelude to a Western strike on Syria. Warning statements from Trump about imminent military action against Damascus and Zasypkin's threat that Russia would respond to any US strike reinforced the need for caution. Most dangerously, multiple global and regional powers had been drawn into the conflict in Syria. Indeed, tensions increased between Moscow and Tel Aviv after the Israeli attack on the Syrian T4 air base on 9 April. Yet, it was unlikely that Israel's action would break down the strategic partnership between both states and spark further escalation as long as Israeli strikes did not endanger Russian personnel on the ground. Given the threat of further Western attacks and after negotiations with Russian military personnel for a deal, the insurgent group Jaish al-Islam withdrew from Douma, and Russia deployed military police to maintain stability.

Despite heightened geopolitical risks, on 14 April the US, France, and Britain launched airstrikes against three Syrian research, storage, and military targets in retaliation for the Syrian regime's suspected chemical attack on Douma.[105] In a marked shift from his recent posture on Syria, Trump was ready to keep the US military engaged if al-Assad were to use chemical weapons again. Given Moscow's warning that it would strike back, the West gave advanced notice to Russia, as it had a year before, to avoid escalation by drawing Russia and Iran into a deeper confrontation with the US in Syria. The strikes would not change the course of the Syrian civil war as Putin headed his new six-year term, which started on 7 May. Although Russia did not engage the incoming missiles, Putin condemned the Western strike as an "act of aggression" that would worsen the humanitarian catastrophe in Syria and that had a "destructive influence on the entire system of international relations."[106] Putin limited his response to calling an urgent meeting of the UN Security Council. Other than that, the Kremlin warned that Russia could supply Syria with the S-300 surface-to-air missile system that was a concern for Israel. Russia was staunchly opposed to regime change fostered by outsiders. Less than a week after the Western missile strike on Syria, the head of Russia's military general staff, Valery Gerasimov, and NATO's supreme allied commander, General Curtis Scaparroti, met in Baku and discussed the war in Syria and "issues related to military posture and exercises" as both sides accused the other of risky deployments in the Baltic States and Eastern Europe.[107] As argued in previous chapters, NATO's attempt to build a strategic partnership with Russia failed in the post-

Cold War era. During his visit to Brussels on 27 April, US Secretary of State Mike Pompeo stressed that NATO should maintain a unified position of "no business as usual" with Russia until it implemented an agreement to end violence in eastern Ukraine and halted destabilizing actions for which it was blamed elsewhere.[108] Russia was also criticized by the EU, NATO, and the US for its construction and opening of the Kerch Strait Bridge between Russia and the Crimea in May 2018.

On 14 May 2018, the Astana talks (Astana IX) began against the background of potential confrontation between Israel and Iran as a result of Iran's attack on Israeli positions in the occupied Golan Height and Israel's retaliation on Iranian positions in Syria and Trump's pull out of the US from the nuclear deal with Iran on 8 May, further complicating the regional picture.[109] Israel was determined to prevent any Iranian military entrenchment in Syria. Trump's dramatic withdrawal from the 2015 Iran nuclear deal was justified in that his predecessor Obama had not addressed Iran's ballistic missile program, its nuclear activities beyond 2025, and Iran's role in regional conflicts like Yemen and Syria. Trump's foreign policy move was heartily supported by Netanyahu and opposed by all other governments that were part of the deal. Trump, who called Iran's government a "regime of great terror," held out the possibility that he could negotiate a tougher deal with Tehran in the future.[110] According to Suzanne Maloney, Trump's move "represented an abdication of American leadership on the international stage that was unparalleled in recent history."[111] The strategy behind Trump's move was probably regime change in Tehran. However, the right strategy to reverse Iran's power grab in the ME would begin with Syria and not by withdrawing from the Iran nuclear deal and maintaining its military position in the east of the Euphrates River and other points in southern Syria. Russia, which was friendly to Israel but was fighting in Syria on the same side as Iran, called on both nations to resolve their differences through diplomatic means. Russia's good relations with Iran, Hizbullah, and the Syrian government made it the sole actor capable of mediating understandings to prevent an Iran-Israel escalation across Syria.[112]

The Astana IX talks did not make progress on a political settlement in Syria and the US did not send a delegation to observe the latest round of the peace talks. As the broader situation in Syria was not getting any better as far as US interests were concerned, Trump intended to reduce the US military and civilian stabilization presence in Syria. However, the State Department, the Pentagon, and intelligence agencies tried to dissuade him from pulling troops immediately. In northeast Syria, US troops were still battling IS and civilian teams from the State Department and the US Agency for International Development were working in newly liberated areas. The regime forces were making inroads against the rebels. Russia was solidifying its influence, and on 17 May 2018 Putin hosted al-Assad, who congratulated the Russian president on his new term after he was elected in March, in Sochi. After meeting al-Assad, Putin vowed that "with the start of the political process in its most active phase, foreign armed forces would withdraw from Syrian territory" including Iran and its proxies.[113] Still, Putin declared that the Russian forces would not withdraw but would remain in place in order "to ensure Russia's interests and its international obligations in an important region of the world."[114] Putin's call was a turning point in Russia's partnership with Iran. Yet, Firouznia disclosed to the author that, "there was no conflict between Russia and Iran about Iran's influence in Syria."[115]

Putin's statement about the withdrawal of foreign forces was a message to Tehran that the Syrian conflict must not escalate to a deadlier confrontation between Iran and Israel. Russia had no interest in establishing an anti-Israeli front along the Golan Heights. Stemming from its role of playing a delicate balancing act between different regional actors, Russia stressed that only the Syrian army should be deployed on the country's southern border with Jordan and Israel. Having taken the last opposition enclaves in Damascus and outside Homs, in the second half of June 2018, Russian-backed regime forces launched an offensive on the rebel-held southern province of Deraa, which was covered by a trilateral de-escalation agreement that had been negotiated by the US, Russia, and Jordan in July 2017.[116] On 7 July, as the rebels agreed to surrender their arms in a Russian-brokered ceasefire deal, the regime forces entered Deraa and regained control of the vital Nassib border crossing with Jordan. On 12 July, Russian military police entered the city. As al-Assad sought victory, there seemed little hope of a negotiated peace with 6 million Syrians abroad as refugees and 6.5 million more displaced internally.

On 18 June, Putin hosted German Chancellor Angela Merkel and told her that the reconstruction of Syria should not be politicized and that the European countries should help Syria if they wanted refugees to return to their country.[117] Putin also hosted Macron in St Petersburg on 24 May. Both leaders expressed concern about the withdrawal of the US from the Iran deal and agreed that the focus in Syria should be on a new constitution and setting up elections that would include all Syrians, including the refugees. Compliant with the agreement reached in Sochi in January 2018 on the formation of a constitutional committee, on 27 May, de Mistura declared that the Syrian government submitted to the UN a list of names as candidates for inclusion in a committee yet to be formed.[118] Meanwhile, Russia, one of the strongest defenders of the Iran deal, tightened its trade ties with Tehran when in Astana the Russian-led Eurasian Economic Union signed an interim trade deal with Iran that lowered tariffs on hundreds of goods.

To avoid confrontation between two NATO members in Syria, on 4 June 2018, the US and Turkey endorsed a roadmap to resolve the dispute over Manbij, which was controlled by US-backed Kurdish fighters. The roadmap envisioned joint Turkish-US patrols around Manbij after the withdrawal of the YPG, the largest part of the SDF, to the east of the Euphrates River, meeting a long-standing Turkish demand.[119] The Manbij plan was a political deal meant to establish a balance of power between Turkey and the US in northern Syria to jointly maintain security and stability after the Kurdish militia withdrew from the town. In November 2018, Turkish and US troops began joint patrols around the town of Manbij on the west bank of the Euphrates to avert clashes between Turkey and the YPG. However, Turkey pressed on with a new offensive to crush the Kurds. For his part, al-Assad kept the door open to negotiations with the SDF on the Kurdish-administered region where the US operated air bases and outposts.

Internationally, at the 8 June 2018 G7 meeting in Quebec's picturesque resort town of La Malbaie, Trump called for Russia's readmission into the group and refused to ease American tariffs on steel and aluminum imports from Canada, the EU, and Mexico, raising the spectre of a global trade war. Russia was ousted from the diplomatic forum after Putin violated international norms by annexing Crimea in 2014 and readmission to the G7 would be a gesture toward Russia's status. During a press conference on the sidelines of the summit Trump said that "it would be an asset to have Russia back in because we should have Russia at the negotiating table. You know, whether you like it or not, and it may not be politically correct, but we have a world to run" he added. Yet, the final communiqué of the G7 issued on 9 June stated, "we stand ready to take further restrictive measures to increase costs on Russia."[120] Evidently, attending summit meetings, state visits, and strategic dialogues were status enhancing markers that could have satisfied Russia's aspiration to be recognized as great power. Attending the G7 was a symbolic indicator of status accommodation. Yet, Lavrov, speaking on Russian television, said that Moscow was not seeking to rejoin the group. Russia was "working fine in other formats." Lavrov added that the G20 "was a mechanism to reach consensus" and the "most promising format for the future."[121]

Years before, Russia had decided on a pivot to the east after ties worsened with the US over the Ukraine conflict and its intervention in Syria. Putin's visit to China on 8 June 2018 came as China-US relations soured over a bitter trade war. Both China and Russia had "resolutely supported each other's core interests … and jointly proactively participated in international affairs and global governance." The two leaders, Xi Jinping and Putin, signed a statement saying that "in conditions of growing global instability and uncertainty" Russia and China would "deepen their consultations on strategic stability issues."[122] For his part, Rouhani, who had criticized American unilateralism in withdrawing from the nuclear deal, hailed the efforts by China and Russia to maintain the deal. Presidents Putin and Xi vowed to "expand counterterrorism cooperation," boost contacts between their militaries, and encourage joint international efforts to fight terrorism "without any double standards."[123]

The prospects for conflict resolution in Syria would depend significantly on the ability of Russia and the US to accommodate their divergent preferences or on Russia's ability to prevail over the US. The results of the Helsinki summit on 16 July 2018 between Putin and Trump concerning Syria were unlikely to be immediate. Trump refused to blame the Russian leader for meddling in the 2016 election and denounced the "foolishness and stupidity" of his own country's policy for the deterioration in relations with Russia.[124] Putin would allow the FBI to interrogate Russian military intelligence officials accused of hacking the 2016 US election campaign. Putin wanted Trump to acknowledge Moscow's influence over its former neighbours and recognize Russia as a global player whose interests and values must be taken into account. Russia's posture was embedded in its assertive foreign policy strategies aimed at pursuing vital regional and global interests. Trump, for his part, wanted Putin to contain Iran's influence in Syria; this was also an Israeli demand. However, Moscow could not compel Iran to leave Syria because Iranian advisers were in Syria at the invitation of the Syrian government. Russia's proposal to Washington to jointly organize the return of the Syrian refugees to their homes and begin reconstruction would foster cooperation between them. Syria was one area where Moscow and Washington could find some common ground. In this regard, after a few days the Russian Defense Ministry sent a proposal to Washington that included setting up a Russian-US-Jordanian monitoring group in Amman and a similar group in Lebanon. The choice of the refugee issue was telling because Russia wanted to solicit the support of Europe and the US for Russia's role in Syria and its presumed importance to them. Yet, Pompeo stressed that the refugees from Lebanon, Turkey, and Jordan would return to their homes at the right time and through a voluntary mechanism.[125]

The summit did not produce a breakthrough, and the Kremlin did not expect that one meeting would bring an end to Western sanctions and a pullback of NATO forces deployed near Russia's borders. As argued in chapters 1 and 2, Washington lost Russia in the 1990s because it did not understand Russia's security perception in the Balkans. In March 1999, the West used force in Yugoslavia against Russia's traditional Slavic/orthodox ally without consulting the Kremlin.[126] In the 1990s Russia was not integrated into the Western world. Yet, Putin, after mid-2000, in his efforts to restore Russia's greatness, had undermined the West and its democratic values. Prior to the Helsinki summit, on 11 July, Netanyahu and Ali Akbar Velayati, a senior advisor to Iran's supreme leader, visited Moscow for talks on the Iranian presence in Syria. It seemed that Israel wanted only regime forces without Iranian personnel to control the Syrian frontier with the Israeli occupied Golan Heights. Israel's *Haaretz* quoted Netanyahu saying, "we never had a problem with the Assad regime. For 40 years not one bullet was fired on the Golan Heights."[127] Russia offered to keep Iranian forces one hundred kilometres from the Golan Heights ceasefire line, but Israel rejected the offer saying that the pullback would be inadequate.[128]

Meanwhile, on 20 July Syrian rebels laid down their weapons and began evacuating their positions in the Qunaitra province near the occupied Golan Heights, paving the way for regime forces to retake their positions along the Israeli frontier for the first time since 2011. Concurrently, Russian military police deployed on the edge of the Israeli occupied Golan Heights after Syrian government forces regained control of the area. Similar to the fate of the opposition in Aleppo and Homs, those who refused to surrender their arms were evacuated to Idlib where Turkey had twelve observation points staffed by its military, ostensibly aimed at monitoring a de-escalation zone and preventing a humanitarian crisis. The deployment of the Turkish military units also served to protect Ankara's geostrategic interests. Given the concerns about an imminent regime offensive, Russia and Turkey were in intense negotiations to ensure that Idlib, home to about 3 million people, did not become a breaking point in their partnership to bring peace to Syria.

Throughout 2018 until mid-2019 the Syrian regime liberated most of the opposition-held areas in the de-escalation zones with the exception of large parts of Idlib. On 22 August 2019, the Syrian army captured Khan Sheikhoun in Idlib province, effectively cutting off Turkish troops at a military post near the town of Morek, seventy kilometres inside Syria.[129] To normalize the situation, Putin hosted Erdogan in Moscow on 27 August. Turkey expected that Russia, as a powerful supporter of al-Assad, would take steps to "alleviate the problem" and necessary measures to prevent a new migrant wave to Turkey. From a Turkish perspective, the Syrian offensive was harming efforts for a resolution of the conflict and posing a "serious threat" to Turkey's security.[130] In a short briefing with Erdogan, Putin said, "we have outlined additional joint steps to neutralize the terrorist's nests in Idlib and normalize the situation there and in the whole of Syria."[131] The discord between the US and Turkey would rehabilitate Russia's relationship with Turkey and extend its diplomatic influence in the region. Concurrently, Turkey's alliance with Russia would ensure that Ankara would play a significant role in deciding the future of the Syrian state.

On 28 August 2018, Cavusoglu led a delegation to Moscow to discuss the Idlib situation and Moscow's planned delivery of its S-400 missile system to Turkey ignoring Washington's concern that the purchase of the S-400 missiles could risk the security of the US-made F-35 warplane.[132] Turkey, who was at odds over the US backing of the SDF in Syria, had agreed to pay $2.5 billion for Russia's S-400 air defense system. Despite US threats to impose sanctions on Ankara for buying Russian military hardware incompatible with NATO systems and the acquisition of which might lead to Turkey's expulsion from an F-35 fighter jet program, Turkey received the first parts of the S-400 on 12 July 2019. For Turkey, "the system was a strategic defense requirement, particularly to secure its southern borders with Syria and Iraq."[133] Russia, for its part, expressed growing impatience and accused extremist groups, such as HTS, for using civilians as human shields and for targeting its forces at Humeimeem from Idlib. In terms of costs, since 2017 Turkey had been unable to bring a full halt to the rebel's provocations, including drone attacks on Russia's Syrian air base apparently launched from Idlib.

Within this context, on 17 September 2018 Putin and Erdogan met in Sochi and agreed to avert what would become a devastating war in rebel-controlled Idlib. According to the deal, a demilitarized zone with a depth of fifteen to twenty kilometres would be created in Idlib by mid-October as a means of separating the armed opposition and regime forces. The deal also envisaged the withdrawal of "radically minded" rebels with their heavy weapons from that zone. The demilitarized zone along the line of contact between Idlib's rebels and regime forces would be patrolled by Russian and Turkish forces.[134] The deal was a win for Russia because Moscow sidelined Iran from the deal and effectively forced Turkey, and by extension the US, to accept Russia's arrangement. In doing so, Russia made itself indispensable to all regional actors in reshaping the political and the diplomatic landscape in Syria. Russia was determined to keep Syria anchored in its sphere of influence. As a matter of fact, Saudi King Salman's first ever visit to Moscow on 10 October underscored Russia's role and growing power in the ME. The Kremlin was seeking support for a political settlement in Syria that guaranteed al-Assad's role.

In terms of costs, certain incidents caused tension between Russia and Israel. On 18 September, after an Il-20 Russian reconnaissance aircraft with fifteen Russians on board was mistakenly shot down by the Syrian anti-aircraft system, Russia held Israel accountable for its "irresponsible actions" because the Israeli jets had used the Russian plane as cover, thereby exposing it to fire from Syrian air defenses. Yet, Netanyahu blamed Syria for the incident.[135] Despite Israeli and American objections, Russia took preventive measures by deploying S-300 antiaircraft missile launchers to Syria to prevent further Israeli attacks on regime facilities and to protect Moscow's geostrategic interests. However, Israel's coordination with Russia on its attacks against Hizbullah and Iranian targets in Syria remained unchanged. Yet, Firouznia stressed to the author that, "Iran would never accept the maintenance of Russian–Israeli interests in Syria."[136] Similarly, the US-led coalition attacks against IS in Syria and Iraq that had begun in August 2014 continued. Yet, the Trump administration still lacked a plan for Syria and Iraq, especially on the crucial question of whether to keep a small residual US force in the country.

Although participants at a Syrian peace conference in Russia in January 2018 had agreed to form a constitutional committee made up of 150 members, in October Moallem aborted the outgoing UN envoy de Mistura's efforts to form the committee saying that "the constitution and everything related to it were purely a sovereign affair that was decided by the Syrian people without any foreign intervention."[137] Control over the constitutional process had been a key point of conflict between the regime and the international community and the Syrian opposition, which considered that the regime did not want to take any steps on the political level. On 29 November 2018, at Astana (Astana XI) where Russia, Turkey, and Iran held talks with representatives of the regime and the opposition, no progress was made on the issues of returning the refugees to their country and the formation of the constitutional committee.[138] Zasypkin disclosed to the author that, "the formation of the constitutional committee was the basis of the political settlement in Syria. However, the Americans were not helpful in this regard." Contrary to Moallem's stance, Zasypkin stressed that, "the participation of all the parties and the UN in its formation was crucial because Russia wanted to secure transparent and genuine elections in the next stage."[139]

In November 2018, seasoned Norwegian diplomat Geir Pederson was appointed by the UN to facilitate an inclusive and credible political solution to Syria's war. However, in the absence of international will and a determination to reach a political solution, the change of envoy would have little impact on the peace process. After Ankara and Moscow brokered a deal to create a demilitarized zone in Idlib, Turkey, on 28 October, hosted an international summit on Syria. A statement released in Istanbul by the leaders of Turkey, Russia, France, and Germany called for "an inclusive, Syrian-led and Syrian-owned political process" and the convening of a constitutional committee by the end of the year to work on several reforms as a prelude to UN-backed free and fair elections.[140] It was apparent that international efforts were currently focused on trying to convene a committee to rewrite Syria's constitution. Yet, many obstacles remained to a peace agreement, including the divided opinions about the fate of al-Assad. According to Putin, a settlement in Syria could not be reached without consultations with Syria and Iran, describing Iran as "a guarantor country of the peace process, the ceasefire, and the establishment of demilitarized zones."[141]

The persistent tension between the US and Russia over issues including Russia's annexation of the Crimea, its role in the war in Syria and eastern Ukraine, and its alleged meddling in the US elections, evidently hindered peacemaking in the ME. Russia and China lashed out at US sanctions and tariffs that they said were undermining the global trading system built by Washington. Since 2017, the US National Security Strategy focused on great power rivalry with China and Russia, designated as America's main competitors. It is out of the scope of this chapter to examine the Chinese economic policy that caused rivalry with the US. From a Chinese and Russian perspective, US trade restrictions revived "protectionism and unilateral approaches" that harmed "the multilateral trade system the core of which was the WTO."[142] The sanctions played an important role leading to the underperformance of the Russian economy. Still, Russia's economy was stagnant and was severely affected by corruption. Putin had pledged after his re-election in March 2018 to accelerate growth to a level that exceeded the global average of 3.7 per cent, but did not achieve his goal. Without building a strong economy Russia's status-seeking strategy would remain stillborn. According to Putin's spokesman, Dmitry Peskov, "rosy prospects for the normalization of U.S.–Russian ties were not visible on the horizon."[143] Indeed, the brief contact between Putin and Trump in Paris on 11 November 2018 on the occasion of marking the centenary of the end of World War I demonstrated no bright prospects for an improvement in US-Russian ties.

In conclusion, I have argued that Syria's civil war had geopolitical implications and scenarios. Although Russia and the US-led coalition defeated IS, there was no sign of a negotiated solution under the auspices of the UN. The Syrian government was not interested in real negotiations either in Geneva or in Astana because the Syrian army backed by Russia and Iran had already liberated most of the rebel-held territories in the de-escalation zones, with the exception of Idlib. The resolution of the Syrian conflict required a combination of regional and international strategies to deal with the communal and geopolitical dimensions of the conflict.

Russia's regional diplomacy highlighted Moscow's method of negotiating regional divides by dealing simultaneously with Turkey, Iran, Saudi Arabia, and Israel which all had divergent geopolitical interests in the ME. Russia was convinced that achieving higher status was connected to its ability to manage international conflicts and contribute to setting the guiding principles of global order. Yet, Moscow's willingness to use military power in its foreign policy as a means to enhance its status seemed unlikely. I have analyzed Russia's power politics vis-à-vis three key factors: identity, opportunity, and costs. The required consensus to resolve the Syrian conflict between the US and Russia was not achieved. Russia's policy of marginalizing the US and going it alone in the ME was based on wishful thinking. Russia did not share the Western view of Iran as a state that sponsored terrorism and criticized Trump for withdrawing the US from the Iranian nuclear deal. While Iran was in a confrontation with the US and Israel, Russia succeeded in preventing an Iranian-Israeli war that would have destabilized Syria further. Iran's geopolitical objective was to create a land corridor extending from Iran to Lebanon through Iraq and Syria against its regional rivals Israel and Saudi Arabia. Syria and Iran were also the backbone of the axis of resistance, an alliance of regional forces, to counter Western hegemony in the region and to ensure the survival of both regimes. Concurrently, the US and Israel would prevent Iran from solidifying its military presence in Syria.

I also argued that Turkey's goals were built around security priorities. Turkey blocked the westward expansion of the US-backed SDF to prevent the Syrian Kurds from establishing an autonomous area near its border, frustrated US military operations east of the Euphrates, worked with Russia to ensure that Syria remained a unitary state, and tried to resettle displaced Syrians in Turkish-controlled territories. Turkey also allied with Russia to ensure that it would play a significant role in deciding the future of the Syrian state. The Kurdish issue left Washington and Ankara struggling to come up with a deal whose centrepiece was a balancing act in Manbij. The US and Turkey engaged in arduous negotiations for the rules of engagement governing the joint patrols around Manbij.

With the Syrian war continuing, the regional and international players would try to shape the outcome of the peace process in line with their geopolitical interests. Russia was determined to keep Syria in its sphere of influence over the long-term as a foothold in the ME. Despite the economic and political costs of Russia's power politics in Syria, Putin did not reverse Russia's assertive foreign policy. Yet, Russia needed to establish dialogue with the US as an equal partner both politically and militarily.

Conclusion

This book has examined Russia's military intervention in Syria in September 2015 from a status-seeking point of view. The Syrian civil war represented the context in which Russia exercised power politics to enhance its status. This book provided a detailed analysis of the causes and foreign policy objectives of Russia's actions in the former Soviet republics and the Middle East (ME). Russia risked conflict by annexing Crimea and supporting the rebels in eastern Ukraine in 2014 to defend its exclusive status in the region and maintain its values and interests. As a matter of fact, annexing Crimea was a revisionist move not typical of status-inconsistent powers. The official justification of Russia's intervention in Syria was to support the Syrian regime in its fight against terrorism and to prevent the collapse of the Syrian state. Yet, Russia sought to preserve its centrality in international conflict management as an embodiment of its international status and to set the guiding principles of the global order. In light of the growing American retreat at the global level, Russia elbowed its way into a changing international system, carved out a sphere of influence in its neighbourhood, and prevented a regime change in Syria, Russia's ally since the Cold War period.

After the demise of the Soviet Union in 1991, Russia lost its great power status, was not respected, and was not treated as an equal by the US. This book highlighted the relationship between status inconsistency and conflict. It also stressed that Russia as a status-inconsistent power used power politics to be recognized as a great power. Yet, power politics played a much greater role in Russia's status-seeking strategy than the material capabilities of the country warranted, particularly when assessed against the backdrop of Russia's economic problems. I argued that Russia's willingness to use military power in its foreign policy as a means to enhance its status seemed very unlikely.

For a better understanding of Russia's intervention in Syria from a status-seeking point of view and to find out what determined Russia's foreign policy options, I tried to give more empirical substance to the measures of attribution, willingness, and capability. With regard to attribution, I examined the factor of identity. With regard to willingness, I discussed the factor of opportunity. Finally, with regard to capabilities, I examined the factor of cost.

From 2011 until September 2015 Russia tried to preserve its influence in Syria and the ME through diplomacy. Russia engaged in international diplomacy as a means to preserve its influence in international politics and as a counterweight to US dominance in the UNSC. Russia had significant influence on the international conflict management in Syria via its UNSC seat. By using its veto power, Moscow prevented the West and the US to intervene militarily in Syria. In September 2015, Moscow's decision to intervene in Syria displayed an underachiever strategy, seeking to enhance its status and influence in Syria and the ME aggressively. In addition to fighting terrorism and preventing a regime change in Syria, another Russian foreign policy objective was to maintain a foothold in the ME.

After nine years of civil war, all but two areas of Syria returned to government control. The opposition-held bastion of the Idlib province in the northwest, where Islamic militants from all over the country were cornered, and the oil-rich area in the northeast, which was held by the US-backed SDF. The Syrian conflict eventually became a proxy war pitting the US, Turkey, and the Gulf countries, which supported the rebels, against Russia, Iran, and Hizbullah, who fought alongside the regime. Since August 2019 a tentative ceasefire between Russian-backed government forces trying to recapture the province and the rebels who hold it has been in place in Idlib. Concurrently, on 1 August the thirteenth round of talks sponsored by Turkey, Russia, and Iran began in Nur-Sultan (previously known as Astana) focused on de-escalation in Idlib and the formation of the constitutional committee.[1] For the first time representatives from Lebanon and Iraq joined the talks as observer parties. Meanwhile, on 7 August Turkish and US military officials, who met in Ankara, agreed to establish a safe zone from the Euphrates River to the Iraqi border to facilitate the return of the 3.6 million displaced Syrians to their home country and provide security to the Turkish border settlements and military outposts. The conflict unleashed a global migrant crisis that continued to affect Europe and the countries neighbouring Syria that opened their borders to millions who sought refuge. Both sides agreed to establish a joint operation centre to provide joint management at a time when the Trump administration reduced the number of US troops in Syria.[2] There were deep differences between Ankara and Washington over the scope and command of the safe zone, which raised the prospect of Turkish military action. Also, Turkey warned against delays in the implementation of the agreement, comparing it to an earlier deal with Washington to withdraw the YPG/PYD fighters from the city of Manbij. However, US Defense Secretary Mark Esper reiterated that any Turkish operation into north Syria would be unacceptable, and the US would prevent unilateral incursions. In early September 2019, although the first joint ground patrol with US counterparts began near the Turkish border town of Tal Abyad, Turkey remained concerned as the US continued to support the YPG, a component of the SDF and a crucial partner in the US-led coalition that defeated IS in Syria.

I argued that Russia was willing to assume responsibilities associated with its conflict management role in the ME as an embodiment of its international status. Russia's willingness was connected to its capabilities to both resolve the conflict and maintain its influence in the region. Both capabilities had status implications. The fifth trilateral summit in Ankara between Erdogan, Putin, and Rouhani on 16 September 2019 and the agreement on 23 September 2019 by the Syrian parties "on the rules and procedures which was facilitated by the Astana guarantors in coordination" with the UN current Syria envoy Geir Pedersen, was a "crucial step that would pave the way for a viable and lasting Syrian-led, Syrian-owned and UN facilitated political process in line with the decisions of the Syrian National dialogue Congress in Sochi and the UNSC resolution 2254."[3] For Putin and Erdogan the situation in Idlib was of utmost importance. While Erdogan expressed growing concern over the Syrian army's military campaign in Idlib, Putin emphasized that Russia would continue its fight against the terrorist groups, such as HTS. As for Rouhani, his main goal at the summit was to gain Russian and Turkish support in light of the potential threats posed by America and Israel resulting from Iran-backed Yemen's Houthi rebel drone and missile attack on Saudi Arabia's oil industry on 14 September, an event that shook global energy markets. At the start of the summit, Rouhani emphasized that the "American forces should leave Syria at once" because their presence in the country "endangered Syria's territorial integrity and sovereignty."[4] Notwithstanding their different priorities, the three guarantors of the Astana format emphasized that the sovereignty, independence, and territorial integrity of Syria should be respected by all sides. Putin seldom missed an opportunity to expose any perceived US weakness. Putin wanted to underscore Russia's growing confidence in projecting influence in the region, building on the role Moscow played in shoring up al-Assad in Syria; managing to deal with Israel and Iran; and selling the S-400 missile system to NATO member Turkey despite US objections.

Since 2015, Russia positioned itself as a key player in shaping the ME. Russia was able to keep cooperative relations with Egypt, Israel, Iran, Turkey, the Palestinians, and the Gulf countries. By maintaining an open line and dialogue with these regional players Putin demonstrated that Russia was a great power able to manage conflicts, form alliances, and prevent deadly confrontation between Israel and Iran and between Saudi Arabia and Iran. An Israeli-Iranian war across Syria and a Sunni-Shiite confrontation in the region was not in the interest of Russia because such conflicts would complicate the Russian-led Astana peace process. Therefore, ambitious Russia proved that it was an indispensable actor able to keep a balance of power in the ME. Still, buoyed by Russian military gains in Syria, Putin, on his first visit to Saudi Arabia on 12 October 2019, signalled Moscow's growing ME clout. After the two sides signed more than a dozen memoranda of understanding in the fields of energy and petrochemicals, and after discussing the conflicts in Syria and Yemen, Putin offered King Salman the Russian S-400 surface-to-air missile system to protect the kingdom's oil facilities from attacks similar to those of 14 September.[5] Geopolitically, Putin could also play a positive role in easing tensions with Tehran given Russia's good relations with both sides.

Yet, domestic political and economic factors would influence Russia's status-seeking strategy in such a way that the costs of action were not calculated consistently. Hence, power politics played a greater role than the country's domestic capabilities warranted. Putin was not without problems at home. He was under pressure to raise living standards, diversify the economy away from oil and improve economic growth. The EU and US sanctions, imposed on Russia after the annexation of Crimea would not be lifted until Russia took steps to resolve the conflict in Ukraine. Peace in Ukraine would improve the battered

US-Russian relations and EU-Russian relations. Putin reminded the European powers and the US that Russia retained geopolitical reach and a readiness to act to protect its values and interests in the FSR. Russia made headway by expanding trade and investment ties with China and by making its influence felt in the ME. However, Anna Borshchevskaya, a senior fellow at the Washington Institute, wrote, "Russia often made gains simply because the U.S. was too risk-averse to challenge it."[6]

On 23 September 2019, on the eve of the seventy-fourth UN General Assembly meeting in New York, UN Secretary General Antonio Guterres announced the creation of a constitutional committee on Syria that included fifty members nominated from the government, fifty members nominated from the opposition, and another fifty nominated by the UN.[7] It took twenty months for the sides to agree on the names. The committee was tasked with drafting a new Syrian constitution. Yet, al-Assad won the war and the regime seemed unlikely to allow external powers and the UN to introduce major changes in the constitution, which had been revised in 2012. Pedersen hoped that the "committee would work on finding a solution that would address the issues that were necessary, and that it would be seen as legitimate by all key actors within Syrian society."[8] The first meeting of the constitutional committee took place in Geneva on 30 October 2019. Each delegation included Kurds, but there was no representation from the SDF. Pedersen in his opening remarks said, "You are here sitting together face-to-face ready to start a dialogue and negotiations," which "I believe is a powerful sign of hope for Syrians everywhere, both inside and outside the country."[9] Syria was scheduled to hold presidential elections in 2021, and the UN hoped the committee could help create a climate and mechanism for holding a fair vote.

I argued in chapters 3, 4, and 5 that numerous rounds of UN-led peace talks at Geneva failed to end the Syrian war mainly because of the strained relations between the US and Russia and the regional competition between Turkey, Iran, and Saudi Arabia in the ME. Although defeating IS and fighting terrorism was a common goal between the US and Russia, Presidents Obama and Trump avoided deeper engagement in the Syrian war. Instead, the US trained moderate rebels, sent Special Operation Forces to stabilize northern Syria, and formed an alliance with the SDF to defeat IS. While Obama advocated economic development and nation building at home, Trump articulated his America First policy. The fate of al-Assad, the voluntary return of the refugees to their homes, reconstruction, and the issue of determining Syria's future were contested issues that prevented a negotiated solution. To end the war, international and regional support was needed. There was also the question of timing and whether the conflict was ripe for resolution. On 3 May 2019, Pedersen met in Geneva with top diplomats from a "small group" of countries. Representatives from Egypt, France, Germany, Jordan, Saudi Arabia, the UK, and the US attended the meeting with Pedersen to revive the Geneva process, which had been stagnant since December 2018.[10] Pedersen, having in mind the failure of the previous three UN envoys, needed a commitment from these actors that they would support the Geneva process. It is worth noting that since 2017, a parallel negotiations track at Astana led by Russia, Turkey, and Iran took precedence.

From Turkey's perspective, the US-Turkey agreement to create a safe zone 440 kilometres long and thirty to thirty-two kilometres deep in northern Syria in order to return the 3.6 million refugees to their homes did not achieve the desired results. Frustrated Turkey, also sought the withdrawal of the SDF from the Syrian side of the border so as to prevent a threat to its national security. On 7 October 2019, following a phone call with Erdogan, the White House issued a statement that surprised everyone. Trump's abrupt decision to withdraw US troops in a chaotic and dangerous manner from northeastern Syria gave the green light to a Turkish invasion on 9 October. Amidst international condemnation of the Turkish assault and strong opposition from the Pentagon and Republican and Democratic lawmakers, Trump appeared to reverse himself by announcing that should Ankara do anything that "I, in my great and unmatched wisdom, consider to be off limits, I will totally destroy and obliterate the economy of Turkey."[11] Trump's green light to Turkey for the assault was seen as a betrayal of Washington's erstwhile Kurdish allies. The danger of the assault lied not only in the revival of IS but also the escape of about eleven thousand IS fighters who were being detained by the SDF. Turkish-backed Syrian rebels participated in the offensive dubbed Operation Peace Spring to enforce the safe zone. After launching the assault with airstrikes and intense artillery fire, Turkish troops crossed the border into the Kurdish-controlled towns of Tal Abyad and Ras al-Ain. Russia urged dialogue between Damascus and Syria's Kurds.

As Turkey extended its military incursion against Turkish militias further south than originally planned, the US withdrew one thousand troops from northern Syria. Turkey ignored US sanctions. As security collapsed in northeastern Syria, hardened IS fighters could escape from camps and prisons that were run by the SDF and renew the terrorist threat against the US, Europe, and Russia that they posed since 2014. The Turkish assault triggered international alarm over the large-scale displacement of civilians it caused. To minimize its human losses and to counter the Turkish onslaught, the SDF sought a deal with Russia.

Russian-backed Syrian forces took advantage of the abrupt US troop withdrawal, deployed inside Kurdish-held territory, and entered Manbij, west of the Euphrates River, where US troops had previously conducted joint patrols with Turkey. Syrian troops and Russian forces also entered Ain al-Arab (Kobani), a strategically important border city. The SDF invited in the government forces, as an emergency step, to help fend off the Turkish assault. Evidently, Washington's decision to abandon a policy it had pursued since 2014 gave Turkey and Russia a free hand to shape the battlefield. The deployment of the Syrian forces near the border with Turkey, a continuous Russian demand, was a victory for al-Assad and Russia because it gave them a foothold in the biggest remaining swath of the country that was outside their control. On 17 October, a ceasefire was announced by US Vice President Mike Pence after talks in Ankara with Erdogan. Accordingly, the YPG was obliged to pull out of the safe zone that was primarily enforced by Turkey.[12] Before the US-Turkish ceasefire expired it was superseded by a Russian-Turkish ceasefire agreement, which both the YPG and Damascus accepted. As the YPG's hold on the area weakened it sought arrangements with the al-Assad regime, through Russia, to gradually reintegrate the area into the Syrian state and preserve its civil and security institutions as much as possible.

Trump's actions in Syria were part of a Middle Eastern policy that, as Martin Indyk explained in *Foreign Affairs*, was in total disarray. "In fact," Indyk said, the Trump administration "understands so little about how the Middle East actually works that its bungling efforts have been a failure across the board. As so often in the past, the cynical locals are manipulating a clueless outsider, advancing their personal agendas at the naïve Americans' expense."[13] Still, Indyk said, "almost three years into his term, Trump has nothing to show for his efforts to counter Iran or promote peace in the Middle East. Instead, his policies have fueled the conflict between Iran and Israel, alienated the Palestinians, supported an unending war and a humanitarian crisis in Yemen, and split the Gulf Cooperation Council, possibly permanently."[14]

Once again, Russia exploited the opportunity and filled the vacuum after the pullback of US troops. On 22 October 2019, after marathon talks in Sochi, Erdogan and Putin agreed to push back the YPG/PKK fighters to a line thirty-two kilometres deep along the entire length of the Turkish-Syrian border (440 kilometres). Turkey was granted the right to remain fully deployed in an Arab majority area it had dubbed a safe zone that was the main objective of the offensive.[15] Turkey put Russia as guarantor for the implementation of the agreement. The agreement entrusted Russian military police and Syrian regime border guards, which had already started returning to the north, with the task of removing YPG fighters and their weapons from a zone extending thirty kilometres south of the Turkish-Syrian border. The Sochi agreement also authorized joint Turkish-Russian patrols along the entire border, to a depth of ten kilometres inside Syria, with the exception of the border city Qamishli, the de facto capital of the defunct Kurdish autonomous region. For the Kurds the agreement was the end of Rojava, the name they gave to their region. At the time of writing (2019), Russia "is walking its own tightrope between two partners that are viscerally hostile toward one another: a regime with which it is closely allied and a country with which it wishes to strengthen relations for a range of geopolitical reasons."[16] It is noteworthy that in early November 2019, US troops began repositioning to the Deir al-Zour province with their SDF fighters "to increase security and continue their mission to defeat IS remnants" and to prevent oil fields from being taken over by IS militant groups. The death of Baghdadi (the leader of IS) in a raid by US Special Forces in northwestern Syria on 27 October may prompt the embattled remnants of IS to seek revenge for their fallen leader. Trump reiterated that a small number of US troops would remain in Syria "where they have the oil."[17] The three influential actors in Syria, Iran, Russia, and Turkey criticized the US decision to maintain a presence near Syrian oil fields. However, the US needed to get back in Syria to reduce, if not eliminate, Iran's influence in there. Iran could stir up trouble not only in Syria but also in Iraq and Lebanon and pose a security threat to Israel.

Turkey's unilateral action in Syria and the position of NATO was also criticized harshly by French President Emmanuel Macron during the G7 summit in Biarritz, France in August 2019. Macron said, "what we are currently experiencing is the brain death of NATO." He also said, "you have an uncoordinated aggressive action by another NATO ally, Turkey, in an area where our interests are at stake."[18] Concerning strategic dialogue with Russia, Macron emphasized that it was crucial to seek a rapprochement with Moscow, which had regarded NATO's expansion into FSR suspicious and a threat to Russia's security and national interests. I argued that since the late 1990s Russia has not been respected by the West and has experienced a status dilemma. Moscow perceived the European partnership programs with Georgia and Ukraine and NATO's enlargement policy as a threat to its values and security and an attempt at regime change in Russia. Another reason that prevented partnership with Europe was that Russia did not share European values: it does not champion democracy and the rule of law. The EU renounced any revision of borders by force, and the ongoing war in Ukraine's Donbas region made a EU-Russia partnership impossible. Russia's annexation of Crimea was a revisionist move, not typical for status-inconsistent powers. Nonetheless, Macron made renewed efforts to improve EU-Russian relations by meeting with Putin in the run-up to the G7 summit in Biarritz.

The problem was that there was no partnership between the US and Russia partly because from the 1990s successive US administrations had treated Russia as a subordinate nation and denied it equal status. Thus, Macron's explosive comments appeared plausible when he said NATO had not re-examined its future in the early 1990s after the collapse of the Soviet Union and "the unarticulated assumption is that the enemy is still Russia." Despite the Kremlin's anti-Western rhetoric and given the limits of its status-seeking strategy, in the long term Russia would need "a partnership with Europe." However, "to rebuild European strategic autonomy," Europe "need to reconsider its position with Russia," Macron said.[19] Russia would benefit economically. But improving economic relations was difficult without progress in the implementation of the Minsk Protocol to end the conflict in Ukraine.

I have argued that peace and security in the ME and at the global level required a deeper understanding between the US and Russia. In a changing international order, Russia advocated multipolarity and sought to have an equal say on global issues. We witnessed a progressive erosion of international cooperation that was demonstrated in the G7/G8 summits and at the level of the UN when both the US and Russia violated international law under the pretext of protecting their national interests. Russia lost prestige when its G8 membership was suspended in 2014. Yet, Russia expressed the desire to restore international law and the UN's key role in that. After all, the UN was Russia's preferred multilateral forum. As a veto-wielding permanent member of the Security Council and a nuclear power, Russia exercised influence and could prevent US unilateral action. It is reasonable to assume that renewed multilateral cooperation through the UN could play to Russia's strengths and satisfy its great power aspirations. Military power aside, Russian diplomacy succeeded in de-escalating the tension between the US and North Korea. Still, Russia as one of the main parties to the Joint Comprehensive Plan of Action (JCPOA), as the Iranian nuclear deal of 2015 is known, managed to bring Iran to the negotiating table through sanctions. In Syria, although Russia's diplomacy against Western intervention was successful in terms of maintaining Moscow's centrality in international conflict management efforts, it did not stop the violence on the ground.

Arms control was another area of US-Russian disagreement. At the moment there is strategic instability between the US and Russia because the two nations barely talk. On 2 August 2019, the US and Russia officially withdrew from the 1987 INF Treaty. Both the US and NATO accused Russia of violating the agreement by deploying the 9M729 land-based intermediate missile and the Burevestnik (Storm Petrel), a nonstrategic nuclear weapon known to NATO as the SSC-8 Skyfall.[20] On 20 August, China and Russia warned that a new US missile test heightened military tensions and risked sparking an arms race. The US missile test came weeks after a deadly explosion at a Russian testing site. The INF's collapse could undermine the last pillar of arms control, the 2010 New START arms control treaty that will expire in 2021 unless renewed. Putin reiterated that if Washington was reluctant to begin talks, "we do not have to extend it. Our systems can guarantee Russia's security for quite a long period of time."[21] According to Sam Nunn, "we need political space for arms control discussions to take place."[22] Failing to address Russia's security concerns and not resuming strategic dialogue with Moscow under the pretext of Russia's intervention in the 2016 presidential election was "not a sensible strategy."[23]

Concerning Russia's status aspirations, it is important to stress that in the twenty-first century military power and nuclear weapons are not sufficient attributes to achieve higher status. True, Russia undertook diplomatic initiatives in the ME and pursued leadership in regional organizations. Putin successfully restored Russia's presence on the world stage. Yet, in a new global order, achieving higher status would be determined by increased economic clout, diversified economy, better healthcare, transparency, additional responsibilities at the global level, and "a wider spectrum of technological capabilities based on digitization."[24]

Russia's intervention in Ukraine and Syria showed ample evidence of status dilemma dynamics. Overall, Russia's hard-power-based status seeking in Ukraine and Syria did not solve the country's status-inconsistency dilemma. Russia's willingness to use military power in its foreign policy and by risking conflict in Syria can form a social status perspective and is perhaps a necessary step to defend its identity as a great power both in the region and in its relations with the West. If we acknowledge that the role of status in the Russian military campaign in Syria was crucial, then it must be taken into account in any solution. This book addressed the two hypotheses that are related to the possibility of according higher status to Russia by the dominant power (the US). If the West is willing to accord Russia a status only in terms of the existing international order, then such recognition would not satisfy Russia's aspirations because Russia rejected the principle of global domination by one power (the US). The post-Cold War global order is undergoing a fundamental change with the rise of China and resurgent Russia. Russia could be accorded higher status if both the US and Russia do not consider each other or do not anticipate each other to emerge as primary threats. The analysis in this book provided evidence that US Presidents Clinton and Bush avoided the potential pitfalls of managing the status aspirations of Russia. I also showed the limits to Russia becoming a status-consistent power and its weaknesses in promoting its soft power, culture, and economy so as to set the guiding principles of global order. Trump expressed willingness to conduct dialogue with Russia but Congress was not in favour of rewarding Russia for its revisionist moves. According Russia higher status could have reduced a great power conflict in the international system and some of the material costs that major powers incur to structure the order and international development necessary for global peace.

While H1 ensures the permissive conditions for the dominant power (the US) to accommodate Russia's status claims, H2 also creates conditions that require an active policy on the part of the dominant power to satisfy Russia's aspirations. The balancing logic means that the US would have preferred integrating Russia into its orbit while it could before dissatisfaction reached a point where Russia refrained from cooperation with regard the primary threat (international terrorism and arms control). Yet, Russia should have realized that the common threat could not be balanced without the help of the US and that joining hands would bring security and status. If the US is less likely to engage in status accommodation, the likelihood of a prolonged status conflict with the West will continue.

APPENDIX A

Provisions Agreed Upon during the Second Inter-Syrian Consultative Meeting. Moscow, 9 April 2015

1. The settlement of the Syrian crisis must be reached through political means on the basis of mutual agreement on the principles of Geneva I, 30 June 2012.
2. The participants appeal to the members of the international community to use their influence on all Arab, regional, and international parties involved in Syrian bloodshed, urging them to fulfill UN Security Council resolutions on counterterrorism and cessation of all actions supporting terrorism, including the promotion of terrorists on Syrian territory, their education and training, providing them with shelter, financial aid and weapons.
3. The participants appeal to the members of the international community demanding immediate and complete lifting of the blockade and unilateral coercive economic measures introduced against the Syrian people and state institutions.
4. Content and results of any political process must be based on national sovereignty and the people's will expressed through democratic mechanisms.
5. The political process is carried out through mutual agreement between the Syrians – government, forces, parties, and movements that are committed to a political solution.
6. The participants express support for a national reconciliation process and eagerness to strengthen it as well as to facilitate the achievement of a political settlement and support of the army and the armed forces in the fight against terrorism.
7. The participants appeal to the members of the international community for assistance in repatriation of Syrian refugees and creation of favourable conditions for the return of IDPs.

8 The fundamental goals of a political process are as follows:
   a Preservation of national sovereignty.
   b Unity of Syrian territory and its people.
   c Preservation of public institutions, improvement and enhancement of their functioning.
   d Rejection of any political settlement built on ethnic, religious, or communal quotas.
   e Strict commitment to liberation of all the occupied Syrian territories.
   f The only way to achieve a political solution is an inter-Syrian national dialogue, led by the Syrians without any external intervention.
9 A political settlement will lead to consolidation and mobilization of the people in countering and defeating terrorism. Such a settlement should result in an exclusive monopoly by state institutions to possess weapons.
10 The participants appeal to the members of the international community to support mutual agreement on a comprehensive political solution to be reached during the Moscow meeting in preparation for its adoption during the Geneva 3 conference.[1]

APPENDIX B

The Russian Eight-Point Plan, November 2015

1 UN Security Council to list ISIS as a terrorist organization.
2 Agree on the additional list of terrorist groups.
3 Adopt a UN Security Council resolution in support of the efforts against ISIS and other terrorist groups, providing legal framework for cooperation of all participants of counterterrorist actions among themselves and with respective governments.
4 Block channels of supply of ISIS and other terrorist groups; stop illegal trade in oil by ISIS in accordance with UNSCR 2199; prevent control of oil fields by terrorists.
5 When considering the issue of ceasefire in Syria, operations against ISIS and other terrorist groups must be excluded.
6 Launch under the auspices of the UN special envoy political process on the basis of the Geneva Communiqué of 30 June 2012 between the Syrian government and a united delegation of the opposition groups. The composition of the opposition delegation has to be agreed beforehand, including on the basis of readiness of respective groups to share the goals of preventing terrorists from coming to power in Syria and of ensuring sovereignty, territorial integrity, and political independence of Syria, as well as secular and democratic character of the state.
7 The Syrian parties at the proposed conference are invited to agree on the following steps: Launch a constitutional reform up to eighteen months; for that purpose, to form a constitutional commission to embrace the entire spectrum of the Syrian society; draft constitution will be submitted to a popular referendum; parliamentary elections planned to take place in the spring of 2016; Syrian government will be formed on the basis of party/electoral

block which receives a majority of the popular vote and will have the functions of commander in chief of the armed forces, control of special services and foreign policy.

8 Convene a Syrian Support Group (SSG) to help prepare the conference and assist Syrian parties during its work in reaching mutual consent. The SSG could include members of P-5, Saudi Arabia, Turkey, Iran, Egypt, Jordan, Oman, Qatar, UAE, Iraq, Lebanon, Germany, Italy, UN Special Envoy, Arab League and OIC, EU.[1]

Notes

INTRODUCTION

1 Volgy, Corbetta, Grant, and Baird, "Major Power Status in International Politics," 10.
2 Simes, "Losing Russia," 36.
3 Tsygankov, "Vladimir Putin's Last Stand," 292.
4 Trenin, "The Revival of Russian Military," 24.
5 Freire and Heller, "Russia's Power Politics in Ukraine and Syria," 1201.
6 Renshon, *Fighting for Status, Hierarchy and Conflict in World Politics*, 59 and 65.
7 See, Larson, Paul, and Wohlforth, "Status and World Order," 3–29.
8 Volgy, Corbetta, Rhamey Jr, Baird, and Grant, "Status Considerations in International Politics," 83.
9 Quoted in Brzezinski, "Putin's Choice," 177.
10 Tsygankov, "Assessing Cultural and Regime-Based Explanations of Russia's Foreign Policy."
11 Freire and Heller, "Russia's Power Politics," 1203.
12 Makarychev, *Russia and the EU in a Multipolar World*, 53.
13 Tsygankov, "Vladimir Putin's Last Stand," 287.
14 Makarychev, *Russia and the EU*, 68.
15 Larson, Paul, and Wohlforth, "Status and World Order," 18.
16 See Tsygankov, "The Frustrating Partnership," 345–54.
17 Freire and Heller, "Russia's Power Politics," 1201.
18 "The Military Doctrine of the Russian Federation approved by the President of the Russian Federation on 25 December 2014," accessed 2 December 2016, http://www.theatrum-belli.com/the-military-doctrine-of-the-russian-federation.

19 Jenkins, "A Revanchist Russia Versus an Uncertain West," 2.
20 Tsygankov, *Russia and the West from Alexander to Putin*.
21 Freire and Heller, "Russia's Power Politics," 1203.
22 Quoted in Brian Whitmore, "The Road from Damascus to Yalta," *Radio Free Europe/Radio Liberty, Russia Report* (hereafter RFE/RL), 15 March 2016.
23 Sergunin, *Explaining Russian Foreign Policy Behavior*, 35.
24 Mankoff, *Russian Foreign Policy*, 62–8.
25 Nizameddin, *Putin's New Order in the Middle East*, 51–2.
26 Sergunin, *Explaining Russian Foreign Policy Behavior*, 99.
27 Sergei Karaganov, "Mutually Assured Deterrence can Save the World," *The Daily Star*, 25 February 2017, 7.
28 See Renshon, *Fighting for Status*, 36.
29 Quoted in ibid., 52.
30 Morgenthau, *Politics Among Nations*, 85.
31 See Shannon and Kowert, *Psychology and Constructivism in International Relations*.
32 Sergunin, *Explaining Russian Foreign Policy Behavior*, 59. See also Forsberg, Heller, and Wolf, "Status and Emotions in Russian Foreign Policy," 261–8.
33 Tsygankov, *Russia and the West from Alexander to Putin*.
34 Levy, *War in the Modern Great Power System*. See also Volgy, Corbetta, Grant, and Baird, *Major Powers and the Quest for Status in International Politics*.
35 Gilpin, *War and Change in World Politics*, 31.
36 Danilovic and Clare, "Global Power Transitions and Regional Interests," 292.
37 Volgy and Mayhall, "Status Inconsistency and International War," 68.
38 Volgy et al., "Major Power Status," 10–2.
39 Wohlforth, "Unipolarity, Status Competition, and Great Power War," 40.
40 Volgy et al., "Major Power Status," 11.
41 See Organski, *World Politics*. See also Organski and Kuglar, *The War Ledger*.
42 Volgy et al., "Major Power Status," 12.
43 Freire and Heller, "Russia's Power Politics." 1192.
44 "The Foreign Policy Concept of the Russia Federation," 28 June 2000, http://fas.org/nuke/guide/russia/doctrine/econcept.htm.
45 Bull, *The Anarchical Society*, 202.
46 Larson and Shevchenko, "Managing Rising Powers," 34–5.
47 Larson and Shevchenko, "Russia Says No," 269–79.
48 Larson and Shevchenko, "Managing Rising Powers," 42.
49 Tajfel, "The Achievement of Group Differentiation," 93–4.
50 Dore, "The Prestige Factor in International Affairs," 190–207.
51 Turner and Brown, "Social Status, Cognitive Alternatives," 201–34.
52 Tsygankov, "The Sources of Russia's Fear," 104.

53 Ibid.
54 Mearsheimer, "Why the Ukraine Crisis is the West's Fault," 83.
55 Westle, "Identity, Social and Political," 1135.
56 Freire and Heller, "Russia's Power Politics," 1185.
57 Ibid.
58 Yost, "The Budapest Memorandum."
59 Tsygankov, "Preserving Influence in a Changing World," 31.
60 Paul and Shankar, "Status Accommodation through Institutional Means," 170.
61 Ibid.
62 Ibid., 171.
63 Bryman, *Quantity and Quality in Social Research*, 45–50.
64 Altaqi and Aziz, "Putin's Game Plan in the Middle East," 2.

CHAPTER ONE

1 Tsygankov, "Self and Other in International Relations Theory," 767.
2 Tsygankov, "Contested Identity and Foreign Policy," 29.
3 Tsygankov, "Preserving Influence," 29.
4 See "New Thinking: Foreign Policy under Gorbachev," accessed 6 November 2018, http://countrystudies.us/russia/17.htm.
5 McCauley, *Gorbachev*, 77.
6 Ibid., 70.
7 Simes, "Losing Russia," 38.
8 Duncan, "The Rebirth of Politics in Russia," 110–11.
9 Malinova, "Russian Political Discourse in the 1990s," 117.
10 Donaldson, Nogee, and Nadkarni, *The Foreign Policy of Russia*, 232.
11 Tsygankov, *Russia's Foreign Policy*, 57.
12 See Malinova, "Russian Political Discourse," 111–20.
13 Tsygankov, "Self and Other in International Relations Theory," 768.
14 Tsygankov, *Russia's Foreign Policy*, 58.
15 Ibid.
16 Quoted in Donaldson, Nogee, and Nadkarni, *The Foreign Policy of Russia*, 237.
17 Ibid.
18 Simes, "Losing Russia," 39–40.
19 Belopolsky, *Russia and the Challengers*, 43.
20 Ibid.
21 Tsygankov, "The Sources of Russia's Fear," 103.
22 Tsygankov, *Russia's Foreign Policy*, 59.

23 Simes, "Losing Russia," 40.
24 See "The Basic Provisions of the Military Doctrine of the Russian Federation," accessed 17 March 2017, https://fas.org/nuke/guide/russia/doctrine/russia-mil-doc.html.
25 Nizameddin, *Putin's New Order*, 39.
26 Rumer, "Dangerous Drift," 7.
27 Lynch, "The Realism of Russia's Foreign Policy," 7–31.
28 Kreutz, *Russia in the Middle East*, 18.
29 See, "Who was Who? The Key Players in Russia's Dramatic October 1993 Showdown," RFE/RL *Russia Report*, 2 October 2018.
30 Quoted in Kreutz, *Russia in the Middle East*, 19.
31 See "Who was Who? The Key Players," 2 October 2018.
32 Donaldson, Nogee, and Nadkarni, *The Foreign Policy of Russia*, 145–6.
33 Kreutz, *Russia in the Middle East*, 19.
34 Concerning Syrian–Russian relations in the Soviet era, see Freedman, *Soviet Policy Toward the Middle East since 1970*.
35 Kreutz, *Russia in the Middle East*, 20.
36 Stent, "America and Russia," 260–80.
37 Alexander J. Motyl, "Dilemmas of Independence: Ukraine after Totalitarianism," Council of Foreign Relations, New York, 1993.
38 Quoted in Simes, "Losing Russia," 40.
39 Concerning emotions in Russia's foreign policy, see Tsygankov, "The Frustrating Partnership," 345–54.
40 Paul and Shankar, "Status Accommodation," 170.
41 Donaldson, Nogee, and Nadkarni, *The Foreign Policy of Russia*, 312.
42 Mankoff, *Russian Foreign Policy*, 121.
43 Richard Boudreaux, "Russia Agrees to Stop Selling Arms to Iran," *Los Angeles Times*, 1 July 1995.
44 Donaldson, Nogee, and Nadkarni, *The Foreign Policy of Russia*, 312.
45 Nizameddin, *Putin's New Order*, 43.
46 Trenin, *What is Russia up to in the Middle East*, 37.
47 Ibid.
48 Tsygankov, *Russia's Foreign Policy*, 67.
49 Smith, "Russia as a Great Power," 358.
50 Ibid.
51 Donaldson, Nogee, and Nadkarni, *The Foreign Policy of Russia*, 245.
52 Baev, *Russian Energy Policy and Military Power*, 9.
53 Sergunin, *Explaining Russian Foreign Policy Behavior*, 85.
54 Mankoff, *Russian Foreign Policy*, 65.
55 Ibid., 66.

56 Fridman, *Russian "Hybrid Warfare,"* 87.
57 Tsygankov, "Self and Other," 768.
58 Stankevich, "Toward a New National Idea," 31–2.
59 Ibid., 24.
60 Mankoff, *Russian Foreign Policy*, 68.
61 Ibid.
62 Lukin, "Russia and its Interests," 115.
63 Malcolm, "New Thinking and After," 167.
64 Clunan, "Historical Aspirations," 285.
65 Tsygankov, *Russia's Foreign Policy*, 67.
66 Skillen, *Freedom of Speech in Russia*, 40.
67 Kreutz, *Russia in the Middle East*, 20.
68 Quoted in Mearsheimer, "Why the Ukraine Crisis is the West's Fault," 78.
69 Donaldson, Nogee, and Nadkarni, *The Foreign Policy of Russia*, 243.
70 Hill and Gaddy, *Mr. Putin, Operative in the Kremlin*, 30.
71 Smith, "Russia as a Great Power," 360.
72 Belopolsky, *Russia and the Challengers*, 161.
73 Quoted in Clunan, "Historical Aspirations," 286.
74 Mankoff, *Russian Foreign Policy*, 30.
75 Paul and Shankar, "Status Accommodation," 171.
76 Donaldson, Nogee, and Nadkarni, *The Foreign Policy of Russia*, 313.
77 Ibid. The five littoral states are Iran, Russia, Turkmenistan, Kazakhstan, and Azerbaijan. It is important to note that these five littoral states have disagreed on how the bottom of the Caspian should be divided between them. The 1921 friendship treaty that was signed between Iran and the Soviet Union, which recognized the two countries' borders in the Caspian Sea, in addition the treaty of March 1940 that provided the legal status of the Caspian Sea until 1989 are not acceptable to post-Soviet Russia.
78 Kandiyoti, *Pipelines, Flowing Oil and Crude Politics*, 165.
79 Donaldson, Nogee, and Nadkarni, *The Foreign Policy of Russia*, 330.
80 Ibid., 314.
81 Mankoff, *Russian Foreign Policy*, 107.
82 Ibid.,108.
83 Forsberg, "Status Conflicts Between Russia and the West," 326.
84 Karaganov, "Russia's Choice," 7.
85 Larson and Shevchenko, "Managing Rising Powers," 38.
86 Clunan, "Historical Aspirations," 286.
87 *Rossiiskaya Gazeta*, 26 December 1997, 4–5. FBIS-SOV-97-364, 30 December 1997.
88 Lo, *Russia and the New World Disorder*, 43.

89 Ibid.
90 Clunan, "Historical Aspirations," 287.
91 Ibid., 286.
92 Simes, "Losing Russia," 42.
93 *Rossiiskaya Gazeta*, 26 December 1997, 4-5. FBIS-SOV-97-364, 30 December 1997.
94 Primakov, *Russia and the Arabs*, 297.
95 Ibid., 299.
96 Ross, *The Missing Peace*, 493–4.
97 Kreutz, *Russia in the Middle East*, 24.
98 Ibid.
99 Ibid., 22.
100 Quoted in Ross, *The Missing Peace*, 498.
101 Zartman, "Conflict Resolution and Negotiation, 329.
102 Renshon, *Fighting for Status*, 58–9.
103 Smith, "Russia as a Great Power," 361.
104 Evangelista, *The Chechen Wars*.
105 Tsygankov, "The Frustrating Partnership," 346.
106 Simes, "Losing Russia," 42.
107 Paul and Shankar, "Status Accommodation," 171–2.
108 Simes, "Losing Russia," 43.
109 Smith, "Russia as a Great Power," 361.
110 Mankoff, *Russian Foreign Policy*, 108.
111 Tsygankov, "The Frustrating Partnership," 347.
112 Tsygankov, "Vladimir Putin's Vision of Russia," 132–58.
113 Nizameddin, *Putin's New Order*, 76.

CHAPTER TWO

1 Sherr, *Hard Diplomacy and Soft Coercion*, 54.
2 Nitoiu, "Aspirations to Great Power Status," 41.
3 Baev, *Russian Energy Policy and Military Power*, 3.
4 Tsygankov, "Russia's International Assertiveness," 39.
5 Laqueur, *Putinism*, 51.
6 Khripunov, "Russia's Weapons Trade," 41.
7 Laqueur, *Putinism*, 112.
8 Vladislavlev and Karaganov, "The Idea of Russia," 36.
9 Tsygankov, "Contested Identity and Foreign Policy," 25.
10 Tsygankov, *Russia and the West from Alexander to Putin*, 4.
11 Vladislavlev and Karaganov, "The Idea of Russia," 33.

12 Nizameddin, *Putin's New Order*, 81.
13 de Hass, *Russia's Foreign Security Policy in the 21st Century*.
14 The National Security Concept of the Russian Federation, approved by Presidential Decree No. 24 on 10 January 2000, accessed 9 November 2018, http://www.mid.ru/en/foreign_policy_documents/assets_publisher.
15 The Foreign Policy Concept of the Russian Federation, approved by President Vladimir Putin on 28 June 2000, accessed 17 March 2017, http://fas.org/nuke/guide/Russia/doctrine/concept.htm.
16 Ibid.
17 Tsygankov, "The Sources of Russia's Fear," 104.
18 The Foreign Policy Concept of the Russian Federation, approved by President Vladimir Putin on 28 June 2000.
19 Leichtova, *Misunderstanding Russia*, 36.
20 Lyne, "Russia's Changed Outlook," 3.
21 Tsygankov, "Preserving Influence," 36
22 Ibid.
23 Makarychev, *Russia and the EU in a Multipolar World*, 94.
24 Donaldson, Nogee, and Nadkarni, *The Foreign Policy of Russia*, 365.
25 Ibid., 366.
26 Mankoff, *Russian Foreign Policy*, 109.
27 Donaldson, Nogee, and Nadkarni, *The Foreign Policy of Russia*, 365.
28 Ibid., 367.
29 "Russia Offers China Joint Projects in Oil Deposits," *Moscow ITAR-TASS*, 22 March 2000. Foreign Broadcast Information Service (hereafter, FBIS-SOV-2000-0322).
30 Belopolsky, *Russia and the Challengers*, 130.
31 "Round One at Shepherdstown," *The New York Times*, accessed 5 December 2018, https//www.nytimes.com/2000/01/12/opinion/round-one-at-shepherdstown.html.
32 Jane Perlez, "In Geneva, Clinton Bet that Assad Would Bend, and Lost," *The New York Times*, accessed 5 December 2018, http://www.nytimes.com/2000/03/28/world/in-geneva-clinton-bet-that-assad-would-bend-and-lost.html.
33 *ITAR-TASS News Agency*, 13 June 2000.
34 Quoted in Mankoff, *Russian Foreign Policy*, 110.
35 Simes, "Losing Russia," 43.
36 Holsti, "National Pole Conceptions," 233–4, 245.
37 See Tsygankov, *Russia and the West*.
38 Goldgeier, *Power and Purpose*, 2.
39 Shay, *The Axis of Evil*, 171.

40 Mankoff, *Russian Foreign Policy*, 125.
41 Baev, *Russian Energy*, 71. It is important to note that Azerbaijan, Belarus, and Georgia joined the CSO in 1993, but in 1999, when the Tashkent Treaty was up for renewal, Azerbaijan, Georgia, and Uzbekistan seceded.
42 Mankoff, *Russian Foreign Policy*, 125.
43 Lyne, "Russia's Changed Outlook," 4.
44 Martin Gilman, "Russia: The Latecomer to G8," *Russia in Global Affairs* 3 (July/September 2007), accessed 6 December 2018, http://eng.globalaffairs.ru/number/n_9128.
45 Paul and Shankar, "Status Accommodation through Institutional Means," 172.
46 Slocombe, "Europe, Russia and American Missile Defense," 19–24.
47 Kimberly Marten, "Reducing Tensions Between Russia and NATO," Council on Foreign Relations, Special report no. 79 (March 2017): 10.
48 Lyne, "Russia's Changed Outlook," 6.
49 Nizameddin, *Putin's New Order*, 84.
50 Goodarzi, *Syria and Iran*, 293.
51 UN Security Council Resolution 1559, S/RES/1559, 2 September 2004.
52 Nizameddin, *Putin's New Order*, 89.
53 See "Russia, France Will not Allow Passage of War Resolution in Iraq," *Interfax*, Moscow, 5 March 2003, FBIS-SOV-2003-0305.
54 Baev, *Russian Energy Policy*, 36.
55 Simon Saradzhyan and Oskana Yablokova, "Putin Calls the Attack a Big Political Mistake," *The Moscow Times*, 21 March 2003, 1.
56 See "Withdrawal of Resolution from UNSC Seen as Declaration of War," *Moscow, ITAR-TASS*, 17 March 2003, FBIS-SOV-2003-0317.
57 Larson and Shevchenko, "Russia Says No," 273.
58 Nixey, "Russian Foreign Policy," 35.
59 Simes, "Losing Russia," 44–5.
60 Wohlforth, "Unipolarity, Status Competition," 40.
61 Jones, *Georgia, A Political History Since Independence*, 139.
62 Lyne, "Russia's Changed Outlook," 7.
63 Tsygankov, "Vladimir Putin's Last Stand," 282.
64 Ibid., 280.
65 Freire and Heller, "Russia's Power Politics," 1191.
66 Tsygankov, *Russia's Foreign Policy*, 155.
67 Simes, "Losing Russia," 44.
68 Donaldson, Nogee, and Nadkarni, *The Foreign Policy of Russia*, 377.
69 UN Security Council Resolution 1483, S/RES/1483, 22 May 2003.
70 Laqueur, *Putinism*, 116.

71 Sergunin, *Explaining Russian Foreign Policy Behavior*, 90.
72 Lyne, "Russia's Changed Outlook," 6.
73 Donaldson, Nogee, and Nadkarni, *The Foreign Policy of Russia*, 327.
74 Lyne, "Russia's Changed Outlook," 8.
75 Tsygankov, "The Sources of Russia's Fear," 108.
76 Ibid.
77 Tsygankov, "Preserving Influence," 38.
78 *Rossiiskaya Gazeta*, 27 May 2004, 3, in the Current Digest of the Post-Soviet Press 56, no. 21 (2004), 1.
79 Alexei Arbatov, "Is a New Cold War Imminent?" *Russia in Global Affairs* 2 (August 2007), accessed 17 December 2018, https://eng.globalaffairs.ru/number/n_9127.
80 Laqueur, *Putinism*, 117–18.
81 Grodeland, "Perceptions of Civil Rights," 318.
82 Donaldson, Nogee, and Nadkarni, *The Foreign Policy of Russia*, 385.
83 Trenin, *What is Russia up to in the Middle East?*, 40.
84 Donaldson, Nogee, and Nadkarni, *The Foreign Policy of Russia*, 329.
85 Hunter, *Iran Divided*, 79.
86 UN Security Council Resolution 1737, S/RES/1737, 23 December 2006.
87 UN Security Council Resolution 1747, S/RES/1747, 24 March 2007.
88 Donaldson, Nogee, and Nadkarni, *The Foreign Policy of Russia*, 389.
89 Ibid., 390.
90 See, Brzezinski, "Putin's Choice," 177.
91 Julia Ioffe, "Putin's Game, What Putin Really Wants," *The Atlantic* (January/February 2018), 75.
92 Speech and the Following Discussion at the Munich Conference on Security Policy, Munich, 10 February 2007, http://en.kremlin.ru/events/president/transcripts/24034.
93 Vladimir Putin, "Daiu Vam Chestone Partiinoe Slovo," *Kommersant*, 30 August 2010.
94 Speech and the Following Discussion at the Munich Conference on Security Policy, Munich, 10 February 2007.
95 Ibid.
96 Andrew E. Kramer and Thom Shanker, "Russia Suspends Arms Agreement over U.S. Shield," *The New York Times*, 15 July 2007.
97 Andrew E. Kramer, "Russia Resumes Patrols by Nuclear Bombers," *The New York Times*, 18 August 2007.
98 Andrew Tully, "Russia: Washington Reacts to Putin's Munich Speech," accessed 13 March 2017, http://www.rferl.org/a/1074671.html.

99 Ibid.
100 Antonenko, "Russia and the Deadlock over Kosovo," 91–106.
101 Tsygankov, "Contested Identity," 27.
102 Dmitry Medvedev, "Europe will Need European Security Treaty Soon or Later," *RIA Novosti*, 1 December 2010.
103 Trenin, *Post-Imperium*, 101–8.
104 Tsygankov, "The Sources of Russia's Fear," 105.
105 Makarychev, *Russia and the EU*, 117.
106 Nixey, "Russian Foreign Policy," 37–8.
107 Tsygankov, "Contested Identity and Foreign Policy," 29.
108 Tsygankov, "Russia and the CIS in 2011," 48.
109 Nixey, "Russian Foreign Policy," 36.
110 Fyodor Lukyanov, "Rossiya Mezhdu Kitayem I Zapadom," *Novoye Vremya* 22, 2 June 2008. See also Aleksandr Khramchikhin, "Sovbes Ozabotilsya National'noi Bezopasnostyu," *Nezavisimoye Voyennoye Obozreniye*, 16 January 2009.
111 Kolvraa and Ifversen, "The European Neighborhood Policy," 50–61.
112 Mearsheimer, "Why the Ukraine Crisis is the West's Fault," 79.
113 Nixey, "Russian Foreign Policy," 35.
114 See "Eurasian Economic Union," accessed 25 December 2018, http://en.wikipedia.org/wik/Eurasian_Economic_Union.
115 Volgy et al., "Status Considerations in International Politics," 64.
116 Nixey, "Russian Foreign Policy," 35.
117 Sergi, "Putin's and Russian-Led Eurasian Economic Union," 54.
118 The Foreign Policy Concept of the Russian Federation, 12 January 2008, http://en.Kremlin.ru/supplement/4116.
119 Ibid.
120 Ibid.
121 German, *Regional Cooperation in the South Caucasus*, 83.
122 Donaldson, Nogee, and Nadkarni, *The Foreign Policy of Russia*, 397.
123 Freire and Heller, "Russia's Power Politics in Ukraine and Syria," 1188.
124 Sergei Lavrov, "America Must Choose Between Georgia and Russia," *Wall Street Journal*, 20 August 2008.
125 D'antonio, *The Legacy of Barack Obama*, 160.
126 Donaldson, Nogee, and Nadkarni, *The Foreign Policy of Russia*, 398.
127 "Obama: U.S. Wants Strong Peaceful Russia," *CNN*, 7 July 2009, http://edition.cnn.com/2009/POLITICS/07/07/obama.moscow/index.html.
128 Peter Baker, "Twists, Turns and Anger on Way to Arms Pact with Russia," *New York Times*, 26 March 2010.

129 "Obama: U.S. Wants Strong Peaceful Russia," 7 July 2009.
130 Ibid.
131 "U.S. Relations: Reset Fact Sheet," White House, Office of the Press Secretary, 24 June 2010, http://obamawhitehouse.archives.gov/realitycheck/the-press-office/us-russia-relations-reset-fact-sheet.
132 Ibid.
133 UN Security Council Resolution 1929, S/RES/1929, on 9 June 2010.
134 Mark Lander, "Clinton Trip to Moscow Exposes Rift on Iran," *New York Times*, 18 March 2010.
135 Stent, *The Limits of Partnership*, 234.
136 "U.S. Relations: Reset Fact Sheet," White House, Office of the Press Secretary, 24 June 2010, http://obamawhitehouse.archives.gov/realitycheck/the-press-office/us-russia-relations-reset-fact-sheet.
137 Ibid.
138 Ellen Barry, "After Competing for Influence in Kyrgyzstan, Big Powers Step Aside," *New York Times*, 19 June 2010. See also Michael Schwirtz, "New Leader Says U.S. Base in Kyrgyzstan Will Be Shut," *The New York Times*, 1 November 2011.
139 Sherr, "A War of Narratives and Arms," 24.
140 Stent, *The Limits of Partnership*, 238.
141 Nixey, "Russian Foreign Policy," 38.
142 Quoted in Larson and Shevchenko, "Russia Says No," 275.
143 Cimbala, "Russia and European Missile Defenses," 10.
144 Alexander Golts, "Medvedev Mollifies the West," *The Moscow Times*, 29 November 2011.
145 Ruslan Pukhov, "Medvedev's Missile Threats are His Plan B," *The Moscow Times*, 1 December 2011.
146 Paul and Shankar, "Status Accommodation," 170.
147 Quoted in Cimbala, "Russia and European Missile Defenses," 13.
148 Jim Nichol, "Russia's December 2011 Legislative Election: Outcome and Implications," Congressional Research Service Report for Congress, R42118, 13 December 2011, 8.

CHAPTER THREE

1 Altaqi and Aziz, "Putin's Game Plan in the Middle East," 2.
2 Makarychev, *Russia and the EU in a Multipolar World*, 187.
3 See Van Dam, *Destroying a Nation*, 69–70.
4 Kozhanov, *Russia and the Syrian Conflict*, 23.
5 Phillips, *The Battle for Syria*, 92.

6 Quoted in "Russia, Iran Diverge on Assad Stance," *The Daily Star*, 4 November 2015, 1.
7 Freire and Heller, "Russia's Power Politics," 1201.
8 See "Reforms in Syria on Back Burner," *The Daily Star*, 31 March 2011, 1.
9 Geukjian, "The Objectives of Russia's Military Intervention," 279.
10 Author interview with Walid Jumblatt, Beirut, 15 November 2018.
11 See "Obama Backs Return to 1967 Borders," *The Daily Star*, 20 May 2011, 1.
12 Ibid., 1.
13 See "Syria's Moallem: Forget Europe," *The Daily Star*, 23 June 2011, 1.
14 See International Crisis Group, "Syria's Mutating Conflict," Middle East Report no. 128 (1 August 2012): 3.
15 Quoted in David Ignatius, "As the Assad Ship Sinks, Washington Changes Gears," *The Daily Star*, 21 July 2011, 7.
16 Freire and Heller, "Russia's Power Politics," 1201.
17 Author interview with Walid Jumblatt, Beirut, 15 November 2018.
18 Presidential Statement adopted by the Security Council (SC/10352), in its 6598th Meeting, 3 August 2011.
19 See, "Syria Testing International Patience," *The Daily Star*, 5 August 2011, 1, 10.
20 Author interview with Russian Ambassador Alexander Zasypkin, Beirut, 26 December 2018.
21 See "Syria's Diplomatic Isolation Grows," *The Daily Star*, 9 August 2011, 1.
22 Joseph Logan, "Saudi Arabia's Calculated Risk on Syria Poses a Major Blow to Iran," *The Daily Star*, 10 August 2011, 6.
23 See *As-Safir*, 10 August 2011, 1, 17.
24 Author interview with Walid Jumblatt, Beirut, 15 November 2018.
25 Joost Hiltermann, "Russia a Reluctant Driver in the Syria War," International Crisis Group, 26 February 2018, 1.
26 Phillips, *The Battle for Syria*, 31.
27 David Ignatius, "In Syria, the U.S. can Pursue Interests and Values," *The Daily Star*, 20 August 2011, 7.
28 International Crisis Group, "Anything But Politics: The State of Syria's Political Opposition," Middle East Report no. 146 (17 October 2013): 3.
29 See Nicholas Blanford, "Russia Banks on Assad's Survival as Billions in Arms Deals Hang in Balance," *The Daily Star*, 21 September 2011, 9.
30 Ibid.
31 Ron Synovitz, "Explainer: Why is Access to Syria's Port at Tartus so Important to Moscow?" *RFE/RL Russia Report*, 19 June 2012.
32 UN Security Council Draft Resolution (SC/10403) at its 6627th meeting, 4 October 2011, http://www.un.org/press/en/2011/sc10403.doc.htm.

33 Ibid.
34 Author interview with Russian Ambassador Alexander Zasypkin, Beirut, 26 December 2018.
35 See "Dim Prospects for Syrian Dialogue," *The Daily Star*, 27 October 2011, 1.
36 See International Crisis Group, "Conflict Risk Alert: Syria's Tipping Point," 3 November 2011.
37 See "Arab League Gives Syria Three Days to End Crackdown, Threatens Sanctions," *RFE/RL Russia Report*, 16 November 2011.
38 Peter Harling and Hugh Pope, "Are There Zero Problems for Turkey?" *The Daily Star*, 29 November 2011, 7.
39 See, "Russia Floats New UN Draft on Syria," *The Daily Star*, 16 December 2011, 1.
40 See *As-Safir*, 20 December 2011, 1.
41 See *As-Safir*, 11 January 2012, 12.
42 See "Assad Vows to Crush Conspiracy," *The Daily Star*, 12 January 2012, 1.
43 Martin Chulov and Mathew Weaver, "Arab League in Disarray on Syria," *The Guardian Weekly*, 2 February 2012, 1.
44 See *An-Nahar*, 23 January 2012, 1, 12.
45 Quoted in Alistair Lyon, "Syria Denounces League Plan," *The Daily Star*, 24 January 2012, 1. Concerning military support, Russia signed a new deal to send Syria nearly forty fighter jet trainers. Damascus would also receive thirty-six Yak-130 aircraft for which it would pay $550 million.
46 See "Fighting Continues Near Damascus; Russia Offers Mediation," *RFE/RL Russia Report*, 30 January 2012.
47 UN Security Council Draft Resolution (SC/10536), at its 6711th meeting, 4 February 2012, http://www.un.org/press/en/2012/sc10536.doc.htm.
48 Quoted in Steve Gulterman, "Putin Backs Gradual Democratic Renewal," *The Daily Star*, 7 February 2012, 11.
49 Stent, *The Limits of Partnership*, 245.
50 Vladimir Putin, "Address to the Federal Assembly," 12 December 2012, en.kremlin.ru/events/president/news/17118.
51 Hussein Abdallah and Lauren Williams, "West, Opposition Dismiss Syria Vote," *The Daily Star*, 27 February 2012, 1.
52 UN Security Council Presidential Statement on Syria adopted at its 6746th meeting, 21 March 2012, http://www.un.org/press/en/2012/sc10601.doc.htm.
53 See "Text of Annan's Six-Point Peace Plan for Syria," 4 April 2012, https://www.reuters.com/article/us-syria-ceasefire/text-of-annans-six-point-peace-plan-for-syria.
54 Ria Daou, "Friends of Syria Steer Clear of Conflict: Expert," *The Daily Star*, 2 April 2012, 9.

55 See "Shaky Truce Tests Monitors in Syria," *The Daily Star*, 17 April 2012, 1. See also "Syria Signs Protocol on Terms for UN Observers," *The Daily Star*, 20 April 2012, 1, 10.
56 Roula Khalaf and Abigail Fielding-Smith, "UN's Syria Plan in Disarray," *Financial Times*, 28 May 2012, 1.
57 Charles Clover, "Russia Shifts Blame from Assad," *Financial Times*, 29 May 2012, 2.
58 Gideon Rachman, "In Syria, Diplomacy is Still Better than Bombs," *Financial Times*, 29 May 2012, 9.
59 Quoted in Fouad Ajami, "For Barack Obama, Syria is Best Forgotten this Election Year," *The Daily Star*, 22 June 2012, 7.
60 See "Obama, Putin Discuss Syria Crisis at G20," *RFE/RL Russia Report*, 19 June 2012.
61 Tsygankov, "Preserving Influence in a Changing World," 38.
62 Charles Clover, "Military Think-Tank Queries Kremlin's Backing for Syria," *Financial Times*, 27 June 2012, 4.
63 Van Dam, *Destroying a Nation*, 139–40.
64 See "Geneva-1 Final Communiqué of the Action Group for Syria; and the Basis for Geneva-2 Meeting," 29 January 2014, http://www.reasonedcomments.org/2014/01/012801geneva1.html.
65 Author interview with Russian Ambassador Alexander Zasypkin, Beirut, 26 December 2018.
66 Roula Khalaf and Michael Peel, "Deadly Bomb Strike at Heart of Assad Regime," *Financial Times*, 19 July 2012, 1.
67 UNSC Draft Resolution on Syria that Threatened Sanctions (SC/10714), at its 6810th Meeting, 19 July 2012, https://www.un.org/press/en/2012/sc10714.doc.htm.
68 Freire and Heller, "Russia's Power Politics," 1201.
69 Kofi Annan, "My Departing Advice on How the World can yet Save Syria," *Financial Times*, 3 August 2012, 9.
70 Roula Khalaf and Geoff Dyer, "Wary US Builds Support for Armed Rebellion," *Financial Times*, 3 August 2012, 9.
71 Ibid.
72 Tabler, "Syria's Collapse," 93.
73 Author interview with the Iranian ambassador to Beirut Mohammad Jalal Firouznia, Beirut, 4 January 2019.
74 Author interview with the Russian ambassador to Beirut Alexander Zasyptin, Beirut, 26 December 2018.
75 See "Turkey Demands Syria Safe Havens at UN Meeting," *The Daily Star*, 31 August 2012, 1.

76 John Irish, "Nations Fail to Agree on Protective Zone Strategy," *The Daily Star*, 1–2 September 2012, 11.

77 See "Brahimi: Assad Clinging to Old Syria," *The Daily Star*, 25 September 2012, 1.

78 See Commentary, "Obama's Realist Foreign Policy," *Financial Times*, 27 September 2012, 12.

79 See "Obama Renews Call for Ouster of Assad," *The Daily Star*, 26 September 2012, 1, 10.

80 Dmitry Zaks, "Russia Unveils $4.2 Billion Iraq Arms Deals as Maliki Visits," *The Daily Star*, 10 October 2012, 9.

81 See "Syrian National Coalition Formed, Seeks International Legitimacy," *The Daily Star*, 12 November 2012, 1.

82 Larson and Shevchenko, "Russia Says No," 275.

83 Stent, *The Limits of Partnership*, 252.

84 See "U.N. Envoy Sees no Return to Assad's Old Syria," *The Daily Star*, 30 November 2012, 8.

85 Commentary, "Russia and Syria," *Financial Times*, 17 December 2012, 8.

86 See "Shadow Over Geneva Talks as Syria Labels Brahimi Biased," *The Daily Star*, 11 January 2013, 1.

87 Michael Peel, "Even-Tempered Emissary Loses Patience with Assad's Rule," *Financial Times*, 11 January 2013, 6.

88 Steve Gutterman and Maria Kiselyova, "Russia Starts Record Naval Exercises, Syria Link Seen," *The Daily Star*, 21 January 2013, 8.

89 Daalder, "Responding to Russia's Resurgence," 32.

90 Jonathon Burch, "NATO Patriot Missile Batteries Arrive in Turkey," *The Daily Star*, 22 January 2013, 8.

91 Quoted in Lauren Williams, "Uncertainty Behind U.S. Escalation on Syria," *The Daily Star*, 20–1 April 2013, 10.

92 Ibid.

93 Gideon Rachman, "Syria and the Undoing of Obama's Grand Strategy," *Financial Times*, 30 April 2013, 9.

94 See "Arab League Agrees to Arm Syria Rebels," *The Daily Star*, 7 March 2013, 1.

95 See "Assad Appeals to BRICS Countries to Help End War," *The Daily Star*, 28 March 2013, 1, 10.

96 See "How Many Chechens are Fighting in Syria," *RFE/RL Russia Report*, 19 June 2013.

97 Sergunin, *Explaining Russian Foreign Policy Behavior*, 99.

98 See "Russia, China Reach $60 Billion Oil Supply Deal," *The Daily Star*, 21 June 2013, 6.

99 Alexei Anishchuk and Timothy Heritage, "Chinese Leader Bolsters Russian Ties," *The Daily Star*, 23–4 April 2013, 5.
100 See "Russia Presents Evidence Syrian Rebels Used Chemical Weapons," *RFE/RL Russia Report*, 9 July 2013.
101 Khaled Yacoub Oweis, "By Relying on Iran, Assad Risks Irrelevance," *The Daily Star*, 22 July 2013, 8.
102 Phillips, *The Battle for Syria*, 186.
103 Christopher R. Hill, "America Must Devise a Plan to help Rescue Syria, and Itself," *The Daily Star*, 30 July 2013, 7.
104 Matthew Rojansky and Nikolas Gvosdev, "The Reset That Wasn't," *The New York Times*, 5 July 2013.
105 Donaldson, Nogee, and Nadkarni, *The Foreign Policy of Russia*, 412.
106 See "Obama Vows to Punish Assad," *The Daily Star*, 31 August 2013, 1.
107 See "Kerry Waves Stick as Talks on Syria Begin," *The Daily Star*, 13 September 2013, 1.
108 Valdimir Putin, "A Plea for Caution from Russia," *The New York Times*, 11 September 2013.
109 UNSC Resolution 2118, S/RES/2118, 27 September 2013.
110 Martin S. Indyk, "The End of the U.S. Dominated Order in the Middle East," Brookings Institution, accessed 18 March 2016, http://www.brookings.edu/blogs/order-from-chaos/posts/2016/03/15-end-of-us-dominated-order-in-the-middle-east.
111 See "The North Caucasus Insurgency and Syria: An Exported Jihad," International Crisis Group, Europe Report no. 238, 16 March 2016.
112 Phillips, *The Battle for Syria*, 185. Among the groups that announced their membership in the Islamic Front were the Tawhid, Ahrar al-Sham, Jaish al-Islam, Suqour al-Sham, al-Haqq, Ansar al-Sham Brigades, and the Kurdish Islamic Front.
113 Anja Manuel, "Is There a Right Path for Washington in Syria?" *The Daily Star*, 22 January 2014, 5.
114 Quoted in Michael Glackin, "The West May Pay for its Inaction in Syria," *The Daily Star*, 17 January 2014, 7.
115 Julian Borger and Saeed KamaliDehghan, "Iran Seals Nuclear Deal with West in Return for Sanctions," *The Guardian*, 24 November 2013, https://www.theguardian.com/world/2013/nov/24/iran-nuclear-deal-west-sanctions-relief.
116 Tsygankov, "Vladimir Putin's Last Stand," 291.
117 Olexiy Haran and Maria Zolkina, "The Demise of Ukraine's Eurasian Vector and the Rise of Pro-NATO Sentiment," PONARS Eurasia Policy Memo no. 458, February 2017, 1.

118 See "EU Says Door Open to Ukraine, not their Leaders," *The Daily Star*, 21–2 December 2013, 9.
119 Agata Wierzbowska-Miazga, Commentary, "Russia Goes on the Offensive Ahead of the Eastern Partnership Summit in Vilnius," Center for Eastern Studies no. 115, 30 September 2013.
120 Vladimir Putin, meeting of the Valdai International Discussion Club, 19 September 2013.
121 Jonathan Saul, "Russia Steps up Military Lifeline to Syria's Assad: Sources," *The Daily Star*, 18–19 January 2014, 10.
122 See *As-Safir*, 23 January 2014, 10.
123 See "Assad Era Over, Jabra Says," *The Daily Star*, 24 January 2014, 10.
124 Jude Dempsey, "The Munich Security Conference. What Security?," 5 February 2014, https://carnegieeurope.eu/strategiceurope/?fa=58971.
125 See "Ukraine Unrest: EU and U.S. Clash with Russia in Munich," *BBC*, 1 February 2014, https://www.bbc.com/news/world-europe-25996453.
126 Mearsheimer, "Why the Ukraine Crisis is the West's Fault," 80.
127 Ibid., 81.
128 Samuel Charap, "Russia's Use of Military Force as a Foreign Policy Tool, is There a Logic?" PONARS Eurasia Policy Memo no. 443, October 2016, 1.
129 Quoted in Tsygankov, "The Sources of Russia's Fear," 108.
130 Tsygankov, "Vladimir Putin's Last Stand," 292.
131 Freire and Heller, "Russia's Power Politics," 1199.
132 Quoted in ibid.
133 Urnov, "'Greatpowerness' as the Key Element," 3–4.
134 Donaldson, Nogee, and Nadkarni, *The Foreign Policy of Russia*, 417.
135 See "Assad Says Russia Re-establishing Multipolar World," 2 April 2014, http://www.naharnet.com/stories/124848-assad-russia-re-establishing-multi-polar-world/print.
136 See "Assad Tells Ex-Russian Prime Minister Syria War Will be Over Next Year," *The Moscow Time*, 7 April 2014.
137 See "Assad Tells Putin He Won't Flee Like Ukraine," 7 April 2014, https://www.timesofisrael.com/assad-tells-putin-he-wont-flee-like-ukraine-leader.
138 Quoted in Ali Wyne, "U.S. Influence Gains from Updating the Liberal International Order," *The Daily Star*, 7 March 2014, 7.
139 Quoted in Warren Strobel, "Chemical Deal Strengthened Assad: U.S. Intelligence Chief," *The Daily Star*, 5 February 2014, 1.
140 Laura Smith-Spark, "P5+1 and Iran Agree on Nuclear Negotiation framework in Vienna," 20 February 2014, https://edition.cnn.com/2014/02/20/world/europe/iran-nuclear-talks/index.html. See also "What Next for Iran

and the P5+1," Middle East Program, Wilson Center, Viewpoints no. 67, November 2014.

141 UN Security Council Resolution 2139, S/RES/2139, 22 February 2014.

142 David B. Ottaway, "A New Chapter in the Tangled U.S.–Saudi Relationship," Middle East Program, Wilson Center, Viewpoints no. 62, September 2014.

143 Peter Apps, "Videos Show First U.S.-Made Rockets in Syria," *The Daily Star*, 16 April 2014, 8.

144 See "Homs, Capital of the Revolution, in the Hands of Regime Forces," *The Daily Star*, 9 May 2014, 1.

145 See "United States Approves Diplomatic Mission for Syria Opposition," *The Daily Star*, 6 May 2014, 1.

146 See "Obama West Point Speech in full with Analysis," *BBC*, 29 May 2014, https://www.bbc.com/news/world-us-canada-27606537.

147 Quoted in Marlin Dick, "U.S. Mulls War on Syria Terror Approach," *The Daily Star*, 6 June 2014, 8.

148 Byman, "Beyond Counterterrorism," 12.

149 Yezid Sayigh, "Syria's Spring Offensive and the Death of Diplomacy," Carnegie Middle East Center, 6 March 2014.

150 See "Syrian Rebels can Play a Role in Iraq: Kerry," *The Daily Star*, 28–9 June 2014, 1.

151 Ibid.

152 Gerges, *ISIS, A History*, 219.

153 Quoted in Ryan Lucas, "Alarm, Ridicule for Declaration of Islamic State," *The Daily Star*, 1 July 2014, 8.

154 Kenneth Katzman, "Iran's Foreign Policy," Congressional Research Service R44017, 25 November 2015.

155 Author interview with Iranian Ambassador to Beirut Mohammad Jalal Firouznia, Beirut, 4 January 2019.

156 Gerges, *ISIS, A History*, 193.

157 See "Iraqi and Kurdish Forces Recapture Mosul Dam from ISIS," *The Guardian*, 18 August 2014.

158 UN Security Council Resolution 2170, S/RES/2170, 15 August 2014.

159 See *As-Safir*, 26 August 2014, 1.

160 See "Syria Offers to Help Fight ISIS but Warns Against Unilateral Air Strikes," *The Guardian*, 26 August 2014.

161 Spencer Ackerman and Nicholas Watt, "Obama Urges Action to Halt ISIS Cancer as UK Steps up Fight Against Jihadists," *The Guardian*, 21 August 2014.

162 Andrew Radin, "Hybrid Warfare in the Baltics: Threats and Potential Responses," RAND Corporation, 2017, 8.
163 Henry E. Hale, "Russian Nationalism and the Logic of the Kremlin's Actions on Ukraine," *The Guardian*, 29 August 2014, https://www.theguardian.com/world/2014/aug/29/russian-nationalism-kremlin-actions-ukraine.
164 "Report from NATO Summit in Newport, Wales, 4–5 September 2014," accessed 23 February 2019, http://www.no-to-nato.org/2014/09/16/report-from-nato-summit-in-newport-wales-4-5-sept-2014.
165 Ibid.
166 Helene Cooper, "Obama Enlists 9 Allies to Help in the Battle Against ISIS," *The New York Times*, 5 September 2014.
167 "Arabs Vow all Needed Measures Against ISIS," 8 September 2014, http://english.alarabiya.net/en/News/middle-east/2014/09/07/Arab-League-moves-against-ISIS.html.
168 See "Kerry Enlists Saudi King in War of Ideas Against ISIS," *Time*, 11 September 2014, http://time.com/3379004/kerry-isis-saudi.
169 David B. Ottaway, "A New Chapter in the Tangled U.S.–Saudi Relationship," Viewpoints, no. 62, Wilson Center Middle East Program, September 2014.
170 Joseph S. Nye, "Devise a Strategy in Order to Manage Russia's Likely Decline," *The Daily Star*, 10 September 2014, 7.
171 Paul and Shankar, "Status: Accommodation Through Institutional Means," 171–2.
172 Quoted in Gabriela Baczynska, "Lavrov: Ties with Washington Need Reset 2.0," *The Daily Star*, 29 September 2014, 11.
173 Julie Pace, "Obama Faces Questions as Campaign Expands," *The Daily Star*, 22 September 2014, 9.
174 UN Security Council Resolution 2178, S/RES/2178, 24 September 2014.
175 Mona Alami, "ISIS Survives Amid Conflicting Agendas," *The Daily Star*, 1 December 2014, 7.
176 See "Turkey Allows Kurdish Fighters into Battle," *The Daily Star*, 21 October 2014, 1, 10.
177 Joana Paraszczuk, "Hints Emerge that Fight Against IS Moving U.S., Russia Closer on Syria," *RFE/RL Russia Report*, 15 October 2014, 1.
178 Ibid., 2.
179 See *As-Safir*, 11 November 2014, 1.
180 Tom Perry, "U.S.-Trained Syrian Rebels Await More Help," *The Daily Star*, 3 December 2014, 8.

181 Lister, *The Syrian Jihad*, 310–11.
182 Trenin, *What Is Russia Up To in the Middle East*, 111–12.
183 Ishaan Tharoor, "How Russia's Putin and Turkey's Erdogan were Made for Each Other," *The Washington Post*, 2 December 2014.
184 Ibid.
185 Freire and Heller, "Russia's Power Politics," 1186.

CHAPTER FOUR

1 Freire and Heller, "Russia's Power Politics," 1201.
2 See, "UN: Syrian Refugees Rise by 704,000 in six months," *The Daily Star*, 8 January 2015, 8.
3 Kozhanov, *Russia and the Syrian Conflict*, 43.
4 See "Turkey and U.S. Agree to Train and Arm Syrian rebels in Fight Against ISIS," *The Guardian*, 19 February 2015.
5 See "Rouhani: No End to Mideast Strife Without Iran," *The Daily Star*, 12 February 2015, 9.
6 Quoted in Marlin Dick, "Louay Hussein Announces Exile," *The Daily Star*, 27 April 2015, 5.
7 See "Assad Lowers Expectations for Moscow Meeting on Syria," *The Daily Star*, 16 January 2015, 1. According to de Mistura, as of January 2015, the Syrian conflict had rendered 12 million people in need, 7.6 million displaced, 3.3 million refugees, and 220,000 deaths.
8 Mark N. Katz, "Elusive as Ever: The State of Iranian-Russian Cooperation," Viewpoints, no. 73, Middle East Program, Wilson Center, March 2015, 1.
9 Ian Black, "Bashar al-Assad Dismisses US Position on Negotiating End to Syria War," *The Guardian*, 16 March 2015.
10 Joanna Paraszczuk, "Lavrov: Fighting IS More Important than Regime Change in Syria," *RFE/RL Russia Report*, 22 January 2015.
11 The US National Security Strategy, February 2015, 2.
12 See "Lavrov: Islamic State is Russia's Main Enemy," *RFE/RL Russia Report*, 22 April 2015.
13 Joanna Paraszczuk, "Lavrov: Fighting IS More Important than Regime Change in Syria," *RFE/RL Russia Report*, 22 January 2015.
14 Robin Wright, "A Victory in Kobani," *The New Yorker*, 27 January 2015, http://www.newyorker.com/news/news-desk/victory-kobani.
15 Author interview with Russian Ambassador Alexander Zasypkin, Beirut, 26 December 2018.
16 See Plenary Session of the 19th St Petersburg International Economic Forum

18–20 June 2015, accessed 12 June 2019, http://en.kremlin.ru/events/president/news/49733.

17 See "Iran Sends 15,000 Fighters to Syria," *The Daily Star*, 4 June 2015, 1.

18 Author interview with Iranian Ambassador Mohammad Jalal Firouznia, Beirut, 4 January 2019.

19 Desmond Balter, "Turkey, Saudi Arabia Set Aside Differences to act Against Assad," *The Daily Star*, 8 May 2015, 11.

20 David Ignatius, "The Arabs and Turkey Align to Topple Assad," *The Daily Star*, 15 May 2015, 7.

21 Lister, *The Syrian Jihad*, 348.

22 Ibid., 357.

23 Martin S. Indyk, "The Regional Implications of a Nuclear Deal with Iran," Brookings Institution, 5 June 2015,

24 Karam Shoumali, Anne Barnard, and Eric Schmitt, "Abductions Hurt U.S. Bid to Train Anti-ISIS Rebels in Syria," *New York Times*, 30 July 2015, https://www.nytimes.com/2015/07/31/world/middleeast/us-trained-islamic-state-opponents-reported-kidnapped-in-syria.html.

25 See "UN Envoy Looks to Revive Syria Talks," *The Daily Star*, 6 May 2015, 8.

26 See "Meeting of BRICS Leaders with Heads of Guest Countries," http://en.kremlin.ru/events/president/news/49901. See also Alvin Cheng-Hin Lim, "2015 BRICS-SCO Summits in Ufa: New Developments in Multilateralism – Analysis," 20 July 2015, www.eurasiaview.com/20072015-2015-brics-sco-summits-in-ufa-new-developments-in-multilateralism.analysis.

27 Tsygankov, "Vladimir Putin's Last Stand," 292.

28 See "Russia, Egypt Support Formation anti-ISIS Coalition with Syria – Putin," 26 August 2015, https://www.rt.com/news/313537-russia-egypt-putin-meeting.

29 Maksymilian Czuperski, John Herbst, Eliot Higgens, Frederic Hof, and Ben Nimmo, "Distract, Deceive, Destroy: Putin at War in Syria," Atlantic Council, April 2016, 9.

30 Quoted in Vladimir Isachenkov, "Putin Jockeying for Deal with U.S. on Syria," *The Daily Star*, 9 September 2015, 9.

31 Arkady Moshes, "EU-Russia Relations: Quo Vadis? Muddling, Normalization, or Deterioration," PONARS Eurasia Policy Memo no. 454 (January 2017): 3.

32 Vladimir Isachenkov, "Putin Jockeying for Deal with U.S. on Syria," *The Daily Star*, 9 September 2015, 9.

33 Joseph S. Nye, "A More Sophisticated U.S. Mideast Policy Must be Discussed," *The Daily Star*, 15 September 2015, 7.

34 Mikhail Troitskiy, "The Need to Massage Egos, Status Politics as a Crucial Element of US-Russia Relations," PONARS Eurasia Policy Memo no. 445, October 2016, 1.

35 Donaldson, Nogee, and Nadkarni, *The Foreign Policy of Russia*, 8.

36 Frederic C. Hof, "Russia and Iran Won't Restrain Assad," accessed 19 September 2017, http://www.atlanticcouncil.org/blogs/menasource/syria-moscow-makes-a-move.

37 See "Russia Deploys 28 Combat Aircraft in Syria," *The Daily Star*, 22 September 2015, 1.

38 David Ignatius, "America's Straddle in Syria was Bound to Fail," *The Daily Star*, 17 December 2016, 7.

39 See "Putin Defends Military Aid to Assad," *The Daily Star*, 16 September 2015, 8.

40 Martin S. Indyk, "The End of the US Dominated Order in the Middle East," Brookings Institution, accessed 18 March 2017, http://www.brookings.edu/blogs/order-from-chaos/posts/2016/03/15-end-of-dominated-order-in-the-middle-east.

41 Quoted in Mathew Lee, "Russian Moves in Syria Flummox United States," *The Daily Star*, 17 September 2015, 8.

42 Jeffrey D. Sachs, "A Resolution in Syria Must Run Through the Security Council," *The Daily Star*, 22 September 2015, 7.

43 Sergei Karaganov, "A Dialogue is Needed Between Europe and Greater Eurasia," *The Daily Star*, 23 September 2015, 7.

44 Freire and Heller, "Russia's Power Politics," 1203.

45 Julia Kollewe, "Sanctions to Push Russia into Recession in 2015 – Business Live," *The Guardian*, 25 May 2017, https://www.theguardian.com/business/live/2014/dec/02/rouble-recovers-as-oil-prices-business-live?page=with:block-547dcd1ce4b0195b12e259f4.

46 Quoted in Lukyanov, "Putin's Foreign Policy," 34.

47 Van Dam, *Destroying a Nation*, 98.

48 David Ignatius, "The Star-Crossed History of CIA Paramilitary Action," *The Daily Star*, 22 July 2017, 7.

49 Author interview with Iranian Ambassador Mohammad Jalal Firouznia, Beirut, 4 January 2019.

50 Vladimir Putin, "Text of Address at Seventieth Session of the UN General Assembly," 28 September 2015, http://en.kremlin.ru/events/president/news/50385.

51 Freire and Heller, "Russia's Power Politics," 1190.

52 Volgy, Corbetta, Grant, and Baird, "Major Power Status in International Politics," 12.

53 Lukyanov, "Putin's Foreign Policy," 35.
54 See "Syria Conflict: Putin Defends Russia's Air Strikes," *BBC*, 12 October 2015, https://www.bbc.com/news/world-middle-east-34502286.
55 Quoted in Michael Totten, "Moscow on the Tigris: Russia Joins the Terror Nexus," accessed 20 November 2016, http://www.worldaffairsjournal.org.
56 Author interview with Russian Ambassador Alexander Zasypkin, Beirut, 26 December 2018.
57 "The Fall of Aleppo: Vladimir Putin's Victory; the West's Failure; and a Warning of What Happens When Interests Triumph Over," *The Economist* (17–23 December 2016): 11.
58 Author interview with Russian Ambassador Alexander Zasypkin, Beirut, 26 December 2018.
59 Farid Zakaria, "Why Would Trump Help Putin Reach Goals," *The Daily Star*, 19 December 2016, 7.
60 Brian Michael Jenkins, "A Revanchist Russia Versus an Uncertain West: An Appreciation of the Situation since the 2014 Ukrainian Crisis," Center for the Study of Democracy, December 2016, 6.
61 International Crisis Group, "Russia's Choice in Syria," Middle East Briefing 47, 29 March 2016, 2.
62 Ekaterina Stepanova, "The Islamic State as a Security Problem for Russia, The Nature and the Scale of the Threat," PONARS, Eurasia Policy Memo no. 393, October 2015.
63 Dmitry Gorenburg, "What Russia's Military Operation in Syria Can Tell us About Advances in its Capabilities," PONARS Eurasia Policy Memo no. 424, March 2016, 1–5.
64 Freire and Heller, "Russia's Power Politics," 1203.
65 "Military Detachment Commander: Syria to be Cleared of Terrorism Soon," *Tass*, 2 February 2016, http://tass.ru/en/world/854037.
66 See "Putin Confident of Military's Prowess," *The Daily Star*, 23 December 2016, 11.
67 See "Moscow Warns against Demands for Assad's Ouster," *The Daily Star*, 10 November 2015, 8.
68 See "NATO Chief Sounds Alarm Over Russian Buildup," *The Daily Star*, 6 November 2015, 11.
69 See "Russia Says Syria Bombing Sharply Cut ISIS Oil Income," *The Daily Star*, 21 November 2015, 1.
70 Quoted in Steve Gutterman, "Russia Likely to Remain Defiant on Syria, the Last of its Surviving Middle Eastern Allies," *The Daily Star*, 17 November 2015, 8.
71 David Ignatius, "Even in Death, Primakov Continues to Inspire Putin," *The Daily Star*, 22 October 2015, 7.

72 Saideman, "Overlooking the Obvious," 72.
73 Author interview with Russian Ambassador Alexander Zasypkin, Beirut, 26 December 2018.
74 Hampson, *Nurturing Peace*, 24.
75 See "Ukraine Ceasefire: New Minsk Agreement Key Points," *BBC*, 12 February 2015, http://www.bbc.com/news/world-europe-31436513.
76 See "14 November 2015, Statement of the International Syria Support Group Vienna," accessed 4 February 2017, http://www.un.org/undpa/en/Speeches-statements/14112015/syria.
77 UN Security Council Resolution 2254, S/RES/2254, 18 December 2015.
78 Quoted in Andrew Osborn, "Hollande Visit May Spur End to Putin's Isolation," *The Daily Star*, 19 November 2015, 11.
79 Nikolay Kozhanov, "The Saudi-Iranian Rift Forces a Difficult Decision on Moscow," 3 February 2016, http://www.chathamhouse.org/expert/comment/saudi-iranian-rift-forces-difficult-decision-on-moscow.
80 Pete Baumgartner, "Possible Russia-West Rapprochement Over Syria Stokes Fears in Europe's East," *RFE/RL Russia Report*, 19 November 2015.
81 See "Russia Strikes Raqqa from Submarine," *The Daily Star*, 9 December 2015, 1.
82 On the text of the Minsk Protocol signed on 2 September 2014, see http://en.wikipedia/wiki/Minsk_protocol.
83 Hampson, *Nurturing Peace*, 17.
84 See "Tensions Soar as Jet Downing Raises Stakes in Syria," *The Daily Star*, 25 November 2015, 1.
85 Jonathan Landay and Warren Strobel, "Goals Met for Russia in Syria so far, U.S. Sees," *The Daily Star*, 29 December 2015, 8.
86 See "Obama and Putin Hold Closed-Door Talks in Paris," 30 November 2015, http://www.rte.ie/news/2015/1130/750129-obama-hollande-paris
87 Tsygankov, "Preserving Influence," 38.
88 Author interview with Iranian Ambassador Mohammad Jalal Firouznia, Beirut, 4 January 2019.
89 "The Fall of Aleppo," 11.
90 Gaorge Gavrilis, "Can Russia's Peace Plan for Syria Work?" PONARS Eurasia Policy Memo, 420, February 2016, 3.
91 See "Russian Strategists Play Big in Syria," *The Daily Star*, 16 February 2016, 8.
92 Salam al-Saadi, "Russia's Role and Talk of a Transition Changed Syria's Opposition," *The Daily Star*, 5 January 2016, 7.
93 Quoted in "Syria Peace Negotiations Hit Trouble," *The Daily Star*, 1 February 2016, 1.

94 See "Syria Talks Run Parallel to Regime Offensive," *The Daily Star*, 2 February 2016, 1.
95 Van Dam, *Destroying a Nation*, 151.
96 See "Turkey's Syrian Refugees: Defusing Metropolitan Tensions," International Crisis Group, Europe Report no. 248, 29 January 2018.
97 See "Syria Talks Run Parallel to Regime Offensive," *The Daily Star*, 2 February 2016, 2.
98 Van Dam, *Destroying a Nation*, 154.
99 Foreign Minister Sergey Lavrov's Speech at the Ministerial Panel Discussion during the Munich Security Conference, Munich, 13 February 2016, www.mid.ru/en/foreign_policy/news/-/asset_publisher/cKNonkJE02Bw/content/id/2086892.
100 Frederic C. Hof, "What's Next after Geneva's Failure?" *The Daily Star*, 9 February 2016, 7.
101 "Moscow: Senior Military Advisor Killed in Syria," *Middle East Monitor*, 4 February 2016, https://www.middleeastmonitor.com/20160204-moscow-senior-military-advisor-killed -in-syria.
102 See "U.S., Russia Agree Syria Cease-fire Starting Saturday," *The Daily Star*, 23 February 2016, 1, 10.
103 Quoted in Andrew Osborn, "Syria Gambit has Placed Russia at the Top Table," *The Daily Star*, 16 March 2016, 8.
104 Ibid.
105 Quoted in Dave Clark and Karim Talbi, "Make-or-Break Syria Cessation of Hostilities Tests Russia–US Cooperation," *The Daily Star*, 27 February 2016, 8.
106 The battlefield around Aleppo was the most complicated that the world had seen for decades. Different combatants and foreign forces were fighting including the Syrian regime forces backed by Russia, Iran, and Hizbullah; the Kurdish rebel forces backed by the US; Turkish forces that were shelling the US-backed Kurds; Arab rebel fighters supported by the CIA and Saudi intelligence; Nusra Front fighters allied with al-Qaeda; and IS fighters who were fighting against all.
107 See Dave Clark and Karim Talbi, "Make-or-Break Syria Cessation of Hostilities Tests Russia–US Cooperation," *The Daily Star*, 27 February 2016, 8.
108 See "Rouhani: Iran, Turkey in Lockstep on Syria Ceasefire," 6 March 2016, http://www.timesofisrael.com/rouhani-iran-turkey-in-locked-on-syria-ceasefire.
109 Author interview with Iranian Ambassador Mohammad Jalal Firouznia, Beirut, 4 January 2019.

110 David Ignatius, "Russia is Now an Essential US Partner in Syria," *The Daily Star*, 14 January 2016, 7.
111 Quoted in M.K. Bhadrakumar, "Putin Throws Down the Gauntlet on Syria. Any Takers?" 15 March 2016, http://urldefense.proofpoint.com/v2/url?u=http-3A_atimes.com.
112 See "US Wary of Russia's Military Moves in Syria," *The Daily Star*, 22 April 2016, 8.
113 See "Putin Orders Syrian Withdrawal, Saying Goals Achieved," *RFE/RL Russia Report*, 14 March 2016, 1.
114 Quoted in Gabrielle Tetrault-Farber, "From Base in Syria, Russia Monitors Truce," *The Daily Star*, 6 May 2016, 8.
115 Tom Miles and Suleiman Al-Khalidi, "Syria Talks Move Toward Assad Question," *The Daily Star*, 21 March 2016, 4.
116 Frederic C. Hof, "Shooting Banks: The West's Syria Policy," *The Daily Star*, 10 June 2016, 7.
117 Quoted in Olga Rotenberg, "West Puzzled by Russia Game Plan in Syria," *The Daily Star*, 29 March 2016, 8.
118 Quoted in Brian Whitmore, "The Road from Damascus to Yalta," *RFE/RL Russia Report*, 15 March 2016, 1.
119 Polina Sinovets, "The European Missile Defense System and Russia: Can there be Dialogue Rather than an Arms Race?" PONARS Eurasia Policy Memo, February 2017.
120 Russia's Updated National Security Strategy, 1 January 2016, http://www.newcoldwar.org/russias-updated-national-security-strategy-for-2016.
121 Sergei Karaganov, "Mutually Assured Deterrence can Save the World," *The Daily Star*, 25 February 2017, 7.
122 Mohamad Rosidin, "ASEAN and Russia: Creating a New Security Architecture," 1 June 2016. https://thediplomat.com/2016/06/asean-and-russia-creating-a-new-security-architecture. See also "Russia-ASEAN Summit," 20 May 2016, http://en.kremlin.ru/events/president/news/51953.
123 Freire and Heller, "Russia's Power Politics," 1203.
124 "The Fall of Aleppo," 11.
125 Frederic C. Hof, "Shooting Blanks: The West's Syria Policy," *The Daily Star*, 10 June 2016, 7.
126 See "Defiant Assad Vows to Liberate Every Inch of Syria," 7 June 2016, https://www.aljazeera.com/news/2016/06/defiant-assad-vows-liberate-inch-syria-160607114315788.html.
127 Quoted in Ashish Kumar Sen, "Keep Door Open to Russia, Former Allied Commander Urges," *The Daily Star*, 14 June 2016, 7.

128 See "Putin: Russia Accepts U.S. is Sole Superpower," RFE/RL *Russia Report*, 17 June 2016.
129 See "US Troops Enter Poland, at Russia's Doorstep," *The Daily Star*, 13 January 2017, 11.
130 Simon Tisdall, "Erdogan's Overtures to Russia Part of Wider Diplomatic Bridge-Building," *The Guardian*, 28 June 2016, http://www.theguardian.com/world/2016/jun/28/erdogan-russia-turkey-foreign-policy.
131 See "Lavrov and Cavusoglu Meet to Repair Ties," *The Daily Star*, 2 July 2016, 9.
132 See "Russia's New Foreign Policy Concept Calls for Broad Anti-Terror Coalition," 1 December 2016, http://sputniknews.com/politics/2016 12011048059451-russia-foreign-policy.
133 See "Russia, Turkey Reach Breakthrough Agreement on Fighting Terrorists in Syria," 2 July 2016, http://sputniknews.com/politics/20160702/1042338086 /russia-turkey-syria-terrorists.html.
134 See "Erdogan Exclusive: New Page in Russia-Turkey Relations," 9 August 2016, http://tass.com/world/893204.
135 See "Trilateral Meeting of the Presidents of Azerbaijan, Iran and Russia," 8 August 2016, http://en.kremlin.ru/events/president/news/52666.
136 Olesya Astakhova and Nick Tattersall, "Putin and Erdogan Move Toward Repairing Ties Amid Tension with West," 9 August 2016, https://www.reuters.com/article/us-russia-turkey-idUSKCN10K19T.
137 See "Turkish Stream Pipe-Laying to Start in 2017, End in Late 2019," 12 October 2016, http://sputniknews.com/business/201610121046252095-turkish-stream-pipe-laying.
138 See "Turkish Army and Allies Thrust Deeper into Syria," *The Daily Star*, 29 August 2016, 1.
139 James Miller, "With Use of Iranian Base, Russia is Trying to send Clear Message," RFE/RL *Russia Report*, 17 August 2016.
140 See "Coalition Scrambles to Defend U.S. Forces from Syrian Bombing," *The Daily Star*, 20 August 2016, 1.
141 Frederic C. Hof and Faysal Itani, "Experts Weigh in on U.S.–Russia Agreement for Syria," 12 September 2016, https://www.newsdeeply.com.
142 See "Aleppo Stakes More Deadly with Massive Regime Ground Assault," *The Daily Star*, 28 September 2016, 1.
143 See "Russia under Fire at UN after Deadly Aleppo Bombing," RFE/RL *Russia Report*, 26 September 2016.
144 See "U.S. Threatens to End Cooperation with Russia Over Aleppo Assault," RFE/RL *Russia Report*, 28 September 2016.

145 See "Obama, Merkel Condemn Russia's Barbarous Behavior in Syria," RFE/RL *Russia Report*, 30 September 2016.
146 Mikhail Troitskiy, "What's Next for Russian Foreign Policy?" 31 October 2016, http://www.europeanleadershipnetwork.org.
147 See "Putin Suspends U.S.–Russia Plutonium Deal, Blaming NATO, Sanctions, Magnitsky Act," RFE/RL *Russia Report*, 3 October 2016.
148 See "U.S. Says Russia's Suspension of Weapons-Grade Plutonium Deal Big Mistake," RFE/RL *Russia Report*, 5 October 2016.
149 See "Russia Confirms Deployment of S-300 Air Defense Missiles to Syria," RFE/RL *Russia Report*, 4 October 2016.
150 See "Moscow Ends Uranium Research Pact with United States," *The Daily Star*, 6 October 2016, 10.
151 See "Russian Airborne Vehicles to Land First in Africa Within Drills With Egypt," 24 October 2016, https://sputniknews.com/military/2016 10241046657973-russia-egypt-drills-airborne.
152 UN Security Council Resolution 12545, S/RES/12545, 8 October 2016.
153 See "Russia Calls Draft French UN Syria Resolution One-Sided," RFE/RL *Russia Report*, 9 October 2016.
154 Mathew Lee, "Presidential Candidates Offer Few Plans for Syria," *The Daily Star*, 12 October 2016, 6.
155 Conley, Mina, Stefanov, and Vladimirov, *The Kremlin Playbook*, x–xi.
156 Quoted in David Ignatius, "Trump Treats Foreign Policy Like a Game of Survivor," *The Daily Star*, 22 October 2016, 7.
157 Haass, *A World in Disarray*, 47.
158 See "Russian-Led CSTO Alliance Vows to Face Down Threats from Europe to Central Asia," 16 October 2016, http://sputniknews.com/politics /201610161046391802.
159 Tsygankov, "The Sources of Russia's Fear," 108.
160 International Monetary Fund, Russian Federation: Selected Issues. IMF Country Report no. 15/212, August 2015.
161 Freire and Heller, "Russia's Power Politics," 1205.
162 See "Putin, Trump Speak by Phone, Agree to Work to Improve Ties," *The Daily Star*, 15 November 2016, 1.
163 Joseph S. Nye, "Foreign Policy Challenges Facing Trump," *The Daily Star*, 16 November 2016, 7.
164 Vladimir Isachenkov, "Russia Projecting Power with Modern Military," *The Daily Star*, 7 December 2016, 6.
165 See "Putin: Russia Will Oppose any Attempts to Break Global Strategic Balance, Including NATO Missile System," 19 November 2016, https://www.rt.com/news/367379-putin-nato-strategic-balance.

166 Foreign Policy Concept of the Russian Federation, approved by the President of the Russian Federation Vladimir Putin on 30 November 2016, http://www.mid.ru/en/foreign_policy/official_documents/article92.
167 Mark Entin, "What kind of Equality does Russia Want in its Relationship with the West?," 6 December 2016, http://www.russia-direct.org /opinion.
168 Presidential Address to the Federal Assembly, 1 December 2016, http://en.kremlin.ru/events/president/news/53379.
169 Alexander Sotnichenko, "The Killing of Russia's Ambassador in Turkey: A Stab in the Back," accessed 3 December 2016, http://www.russia-direct.org /opinion/assassination-russian-ambassador-turkey-stab-back.
170 See "Russia, Iran, and Turkey Agree to Work Toward Syria Accord, Serve as Guarantors," *RFE/RL Russia Report*, 20 December 2016.
171 Foreign Policy Concept of the Russian Federation, approved by President of the Russian Federation Vladimir Putin on 30 November 2016, http://www.mid.ru/en/foreign_policy/official_documents/article92.
172 See "Ankara Says it has Syria Ceasefire Plan," *The Daily Star*, 29 December 2016, 1.
173 Neil MacFarquhar, "With Trump, Russia Goes from Thursday's Foe of US to Friday's Friend," *The New York Times*, 31 December 2016.
174 Quoted in "Russia Refrains from Expulsions Over U.S. Sanctions," *The Daily Star*, 31 December 2016, 1.
175 Neil MacFarquhar, "Vladimir Putin Won't Expel US Diplomats as Russian Foreign Minister Urged," *The New York Times*, 3 January 2017.
176 Ibid.
177 See Deyermond, "Russia's Trump Card?," 2–4.
178 Neil MacFarquhar, "Vladimir Putin Won't Expel US Diplomats as Russian Foreign Minister Urged," *The New York Times*, 3 January 2017.
179 Mikhail Troitskiy, "The Need to Message Egos, Status Politics as a Crucial Element of US-Russia Relations," PONARS Eurasia Policy Memo no. 445, October 2016, 3.
180 Alexander Bratersky, "Russian Public Perception Pressuring Putin to Wrap up Syria Operation," *Syria Deeply*, 21 March 2017, 3.
181 Noah Bonsay, "What's at Stake in the Syrian Peace Talks in Astana?" Commentary, Middle East and North Africa, International Crisis Group, 24 January 2017, 1–10.
182 See "Assad Allies, Turkey Agree to Oversee Truce Deal," *The Daily Star*, 25 January 2017, 1.
183 Author interview with Iranian Ambassador Mohammad Jalal Firouznia, Beirut, 4 January 2019.

184 See "Syria Sides at Odds as Truce Conclude in Astana," *RFE/RL Russia Report*, 24 January 2017.
185 Quoted in "Assad Allies, Turkey Agree to Oversee Truce Deal," *The Daily Star*, 25 January 2017, 10.
186 King, *Ending Civil Wars*, 57.
187 Jentleson, "Preventive Diplomacy and Ethnic Conflict," 303.
188 Saideman, "Overlooking the Obvious," 70.
189 Jasmine El-Gamal, in Alessandria Masi and Kim Bode, "Expert Views: does a United Syria Contradict de-Escalation Zones?," 18 August 2017, https://www.newsdeeply.com.
190 See "Syrian Militias Receive More U.S. Support for Daesh Fight," *The Daily Star*, 1 February 2017, 1.
191 See "Putin Says Russian, U.S. Intelligence Agencies Should Restore Ties," *RFE/RL Russia Report*, 16 February 2017.
192 See "Lavrov Says Russia Wants Military Cooperation with NATO, Pragmatic U.S. Ties," *RFE/RL Russia Report*, 18 February 2017.
193 Pavel K. Baev, "Tenth Anniversary of Putin's Munich Speech: A Commitment to Failure," 13 February 2017, https://jamestown.org/analyst/pavel-k-baev.
194 See "UN Plays Down Hopes for Geneva Talks," *The Daily Star*, 20 February 2017, 1.
195 Quoted in Catherine Lucey and Robert Burns, "New NSC Chief McMaster a Soldier-Scholar," *The Daily Star*, 22 February 2017, 7.
196 See "Putting out the Flames of War in Syria," 14 March 2017, http://sputniknews.com/middleeast/201703141051574554-syria-peace-talks.
197 Quoted in "Facing Political Reality: Washington Changes Mind about Assad, Middle East," 1 April 2017, http://sputniknews.com/world/201704011052186268-syria-middle-east-united-states-strategy.
198 Peter Baker and Mark Landler, "Trump, Meeting Netanyahu, Backs Away from Palestinian State," *The New York Times*, 15 February 2017.
199 Saideman, "Overlooking the Obvious," 66.
200 Robert Burns and Lolita C. Baldor, "US May Deepen Involvement in Syria," *The Daily Star*, 28 February 2017, 8.
201 See "US Enters Manbij to Keep Feuding Parties Apart," *The Daily Star*, 7 March 2017, 1.
202 See "Netanyahu: No Syrian Peace if Iran Present," *The Daily Star*, 10 March 2017, 1.
203 See "Israel Threatens to Destroy Syrian Air Defense Systems," *The Daily Star*, 20 March 2017, 1.

204 Author interview with Iranian Ambassador Mohammad Jalal Firouznia, Beirut, 4 January 2019.

205 See "Turkey Seeks Alliance with Russia in Syria," *The Daily Star*, 11 March 2017, 8. See also "Putin, Erdogan Pledge Cooperation to Help Bring End to Syrian Conflict," *RFE/RL Russia Report*, 10 March 2017.

206 See "Russia, Iran Ink Deals as Rouhani Visits Moscow," *The Daily Star*, 29 March 2017, 8.

207 See "Saudi King, Putin Agree Deals on Historic Russia Trip," *Al Jazeera*, 6 October 2017.

208 See "Syrian Fighters Reach Daesh-Held Dam," *The Daily Star*, 25 March 2017, 10.

209 Lake and Rothchild, "Containing Fear," 123.

210 Ibid.,125.

211 See "US Submitted Draft Resolution on Syria to UNSC Based on Fake Reports – Moscow," 5 April 2017, https://sputniknews.com/middleeast/201704051052321244-unsc-russia-syria-idlib.

212 See "Remarks at a UN Security Council Meeting on the Situation in Syria," 7 April 2017, https://usun.state.gov/remarks/7755.

213 See "Kremlin on Idlib Attack: Russia to Continue Supporting Assad in War on Terror," 5 April 2017, https://sputniknews.com/poltics/201704051052316233-kremlin-idlib-attack-assad.

214 See "Syria after the U.S. Strike: What Should Come Next," Statement/Middle East and North Africa, *International Crisis Group*, 11 April 2017.

215 Quoted in "Russia Suspends Air Safety Deal with US after Syria Strike," *Asharq Al-Awsat*, 7 April 2017.

216 See "Macron Sticks to His Guns in Putin Talks," *The Daily Star*, 30 May 2017, 1.

217 Vladimir Frolov, "Russia has Backed itself into a Corner in Syria," 7 April 2017, http://themoscowtimes.com/articles/russia-has-backed-itself-into-a-corner-in-syria.

218 Robert Skidelsky, "Trump's War Policy in Syria," *The Daily Star*, 24 April 2017, 7.

219 Frederic C. Hof, "Syria: Thinking Strategically, Going Beyond one-off Actions," *The Daily Star*, 20 April 2017, 7.

220 See "US, Russia Still Far Apart as Syria Haunts Talks," *The Daily Star*, 13 April 2017, 1.

221 See "Montenegro Joins NATO as 29th Ally," 5 June 2017, http://www.nato.int/cps/ennatohq/news_144647.htm.

222 See "United States Beefs up Russia Sanctions," *The Daily Star*, 21 June 2017, 1.

223 See "US Arms Supplies to Syrian Kurds is Geopolitical Project, Part of a Larger Plan," 14 May 2017, https://sputniknews.com/middleeast/201705141053606640-us-supplies-syrian-kurds.

224 See "Coalition Again Strikes Pro-Assad Forces Near Al-Tanf," *The Daily Star*, 7 June 2017.

225 See "Explainer: The Very Bad History of Safe Zones," *RFE/RL*, 5 May 2017.

226 See "US to Step up Sanctions on Iran, Syria, North Korea," *The Daily Star*, 25 May 2017, 10.

227 Author interview with Russian Ambassador Alexander Zasypkin, Beirut, 26 December 2018.

228 Seymour M. Hersh, "Trump's Red Line," 25 June 2017, http://www.welt.de/politik/ausland/article165905578/Trump-s-Red-Line.html.

229 See "Deraa de-Escalation Zone under Review," *The Daily Star*, 10 June 2017, 8.

230 See "Russia Says Military Police Deployed to Monitor Syria Ceasefire," 24 July 2017, https://www.rferl.org.

231 See "Syrian Rivals Weigh UN Plan for New Constitution," *The Daily Star*, 18 May 2017, 1.

232 See "Alleged Arab NATO Plan against Iran in Progress," *Daily Sabah*, 27–8 May 2017, 10.

233 See "Trump Rails Against Iran and Hizbullah," *The Daily Star*, 22 May 2017, 10.

234 See "Russia Criticized U.S. Missile Deployment in Syria," *RFE/RL Russia Report*, 15 June 2017.

235 See "Putin Says Russia to Beef up Syrian Army," *The Daily Star*, 16 June 2019, 1.

236 Stedman, "Spoiler Problems in Peace Processes," 7.

CHAPTER FIVE

1 See "White House Says Trump Had Second Talk with Putin at G-20 Summit," 19 July 2017, https://www.rferl.org.

2 See "This is How the G-20 Summit Helped Trump and Putin Claim Victories," accessed 17 July 2017, http://nationalinterest.org.

3 See "Trump Fully Supported Idea of US-Russia Cyber Security Unit at G20," accessed 26 July 2017, https://sputniknews.com/politics/2017 07101055417176-trump-putin-cyversecurity.

4 Quoted in Vivian Salama, "Russia Sanctions Bill Exposes Trump's Legislative Tug of War," *The Daily Star*, 28 July 2017, 6.
5 See "US, Russia Agree Deal on Syria Ceasefire," *The Daily Star*, 8 July 2017, 8.
6 See "France Sees Syria Opportunity through Dialogue with Russia," *The Daily Star*, 30 June 2017, 1.
7 Philip Issa, "Opposition Told to Come to Terms with Assad Survival," *The Daily Star*, 25 August 2017, 8.
8 See International Crisis Group, "Keeping the Calm in Southern Syria," Middle East Report no. 187, 21 June 2018.
9 See "Key Powers Fail to Nail Syria Safe Zones Plan," *The Daily Star*, 6 July 2017, 1.
10 See "Turkey: We Were Buying Both Russian and European Air Defense," accessed 18 July 2017, http://www.eurasianet.org/print/84386.
11 Torrey Taussig, "The Serpentine Trajectory of Turkish-Russian Relations," 4 October 2017, https://www.brookings.edu.
12 See "U.S. Puts New Sanctions on Iran Over Missile Program," *The Daily Star*, 19 July 2017, 1.
13 David Ignatius, "The Star-Crossed History of CIA Paramilitary Action," *The Daily Star*, 22 July 2017, 7. See also Fabrice Balanche, "The End of the CIA Program in Syria: Washington Cedes the Field," 2 August 2017, https://www.foreignaffairs.com.
14 See "On Hot Mic, Netanyahu Admits Syria Strikes, Raps Crazy EU," *The Daily Star*, 20 July 2017, 1.
15 Author interview with Iranian Ambassador Mohammad Jalal Firouznia, Beirut, 4 January 2019.
16 Ibid.
17 See "Russia Orders U.S. Embassy Staff Cuts in Sanctions Retaliation," *The Moscow Times*, 28 July 2017.
18 Vladimir Frolov, "Russia's Responses to Sanctions Shows Restraint op-ed," *The Moscow Times*, 29 July 2017.
19 See "After Retaliation against U.S. Sanctions, Moscow Says Cooperation Still Possible," *RFE/RL Russia Report*, 29 July 2017.
20 See "Putin: We Will Have to Retaliate against Sanctions," *The Daily Star*, 28 July 2017, 6.
21 See "Trump Signs Russia Sanctions Bill but Slams it as Flawed," *The Daily Star*, 3 August 2017, 1.
22 Mark Lander and Gardiner Harris, "In Retaliation, U.S. Orders Russia to Close Consulate in San Francisco," *The New York Times*, 31 August 2017.

23 Eugene Rumer and Andrew S. Weiss, "Vladimir Putin's Russia Goes Global," 4 August 2017, http://carnegieendowment.org.

24 See "Putin Signs Deal Cementing Russia's Long-Term Military Presence in Syria," *RFE/RL Russia Report*, 27 July 2017.

25 Author interview with Russian Ambassador Alexander Zasypkin, Beirut, 26 December 2018.

26 See "Agreement Reached on Third Syrian De-Escalation Zone North of Homs," 3 August 2017, http://tass.com/defense/958881.

27 Walter, "The Critical Barrier to Civil Settlement," 336.

28 Philip Issa, "Opposition Told to Come to Terms with Assad Survival," *The Daily Star*, 25 August 2017, 8.

29 Frederic C. Hof, "Washington Makes Room for Rivals in Eastern Syria," 18 August 2017, https://www.newsdeeply.com.

30 Quoted in Mike Eckel, "Russia's Medvedev Says US Sanctions Bill Ends Hope for Better Ties," *RFE/RL Russia Report*, 3 August 2017.

31 See "Averting Disaster in Syria's Idlib Province," International Crisis Group Briefing No. 56, 9 February 2018, 2.

32 Ronald J. Fisher, "Methods of Third Party Intervention," accessed 20 July 2018, http://www.berghof-foundation.org/nc/nr/publications/handbook/berghof-handbook-for-conflict-transformation.

33 See "Final De-Escalation Zones Agreed On in Astana," *Al Jazeera*, 15 September 2017, https://www.aljazeera.com/news/2017/9/15/final-de-escalation-zones-agreed-on-in-astana.

34 See "Russian Nuclear Bombers Fly Near North Korea," *The Daily Star*, 26 August 2017, 11.

35 Quoted in "As Trump Returns from Asia, America Retreats from World," *The Daily Star*, 16 November 2017, 7.

36 See "BRICS Leaders Xiamen Declaration," 8 September 2017. Available at https://brics2017.org/English/Headlines/201709/t20170908_2010.html.

37 Tsygankov, "Preserving Influence," 38.

38 See "BRICS Urges UN Reform, Anti-Terror Cooperation," *The Daily Star*, 5 September 2017, 11.

39 See Rouhani's address to the UN General Assembly, 20 September 2017, https://gadebate.un.org/en/72/iran-islamic-republic.

40 See "In Defiance of U.S., Iran Unveils Latest Missile at Parade," *The Daily Star*, 23 September 2017, 9.

41 Trenin, *What is Russia up to in the Middle East*, 112.

42 See "Riyadh, Moscow Cement Ties with King Salman's Visit," *The Daily Star*, 6 October 2017, 1.

43 See David Ignatius, "Trump Applies his Business Style to Iran Dealings," *The Daily Star*, 17 October 2017, 7.

44 See "Averting Disaster in Syria's Idlib Province," International Crisis Group, Middle East Briefing no. 56, 9 February 2018, 2.

45 See "US–Allied Fighters Takes Syria's Largest Oil Field," *The Daily Star*, 23 October 2017, 1.

46 See "Rouhani, Iran's Regional Status has Never been Stronger," *The Daily Star*, 24 October 2017, 8.

47 Author interview with Iranian Ambassador Mohammad Jalal Firouznia, Beirut, 4 January 2019.

48 Buzan, "Third World Regional Security," 37.

49 Corbetta and Melin, "Exploring the Threshold Between," 1–27.

50 See "Fresh Syria Peace Talks Open in Astana," *The Daily Star*, 31 October 2017, 1.

51 See "Putin Offers Support for Iran Nuclear Deal, Hails Cooperation on Syria," RFE/RL *Russia Report*, 1 November 2017.

52 See "Israel Signals Free Hand in Syria as U.S., Russia Expand Truce," *The Daily Star*, 13 November 2017, 1.

53 Josh Cohen, "The Mideast War Risk Trump Can't Ignore," *The Daily Star*, 13 November 2017, 7.

54 See "Russia Conducts Ballistic Missile Tests," RFE/RL *Russia Report*, 27 October 2017.

55 See "Turkey, Russia Agree to Deepen Relations," 14 November 2017, http://hurriyetdailynews.com/turkey-russia-agree-to-deepen-relations-122383.

56 Author interview with Iranian Ambassador Mohammad Jajal Firouznia, Beirut, 4 January 2019.

57 See "Trump, Putin Discuss Need for Peace in Syria, Ukraine in Phone Call," RFE/RL *Russia Report*, 22 November 2017.

58 See *Al-hayat*, 23 November 2017, 3. See also Andrew Parasiliti, Kathleen Reedy, and Becca Wasser, "Preventing State Collapse in Syria," RAND Corporation, January 2017.

59 See "Syria Opposition Seeks Direct Talks with Government," *The Daily Star*, 24 November 2017, 1.

60 See "Syrian Opposition, UN Open Talks in Geneva," *The Daily Star*, 29 November 2017, 10.

61 See "Syrian Government Negotiator Quits Geneva, Says May not Return," *The Daily Star*, 2 December 2017, 1.

62 Patrick Wintour, "Golden Opportunity Lost as Syrian Peace Talks Collapsed," *The Guardian*, 14 December 2017.

63 Andrew Osborn, "Putin, in Syria, Says Mission Accomplished, Orders Partial Russian Pull-Out," 11 December 2017, https://www.reuters.com/article/us-mideast-crisis-syria-russia-putin-idUSKBN1E50X1.
64 See "Putin Announced Re-Election Bid, Appears Certain to Win," *The Daily Star*, 7 December 2017, 10.
65 See "Trump Defies World Over Jerusalem," *The Daily Star*, 7 December 2017, 1.
66 Quoted in Gemma Fox, "Russia as Palestine Patron Unlikely Without U.S.," *The Daily Star*, 30 December 2017, 8.
67 See summary of the 2018 National Defense Strategy of the USA, 18 December 2017, 1–2.
68 See "Trump's New Security Strategy to Keep Russia and China as Main Competitors," 10 December 2017. Posted at https://www.rt.com/usa/413506-russia-china-us-competitors-strategy.
69 Quoted in Daniel Fried, "McMaster Accuses Russia of Subversion," *The Daily Star*, 19 December 2017, 7.
70 Hampson, *Nurturing Peace*, 17.
71 Daniel Fried, "McMaster Accuses Russia of Subversion," *The Daily Star*, 19 December 2017, 7.
72 See "China, Russia Slam American Cold War Mentality," *The Daily Star*, 20 December 2017, 10.
73 See "Russia Calls U.S. Security Strategy Imperial, China Denounces Cold War Thinking," *RFE/RL Russia Report*, 19 December 2017.
74 See "Russia Harshly Criticized New U.S. Nuclear Posture Document," *RFE/RL Russia Report*, 3 February 2018.
75 See "EU Officially Extends Ukraine-Related Sanctions Against Russia for Six Months," *RFE/RL Russia Report*, 21 December 2017.
76 See "Russia to Host Syria Talks in Sochi Next Month," *The Daily Star*, 23 December 2017, 1.
77 Reid, "Finding a Peace that Lasts," 1402–3.
78 See "Russia, Turkey Slam Plan for Kurdish-Led Syrian Border Guards," *RFE/EL Russia Report*, 16 January 2018.
79 See David Ignatius, "US Learning from Mistakes," *The Daily Star*, 22 January 2018, 7.
80 See *Al-joumhouria*, 22 January 2018, 15.
81 See "Turkey Infuriated by Unilateral US Actions in Syria: Russian FM Lavrov," 22 January 2018, https://www.hurriyetdailynews.com/turkey-infuriated-by-unilateral-u-s-actions-in-syria-russian-fm-lavrov-126094.
82 Amanda Sloat, "Turkey Wants to Crush US Allies in Syria. That Shouldn't Surprise anybody," 24 January 2018, https://www.brookings.edu/blog/order-

from-chaos/2018/01/24/turkey-wants-to-crush-us-allies-in-syria-that-shouldnt-surprise-anybody.

83 See "Western, Arab States Sidestep Assad in Syria Proposals," *The Daily Star*, 27 January 2018, 1.

84 See "Russia-Hosted Syria Conference Calls for Democratic Path," RFE/RL *Russia Report*, 30 January 2018.

85 Haass, *Conflicts Unending*, 6.

86 Ibid., 27–8.

87 Quoted in Ola Cichowlas, "Russia's Syria Peace Strategy in Question," *The Daily Star*, 1 February 2018, 8.

88 See "Turkey Warns U.S. Troops Over Syria Clash Risk," *The Daily Star*, 5 February 2018, 8.

89 Christopher R. Hill, "What is the Endgame for the US in Syria," *The Daily Star*, 21 February 2018, 7.

90 See "Russian Warplane Shot Down in Syria by Rebels, Defense Ministry Says," RFE/RL *Russia Report*, 3 February 2018.

91 See "Syria Says Rare U.S. Strike an Effort to Support Terrorism," *The Daily Star*, 9 February 2018, 1.

92 David Ignatius, "In Syria, Russian Bad Faith on the Ground Turns Fatal," *The Daily Star*, 14 February 2018, 7.

93 Joost Hiltermann, "Russia a Reluctant Driver in the Syrian War," International Crisis Group, 26 February 2018, 2.

94 Quoted in Tony Wesolowsky, "Listen to us Now: Putin Unveils Weapons, Vows to Raise Living Standards in Fiery Annual Address," RFE/RL *Russia Report*, 1 March 2018.

95 Quoted in "Putin: New Nuclear Weapons Not a Bluff," *The Daily Star*, 2 March 2018, 10.

96 Ibid.

97 See "Turkey Will not Stop in Syria until Terror Threat Ends: Erdogan," 21 March 2018, https://www.hurriyetdailynews.com/turkey-will-not-stop-in-syria-until-terror-threat-ends-erdogan-129121.

98 David Ignatius, "The Turks Have Taken Afrin. Let's not Let Manbij Fall Next," *The Daily Star*, 21 March 2018, 7.

99 See "Putin Softens Rhetoric Toward West Amid Criticism Over Landslide Victory," RFE/RL *Russia Report*, 19 March 2018.

100 Mark Landler, "Trump Congratulates Putin, but Doesn't Mention Meddling in U.S.," *The New York Times*, 20 March 2018.

101 Angela Charlton, "What to Expect from Putin and a Resurgent Russia," *The Daily Star*, 20 March 2018, 10.

102 See "Turkey, Iran, Russia Pledge Syria Stability," *The Daily Star*, 5 April 2018, 1.

103 Hampson, *Nurturing Peace*, 66.

104 See "Editorial: In Syria, Trump Faces the Limits of Bluster," *The New York Times*, 9 April 2018.

105 Peter Baker and Rick Gladstone, "President Trump Talked Tough. But His Strike on Syria Was Restrained," *The New York Times*, 13 April 2018.

106 Quoted in Vladimir Isachenkov, "Putin Sits Back as United States, Allies Strike Syria," *The Daily Star*, 16 April 2018, 8.

107 See "Top Russian, U.S. Generals Meet in Baku, Discuss NATO, Syria," *RFE/RL Russia Report*, 19 April 2018.

108 See "Remarks: Secretary of State Mike Pompeo at a Press Availability, April 27," http://ge.usembassy.gov/remarks-secretary-of-state-mike-pompeo-at-a-press-availability-april-27.

109 See "Syria Talks Renew in Astana as Regional Tensions Rise," *The Daily Star*, 15 May 2018, 8.

110 Josh Lederman, "Trump's Opposite Approaches to Iran, North Korea," *The Daily Star*, 10 May 2018, 9.

111 Suzanne Maloney, "After Dumping the Nuclear Deal, Trump has no Strategy for Iran," Brookings, 9 May 2018.

112 See International Crsis Group, "Israel, Hizbullah and Iran: Preventing Another War in Syria," Middle East Report no. 182, 8 February 2018.

113 Quoted in Eric Randolph, "Questions Over Russia-Iran Alliance in Syria," *The Daily Star*, 24 May 2018, 8.

114 See "Putin: Will Stay in Syria as Long as Beneficial," *The Daily Star*, 8 June 2018, 1.

115 Author interview with Iranian Ambassador Mohammad Jalal Firouznia, Beirut, 4 January 2019.

116 See International Crisis Group, "Keeping the Calm in Southern Syria," Middle East and North Africa, Report no. 187, 21 June 2018.

117 For a detailed report about reconstruction in Syria, see Steven Heydemann, "Beyond Fragility: Syria and the Challenges of Reconstruction in Fierce States," The New Geopolitics of the Middle East, Brookings, June 2018.

118 See *Al-joumhouria*, 29 May 2018, 14.

119 See "Turkey, U.S. Endorse Road Map for Syrian City of Manbij," *The Daily Star*, 5 June 2018, 8.

120 See "Trump Repeats Call for Russia's Return to G-7, But Final Communiqué Assails Moscow," *RFE/RL Russia Report*, 9 June 2018.

121 Ibid.

122 See "Chinese Leader Hails Russia Ties as Putin Visits Beijing," *RFE/RL Russia Report*, 8 June 2018.

123 See "Putin: Cooperation with China at Unprecedented Level," *The Daily Star*, 9 June 2018, 11.
124 See "Shock as Trump Backs Putin on U.S. Election Meddling," *The Daily Star*, 17 July 2018, 1.
125 See "Russia Sends Syrian Refugee Proposal to U.S.," *The Daily Star*, 21 July 2018, 1
126 Headley, *Russia and the Balkans*.
127 See "Netanyahu Says No Problem with Syria's Assad Staying in Power," 12 July 2018, https://www.i24news.tv/en/news/israel/179306-180712-netanyahu-says-no-problem-with-syria-s-assad-stayingin-power.
128 See "Iran Pulls Back from Golan in Syria, Israel Not Satisfied," *The Daily Star*, 2 August 2018, 1.
129 See "Syria Offensive Puts Turkish Troops, Border Plan's in Peril," *The Daily Star*, 23 August 2019, 1.
130 See "Syria Retakes Territory Held by Rebels Since 2012," *The Daily Star*, 24 August 2019, 1.
131 See "Russia, Turkey Agree Steps to Tackle Militants in Idlib," *The Daily Star*, 28 August 2019, 1
132 See "Russia Says it Will Start Delivering S-400 Defense System to Turkey in 2019," *RFE/RL Russia Report*, 21 August 2018.
133 See "In Challenge of U.S., NATO, Turkey Starts Getting S-400s," *The Daily Star*, 13 July 2019, 7.
134 See "Russia, Turkey Agree to Create Buffer Zone in Idlib," *RFE/RL Russia Report*, 17 September 2018.
135 See "Moscow Blames Israel after Syria Shoots Down Russian Military Plane," *The Guardian*, 18 September 2018.
136 Author interview with Iranian Ambassador Mohammad Jalal Firouznia, Beirut, 4 January 2019.
137 See "Syria to U.N. Envoy: Stay out of Constitution," *The Daily Star*, 25 October 2018, 8. The committee was expected to include 150 members. The Syrian government objected to a third fifty-member delegation that the UN put together representing Syrian experts, civil society, independents, tribal leaders, and women.
138 See *Al-joumhouria*, 30 November 2018, 14.
139 Author interview with Russian Ambassador Alexander Zasypkin, Beirut, 26 December 2018.
140 See "Russia, Germany, France and Turkey Call for Lasting Ceasefire, Constitutional Meeting for Syria," 29 October 2018, https://www.euractiv.com/section/g;obal-europe/news/russia-germany-france-and-turkey-call-for-lasting-ceasefire-constitutional-meeting-for-syria.

141 See "Istanbul Summit Ends With Call for UN-Backed Process to End Syrian War," *RFE/RL Russia Report*, 27 October 2018.
142 See "Russia, China Lash Out at U.S. Sanctions While Forging Closer Ties," *RFE/RL Russia Report*, 8 November 2018.
143 Quoted in "Kremlin Says Has Little Hope for Better U.S. Ties," *The Daily Star*, 8 November 2018, 9.

CONCLUSION

1 Mariana Belenkaya, "Astana Talks Show Russia to Keep Plugging Away at Idlib," *Al-Monitor*, 5 August 2019.
2 See "Turkey Readies for Action as U.S. Talks on Syria Falter," *The Daily Star*, 7 August 2019, 1.
3 Joint Statement by the Ministers of Foreign Affairs of the Islamic Republic of Iran, the Russian Federation and the Republic of Turkey on Syria, New York, 24 September 2019, https://www.rusemb.org.uk/fnap/6920.
4 See "Erdogan Hosts Putin, Rouhani for Syria Talks," *The Daily Star*, 17 September 2019, 5.
5 See "Russia, Saudi Arabia Seal Billions in Deals During Putin's Visit," *RFE/RL Russia Report*, 14 October 2019.
6 Quoted in Luke Baker, "Russia Makes Presence Felt after Saudi Attacks," *The Daily Star*, 1 October 2019, 5.
7 See "UN to Form Constitutional Committee on Syria," *The Daily Star*, 24 September 2019, 5.
8 "Moving Forward: Geir O. Pedersen on Developments in Syria," Oslo Forum, Center for Humanitarian Dialogue, May 2019.
9 Quoted in Stephanie Nebehay, "Syria Opposition Urges Justice as Peace Panel Opens," *The Daily Star*, 31 October 2019, 5.
10 See "Small Group on Syria Meets in Geneva," *Asharq al-Awsat*, 13 September 2019.
11 See "The Guardian View on Trump and Syria: Damage has been Done," *The Guardian*, 8 October 2019.
12 See *Al-joumhouria*, 18 October 2019, 13.
13 Indyk, "Disaster in the Desert," 12.
14 Ibid., 20.
15 See "Full Text of Turkey, Russia Agreement on Northeast Syria," *Al Jazeera*, 22 October 2019, https://www.aljazeera.com/news/2019/10/full-text-turkey-russia-agreement-northeast-syria-191022180033274.html.

16 International Crisis Group, "Steadying the New Status Quo in Syria's North East," Middle East Briefing no. 72, 27 November 2019, 12.

17 See "U.S. Forces Seen Patrolling in Syria near Turkish Border," *The Daily Star*, 1 November 2019, 5.

18 See "Macron Says NATO Experiencing Brain Death," *The Daily Star*, 8 November 2019, 6.

19 Ibid.

20 See "Fears of New Arms Race as U.S., Russia Left Historic INF Treaty Lapse," *RFE/RL Russia Report*, 2 August 2019.

21 See "Putin Says Russia Prepared to Drop Arms Control Treaty if U.S. not Interested in Renewal," *RFE/RL Russia Report*, 6 June 2019.

22 Quoted in David Ignatius, "Trump is Ignoring Arms Control," *The Daily Star*, 14 October 2019, 4.

23 Ibid.

24 Joschka Fischer, "With a New Global Order, Who Will Win the 21st Century," *The Daily Star*, 2 August 2019, 6.

APPENDIX A

1 Nikolay Kozhanov, *Russia and the Syrian Conflict: Moscow's Domestic, Regional and Strategic Interests* (Germany: Gerlach Press, 2016), 120–1.

APPENDIX B

1 "Text of Russia's Draft Proposals on Syrian Crisis," *The Daily Star*, 12 November 2015, 8.

Bibliography

ARCHIVES

Foreign Policy Concept of the Russian Federation. 28 June 2000.
– 12 January 2008.
– 30 November 2016.
ITAR-TASS News Agency (in English). FBIS-SOV-2000-0612, 12 June 2000
– FBIS-SOV-2003-0317, 17 March 2003.
Military Doctrine of the Russian Federation. 22 April 2000.
– 5 February 2010.
– 25 December 2014.
National Defense Strategy of the USA. 18 December 2017.
National Security Concept of the Russian Federation. 10 January 2000.
Rossiiskaya Gazeta. 26 December 1997. Foreign FBIS-SOV-97-364, 30 December 1997.
– 27 May 2004. Current Digest of the Post-Soviet Press 56, no. 21 (2004), 1.
– "Russia and France Will not Allow Passage of War Resolution in Iraq." FBIS-SOV-2003-0305, 5 March 2003.
Russia's Updated National Security Strategy. 1 January 2016.
United Nations Security Council. Resolution 1483, S/RES/1483. Adopted by the Security Council at its 4761st meeting, 22 May 2003.
– Draft Resolution 10403, S/RES/10403. Considered by the Security Council at its 6227th meeting, 4 October 2011.
– Draft Resolution 10536, S/RES/10536. Considered by the Security Council at its 6711th meeting, 4 February 2012.
– Draft Resolution 10714, S/RES/10714. Considered by the Security Council at its 6810th meeting, 19 July 2012.

– Resolution 1559, S/RES/1559. Adopted by the Security Council at its 5028th meeting, 2 September 2004.
– Resolution 1737, S/RES/1737. Adopted by the Security Council at its 5612th meeting, 23 December 2006.
– Resolution 1747, S/RES/1747. Adopted by the Security Council at its 5647th meeting, 24 March 2007.
– Resolution 1929, S/RES/1929. Adopted by the Security Council at its 6335th meeting, 9 June 2010.
– Resolution 2118, S/RES/2118. Adopted by the Security Council at its 7038th meeting, 27 September 2013.
– Resolution 2139, S/RES/2139. Adopted by the Security Council at its 7116th meeting, 22 February 2014.
– Resolution 2170, S/RES/2170. Adopted by the Security Council at its 7242nd meeting, 15 August 2014.
– Resolution 2178, S/RES/2178. Adopted by the Security Council at its 7271st meeting, 24 September 2014.
– Resolution 2254, S/RES/2254. Adopted by the Security Council at its 7588th meeting, 18 December 2015.

PRINTED SOURCES

Altaqi, Samir, and Esam Aziz. "Putin's Game Plan in the Middle East." *Middle East Briefing* 130, no. 9 (June 2016): 1–2.

Antonenko, Oskana. "Russia and the Deadlock Over Kosovo." *Survival* 49, no. 3 (July 2007): 91–106.

Baev, Pavel K. *Russian Energy and Military Power, Putin's Quest for Greatness.* London and New York: Routledge, 2008.

Belopolsky, Helen. *Russia and the Challengers: Russian Alignment with China, Iran, and Iraq in the Unipolar Era.* Houndmills and Basingstoke: Palgrave Macmillan, 2009.

Bryman, Alan. *Quantity and Quality in Social Research.* London and New York: Routledge, 1996.

Brzezinski, Zbigniew. "Putin's Choice." In *Global Power in the 21st Century: Strategies and Relations*, edited by Alexander T.J. Lennon and Amanda Kozlouski, 175–200. Cambridge: The Center for Strategic and International Studies and Massachusetts Institute of Technology, 2008.

Bull, Hedley. *The Anarchical Society: A Study of Order in World Politics.* New York: Columbia University Press, 1978.

Buzan, Barry. "Third World Regional Security in Structural Perspective." In

The Insecurity Dilemma: National Security of Third World States,edited by Brian L. Job, 167–89. Boulder, CO: Lynne Reinner, 1992.

Byman, Daniel. "Beyond Counterterrorism, Washington Needs a Real Middle East Policy." *Foreign Affairs* 94, no. 6 (November/December 2015): 11–18.

Christensen, Alessandra N. *The Making of the European Neighborhood Policy*. Baden-Baden: Nomos, 2011.

Cimbala, Stephen J. "Russia and European Missile Defenses, Reflexive Reset?" *Joint Force Quarterly* 68, 1st quarter (January 2013): 10–17.

Clunan, Anne L. "Historical Aspirations and the Domestic Politics of Russia's Pursuit of International Status." *Communist and Post-Communist Studies* 47, nos. 3–4 (2014): 281–90.

Conley, Heather A., James Mina, Ruslan Stefanov, and Martin Vladimirov. *The Kremlin Playbook: Understanding Russian Influence in Central and Eastern Europe*. Boulder and New York: Rowman & Littlefield, 2016.

Corbetta, Renato, and Molly M. Melin. "Exploring the Threshold Between Conflict Management and Joining in Biased Interventions." *Journal of Conflict Resolution* 62, no. 10 (November 2018): 2205–35.

Daalder, Ivo H. "Responding to Russia's Resurgence, not Quiet on the Eastern Front." *Foreign Affairs* 96, no. 6 (November/December 2017): 30–8.

Danilovic, Vesna, and Joe Clare. "Global Power Transitions and Regional Interests." *International Interactions* 33 (2007): 289–304.

D'antonio, Michael. *The Legacy of Barak Obama: A Consequential President*. New York: St Martin's Press, 2016.

De Hass, Marcel. *Russia's Foreign Security Policy in the 21st Century: Putin, Medvedev and Beyond*. Abingdon: Routledge, 2011.

Deyermond, Ruth. "Russia's Trump Card? The Prospects for Russia–US Relations After the Election of Donald Trump." *Russian Analytical Digest* 194 (9 December 2016): 2–4.

Donaldson, Robert H., Joseph L. Nogee, and Vidya Nadkarni. *The Foreign Policy of Russia: Challenging Systems, Enduring Interests*. Fifth edition. London and New York: M.E. Sharpe, 2014.

Dore, P.R. "The Prestige Factor in International Affairs." *International Affairs* 51, no. 2 (April 1975): 190–207.

Duncan, Peter S.J. "The Rebirth of Politics in Russia." In *The Road to Post-Communism, Independent Political Movements in the Soviet Union 1985–1991*, edited by Geoffrey A. Hosking, Jonathan Aves, and Peter S.J. Duncan, 67–120. London and New York: Printer Publishers, 1992.

Evangelista, Matthew. *The Chechen Wars: Will Russia Go the Way of the Soviet Union?* Washington, DC: The Brookings Institution, 2002.

Forsberg, Tuomas, Regina Heller, and Reinhard Wolf. "Status Conflicts Between Russia and the West: Perceptions and Emotional Biases." *Communist and Post-Communist Studies* 47, nos. 3–4 (2014): 323–31.

– "Status and Emotions." *Communist and Post-Communist Studies* 47, nos. 3–4 (2014): 261–8.

Freedman, Robert O. *Soviet Policy Toward the Middle East Since 1970*. New York and London: Praeger, 1978.

Freire, Maria R., and Regina Heller. "Russia's Power Politics in Ukraine and Syria: Status-Seeking between Identity, Opportunity and Costs." *Europe-Asia Studies* 70, no. 8 (2018): 1185–212.

Fridman, Ofer. *Russian "Hybrid Warfare" Resurgence and Politicization*. London: Hurst & Company, 2018.

Gaddy, Clifford G., and Andrew C. Kuchins. "Putin's Plan." In *Global Power in the 21st Century: Strategies and Relations*, edited by Alexander T.J. Lennon and Amanda Kozlowski, 201–16. Cambridge: MIT Press, 2008.

Gerges, Fawaz A. *ISIS, A History*. Princeton and Oxford: Princeton University Press, 2016.

German, Tracy. *Regional Cooperation in the South Caucasus, Good Neighbours or Distant Relatives?* London and New York: Ashgate, 2012.

Geukjian, Ohannes. "The Objectives of Russia's Military Intervention in Syria." *The Maghreb Review* 42, no. 3 (2017): 274–306.

Giles, Keir, Philip Janson, Rideric Lyne, James Nixey, James Sherr, and Andrew Wood. *The Russian Challenge*. London: Chatham House Report, June 2015.

Gilpin, Robert. *War and Change in World Politics*. Cambridge: Cambridge University Press, 1981.

Goldgeier, James M. *Power and Purpose: US Policy Toward Russia after the Cold War*. Washington, DC: Brookings Institute Press, 2003.

Goodarzi, Jubin M. *Syria and Iran: Diplomatic Alliance and Power Politics in the Middle East*. London and New York: I.B. Tauris, 2009.

Grodeland, Ase B. "Perceptions of Civil Rights, Security and the War on Terror." *Communist and Post-Communist Studies* 48, no. 4 (December 2015): 317–35.

Haass, Richard. *Conflicts Unending: The United States and Regional Disputes*. New Haven: Yale University Press, 1990.

– *A World in Disarray: American Foreign Policy and the Crisis of the Old Order*. New York: Penguin Press, 2017.

Hampson, Osler. *Nurturing Peace, Why Peace Settlements Succeed or Fail*. Washington, DC: USIP Press, 1996.

Headley, James. *Russia and the Balkans.* New York: Columbia University Press, 2009.

Hill, Fiona, and Clifford G. Gady. *Mr. Putin, Operative in the Kremlin*. Washington, DC: Brookings Institution Press, 2015.

Holsti, Kalevi K. "National Pole Conceptions in the Study of Foreign Policy." *International Studies Quarterly* 14, no. 3 (1970): 233–309.

Hunter, Shireen T. *Iran Divided: The Historical Roots of Iranian Debates on Identity, Culture, and Governance in the Twenty-First Century*. London and New York: Rowman and Littlefield, 2014.

Indyk, Martin. "Disaster in the Desert: Why Trump's Middle East Plan Can't Work." *Foreign Affairs* 98, no. 6 (November/December 2019): 10–20.

Jenkins, Brian M. "A Revanchist Russia Versus an Uncertain West: An Application of the Situation Since the 2014 Ukrainian Crisis." Center for the Study of Democracy, Working Paper, December 2016, 1–22.

Jentleson, Bruce. "Preventive Diplomacy and Ethnic Conflict: Possible, Difficult, Necessary." In *The International Spread of Ethnic Conflict: Fear, Diffusion, Escalation*, edited by David A. Lake and Donald Rothchild, 293–316. Princeton, NJ: Princeton University Press, 1998.

Jones, Stephen. *Georgia, A Political History Since Independence*. London and New York: I.B. Tauris, 2013.

Kandiyoti, Rafael. *Pipelines, Flowing Oil and Crude Politics*. London and New York: I.B. Tauris, 2008.

Karaganov, Sergei. "Russia's Choice." *Survival* 52, no. 1 (February/March 2010): 5–10.

Katz, Mark N. "Elusive as Ever: The State of Iranian-Russian Cooperation." Viewpoints. Middle East Program, Wilson Center no. 73 (March 2015): 1–3.

Khripunov, Igor. "Russia's Weapon's Trade: Domestic Competition and Foreign Markets." *Problems of Post-Communism* 46, no. 2 (March 1999): 39–48.

King, Charles. *Ending Civil Wars*. Oxford and New York: Oxford University Press, 1997.

Kolsto, Pal, and Helge Blakisroad, eds. *Nation-Building and Common Values in Russia*. Boulder and Oxford: Roman and Littlefield, 2004.

Kolvraa, Christopher, and Jan Ifversen. "The European Neighborhood Policy: Geopolitics or Value Export." In *The Frontiers of Europe: A Transatlantic Problem?*, edited by Federica Bindi and Irina Angelescu, 45–68. Rome and Washington: Scuola Superiore della Pubblica Amministrazione and Brookings Institute Press, 2011.

Kozhanov, Nikolay. *Russia and the Syrian Conflict, Moscow's Domestic, Regional and Strategic Interests*. Berlin: Gerlach Press, 2016.

Kreutz, Andrej. *Russia in the Middle East, Friend or Foe?* Westport and Connecticut: Praeger, 2007.

Lake, David A., and Donald Rothchild. "Containing Fear: The Origins and Management of Ethnic Conflict." In *Nationalism and Ethnic Conflict*, edited by Michael E. Brown, Owen R. Cote Jr, Sean M. Lynn-Jones, and Steven Miller, 97–131. Cambridge and London: The MIT Press, 1996–97.

Laqueur, Walter. *Putinism: Russia and its Future with the West*. New York: St Martin's Press, 2015.

Larson, Deborah W., Thomas V. Paul, and William C. Wohlforth. "Status and World Order." In *Status in World* Politics, edited by Thomas V. Paul, Deborah W. Larson, and William C. Wohlforth, 3–29. Cambridge: Cambridge University Press, 2014.

Larson, Deborah W., and Alexei Shevchenko. "Managing Rising Powers: The Role of Status Concerns." In *Status in World Politics*, edited by Thomas V. Paul, Deborah W. Larson, and William C. Wohlforth, 33–57. Cambridge: Cambridge University Press, 2014.

– "Russia Says No: Power, Status, and Emotions in Foreign Policy." *Communist and Post-Communist Studies* 47, nos. 3–4 (2014): 269–79.

Leenders, Reinoud, and Steven Heyderman. "Popular Mobilization in Syria: Opportunities and Threat, and the Social Networks of the Early Riser." *Mediterranean Politics* 17, no. 2 (July 2012): 139–59.

Leichtova, Magda. *Misunderstanding Russia: Russian Foreign Policy and the West*. Farnham, MD: Ashgate, 2014.

Levy, Jack S. *War in the Modern Great Power System*. Lexington: Kentucky University Press, 1983.

Lister, Charles R. *The Syrian Jihad, Al-Qaeda, the Islamic State and the Evolution of an Insurgency*. London: Hurst and Company, 2015.

Lo, Bobo. *Russia and the New World Disorder*. Washington, DC: Brookings Institution Press, 2015.

Lukin, Vladimir. "Russia and its Interests." In *Rethinking Russia's National Interest*, edited by Stephen Sestanovich, 106–15. Washington, DC: Center for Strategic and International Studies, 1994.

Lukyanov, Fyodor. "Putin's Foreign Policy, The Quest to Restore Russia's Rightful Place," *Foreign Affairs* 95, no. 3 (May/June 2016): 30–7.

Lynch, Allen C. "The Realism of Russia's Foreign Policy." *Europe Asia Studies* 53, no. 1 (2001): 7–31.

Lyne, Roderic. "Russia's Changed Outlook on the West: From Convergence to Confrontation." In *The Russian Challenge*, by Keir Giles, Philip Janson, Roderic Lyne, James Nixey, James Sherr, and Andrew Wood, 2–13. London: Chatham House Report, June 2015.

Makarychev, Andrey. *Russia and the EU in a Multipolar World: Discourses, Identities, Norms*. Stuttgart: Ibidim-Verlag, 2014.

Malcolm, Neil. "New Thinking and After: Debate in Moscow about Europe." In *Russia and Europe: an End to Confrontation*, edited by Neil Malcolm, 151–81. London and New York: Printer Publishers, 1994.

Malinova, Olga. "Russian Political Discourse in the 1990s: crisis of Identity and Conflicting Pluralism of Ideas." In *Identities and Politics During the Putin Presidency: The Foundations of Russia's Stability*, edited by Philipp Casula and Jeronim Perovic, 107–24. Stuttgart: Ibidim-Verlag, 2009.

Mankoff, Jeffrey. *Russian Foreign Policy, the Return of Great Power Politics*. Boulder and New York: Rowman & Littlefield Publishers, 2009.

McCants, William. *The ISIS Apocalypse: The History, Strategy, and Doomsday Vision of the Islamic State*. New York: St Martin's Press, 2015.

McCauley, Martin. *Gorbachev*. London and New York: Longman, 1998.

Mearsheimer, John J. "Why the Ukraine Crisis is the West's Fault: the Liberal Delusions that Provoked Putin." *Foreign Affairs* 93, no. 5 (September/October 2014): 77–89.

Morgenthau, Hans. *Politics Among Nations: The Struggle for Power and Peace*. New York: Alfred A. Knopf, 1978.

Nitoiu, Cristian. "Aspirations to Great Power Status: Russia's Path to Assertiveness in the International Arena under Putin." *Political Studies Review* 15, no. 1 (2017): 39–48.

Nixey, James. "Russian Foreign Policy Towards the West and Western Responses." In *The Russian Challenge*, by Keir Giles, Philip Janson, Rideric Lyne, James Nixey, James Sherr, and Andrew Wood. London: Chatham House Report, June 2015.

Nizameddin, Talal. *Putin's New Order in the Middle East*. London: Hurst & Company, 2013.

Organski, A.F.K. *World Politics*. New York: Knopf Press, 1958.

Organski, A.F.K., and J. Kuglar. *The War Ledger*. Chicago: Chicago University Press, 1980.

Ottaway, David B. "A New Chapter in the Tangled U.S.–Saudi Relationship." Viewpoints. Middle East Program, Wilson Center no. 62 (September 2014): 1–3.

Paul, Thomas V., and Mahesh Shankar. "Status Accommodation through Institutional Means: India's Rise and the Global Order." In *Status in World Politics*, edited by Thomas V. Paul, Deborah W. Larson, and William C. Wohlforth, 165–91. Cambridge: Cambridge University Press, 2014.

Phillips, Christopher. *The Battle for Syria: International Rivalry in the New Middle East*. New Haven and London: Yale University Press, 2016.

Primakov, Yevgeny. *Russia and the Arabs: Behind the Scenes in the Middle East from the Cold War to the Present*. New York: Basic Books, 2009.
– *Russian Crossroads*. New Haven and London: Yale University Press, 2004.
Radin, Andrew. "Hybrid Warfare in the Baltics: Threats and Potential Responses." RAND Corporation, 2017. 1–47.
Reid, Lindsey. "Finding a Peace that Lasts: Mediator Leverage and Durable Resolution of Civil Wars." *Journal of Conflict Resolution* 6, 7 (October 2015): 1402–27.
Renshon, Jonathan. *Fighting for Status, Hierarchy and Conflict in World Politics*. Princeton and Oxford: Princeton University Press, 2017.
Ross, Dennis. *The Missing Peace, the Inside Story of the Fight for Middle East Peace*. New York: Farrar, Straus and Giroux, 2004.
Rumer, Eugene B. "Dangerous Drift: Russia's Middle East Policy." Policy Paper no. 54, Washington, DC: Washington Institute of Near East Policy, 2000.
Saideman, Stephen M. "Overlooking the Obvious: Bringing International Politics Back into Ethnic Conflict Management." *International Studies Review* 4, no. 3 (Autumn 2002): 63–86.
Sergi, Bruno S. "Putin's and Russian-Led Eurasian Economic Union: A Hybrid Half-Economics and Half-Political Janus Bifrons." *Journal of Eurasian Studies* 9, no. 1 (January 2018): 52–60.
Sergunin, Alexander. *Explaining Russian Policy Behavior*. Stuttgart: Ibidim-Verlag 2016.
Shannon, V., and P. Kowert, eds. *Psychology and Constructivism in International Relations*. Ann Arbor: The University of Michigan Press, 2012.
Shay, Shaul. *The Axis of Evil: Iran, Hizbullah, and the Palestinian Terror*. New Brunswick and London: Transactions Publishers, 2005.
Sherr, James. *Hard Diplomacy and Soft Coercion: Russia's Influence Abroad*. London: Royal Institute for International Affairs, 2013.
– "A War of Narratives and Arms." In *The Russian Challenge*, Keir Giles, Philip Hanson, Roderic Lyne, James Nixey, James Sherr, and Andrew Wood, 23–32. London: Chatham House Report, June 2015.
Shevtsova, Lili. *Russia: Lost in Transition, the Yeltsin and Putin Legacies*. Washington, DC: Carnegie Endowment for International Peace, 2007.
Simes, Dimitry K. "Losing Russia, the Costs of Renewed Confrontation." *Foreign Affairs* 86, no. 6 (November/December 2007): 36–52.
Skillen, Daphne. *Freedom of Speech in Russia: Politics and Media from Gorbachev to Putin*. Routledge: London and New York, 2017.
Slocombe, Walter B. "Europe, Russia and American Missile Defense." *Survival* 50, no. 2 (April/May 2008): 19–24.

Smith, Hanna. "Russia as a Great Power: Status Inconsistency and the Two Chechen Wars." *Communist and Post-Communist Studies* 47, nos. 3–4 (2014): 355–63.

Stankevich, Sergei. "Toward a New National Idea." In *Rethinking Russia's National Interest*, edited by Stephen Sestanovich, 24–32. Washington, DC: Center for Strategic and International Studies, 1994.

Stedman, Stephen J. "Spoiler Problems in Peace Processes." *International Security* 22, no. 2 (Fall 1997): 5–53.

Stent, Angela E. "America and Russia: Paradoxes of Partnership." In *Russia's Engagement with the West: Transformation and Integration in the Twenty-First Century*, edited by Alexander J. Motyl, Blair A. Ruble, and Lila Shevtsova, 272–92. New York: M.E. Sharpe, 2005.

– *The Limits of Partnership: U.S.–Russian Relations in the Twenty-First Century.* Princeton and Oxford: Princeton University Press, 2014.

Tabler, Andrew J. "Syria's Collapse and How Washington Can Stop it," *Foreign Affairs* 92, no. 4 (July/August 2013): 93.

Tajfel, Henri. "The Achievement of Group Differentiation." In *Differentiation Between Social Groups: Studies in the Social Psychology of Intergroup Relations*, edited by Henri Tajfel, 77–98. London: Academic Press, 1978.

– "The Psychological Structure of Intergroup Relations." In *Differentiation Between Social Groups: Studies in the Social Psychology of Intergroup Relations*, edited by Henri Tajfel, 27–98. London: Academic Press, 1978.

Trenin, Dmitri. *Post-Imperium: A Story*. Washington, DC: Carnegie Endowment 2011.

– "The Revival of Russian Military: How Moscow Reloaded." *Foreign Affairs* 95, no. 3 (May/June 2016): 23–9

– *What Is Russia Up To in the Middle East*. Cambridge: Polity Press, 2018.

Tsygankov, Andrei P. "Assessing Cultural and Regime-Based Explanations of Russia's Foreign Policy: Authoritarian at Heart and Expansionist by Habit?" *Europe–Asia Studies* 64, no. 4 (June 2012): 695–713.

– "Contested Identity and Foreign Policy: Interpreting Russia's International Choices." *International Studies Perspectives* 15 (2014): 19–35.

– "The Frustrating Partnership: Honor, Status, and Emotions in Russia's Discourses of the West." *Communist and Post-Communist Studies* 47, nos. 3–4 (2014): 345–54.

– "Preserving Influence in a Changing World." *Problems of Post-Communism* 58, no. 2 (2011): 28–44.

– "Russia and the CIS in 2011: Uncertain Economic Recovery." *Asian Survey* 52, no. 1 (January/February 2012): 42–51.

– *Russia and the West from Alexander to Putin: Honor in International Relations*. Cambridge: Cambridge University Press, 2012.

– *Russia's Foreign Policy: Change and Continuity in National Identity*. Boulder and New York: Rowman & Littlefield Publishers, 2006.

– "Russia's International Assertiveness: What Does it Mean for the West?" *Problems of Post-Communism* 55, no. 2 (March/April 2008): 38–55.

– "Self and Other in International Relations Theory: Learning from Russian Civilizational Debates." *International Studies Review* 10 (2008): 762–75.

– "The Sources of Russia's Fear of NATO." *Communist and Post-Communist Studies* 51, no. 2 (2018): 101–11.

– "Vladimir Putin's Last Stand: The Sources of Russia's Ukraine Policy." *Post-Soviet Affairs* 31, no. 4 (2015): 279–303.

– "Vladimir Putin's Vision of Russia as a Normal Great Power." *Post-Soviet Affairs* 21, no. 2 (2005): 132–58.

Turner, J., and R. Brown. "Social Status, Cognitive Alternatives, and Intergroup Relations." In *Differentiation between Social Groups: Studies in the Social Psychology of Intergroup Relations*, edited by Henri Tajfel, 201–34. London: Academic Press, 1978.

Urnov, Mark. "'Greatpowerness' as the Key Element of Russia Self-consciousness under Erosion." *Communist and Post-Communist Studies* 47 (2014): 305–22.

Van Dam, Nikolas. *Destroying a Nation: The Civil War in Syria*. London and New York: I.B. Tauris, 2017.

Vladislavlev, Alexander, and Sergey A. Karaganov. "The Idea of Russia." *International Affairs* 38, no. 12 (1992): 22–40.

Volgy, Thomas J., Renato Corbetta, Keith A. Grant, and Ryan G. Baird. "Major Power Status in International Politics." In *Major Powers and the Quest for Status in International Politics: Global and Regional Perspectives*, edited by Thomas J. Volgy, Renato Corbetta, Keith A. Grant, and Ryan G. Baird, 1–26. New York: Palgrave, 2011.

Volgy, Thomas J., Renato Corbetta, Patrick J. Rhamey Jr, Ryan G. Baird, and Keith A. Grant. "Status Considerations in International Politics and the Rise of Regional Powers." In *Status in World Politics*, edited by Thomas V. Paul, Deborah W. Larson, and William C. Wohlforth, 58–84. Cambridge: Cambridge University Press, 2014.

Volgy, Thomas J., and Stacey Mayhall. "Status Inconsistency and International War," *International Studies Quarterly* 39, no. 1 (March 1995): 67–84.

Walter, Barbara F. "The Critical Barrier to Civil Settlement." *International Organization* 51, no. 3 (Summer 1997): 335–65.

Westle, Betlina. "Identity, Social and Political." In *International Encyclopedia of Science*, edited by Bertrand Badei, 1132–43. Thousand Oaks: SAGE Publications, 2011.

"What Next for Iran and the P5+1." Viewpoints. Middle East Program, Wilson Center no. 67 (November 2014): 1–32.

Wierzbowska-Miazga, Agata. Commentary. "Russia Goes on the Offensive Ahead of the Eastern Partnership Summit in Vilnius." Center for Eastern Studies no. 115 (30 September 2013): 1–7.

Wohlforth, William C. "Unipolarity, Status Competition, and Great Power War." *World Politics* 61, no. 1 (January 2009): 28–57.

Yost, David S. "The Budapest Memorandum and Russia's Intervention in Ukraine," *International Affairs* 91, no. 3 (2015): 505–38.

Zartman, William I. "Conflict Resolution and Negotiation." In *The SAGE Handbook of Conflict Resolution*, edited by Jacob Bercovitch, Victor Kremenyulk, and William I. Zartman, 322–39. London and New Delhi: SAGE Publications, 2009.

Index